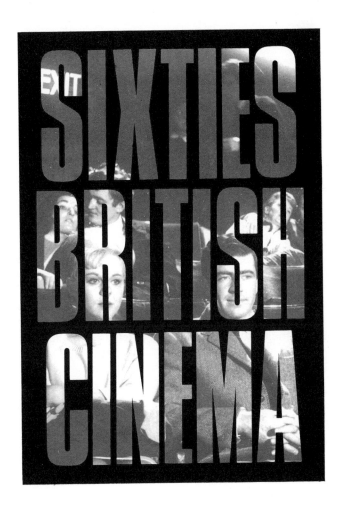

Robert Murphy

BFI PUBLISHING

First published in 1992 by the
British Film Institute
21 Stephen Street
London W1P 1PL

Research for this book was made possible by a generous grant from
the Pinewood Foundation, New York, towards the cost of a series of
volumes on the history of the British cinema since 1939.

British Library Cataloguing in Publication Data

Murphy, Robert, *1947*–
    Sixties British cinema. – (The history of the
    British film)
    I. Title   II. Series
    791.430941

ISBN 0–85170–309–7
ISBN 0–85170–324–0 pbk

Cover design by DREAM ASSOCIATES
Still: Alan Bates and June Ritchie in *A Kind of Loving*
(John Schlesinger, 1962)

Typeset in 10·5 on 12 pt Plantin by
Fakenham Photosetting Limited,
Fakenham, Norfolk
and printed in Great Britain by
The Trinity Press, Worcester

For Clare and Edward

CONTENTS

ACKNOWLEDGMENTS

I would like to thank my students – Lisa Bush, Ben Norrington, Steve Plesniak, Zoe Waterson, Dan O'Brien, Fiona Curtis, Ginnie Keith, Stefan Waters, Susannah Garrett, Stuart Hollis, Sophie Nauman, Paul Anderson, Rachel Simnett, Steve Turner, Jeff Canavan, Julie Nisargand, Melanie Myers, Harriet Willis, Nicky Wilson and Gavin Emerson – who helped me during 1987 and 1988 make some sense of an area of cinema which was almost as new to me as it was to them; Barry Curtis for allowing me to borrow his ideas from his M.A. thesis on *Morgan*, and Richard Dacre for letting me consult prior to publication his monograph on Norman Wisdom and his films; Allen Eyles, Sheila Taylor, Linda Wood, Ian Aitken, Julian Petley, Guy Phelps, Erik Hedling, Peter Todd, for a variety of advice and favours; Kim Newman for lending me a copy of *The Reptile*, Michael Jackson for lending me a copy of his Channel 4 series on the 60s; Maureen Humphries and the staff of the University of Kent Audio-Visual Service, the staff of the BFI Library, BFI Stills, Posters and Designs the UKC Library, Flashbacks, and the National Film Archive and in particular Elaine Burrows and Jackie Morris who have made valiant efforts to retrieve rare and forgotten films for me; Keith Robertson and Sir John Woolf for granting me long interviews; Steve Neale, John Hill and Jeffrey Richards for reading and making useful comments and corrections on an earlier version of this book which I submitted as a Ph.D at the University of Kent; Geoffrey Nowell-Smith, my editor at the BFI, for urging me to clarify my arguments and curb my more unreasonable criticisms; Christine Gledhill for her last-minute corrections; and finally Clare Noel, who bore two children while I wrote this book.

R.M.

INTRODUCTION

> Whatever the Swinging Sixties are going to be remembered
> for it won't be films. The moment you saw a red London
> bus go through the shot you knew you were in for a rotten
> time. (Alan Parker, *A Turnip-Head's Guide to British
> Cinema*, 1986)[1]

The nature of 1960s society is, even now, a contentious issue and
interpretations tend to be more subjective and unreliable than those of
most periods. In 1978, Peter York made the point that:

> when asked about the sixties, there seems to be a qualitative differ-
> ence in people's response – they seem to be confused about what
> really happened [to them] and what the media had said was happen-
> ing. This kind of conceptualizing seems true across the social board.
> Most people under forty, in describing the sixties, at least defer to
> the media sixties.[2]

But the media interpretations are mutually incompatible. Christopher
Booker's influential history of the 1960s, *The Neophiliacs*, shows
Britain as a recklessly decadent, fantasy-ridden society, an image
eagerly seized upon by Margaret Thatcher and the Conservative Party
as a contrast to the 'realism' they imposed upon the country after 1979.
To unreconstructed liberals and the ageing glitterati of the period, it is
a golden age when Vidal Sassoon haircuts, Mary Quant clothes and the
Beatles made Britain the cultural centre of the world.

Similarly simplistic myths surround the films. Paul Willemen, in
reviewing John Hill's *Sex, Class and Realism*, complains that 'it is
unfortunate that it deals with British cinema from 1956 to 1963, the
drabbest period in an already drab national cinema.'[3] And though
Willemen can hardly be said to represent critical orthodoxy, the image
of the 'Kitchen Sink' films as glum, drab and visually boring still
lingers.

1

Lindsay Anderson, in a polemical defence of what he calls the 'tradition of Free Cinema', claims that his films, along with those of Karel Reisz and Tony Richardson, have been dismissed as 'unimaginative social realism or dreary political propaganda'.[4] This is a half-truth: with the exception of Richardson's untidy adaptation of *The Entertainer* and his more unjustly maligned *The Loneliness of the Long Distance Runner*, the balance of critical opinion was in favour of the 'Kitchen Sink' films; and when, after a period of neglect, interest in British cinema among film critics and historians revived, the socially concerned cinema of the early 60s became a site for critical debate. Ironically, in view of Anderson's resolutely anti-Establishment position, most of the criticism has been of their limited, reformist aims. R. Barton Palmer, in her study of *Room at the Top*, concludes that:

> A thoroughgoing examination of New Wave films will, I believe, reveal the movement's unquestioning endorsement of the traditional fictionalising function of British cinema: to provide 'closed texts' that preserve the goal of entertaining a mass audience by processing effectively any challenge to the 'neutral and integrative function of public opinion'.[5]

And Hill's *Sex, Class and Realism*, which is undeniably thoroughgoing, judges that 'the films, and the views of the world which they promoted, may well have obscured as much as they enlightened, and obstructed as much as they initiated the potential for social change and reconstruction.'[6]

If the films have sometimes become entangled in theoretical thickets, the realist cinema of the late 1950s and early 60s is at least critically acknowledged as an important movement. Most of the rest of 60s British cinema – crime films, horror films, comedies, spy films, science-fiction, musicals, youth films, and the cycle of films associated with Swinging London – have received such cursory treatment that it is less a matter of arguing against established critical positions than of dispersing clouds of ignorance and prejudice. 'Swinging London' films, for example, have fared particularly badly. In contrast to the Kitchen Sink and social problem films, which can be assimilated into a respectable, albeit increasingly unfashionable, tradition of socially concerned realism, the Swinging London films – frivolous, ephemeral, unrealistic, extravagant – seemed to represent all that was worst about mass culture, and attracted derision and abuse from film critics.

Philip French, John Russell Taylor, Eric Rhode, David Robinson and other *Sight and Sound* luminaries laid into films as various as *Darling, Morgan, Poor Cow* and *Here We Go Round the Mulberry Bush* for hastening the decline of Western civilisation, and Penelope Houston, summing up the decade, gloomily pronounced that British cinema

2

'has suggested another jaded party, dragging exhaustedly on into the night in its bedraggled fancy dress surrounded by its odds and ends of boutique bric-à-brac, and deaf to the ambulance sirens coming louder up the street.'[7] Thomas Guback, examining the infusion of American capital into British films, was 'forced to wonder whether the British industry has not lost something in the trade – if it has not exchanged autonomy and the chance to manifest its own culture for the appetizing appeal of financial success with many "mid-Atlantic" productions.'[8] Yet in retrospect British films of the 60s seem at least as illuminating of the society in which they were made as those of any earlier decade. The sort of mid-Atlantic film feared by Guback (*To Sir, With Love* or *Prudence and the Pill*, for example) was, if anything, less common and less offensive than in the preceding and following decades. What upset British critics was less an invasion of American ideas and techniques than what they saw as an indigenous degeneration in film style: 'the disregard of form and structure, the visual extravagance, the devices used like purple phrases and exclamation marks in schoolgirl prose, the tourist fantasies of a colour-supplement Britain.'[9]

Barry Curtis argues that the key characteristic of 60s style was a fluidity stemming from the disordering of social hierarchies, 'a loss of "aura" hitherto relied on to mark off the "important" figures and commodities.'[10] In dealing with such a disparate body of films it is difficult to sustain generalisations: David Greene and Peter Collinson, for example, rely on tight cutting, unusual locations and a restless and intrusive camera style, techniques which rapidly became standard for mainstream, medium-budget action pictures. In Greene's 60s films, however, there is a persistent undermining of what seems to be 'reality', and Curtis' argument is borne out by the most clearly marked feature of late 60s cinema, the disruption of the narrative. Fantasy sequences (in which everything becomes possible), slapstick (in which the world collapses into chaos), outrageous visual jokes, distancing devices such as the use of a narrator, inter-titles or direct address to camera spread across films as different as *The Bliss of Mrs Blossom* and *Poor Cow, Here We Go Round the Mulberry Bush* and *If.* . . .

Apart from Curtis' unpublished thesis, there has been little attempt to challenge the view handed down by the world-weary middlebrow critics of *Sight and Sound*. Even a serious film historian like Jeffrey Richards writes of Swinging London as 'an increasingly frenzied saturnalia whose cult was the new and the now'. He goes on to complain:

Sober realism and earnest social comment gave way to fantasy, extravaganza and escapism; black-and-white photography and Northern locations to colour and the lure of the metropolis; Puritanical self-discipline to hedonistic self-indulgence; plain truthful settings to flamboyant, unrealistic decorativeness. Films became

3

locked in a heady spiral of mounting extravagance, febrile excitement and faddish innovation.[11]

My own attitude to the 'Swinging Sixties' ought to be equally hostile. During 1967's 'Summer of Love' I was working as a filleter's labourer in a fish factory in Grimsby, and when I came down to London in 1968 it might still have been swinging but, living in cheap bed-sits with building workers and kitchen porters for neighbours, I hardly noticed. Painfully aware of the discrepancy between my own experience and the colourful dream of Swinging London, I did not look forward to watching innumerable films celebrating pleasures I shared no part of. But the idea that most films between 1965 and 1970 promoted a mindlessly optimistic view of the world is more of a myth than the myth the films are assumed to convey. *Repulsion*, Roman Polanski's bleak vision of madness, came out at virtually the same time as Richard Lester's *The Knack* (January and May 1965 respectively), and many of the films associated with Swinging London (*Morgan, Blow Up, I'll Never Forget What's 'Is Name, Joanna, Sebastian, Up the Junction*) have disturbing undertones. By the end of the decade the mood was one of downbeat realism, with films like *The Strange Affair* and *The Reckoning* making grim comments on the price paid for the affluent and permissive society.

Films of the 1960s have retained a popular appeal denied to most British films: over four hundred 60s feature films have been shown on television (and dozens of B-films and shorts) over the past five years, some of them several times. There has been little attempt to chart this vast sea of films. Alan Lovell, in a 1969 paper entitled 'British Cinema: The Unknown Cinema', suggested that as British cinema boasted few outstanding *auteurs* a good way of studying it was through its genres. A start to this process was made in 1973 by Dave Pirie in his book *A Heritage of Horror*, but there has been little attempt to follow up his example. Intelligent appreciation of British horror films certainly exists – Paul Willemen's contributions to the *Aurum Encylopedia of Horror*, for example – but it remains outside the stockade of academic respectability. There is still no monograph on Terence Fisher, and the best history of Hammer is *The Little Shoppe of Horror*'s valiant, but inevitably patchy, poorly co-ordinated and difficult-to-come-by eighty-five page feature article 'Hammer: Yesterday, Today and Tomorrow'.[12] Other genres such as crime and comedy remain almost virgin territory.

Vincent Porter writes that 'No film ... can be studied without a complete understanding of the specific economic, political, industrial, generic, authorial and ideological conjuncture in which it was both produced and consumed.'[13] This commitment to total history is admirable as a guide to detailed studies of individual films, but it is hardly

4

possible when dealing with large numbers of films over a period of time. In practice, general film history tends to rely on what Ben Brewster calls the '100 best films approach':

> This approach assumes a process of historical selection in which the many works produced at any one time either 'die' or 'survive' to constitute a canon, which can then be written back into the chronological sequence as a series of 'innovations', 'developments' and 'advances', and linked together by 'influences'. The art form thus becomes a 'Tradition' . . .

Once established, this 'tradition' becomes self-perpetuating:

> only the films sanctioned by it are made available or even preserved at all; writing about the cinema returns again and again to the same works and historical moments, endlessly reinterpreting them, but not really displacing or reorganising them.[14]

As Steve Neale and Andrew Higson point out about the 1980s upsurge of interest in British cinema:

> while the new work has adopted much that is new in its theoretical framework and terminology, the films it tends to focus on (and the films it tends to exclude or to marginalise from its analyses) remain substantially the same . . . In other words, the work is still orientating itself by a map of British cinema drawn up many years ago.[15]

Taking the advice of Lawrence Alloway that 'The proper point of departure for a film critic . . . is an approach that accepts obsolescence and in which judgements derive from the sympathetic consumption of a great many films', I have tried to draw my own map.[16]

Alloway was writing at a time of rapid cultural change when the past, including the great mass of popular cinema, seemed in danger of being swept away as outdated ephemera. Now the problems are different, and an essential task of any general survey would seem to be to act as a guide through the backlog of films unexpectedly made permanently accessible by the evolution of television and video technology. I have tried to reconcile the clash between the demands of narrative coherence and the desire to be comprehensive by watching as many films as possible and at least mentioning all those films which for social, financial or aesthetic reasons seem important. The first two chapters try to cover the realist films of the late 50s and early 60s which seemed to promise a new dawn for creative British film-making, and Chapters Eight, Nine and Ten deal with horror, crime and comedy, the three key genres in 1960s British cinema. Chapter Three deals with

5

the critical debates of the early 60s and the development of a vigorous film culture, and Chapter Four examines the possibility of constructing a tradition of 'art cinema' from among British films. Chapter Five deals with the organisation of the industry, and Chapters Six and Seven try to come to terms with the post-Kitchen Sink films and the phenomenon of Swinging London.

Inevitably there are gaps and omissions. With the exceptions of Michael Powell, Joseph Losey, Alexander Mackendrick, Val Guest, Clive Donner and Terence Fisher, I have made no attempt to deal with directors as *auteurs* or to follow the careers of even key 60s actors like Albert Finney, Peter O'Toole and Michael Caine. There is also a bias against big-budget epics like *Lawrence of Arabia*, *Becket*, *Lord Jim*, *The Night of the Generals* and *The Lion in Winter*, which though technically British belong to an international, Hollywood-dominated cinema.[17]

Despite the help of the National Film Archive, there are a handful of important films which I have been unable to see. Guy Green's follow-up to *The Angry Silence*, *The Mark* (1961), with Stuart Whitman as a former sex offender trying to turn over a new leaf, and Hammer's *Never Take Sweets from a Stranger* (1960) with Felix Aylmer suspected of being a paedophile in a small Canadian town, would certainly have found a place among the social problem films, as would Dearden and Relph's *A Place to Go*, had I been able to see them. And for the same reason *The Small World of Sammy Lee* (1963, d. Ken Hughes) and *I Start Counting* (1969, d. David Greene) have been omitted from the crime film chapter. Tony Richardson's later films have also proved elusive and I have had to rely on received opinion for my account of *Mademoiselle*, *The Sailor from Gibraltar*, *Laughter in the Dark* and *Ned Kelly*; though personally I am more disappointed at not having been able to catch up with *Gonks Go Beat*, *Secrets of a Windmill Girl* and *The Viking Queen*.

Certain genres – costume films and war films – begin to look rather mangy in the 1960s. *Tom Jones* did revive the bawdy tradition of *The Wicked Lady* and *The Man in Grey*, but with its bright young stars, Albert Finney and Susannah York, it was also very much a contemporary film, and follow-ups like *The Amorous Adventures of Moll Flanders* and *Lock Up Your Daughters* were commercially and artistically less successful. The visually impressive (and very costly) costume films of the later 60s – *Far from the Madding Crowd*, *Where's Jack?*, *Alfred the Great*, *Cromwell* and *Ryan's Daughter* – have some economic importance in hastening the departure of the Americans and they have received more attention here than early 60s films like Peter Ustinov's *Billy Budd* and Lewis Gilbert's *HMS Defiant*, which in thematic terms are almost as interesting. War films, tremendously important in the 50s, are of decreasing interest after 1958. It is certainly possible to trace a development from the disillusioned realism of late 50s films like *Orders*

6

to Kill, *Yesterday's Enemy* and *The Long and the Short and the Tall*, through belated attempts at war heroics in *The War Lover*, *The Guns of Navarone*, *Operation Crossbow*, *633 Squadron*, *Mosquito Squadron*, *The Heroes of Telemark* and *Where Eagles Dare*, to the vociferous anti-war films of the late 60s – *How I Won the War*, *The Charge of the Light Brigade* and *Oh What a Lovely War!* But apart from Peter Collinson's *The Long Day's Dying*, the two most complex and interesting war films of the decade – *The Blue Max* and *The Night of the Generals* – are, despite their British registration, essentially American films, and gain their originality by looking at the First and Second World Wars from a German perspective.

With so many films being financed by American companies in the 60s it is not always easy to recognise a 'British' film. I have taken Denis Gifford's *The British Film Catalogue 1895–1985* – which relies on the Board of Trade's definition of whether or not a particular film is eligible for the British film quota – to be the authoritative arbiter on this matter. But where a Hollywood film, like William Wyler's *The Collector*, is partly shot in England, uses British actors and appears to deal with themes which are integral to British society, I have included it at the expense of films like *The Sundowners* and *The Dirty Dozen* which are British only because British technicians worked on them. Films made by British directors in Hollywood such as Peter Yates's *Bullitt*, John Boorman's *Point Blank* and John Schlesinger's *Midnight Cowboy*, important though they are in terms of international cinema, seem irrelevant here, though along with Richard Lester's *Petulia* (which is technically British despite its American director, setting and finance) they might be taken as indicators of the shift in creative energy back from England to Hollywood.

I have tried to acknowledge craftsmanship where it becomes a dominant element in the film. Arthur Grant's cinematography on Val Guest's location thrillers and Hammer's horror films is so important that it can scarcely be ignored, and Walter Lassally makes a similarly significant contribution to *A Taste of Honey*, *The Loneliness of the Long Distance Runner*, *Tom Jones* and *Joanna*. Alex Vetchinsky's art direction adds an extra dimension to *Flame in the Streets* and *Life for Ruth* and even seems to liven up those *Carry On* films he worked on, and Ken Adam's collaboration on the Bond films is generally acknowledged to have been crucial in ensuring their success. But comprehensiveness would leave little room for anything other than a detailed list of films and an endless cataloguing of the contributions made by the various people who worked on them. Giving actors their due is even more of a problem. The 60s were unique in producing an array of British actors who became internationally popular – Albert Finney, Michael Caine, Peter Sellers, Terence Stamp, Julie Christie, Vanessa Redgrave, Peter O'Toole, Richard Harris – but here I have found little

7

Sinister husbands, scheming wives. Dudley Foster and Maxine Audley, *Never Mention Murder*

space to comment on their performances. Character actors have been similarly taken for granted, though the odd, slightly sinister men played by Dudley Foster or Jeremy Kemp and the scheming *femmes fatales* and faithless wives portrayed by Barbara Shelley, Maxine Audley, Moira Redmond and Adrienne Corri bring to life even the dullest films.

The 1960s is a very well-documented decade. Christopher Booker's *The Neophiliacs* and Bernard Levin's *The Pendulum Years*, for all their reliance on *Old Moore's Almanac* for philosophical inspiration, are full of insight and inside information on British or at least London society in the 60s. George Melly's *Revolt into Style* and Jeff Nuttall's *Bomb Culture* approximate much more to my own view of the 60s, though for the purposes of general information they are less useful than Booker or Levin. Robert Hewison's *Too Much*, like his two earlier volumes on the history of post-war British culture, is difficult to digest but absolutely invaluable as a summary of the important cultural trends of the period. For the films themselves, Raymond Durgnat's *A Mirror for England* tries to limit itself to the heyday of British middle-class cinema between 1945 and 1958 but frequently strays beyond those borders and is an essential guide to the highways and byways of British cinema. John Hill's *Sex, Class and Realism* looks at the Kitchen Sink and social problem films of the late 50s and early 60s, and though his

8

Marxist perspective leads him to condemn their well-meaning liberalism as ideologically pernicious, Hill's analysis of the films remains open-minded and perceptive. The 60s film industry is well-covered from an economic history point of view: John Spraos's *The Decline of the Cinema* and Terence Kelly's *A Competitive Cinema* are dry but valuable accounts of the main economic developments in the first half of the decade, and Alexander Walker's *Hollywood, England* covers the key story of the later 60s – the American takeover of British film production – in illuminating detail. Walker leans too heavily on the apocalyptic framework of Booker's *The Neophiliacs*, but he interviewed the leading figures in the 60s film industry when events were still fresh in their minds (the book was first published in 1974) and he pieces together the story of America's brief but spectacular take-over of the British film industry with clarity and precision. I have refrained from trying to tell the same story, and my chapter on 'Hollywood's England' merely attempts to show which American companies made what films and whether some were more successful than others in the choices they made.

All dates for films are release rather than production dates and are taken from Denis Gifford's *The British Film Catalogue*. Except when a film is to be dealt with in more detail later, dates are included alongside the film when it is first mentioned.

1

A SAVAGE STORY OF LUST
AND AMBITION

Though, as always, there were long thin tendrils, reaching
to the war, reaching to the Movement, reaching to the slow
rise of living standards and the abolition of rationing in the
earlier fifties, reaching to the crisis of Suez, the critical point
of change, as near as one can ever get to these things, hinges
on the year 1959. (Arthur Marwick, *Journal of Contemporary History*, 1984)[1]

Stagnant Cinema

British cinema of the 1950s has a reputation for stagnant complacency
which is not entirely undeserved. The war films are solid and serious,
the comedies funny, and the substratum of crime and horror B movies
a treasure trove of cinematic delights; but as Lindsay Anderson complained in 1957:

To counterbalance the rather tepid humanism of our cinema, it
must also be said that it is snobbish, anti-intelligent, emotionally
inhibited, wilfully blind to the conditions and problems of the
present, dedicated to an out-of-date, exhausted national ideal.[2]

It is easy to sympathise with Anderson's anger and frustration. He had
helped launch *Sequence*, a lively, adventurous film journal, in 1947
when there were still legitimate expectations that British cinema would
become internationally significant, expectations that were firmly
squashed two years later when the Rank Organisation abandoned its
attempt to crack the American market and concentrated its resources
on safe, innocuous films at Pinewood. Entry into the industry as a
director was difficult, particularly for an intellectual like Anderson.
Apart from the little band of liberals and ex-documentary film-makers
who sheltered under the umbrella of John Baxter and John Grierson's

10

Group Three, most of the directors who made their breakthrough between 1950 and 1959 were pragmatically commercial and had generally served a long apprenticeship in other branches of the industry.[3] Anderson, along with two other young, ambitious film-makers he became associated with – Karel Reisz and Tony Richardson – was too uncompromising to fit into the cosily conformist environs of Elstree, Ealing and Pinewood and too highbrow to seek a career in the film factories of Twickenham, Bray and Merton Park.[4]

In February 1956, Anderson, Reisz and Richardson launched Free Cinema. Between 1956 and 1959 six programmes of films were shown under the Free Cinema banner at the National Film Theatre, three of them remarkably prescient examples of 'New Wave' film-making in Poland, France and the United States, three made up of low-budget films made in Britain. All the British films, except for Lorenza Mazzetti's *Together*, were documentaries, but documentaries different in spirit, technique and context from the mainstream of British documentary. Free Cinema was accepted as a movement because, despite their disparity, most of the film-makers involved shared a common outlook and common interests. As Alan Lovell argues:

> ... the views of the world which emerge from Free Cinema films are recognisable, the result of preoccupations common among intellectuals in the second half of the 1950s. Broadly, these preoccupations were: a sympathetic interest in communities, whether they were the traditional industrial one of *Wakefield Express* or the new, improvised one of the jazz club in *Momma Don't Allow*; fascination with the newly emerging youth culture (*Momma Don't Allow, We Are the Lambeth Boys, Nice Time*); unease about the quality of leisure in an urban society (*Nice Time, O Dreamland*); and respect for the traditional working class (*Enginemen, Every Day Except Christmas*).[5]

Anderson's Free Cinema manifesto, the film programmes, and the articles written by Karel Reisz and other members of the Free Cinema group (such as the cameraman Walter Lassally) created considerable media interest, but their intellectual preoccupations had not yet permeated the film business and doors into the commercial film industry remained jealously closed. Ironically, the breakthrough into a new kind of cinema came from within.

Room at the Top

John and James Woolf, the producers, and Jack Clayton, the director of *Room at the Top*, were not the sort of people one would envisage starting a cinematic revolution. Clayton had served a traditional apprenticeship in the commercial cinema, beginning as a tea-boy at

Denham studios in 1936, rising to become an editor and then a producer, and proving his ability to direct with a short fiction film, *The Bespoke Overcoat*, in 1955. The Woolf brothers were the sons of C. M. Woolf, a key figure of the pre-war film industry. He died in 1942, leaving his sons financially well-endowed but with the family firm, General Film Distributors, tightly ensconced within the Rank empire (GFD's symbol was a muscle-man striking a gong). John Woolf worked for Rank when he came out of the army, but was less than happy as an organisation man and left in 1948 to join his brother in setting up their own distribution and production company.[6]

In contrast to the increasingly staid and conventional Rank Organisation, the Woolfs were prepared to take risks. The investigations of the House of Representatives Un-American Activities Committee had made it difficult, unpleasant or impossible for left-wing film-makers to continue working in Hollywood. Britain, though not immune from its own anti-Communist hysterics, provided a more congenial climate. In 1950 the Woolfs brought over Ava Gardner, James Mason and Albert Lewin to make the wildly exotic *Pandora and the Flying Dutchman*, and despite its disappointing box-office performance, persisted with their experiment in Anglo-American production and scored a big success with *The African Queen*. Several more Anglo-American co-productions followed. By the mid-50s the Woolfs were financially secure enough to bail out Sir Alexander Korda and help him set up his last four films – *A Kid for Two Farthings*, *Richard III*, *Summer Madness* and *Storm Over the Nile* – prestige British films which turned out to be uncharacteristically profitable.

What distinguished the Woolfs from other entrepreneurial partnerships was their combination of financial acumen with artistic flair. John Woolf, born and brought up in the film industry and married to the daughter of producer/director Victor Saville, had strong views about what sort of films he wanted to make as well as a canny perception of what would be commercially successful. But it was James, despite his shyness and poor health, who inherited Korda's ability to recognise and foster talent.[7] Among his protégés was the Lithuanian-born actor Lauruska Mischa Skikne, better known as Laurence Harvey. Harvey's biggest film part had been as the vaguely asexual hero of *I Am a Camera* (1955), an adaptation of Christopher Isherwood's Berlin stories (which would later be re-made as *Cabaret*). Despite his reputation as 'an exotic butterfly', the Woolfs cast him as the working-class hero of *Room at the Top*.[8]

John Braine's novel *Room at the Top*, published in 1957, was a bestseller. It combined the realism of situation, character and setting of earlier 50s novels like John Wain's *Hurry On Down* and Kingsley Amis's *Lucky Jim* with the bitterness and aggression of John Osborne's play *Look Back in Anger*. Braine's hero is working-class but he has had a grammar school education and he works in the Borough Treasurer's office, and as Braine pointed out:

> Most ambitious working-class boys want to get to hell out of the working class. That was a simple truth that had never been stated before. The English working classes are the least politically-minded in the world; they always have been. Give the English working-class man half a chance and he becomes a bourgeois.[9]

Such a viewpoint chimed well with 'never had it so good' attitudes in the late 50s, and the novel was serialised in the *Daily Express*.[10] But the book was no complacent celebration of affluence: its story of a young man who uses his charm and good looks to gain advancement in a class-bound society expressed the resentment of that first generation of working-class children to benefit from the 1944 Education Act, when they emerged into a world far removed from the classless, populist utopia they had been promised.

Joe Lampton moves from the grim northern industrial town of Dufton to take up a job in the much cleaner and more prosperous town of Warnley. He joins an amateur dramatics society and resolves to win the hand of fellow thespian Susan Brown, the pretty daughter of a local industrialist, partly because he is genuinely attracted to her, partly because he sees her as a passport to a better way of life. Though he makes some slow progress towards his goal, he also drifts into a fulfilling love affair with an older woman, Alice Aisgill. Ironically, the social pressures which make his relationship with Susan seem impossible conspire, after he has realised his destiny lies with Alice, in forcing him into marriage with Susan. Alice commits suicide and Joe looks forward to a loveless marriage for which material rewards and a promising career seem insufficient compensations.

Unlike literary predecessors such as Julian Sorel in Stendhal's *Le Rouge et le Noir* or Clyde Griffiths in Dreiser's *An American Tragedy*, whose refusal to accept their humble situation in society provokes bloody retribution by the forces of order, Joe Lampton is congratulated on his success. In 1950s British society his ambitions – a sports car, a glamorous girlfriend, a job with an expense account – are reasonable and legitimate, but *Room at the Top* implies that they are realisable at a high cost in honesty and integrity. Alexander Walker complains that 'what one feels most strongly in *Room at the Top* isn't anger –but envy – the envy of a have-not for what he wants to acquire.'[11] This is misleading. Braine is very specific about Joe's attitude: 'I tasted the sourness of envy. Then I rejected it. Not on moral grounds, but because I felt then, and still do, that envy's a small and squalid vice . . . This didn't abate the fierceness of my longing. I wanted an Aston-Martin, I wanted a three-guinea linen shirt, I wanted a girl with a

A fulfilling love affair with an older woman: Simone Signoret and Laurence Harvey, *Room at the Top*

Riviera suntan – these were my rights, I felt, a signed and sealed legacy.'[12] Joe has a sense of his own value which makes envy irrelevant, and in the film the casting of Laurence Harvey – a prince very thinly disguised as a frog – reinforced the feeling that Joe has a right to the good things in life.

John Braine – a Bradford librarian – identifies with his hero, but he maintains a certain critical distance. In the film, this disappears. Implicit approval is given to Joe's transgression of class boundaries: his aunt and uncle in Dufton who warn him of the dangers of not sticking to his own kind seem like relics from a past age, and the upper-crust characters – Alice's husband, Susan's mother and her chinless wonder of a boyfriend – who are vaguely unpleasant in the book, assume a nightmarish awfulness.[13] The film's morality is tied up in the relationship Joe forms with Alice Aisgill. In the novel the reader is invited to share Joe's reservations about his ageing lover and his attraction to the young and desirable Susan, but by making Alice a foreigner the film-makers put her outside the English class system and change her into a symbol of honesty and true love.[14] It is not second thoughts on Joe's part but external circumstances which make him break off the relationship: Alice's husband refuses to divorce her and threatens to lose Joe his job; Susan gets pregnant and her father makes Joe an offer he cannot refuse. Alice dies, horribly, and Joe is congratulated on achieving his ambitions, his tears on his wedding day mistaken by his young

14

wife for tears of happiness. A radical novel flawed by cynicism and sentimentality is transformed into a film which displays the tragedy of a man stuck in a rigid hierarchical society where ambition and enterprise are turned into self-destructive weapons.

The sexual element is much stronger in the film than in the book. Clayton inserts no extra sex scenes, but they are shot with a frankness and sensuality unusual enough in British cinema at the time for the British Board of Film Censors to saddle the film with an 'X'certificate. The X category had originally been introduced in 1951 as a means of allowing films unsuitable for children to be seen by discerning adults, but it had very quickly acquired an aura of disreputability and the Secretary of the BBFC, John Trevelyan, saw *Room at the Top* as an ideal opportunity to re-establish its respectability.

Romulus had made X films before (*Cosh Boy, I Am a Camera*), but for a 'quality' film like *Room at the Top*, the X certificate could be a considerable handicap. As Rank and ABC, the two major circuits, only rarely gave playing time to X films they tended to be confined to the more down-market cinemas. The Woolfs, who believed in the Hollywood practice of sneak previews, tried the film out in the Bruce Grove Cinema at Tottenham, a rough area of north London, substituting it for either *Dracula* or *The Curse of Frankenstein* in a typical X-rated double bill. The audience reacted with scorn and derision and the Woolfs began to think they had a commercial disaster on their hands. As the big circuits were wary of taking the film, it was opened at Paramount's West End showcase, the Plaza in Lower Regent Street. Critical reaction was by no means universally favourable, but there was general agreement on the film's sincerity, and Frank Jackson in *Reynolds' News* endorsed Trevelyan's attempt to rehabilitate the X certificate, welcoming 'At long last a British film which is truly adult. *Room at the Top* has an X certificate and deserves it – not for any cheap sensationalism but because it is an unblushingly frank portrayal of intimate human relationships.'[15] John Woolf, still unconvinced that the film would reach a 'quality' audience, advertised it as 'a savage story of lust and ambition', but at the end of 1959 *Room at the Top* emerged as the fourth most popular film of the year (behind *Carry On Nurse, I'm All Right Jack* and *The Inn of the Sixth Happiness*) and was acclaimed around the world as the harbinger of a new British cinema.[16] There was going to be no massive infusion of new blood, but cracks were beginning to appear in the British film industry's facade of bland conformity.

Life at the Kitchen Sink
Tony Richardson had begun his career as a television director with the BBC in the early 50s. He left to make *Momma Don't Allow* with Karel Reisz in 1955 and then, seeing no openings in the film industry, joined

15

George Devine in setting up the English Stage Company at the Royal Court. If the British film industry in the mid-50s was uninvitingly stagnant, the stage, where Terence Rattigan was regarded as Britain's best dramatist and Sandy Wilson's nostalgic musicals were seen as excitingly original, was even more of a backwater. As Kenneth Tynan put it in 1954: 'The bare fact is that apart from revivals and imports there is nothing in the London theatre that one dares discuss with an intelligent man for more than five minutes.'[17] In this context Richardson's production of John Osborne's *Look Back in Anger* in May 1956 had the effect of a bombshell, and Richardson determined to use the play as a Trojan horse to get himself and his Free Cinema collaborators into the film industry.[18] With John Osborne and the experienced American producer Harry Saltzman, he formed a production company, Woodfall; and when Richard Burton expressed a desire to play Jimmy Porter, Warner Brothers agreed to finance a film version of *Look Back in Anger*.[19]

Along with fictional precursors like John Wain's Charles Lumley and Kingsley Amis's Jim Dixon and real-life contemporaries such as the self-taught philosopher Colin Wilson, Jimmy Porter and his creator were taken to represent a new type – the Angry Young Man. But by 1959, when the film of *Look Back in Anger* was released, Wilson had fallen from favour, Amis, Wain and Osborne were tucking in to the fruits of fame, and Angry Young Men no longer seemed so significant. Thus changes wrought on the play by a commercially nervous film industry – established stars, greater emphasis on sex and less on politics, insistence on conventional studio film-making under the control of an experienced lighting cameraman – were less harmful than they might have been.

As a director's first film, *Look Back in Anger* is less assured and accomplished than *Room at the Top*, but the comparison is not entirely fair. Whereas Jack Clayton is a meticulous craftsman whose infrequent films are highly polished and complete, Richardson has an impatient disregard for technical standards:

> the whole tone of the picture business is to strive for technical perfection, but we all know this doesn't matter a tiny damn – the thing can be appalling in many ways technically and yet still be a wonderful and marvellous film. Gloss guarantees nothing ... whereas the cost of technical perfection hampers the industry.[20]

It is not surprising, then, that Richardson's films rarely achieve a harmonious artistic unity, but his constant willingness to experiment deserves more credit than it generally receives. Apart from a few bravura touches at the beginning, *Look Back in Anger* is surprisingly disciplined, and with the help of Oswald Morris's sensitive studio photography Richardson evokes a bed-sitter world where it is always Sunday and always raining. The new characters introduced to open out the play – a lacklustre Indian underwear salesman and a fruity old Cockney played by Edith Evans – seem irrelevant, but they function as outlets for Jimmy's political and social conscience, allowing Richardson to cut his tirades and concentrate attention on the relationship between Jimmy and Alison: a battlefield of selfishness, indulgence, immaturity, passion and boredom. One can regret that in comparison with, say, *Brief Encounter* (which is remarkably close to *Look Back in Anger* in its claustrophobic intensity) passion is reduced from something that lights up the world or casts it into deep shadow to a weary game of make-believe, but the change encompasses an impatient dismissal of the static, repressed, over-civilised world of the upper-middle classes. As the American critic Stanley Kauffman argued: 'To be stripped of the earthly and cosmic certainties of the past is to be lonely indeed, but it is also to be free of illusions . . . If there is no longer a comfy old world, there is room to make another. If there is no God, there is still man.'[21]

One does, briefly, glimpse a kitchen sink in *Look Back in Anger*, but the film has little to do with either the working class or with the realist tradition in British cinema. That Osborne was not a working-class realist writer was confirmed by his second play, *The Entertainer*, filmed by Richardson in 1960. Laurence Olivier's performance as the down-at-heel music hall comedian Archie Rice turned the play into a big success, but it was a difficult subject to film. Osborne draws parallels between the state of Britain, on its last legs as an imperial power after the Suez debacle, and that of the music hall, declining into a decrepitude of girly shows and TV spin-offs, but these parallels were easier to maintain in the theatre than in the cinema – particularly in the realistically inclined cinema of Tony Richardson.

Much of the film was shot on location (at the Lancashire seaside town of Morecambe), but Archie and his ill-matched family look as if they have been retrieved from the baggage of a pre-war touring theatre company and are oddly out of place among the fresh air and fun. The exception is Archie's father, Billy Rice, a music hall performer of the old school who copes with the humiliations and disappointments of old age secure in the knowledge that he lived life to the full when he had the chance. In the play he is a sympathetic but insignificant old wreck, living in a dream world of nostalgia for the Good Old Days of the music hall's heyday. As played by Roger Livesey, he becomes a much more significant figure. Livesey, himself the son of an old character actor, had almost twenty years earlier made his mark in *The Life and Death of Colonel Blimp*, progressing in the space of the film's 163 minutes from dashing young subaltern to the walrus-like old gentleman made famous by David Low's cartoons. By 1960 he didn't need to age himself and it is his presence, inadvertently dominating the squabbling household, which brings the film to life. His rendering of the ridiculously jingoistic 'Don't Let Them Scrap the British Navy' is moving rather than embarrassing, but it fatally unbalances the film, making Archie's moment of truth, his memory of an 'old fat negress getting up to sing about Jesus or something', look like sentimental twaddle. Billy's death in the wings of the theatre minutes before a comeback intended to rescue his rascally son from bankruptcy effectively closes the film, and one shares the disappointment and frustration of the theatre audience as they slowly file out while Archie does his 'the show must go on' routine.

With nothing equivalent to Richard Burton's box-office appeal and the 'sex angle' of *Look Back in Anger*, *The Entertainer* faced a hostile reception from the film trade. There were delays in releasing the film, and support from the critics was too lukewarm to boost audiences when the film was shown. With Woodfall's fortunes at a low ebb, Richardson shelved his ideas of directing Shelagh Delaney's *A Taste of Honey* and Colin MacInnes's *City of Spades* and accepted an offer from 20th Century-Fox to make a film in Hollywood (an adaptation of William Faulkner's *Sanctuary*). Karel Reisz was brought in to direct *Saturday Night and Sunday Morning* on a budget of £117,000, little more than half that of *The Entertainer* and *Look Back in Anger*.[22]

The novel, by Alan Sillitoe, had been a success and aroused considerable interest in left-wing circles, but it was not considered to have the same popular appeal as *Room at the Top*.[23] One producer, Joseph Janni, had already tried and failed to find a financial backer, but Michael Balcon's Bryanston consortium was anxious to encourage new blood and agreed to put up the money for Woodfall. The low budget had no ill effects on the look of the film (though the six-week shooting schedule was so tight that Reisz had to go to bed for a week to recover from his exertions), the main saving being on the cast.[24] Only Shirley Ann Field, who had appeared in a number of starlet roles and as the stage-struck beauty queen seduced by Archie in *The Entertainer*, could be considered an established film actress. Albert Finney had made his debut in *The Entertainer*, but in a small part memorable only in retrospect and he was best known for his Shakespearean acting and his West End success as Billy Liar. Rachel Roberts had played several minor film roles but she too was better known for her stage work, and many of the other actors – Bryan Pringle, Colin Blakely, Hylda Baker – were making their film debuts.

The film opens with the sort of sequence one might expect from a documentary-maker with an interest in the working class. In a busy, noisy factory a worker toiling at his lathe expresses his attitude to work and the world at large. But in contrast to the patronising bonhomie of the orthodox documentary, this worker expresses attitudes which are a deliberate affront to middle-class sensibilities: 'No use working every minute God sends, that's my motto. Don't let the bastards grind you down. That's one thing I've learned ... I'd like to see anybody try to grind me down. That'd be the day. What I want is a good time. All the rest is propaganda.' Karel Reisz had come to England from Czechoslovakia as a teenager in the 1930s. As a middle-class, mid-European Jew he had little in common with Arthur Seaton the bolshie Nottingham factory worker, and he later confessed he had little sympathy for him: 'In a metaphorical way Arthur embodied what was happening in England: he was a sad person, terribly limited in his sensibilities, narrow in his ambitions and a bloody fool into the bargain, by no means a standard-bearer for any ideas of mine.'[25] But Reisz's detachment, his position outside the English class system, allowed him to give objective expression to a voice hitherto unheard in British cinema. As Alan Lovell acutely points out:

> Karel Reisz gets his main effect from the style he uses. It's almost an anti-style. The camera does only enough work to tell the story as simply and directly as possible. Because of this the audience is encouraged to make judgments for itself. Just how important this is has gone unnoticed. Very few contemporary films, whatever their quality, leave their audience alone. Nearly every director, either

A young rebel twisting and turning in the trap of dead-end working-class life: Albert Finney, *Saturday Night and Sunday Morning*

19

serious or hack, tries to bludgeon his audience by his technical skill or his dramatic talents. Because of their uncertainty about their relationship with the audience, directors seem constantly to be saying 'Look I'm here and I'm good'. Very few film-makers have enough confidence in the audience just to assume their co-operation. Karel Reisz does just this.[26]

The analytical approach evident in his book *The Technique of Film Editing* (and the fact that he was able to call on the services of Seth Holt to edit the film) stood him in good stead. But unlike Richardson, who had to work with two idiosyncratic, stylised stage plays, Reisz had a good script from a very filmic novel to work from.

Alan Sillitoe shared characteristics with writers like John Braine, Stan Barstow, Keith Waterhouse and David Storey, all of whom came from the north of England, all of whom wrote about working-class characters. But Sillitoe had been pensioned out of the RAF with tuberculosis at the age of twenty-two, and rather than return to the damp slums of Nottingham where he was born, he eked out his pension in the warmer (and cheaper) climes of France and Spain. There he learnt French, Spanish and Catalan and tried to be a writer. *Saturday Night and Sunday Morning* was begun under an orange tree in Majorca in 1955, and Sillitoe's literary mentors were J. D. Salinger and Norman Mailer rather than Kingsley Amis and John Wain.[27] He had originally intended to write short stories rather than a novel, and *Saturday Night and Sunday Morning* is primarily a series of episodes built round the character of Arthur Seaton, a young rebel twisting and turning in the trap of dead-end working-class life. Unlike Joe Lampton, who aspires to the middle class, or Jimmy Porter, cut off from his working-class roots by his university education, Arthur's way out is not into another class but in an arrogant refusal to surrender his individual identity:

> What am I? he wondered. A six-foot pit prop that wants a pint of ale. That's what I am. And if any knowing bastard says that's what I am, I'm a dynamite dealer, sten-gun seller, hundred-ton tank trader, a capstan-lathe operator waiting to blow the Army to Kingdom Cum. I'm me and nobody else; and whatever people think I am or say I am, that's what I'm not, because they don't know a bloody thing about me.[28]

In the book, and as played by Albert Finney in the film, Arthur escapes any attempt to pity him or to moralise about him.

The film ends with Arthur and Doreen, the young woman he has agreed to settle down with, walking in the fields outside the city which are being encroached upon by new housing estates. Arthur throws stones at the houses and when reproved by Doreen tells her that it won't be the last stone he throws. To Reisz, this was a downbeat ending showing the inevitability of Arthur being tamed by the system. But Sillitoe had a more positive interpretation:

> These last scenes stamp Arthur as having changed from when we first saw him at the beginning of the film; yet they also show him to be basically the same person, to the extent that he is still going to be someone with a mind of his own, a mind that can't be so easily got at as most people's seem to be. It is also obvious that for him, life is just beginning.[29]

Despite favourable advance publicity and optimism from publishers – Pan launched a paperback edition before the film was released, hoping to sell 250,000 copies – the film trade was as hostile to *Saturday Night and Sunday Morning* as they had been to *The Entertainer*.[30] Fortunately, when the film did secure a West End release, the critics recognised it as a landmark in British cinema. Even 'old squares' like Fred Majdalany in the *Daily Mail*, while deploring the film's morality, acknowledged its significance, and audiences flocked to see it. In its three-week run round the London circuit cinemas *Saturday Night and Sunday Morning* became the first film to take in more than £100,000, outgrossing even the lavishly promoted *Hercules Unchained*.[31] Woodfall was at last financially secure and Richardson was able to fulfil his desire to make *A Taste of Honey* as an all-location film.

In financial terms Woodfall was a conventional film production company operating within the commercial network of the industry, but Richardson was not content to make films in the conventional way. In particular he disliked the artificiality of making films in studios. He told Colin Young in 1960:

> I hate studios. I no longer want to shoot even interiors in a studio, I would rather work in the limited conditions which a location imposes upon you. For the sort of realistic films I want to make, by improvising one's way out of the impossibilities of real conditions you get something on the screen that is more true, somehow, than something contrived on a set ... once inside a studio you start taking walls out, you start thinking 'wouldn't it be fun if we tracked from here to there, pan round there?' – and you know, do a lot of fancy stuff. One is getting in fact less of the human reality.[32]

The Entertainer and *Saturday Night and Sunday Morning* had been partly shot on location but they were still studio-based and he was determined that *A Taste of Honey* would be made entirely on location. According to the cameraman Walter Lassally, this had special advantages to a maverick like Richardson:

On location in Manchester: *A Taste of Honey*

> By not being based on a major studio we were able to hand-pick our crew, particularly the electricians, carpenters and grips, and thus got not a smaller, but a much more enthusiastic group of colleagues together, whilst still complying faithfully with union minimum crew requirements.[33]

Lassally was the cameraman on Anderson, Reisz and Richardson's Free Cinema films and was respected in Europe for his three films with the Greek Cypriot director Michael Cacoyannis – *A Girl in Black*, *A Matter of Dignity* and *Electra*. But in Britain he was vetoed from *Look Back in Anger* and *The Entertainer* and was only able to find work on 'B' films like Edmond T. Gréville's *Beat Girl*. *A Taste of Honey* was as important to him as it was to Richardson, and their collaboration proved extremely fruitful.

Much more than the other films made by Richardson, Reisz and Anderson, *A Taste of Honey* inherits the 'poetic realism' of Free Cinema: its playground-game theme music echoes *The Singing Street*, its excursion to a seaside amusement parlour *O Dreamland*, its affection for gloomy slumland streets *Together*, and its young lovers are not far removed from the working-class youth of *Momma Don't Allow* and *We Are the Lambeth Boys*. As Lassally points out, despite its grim setting and unhappy ending it is 'above all a romantic and lyrical

22

film'.[34] Back in 1959 Richardson, exposing 'The Man behind the Angry Young Man', asserted that 'There is a general conception that entertainment is escape, a sweet sentimental dream remote from any sense of reality. There is a definite resistance in both the cinema and the theatre to the "sordid". It's the easiest dirty label that conservative opinion has always used.'[35] *A Taste of Honey* was Richardson's first venture into the industrial slumland of the North, but there is little of the anger and disgust of the earlier Kitchen Sink films. Jo, the heroine (Rita Tushingham), is a schoolgirl and the soundtrack is haunted by children's songs; her pregnancy is accepted as the casual consequence of a childish romance, and her subsequent relationship with a young homosexual results in sadness and compromise but not tragedy.

A Taste of Honey was a commercial success, and with Lassally and the same team of technicians Richardson turned to Sillitoe's short story *The Loneliness of the Long Distance Runner*. Filmed with the sort of boisterous gimmickry which Richardson was to take even further in *Tom Jones*, the film attracted almost universal condemnation for what were considered excessive and inappropriate borrowings from the French *nouvelle vague*. The *Monthly Film Bulletin* complained of its 'restless trickery' and expressed a 'reactionary longing . . . for some solid, dramatic meat of the most old-fashioned kind.'[36] And *Sight and Sound*, in a full-scale assault on the film, insisted that: 'Instead of subtly evoking a minutely personal yet symptomatic state of mind, the film's vision has been narrowed to an examination of a social situation, and to the offering of an analysis which rings disquietingly false.'[37] Attacks on Richardson were sometimes coupled with querulous protests at the sympathy extended to working-class youths with no sense of their responsibilities, and complaints that the Kitchen Sink films 'succeeded in presenting us less with the unique quality of individual life than with the broad general outlines of sociological types.'[38]

The reception of *The Loneliness of the Long Distance Runner* marks a critical turning away from realism, though ironically, in style if not in content, the film can be seen as the first of the 'Swinging Sixties' films. It is by no means an unflawed masterpiece, and there is some justification for critical irritation with whirling tree-top shots, heavy-handed montage sequences and an over-insistent score. But some of Lassally and Richardson's experiments are wonderfully effective – Colin's early morning run across the horizon from the dying moon in one corner of the frame to the rising sun in the other; the dissolve from Skegness beach, where Colin has spent a windswept interlude of happiness, to the waterlogged woods where he does his training; the sequence after the funeral where Colin goes through the living room to the back bedroom (the house is a pre-fab bungalow), looks at the bed on which his father died, and burns one of the pound notes his mother has given him from the compensation money as a sacrificial offering to the dead.

In Sillitoe's story Colin Smith is similar to Arthur Seaton but even more of a nihilist with his criminal's alienation from society. As developed by Tom Courtenay in the film, Colin pursues a more rational and considered rebellion. Predictably, some critics complained that Colin's character had been politicised, finding it unbelievable that a working-class youth could be capable of rational political thought.[39] In fact Courtenay's Colin was something of a portent for the future, a fictional precursor of those intelligent working-class rebels who would flirt with Trotskyism in the later 1960s and early 1970s.

The Loneliness of the Long Distance Runner shares with *A Taste of Honey* a casualness which enables it to deal with emotive subjects without becoming sentimental, and an array of vital, idiosyncratic characters. Courtenay's performance was praised in even the most hostile reviews, but the supporting characters – who have hardly any independent existence in Sillitoe's story – are also vividly brought to life. The film's strength, though, comes not from virtuoso performances but from its authenticity and emotional honesty. Thus the Borstal and its inhabitants – the dim shed where the lads stand in line dismantling gas masks, the caricature of a governor and of the new type of 'progressive' prison officer – capture the aura of criminal autobiographies like Mark Benney's *Low Life* and Frank Norman's *Bang to Rights*.[40] The cramped home presided over by Avis Bunnage's tough working-class mum – as determined as Arthur Seaton not to be 'ground down' and as hostile as her son to the police and the bosses – has an untidiness which reflects Colin's disregard of the material world.[41] The scenes with the girls – the casual pick-up in the stolen Ford Prefect, the trip to Skegness with James Bolam pairing off with bubbly, blonde Julia Foster, while Colin makes the best of the moody, cautious girl played by Topsy Jane – are exemplary in concisely sketching out situations and relationships which give depth and subtlety to Colin's character.[42]

Raymond Durgnat, in one of the few sympathetic assessments of Richardson's work, argues that, like Shakespeare and Dickens, Richardson 'works on the "fruit cake" principle of piling into every context as many dense, lyrical, chunky, nourishing details as he can. Perhaps his basic artistic problem is an emotional, impetuous (as contrasted to a cold, closed) dogmatism: he wants to combine simple social messages with a wealth of dramatic complexity.'[43] If one accepts this viewpoint, a film like *A Taste of Honey* which does form a harmonious whole is an accidental fluke and untypical of Richardson's flawed but interesting films. What *The Loneliness of the Long Distance Runner* does share with Richardson's other films is a sincerity which commands respect.

Dreams of Leaving

A Kind of Loving, the other crucially important film in the Kitchen Sink series, was as different as the Woodfall films from the output of the mainstream industry. But as with *Room at the Top*, the production company responsible for it was a thoroughly commercial set-up. The producer, Joseph Janni, an Italian who came to Britain before the war, had been responsible for a mixed bunch of interesting films and, like the Woolfs, he was quick to see the potential of the New Wave writers.[44] He had acquired an option on *Saturday Night and Sunday Morning*, but after failing to find a financial backer had been forced to relinquish it to Woodfall. Fearing that the same thing would happen with *A Kind of Loving*, he turned to a small but dynamic production/distribution company, Anglo Amalgamated, run by two shrewd Jewish businessmen, Nat Cohen and Stuart Levy. Most of Anglo Amalgamated's own productions were low-budget crime thrillers and comedies (they had initiated the *Carry On* series) but they were prepared to take risks occasionally and Janni was able to convince them that money could be made from Kitchen Sink realism. John Schlesinger, the director chosen by Janni, was not unlike Richardson and Anderson in background and interests. He had made low-budget films while at Cambridge, acquired a reputation for inventiveness as a television director, and directed a prize-winning documentary about Waterloo railway station, *Terminus*. But he had also worked as Basil Dearden's assistant on the television film series *The Four Just Men* and seemed more safely conventional than the Free Cinema directors.

A Kind of Loving is the most realistic, least melodramatic of the Kitchen Sink films. In contrast to the aggressive male heroes of *Look Back in Anger*, *Saturday Night and Sunday Morning* and *This Sporting Life*, and the social misfits of *A Taste of Honey* and *The Loneliness of the Long Distance Runner*, the hero and heroine of *A Kind of Loving* are almost painfully ordinary. Vic (Alan Bates) and Ingrid (June Ritchie) are working-class, but they have moved into comfortable white-collar jobs and have no fundamental grudge against the world. The interest which Vic shows in high culture in Stan Barstow's novel has disappeared in the film, replaced only by a vague apprehension that there might be something better than the sort of life he seems to be heading for. The class differences which are explored are those within the working class and assume the form of domestic rows rather than tragic gestures, of petty snobberies and mixed loyalties rather than oppression and injustice. The film ends with Ingrid reluctantly giving up her ideas of a smart semi-detached home and Vic trying to overcome his dirty postcard view of women, but what is celebrated is not conformism and repression but the necessity of respect and understanding in a relationship. Their decision to try to make their marriage work – beyond the baleful eye of Ingrid's mother – seems like a triumph of emotional courage and honesty over egotistical selfishness, rather than a lapse into stultifying conformity.

Except for its North of England setting and the inexperience of its director, there would seem little reason to categorise *A Kind of Loving* with the Woodfall films rather than with other adaptations of popular realist novels like Peter Glenville's *Term of Trial* and Bryan Forbes's *The L-Shaped Room*. In fact Schlesinger, the first major British director to cut his teeth on television, was a pioneer of a different type of documentary realism. His discursive objectivity, his refusal to get too close to his characters, is very different from Richardson's more visceral style, but the two directors share a sympathetic and unpatronising attitude to young people and an urge to get out of the studios and shoot their films in real places. This is more clearly evident in Schlesinger's next film, *Billy Liar!* (1963). Billy, played by Tom Courtenay, has the same sort of low status white-collar job as Joe Lampton and Vic Brown. But he inhabits a world which is being rebuilt around him. Old buildings are being torn down to make way for offices and supermarkets, and if this brave new world is welcomed only half-heartedly there is little nostalgia for the past. The old figures of authority – Leonard Rossiter's office tyrant, Finlay Currie's pompous alderman, Wilfred Pickles's crumpled patriarch – are afforded little respect, and hope for the future is embodied in Liz (Julie Christie), the footloose girl who breezes into Billy's life and generously offers him an escape route.

Life and Art
The Loneliness of the Long Distance Runner was Woodfall's last Kitchen Sink film; its natural successor, *This Sporting Life*, was bought by Leslie Parkyn and Julian Wintle, the independent producers who ran Beaconsfield studios. They had strong links with the Rank Organisation and persuaded Rank to put up £350,000 (a high budget for a debut film) for Karel Reisz to produce and Lindsay Anderson to direct the film. By early 1963, when the film was released, the tide was running against the New Wave. Carol Reed (in defending his own poorly conceived and poorly received film *The Running Man*) protested that cinemagoers didn't want 'to look for an hour or two at a kitchen sink, a one-set movie, the greasy dishes and the mental and moral miasma of certain elements in society', and critical opinion on *This Sporting Life* was divided between those who found it portentous and overwrought and those who thought it a masterpiece.[45] Condemnation of the film's complex system of flashbacks and its lack of entertainment value now seems simple-minded. But the point made by Peter Armitage, that Anderson's stress on the artistic and personal rather than the sociological and general constricts the film's universality, deserves more serious consideration.[46]

26

On location in Bradford: *Billy Liar!*

David Storey's novel, which sets its unhappy love affair against the rough male world of a North of England Rugby League club, is much grimmer than *Saturday Night and Sunday Morning* and *A Kind of Loving*. Its hero, Arthur Machin, enjoys the fruits of affluence – a Jaguar, well-cut clothes – but the world of shabby back-to-backs and industrial squalor in which he operates is still ruled by values and class relations which are essentially Victorian. Where Alan Sillitoe and Stan Barstow look back with affection to working-class warmth and wisdom, Storey paints a darker picture of lives ruined by poverty and sexual repression, the world Joe Lampton was so anxious to leave behind when he moved from Dufton to Warnley.[47]

Anderson retains the bleak atmosphere of the book but – with Storey's collaboration as scriptwriter – he made a conscious effort to play down the 'sociological' aspects of his subject. In an interview with *Films and Filming* shortly before the film was released he announced that:

> *This Sporting Life* is not a film about sport. Nor is it to be categorised as a 'North Country working class story'. ... It is a film about a man. A man of extraordinary power and aggressiveness, both temperamental and physical, but at the same time with a great innate sensitiveness and a need for love of which he is hardly aware.[48]

In Storey's novel the doom-laden relationship between Machin and his

27

widowed landlady, Mrs Hammond, is seen through Machin's eyes, and as he loves her without understanding her she is inevitably a shadowy figure. In the film she is brought to life by Rachel Roberts. Her brooding, witchlike presence haunts the little house she shares with Richard Harris's hulking Machin almost as intensely as Linda Blair does her possessed bedroom in *The Exorcist*. Their guilt-ridden romance – the first sexual encounter is virtually a rape – dominates the film, and ironically, in view of Anderson's background in documentary, what is missing is Storey's evocation of life in a northern industrial town – the grimness, the dirt, the brusque class hostility, the shortened horizons. The sequences in the pub, the restaurant, the boardroom, the Christmas party, are stiff and unconvincing. And the sequences outside Mrs Hammond's home which do work – the glum, masculine brutality of the rugby pitch, the idyllic interlude where Machin drives out into the country with Mrs Hammond and the children – have a dreamlike quality (emphasised by Roberto Gerhard's dissonant score) which distances them from the real world in which the novel is set.

In contrast to the earlier Kitchen Sink films which had been grubbily optimistic, *This Sporting Life* seemed gloomy and defeatist and did poorly at the box-office.[49] Ironically, its commercial failure was used as an excuse for turning against the sort of 'social cinema' from which Anderson and Storey had tried to distance themselves. Sir John Davis, managing director of the Rank Organisation, which had provided *This Sporting Life*'s substantial budget, told his cinema managers:

> We cannot, as a consistent policy, play films which are unacceptable to the public as entertainment. This would lead to disaster for everyone. I do feel that independent producers should take note of public demand and make films of entertainment value. The public has clearly shown that it does not want the dreary kitchen sink dramas.[50]

In fact the opposite was true: those films which kept closest to low-life naturalism – from *Saturday Night and Sunday Morning* to *Up the Junction* – proved popular at the box-office. But it was the changing ambitions and inclinations of the film-makers themselves as much as pressure from the industry which brought the Kitchen Sink cycle to a close.[51]

Class and Femininity

Geoffrey Gorer's brief but influential article 'The Perils of Hypergamy', published in the *New Statesman* in 1957, attempted an anthropological explanation for the aggressive behaviour of Angry Young Men towards women. Gorer argues that in life as in fiction, liaisons between working-class men and middle-class women had hitherto resulted either in the women being reluctantly submerged in the working class (Mrs Morrell in Lawrence's *Sons and Lovers*, for example) or in the man – generally marked by exceptional vigour or talent – being accepted into the middle classes. What distinguishes Jimmy Porter and his ilk is that they don't *want* to be accepted. For Jimmy, Alison's family, far from representing the cultured, intelligent, civilised lifestyle that he, with his university education, can legitimately aspire to, are members of an emotionally sterile, intellectually bankrupt, morally repugnant elite. When Osborne himself called the Royal Family 'a gold filling in a mouthful of decay', it was merely an extension of Jimmy's inveterate hostility towards the Establishment.[52]

In his book *Sex, Class and Realism*, John Hill argues that the real subject of *Look Back in Anger* 'was neither social injustice nor hypocrisy but the debasement and degradation of women'.[53] It is a temptingly bold judgment but it ignores the historical context in which the play and the film first appeared. Jimmy's abuse of Alison is not due to some outdated, sadistic misogyny but because he is incapable of resolving the dilemma his wife poses for him in terms of values and principles, and Alison is too conventional – she sees nothing wrong with the values her parents represent – to meet him halfway. Women do come heavily under attack from the Angry Young Men, but as D. E. Cooper points out, it is less women as such than the ethos of 'effeminacy' which they object to. As Cooper puts it: 'Effeminacy is simply the sum of those qualities which are supposed traditionally, with more or less justice, to exude from the worst in women: pettiness, snobbery, flippancy, voluptuousness, superficiality, materialism.'[54] Women like Alison's mother can be seen as the last pallid upholders of outmoded ideas and institutions – the Church, the Royal Family, the Army, the Public Schools, Harrods – which their menfolk have quietly stopped believing in.

A second anti-feminine argument, articulated as early as 1955 by Martin Green, associates women with the trivial values of the affluent society. Green, a young teacher whose sojourns in Turkey and North America helped him to make uncannily acute observations on the nature of British society in the 1950s, complained that the increasing attention given to gossip in the newspapers and the feeble gentility of the BBC ('Auntie') indicated an erosion of vigorous masculine values:

It is a natural consequence, I'd suggest, of this feminization, that so many personalities in the public eye affect eccentricities – Peter Ustinov, Robert Morley, Gilbert Harding. They are driven to affectation because there is not enough room for self-assertion in the masculine role as socially defined. To be merely a man is too nearly to limit yourself to the scope of Sir Anthony Eden or Lord Attlee.

Defining femininity: Murray Melvin and Dora Bryan, *A Taste of Honey*

Young men do not know how to become individual, in a feminine society.[55]

For John Hill, the Kitchen Sink films in general and *A Kind of Loving* in particular, where 'the superficial values of the new "affluence" are linked inextricably with women, whose obsession with house, television, clothes and physical appearance is persistently emphasised throughout the film', express a similar anxiety about the erosion of masculinity.[56] Vic is rendered impotent in the home of his dragon-like mother-in-law (Thora Hird) and brow-beaten into watching television trash like 'Spot Quiz' instead of enjoying the virile virtues of a brass band concert.

The products of affluence – labour-saving devices, more comfortable homes, even the television set – tended to benefit working-class women more than it did their husbands, who had had their hobbies, allotments, sporting and drinking activities to get them out of the home. But for young working-class men affluence opened up new horizons. Arthur Seaton, 'terribly limited in his sensibilities' and 'narrow in his ambitions' though he is, is still able to take advantage of full employment and a fat wage packet to assume a belligerent, devil-may-care attitude to the world. For working-class grammar-school boys like Joe Lampton, Vic Brown and Billy Fisher, and the teenage protagonists of Colin MacInnes's *Absolute Beginners* and Ray Gosling's *Sum Total*, the benefits are less straightforward. They don't have to follow their father's footsteps into mines and factories, but in breaking away from traditional working-class culture they find themselves adrift in a world where the rules are uncertain. They retain a defensive affection for old values while recognising that they themselves have to find a new path.

Hill argues that the Kitchen Sink films belie their status as progressive films by their misogynist attitude to women, but his Marxist puritanism leads him into dangerously wide generalisations.[57] *Room at the*

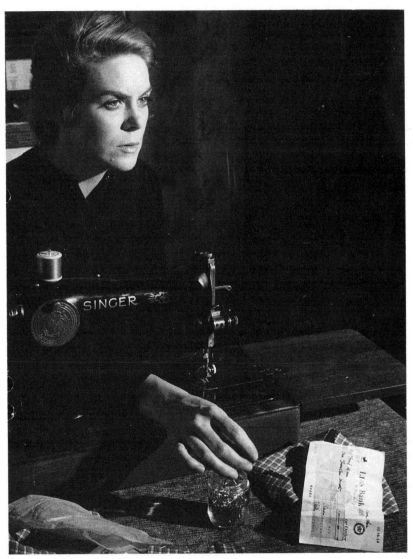

Incandescently intense women: Rachel Roberts, *This Sporting Life*

Top's Lawrentian romanticism is worlds apart from the raw working-class pragmatism of *Saturday Night and Sunday Morning* and the erotic adolescent daydreams of *A Kind of Loving* and *Billy Liar!*, and none of them has much in common with the love/hate relationship Jimmy Porter has with women (and the world). But these working-class heroes do share an almost obsessive interest in women, particularly when contrasted with their urbane predecessors (Dirk Bogarde, Jack Hawkins, Kenneth More, John Mills), who were too busy with wars and good-deeds-for-the-day to worry about women. Geoffrey Gorer points out that migrants from the working class tend to seek security and reassurance in sexual prowess:

> In their secondary school days the future university students are likely to have undergone a good deal of mockery and self-questioning for their studious abstention from the pursuit of money and pleasure which their mates enjoy from the age of fifteen; and consequently they feel driven to emphasise their manliness in such ways as are open to them, perhaps by surliness or pugnacity, but certainly by frequent copulation or attempts thereat.[58]

One searches in vain for such a character in the Kitchen Sink films, and later working-class Lotharios like Michael Caine's Alfie and Ray Brooks's Tolen in *The Knack* don't quite fit Gorer's pattern. Joe Lampton and Jimmy Porter are locked into passionately destructive monogamous relationships which they evade only at great spiritual cost. Vic Brown, Colin Smith and Billy Fisher are not socially mobile enough to mix with middle-class girls and seek the sort of exciting but equal relationship which unconventional, classless young women like Liz in *Billy Liar!* seem to promise.

Arthur Seaton in *Saturday Night and Sunday Morning*, with his fourteen suits and his insistence on having a good time, seems to represent a more traditional working-class machismo. But in his attitude to women he performs a moral balancing act whereby guilt about illicit sex is assuaged by a careful attention to the feelings and sexual needs of the woman:

> Arthur classified husbands into two main categories: those that looked after their wives, and those that were slow. ... He had no pity for a slow husband. There was something lacking in them, not like a man with one leg that could in no way be put right, but something they, the slow husbands, could easily rectify if they became less selfish, brightened up their ideas, and looked after their wives a bit better. For Arthur, in his more tolerant moments, said that women were more than ornaments and skivvies: they were warm wonderful creatures that needed and deserved to be looked

after, requiring all the attention a man could give, certainly more than the man's work or a man's own pleasure.[59]

Admittedly this ethos is more strongly expressed in the book than in the film, but the simplification of Arthur's moral complexity is counterbalanced by the more prominent roles given to Brenda (who shares Arthur with her sister in the book) and Doreen (who makes her appearance much earlier in the film).

Women in the Kitchen Sink films suffer interminably. Brenda (Rachel Roberts) is a willing partner in her sexual liaison with Arthur, but when it comes to the consequences the price she has to pay is immeasurably greater. The BBFC refused to allow the sequence where she tries to terminate her pregnancy by drinking gin while soaking herself in a hot bath, but her predicament is vividly illuminated in the anxiety-ridden meetings with Arthur and the final guilty encounter at the fair. Like Ingrid in *A Kind of Loving*, Alison in *Look Back in Anger*, Susan in *Room at the Top*, Jo in *A Taste of Honey*, her independence is abruptly curtailed by pregnancy. Like Mrs Hammond in *This Sporting Life* and Alice Aisgill in *Room at the Top*, the happiness she finds in a sexual relationship with a man is soon clouded by tragedy. Nevertheless, to complain as Hill does that the Kitchen Sink films were all too often 'content to abandon their female characters to the confinement of familiar domestic and marital roles and even inflict a "punishment" on those who chose to stray beyond', is to miss the fact that these incandescently intense women have a seriousness, an emotional weight, altogether lacking in the pathetically trivial roles women had to play in most 1950s British films.[60]

2

80,000 PROBLEMS

If people want to leave the earth because neither desperate necessity nor clear hopes are there to keep them on it, then to be in the midst of life ... will be considered boring, unentertaining, old-fashioned and grim. ... Every time an art needs to revitalise itself after a period of formalism – and prestige art is always formalist – artists will turn back to reality; but their attitude to reality, and the way they interpret it, will depend upon the particular needs of their time. That is why realism can never be defined as a style, and can never mean an acquiescent return to a previous tradition. (John Berger, *Sight and Sound*, 1957)[1]

Realism

From the Second World War until the mid-1960s the dominant critical tendency was to see realism as desirable and progressive, but since then critical favour has shifted in the opposite direction. This has made possible the rehabilitation of directors like Michael Powell and Douglas Sirk and a questioning of the orthodox canon of film classics. On the other hand there has been a simplistic assumption that British cinema is dominated by a realist tradition which is both dull and ideologically pernicious. The effect on contemporary British filmmakers is to encourage them to abandon the attempt to come to terms with dense, meaningful narratives and concentrate on creating a dazzling visual surface. (One could cite the progressive evacuation of serious content from the films of Nicolas Roeg after *Bad Timing* and Ken Russell after *Tommy*, or the rapid descent into bathos of Great White Hopes like Neil Jordan and Julian Temple). In mounting a defence of the realist tradition it is necessary to define its characteristics. Essentials would seem to be: psychologically rounded characters; editing and photography that present a coherent view of the world; settings that look real; acting which is naturalistic (the actors look and sound like people one might meet in real life); stories that are not far removed from what might happen to ordinary people. All these qualities are present in some of the Kitchen Sink films – *A Kind of Loving* for example – and some of them are present in all of them. But in Tony Richardson's films restless camera movements and obtrusive sound-tracks tend to disrupt the realist illusion, and in *Room at the Top* and *This Sporting Life* the doomed, melodramatic romances pursued by Joe Lampton and Frank Machin hardly seem to belong to a realist ethos. However, Raymond Williams insists that realism has a political dimension which overrides technique: the bringing of hitherto neglected groups, hitherto unsaid truths, hitherto unexpressed attitudes on to the screen.[2] Working-class characters had occasionally played major roles in British films – Emlyn Williams's ex-convict on the run in *They Drive By Night*, Eric Portman's gutsy foreman in *Millions Like Us* – but Joe Lampton's 'I'm working-class and proud of it' (something he doesn't say in the book) and Arthur Seaton's 'Don't let the bastards grind you down' expressed an aggressiveness which seemed to spell trouble for the old order.

John Berger argues that art alternates between periods of realism and periods of formalism and that the return to realism involves a revitalisation. The Kitchen Sink films were only a tiny minority of the output of the British film industry, but it would be a mistake to underrate their commercial or creative influence or to think of them as esoteric or isolated. Bearing in mind the fact that what is gained tends to seep away, so that it would be optimistic to expect, say, most 1960s films to be better than most 1940s films, the wave of realism which swept through the British film industry in the early 60s did leave behind a residue of real gains in terms of acting, writing and film-making technique as well as in a more imaginative and challenging exploration of the world.

British cinematography and art direction had flowered with unexpected brilliance in the 1940s: cameramen like Robert Krasker, Otto Heller, Guy Green and Jack Cardiff, abetted by such idiosyncratically original art directors as John Bryan, Alfred Junge, Hein Heckroth, Alex Vetchinsky and Andrew Mazzei, adapted expressionist techniques used by German film-makers of the 20s in a subtle, flexible way exemplified by Heller's *Temptation Harbour* and *They Made Me a Fugitive*, Cardiff's *Black Narcissus* and *The Red Shoes*, Green's *Madeleine* and *The Passionate Friends*, Krasker's *Brief Encounter* and *The Third Man*. Sixties style was less exact, less meticulous, a more carefree and adventurous poetry of reality. Location filming introduced a new flexibility, breaking up studio conventions which had become stale and clichéd. Freddie Francis in *Saturday Night and Sunday Morning* and *Room at the Top*, Walter Lassally in *A Taste of Honey* and *The Loneliness of the Long Distance Runner*, Denys Coop in *A Kind of Loving* and

This Sporting Life, Larry Pizer in *Four in the Morning*, *The Party's Over* and *The World Ten Times Over* challenged and stretched the old conventions.

Writers like Frederic Raphael and Harold Pinter brought a complexity and sophistication to screenwriting which had been absent from the British film industry since the heyday of Emeric Pressburger and Launder and Gilliat in the late 40s, but original screenplays continued to be greatly outnumbered by adaptations of novels and plays. A wider range of acting talent came into the film industry and was allowed to flourish in a much less restricted way. Fifties leading men – Richard Todd, Bill Travers, Tony Britton, Donald Sinden, Anthony Steel – tended to be difficult to distinguish from one another, and even Dirk Bogarde, Kenneth More and Jack Hawkins were allowed only a very limited repertoire. In contrast – whatever their later misdemeanours – Albert Finney, Tom Courtenay, Peter Finch, Alan Bates, Terence Stamp, Peter O'Toole, Richard Harris, Michael Caine, Tom Bell, David Hemmings, Sean Connery, Stanley Baker, David Warner, Nicol Williamson, represented something new and exciting. Women had a harder time and the casualty rate was much higher, but while it lasted a cinema which could boast Rachel Roberts, June Ritchie, Sarah Miles, Susannah York, Julie Christie, Lynn and Vanessa Redgrave, Barbara Ferris, Ann Lynn, Janet Munro, Virginia Maskell, Billie Whitelaw and Rita Tushingham had much to be proud of.[3]

The transformation in the sort of films made in Britain after 1958 was inevitably a gradual one. Raymond Durgnat's *A Mirror for England*, though avowedly about the middle-class cinema of the 1945 to 1958 period, continually strays into the 60s. But throwbacks, contradictions, overlaps do not invalidate the real changes that occurred. The change from the beautifully frozen emotions of an indigenous British 50s film like *Mandy* or the frothy sexlessness of the Hollywood-British *Indiscreet* to post-*Room at the Top* films like Robert Siodmak's erotic *The Rough and the Smooth*, or even the glossy Anglo-American adaptations of Tennessee Williams's *Suddenly Last Summer* (1959) and *The Roman Spring of Mrs Stone* (1961), is remarkable.

In war films stiff upper lip attitudes, still intact in such 1958 films as *Sea of Sand*, *I Was Monty's Double*, *The Battle of the V1* and *Ice Cold in Alex*, gradually began to crumble. The new model army of the 60s was made up of Hollywood-style epics, from *The Guns of Navarone* to *The Heroes of Telemark*, and smaller, sourer films tinged with a bitter realism – from Anthony Asquith's *Orders to Kill* in 1959 to Peter Collinson's *The Long Day's Dying* in 1969. These war films were not necessarily better than 50s films like *The Cruel Sea* and *The Dam Busters* but they had a more critical, less reverential view of war which expressed an impatience with the unquestioning conformity of the 50s. There was a similar progression in the crime film. By 1950 the spiv cycle which had enlivened British cinema in the late 40s had been killed off, and the 50s was dominated by what Raymond Durgnat calls 'copperolatry'. The hard-working, flintily honest Scotland Yard detective (exemplified by Jack Hawkins in *The Long Arm* and *Gideon's Day*) replaced the flashily evil spiv as the centre of attention, and law and order ruled. By the end of the decade, however, cracks were beginning to appear. Films like *Blind Date, Beyond This Place, Never Let Go* and *The Criminal* showed the police as fallible, corrupt, and discontented with their jobs and lifestyle.

Even in the horror genre there was a turn towards realism. In contrast to Hollywood's supernatural melodramas, Hammer's films, particularly those directed by Terence Fisher, were made with a neat, unpretentious realism, their horror generated by perilous situations and sudden incursions of gory details. This turn to realism is typical of costume films generally. The popular Gainsborough melodramas of the 40s paid little attention to historical detail, using the past as a fantasy world in which impossible dreams of danger and romance could be lived out. The Technicolor swashbucklers made in England by MGM and Disney in the 50s were equally remote from reality, but the 60s also saw an extraordinary cycle of historical films – from *Billy Budd* and *HMS Defiant* at the beginning of the decade to *Alfred the Great* and *Cromwell* at the end – which tried to combine painstaking historical accuracy with an attempt to make their protagonists and their problems relevant to modern society.

The old and the new British cinema can be seen side by side in the two films made about Oscar Wilde released simultaneously in May 1960. Gregory Ratoff's *Oscar Wilde* is a modestly budgeted black and white film bearing a family resemblance to John Croydon and Robert Day's two horror/social problem films *Corridors of Blood* and *Grip of the Strangler*, which combine sensationalism with a reforming social message. Here the sensationalism is only hinted at, with Robert Morley playing Wilde as an ageing man with an avuncular affection for fragile, neurotic Lord Alfred Douglas. Ken Hughes's *The Trials of Oscar Wilde* is on a different scale altogether: over two hours long, in CinemaScope and Technicolor, and with sets designed by Ken Adam, whose flair for sumptuous production design on a limited budget was to prove so successful on the James Bond films.[4] *Oscar Wilde*, despite being made by a Hollywood veteran for 20th Century-Fox, has that modest, not-really-trying quality that characterises much of the output of the British film industry in the 50s. Except when facing Ralph Richardson's implacably bigoted Edward Carson in the courtroom, Morley's Wilde dominates the film, reducing the other characters – Phyllis Calvert as Constance, John Neville as Lord Alfred Douglas, Edward Chapman as Queensberry – to ciphers. He delivers Wilde's epigrams wittily but captures nothing of the man.

In *The Trials of Oscar Wilde*, Peter Finch creates an arrogant, talented, doomed character brought low by malice and small-minded prejudice. Finch's Wilde is charismatic but vulnerable, with feelings susceptible to the people around him. Consequently there is room for the other characters to achieve a life of their own. Yvonne Mitchell and Maxine Audley playing Wilde's sophisticated, spirited but cold women, Lionel Jeffries' grumpily psychotic Queensberry, and John Fraser's fatally attractive Lord Alfred, grow into major characters who help to distance us from Wilde without diminishing our sympathy for him. Nothing is admitted – indeed the whole film is built around Wilde's attempt to clear his name from Queensberry's insinuations – but his relationship with Lord Alfred, culminating in a noisy, tearful row in a Brighton lodging house, shows a startlingly vivid picture of the perils and attractions of love between men.

Gentlemen's Agreements

In terms of authentic dialogue and settings and emotionally convincing characters the development of realism can be traced in thrillers, war films, melodramas, even comedies. But there was a particular tradition of social problem realism in British cinema. Beginning with the moral homilies of films sponsored by the Temperance movement and low-life melodramas of the silent period, it matured in the 1930s with such films as John Baxter's *Doss House*, Victor Saville's *South Riding* and Carol Reed's *Bank Holiday* and *The Stars Look Down*. In the 40s the Ealing films of Basil Dearden and Michael Relph, and the sensationalised modern melodramas made by Sydney, Muriel and Betty Box at Gainsborough, kept the tradition alive. Dearden and Relph's *The Captive Heart*, *Frieda*, *The Blue Lamp*, *Pool of London*, *I Believe in You*, dealt variously with the problems of prisoners-of-war separated from their families, race and colour prejudice, juvenile delinquency, and post-war adjustment. After 1952 their work seemed to lose its impetus, but a fruitful collaboration with the writer Janet Green led to three films equal in intensity and resonance to the best of their earlier films – *Sapphire* (1959), *Victim* (1961), and *Life for Ruth* (1962).

Sapphire and *Victim* were well received by the industry (*Sapphire* was the British Film Academy's Best Film of the Year) and by the critical establishment. But younger, more radical critics like Victor Perkins saw Dearden and Relph as representative of everything that was wrong with the British film industry:

Their method is to devise a number of stereotypes to represent every possible attitude to the matter in hand; they have no success in their attempts to pass these stereotypes off as human beings. These pictures are particularly offensive in assuming that their holy platitudes are too loftily intellectual to be accepted by audiences unless

In the City of Spades: Michael Craig, *Sapphire*

the pill of wisdom is sweetened with spurious excitement. Thus in *Sapphire* and *Victim*, Basil Dearden and his scriptwriter Janet Green have produced thriller-problem films which work neither as thrillers nor as examinations of a problem, and particularly not as films.[5]

Dearden and Relph's style of film-making does now look stiff and old-fashioned and their approach to social problems simplistic. But the sincerity, the gravity, they bring to their films commands respect, and once one accepts the conventions they rely on, the films are satisfyingly well-made.

Sapphire begins as a conventional British thriller with a woman's body being dumped on Hampstead Heath and two Scotland Yard detectives (Nigel Patrick and Michael Craig) investigating her murder. When they discover that despite her appearance the girl, Sapphire Robbins, is black, the film subtly changes gear as it explores what Colin MacInnes called the City of Spades.[6] The *Sunday Express* commented approvingly that: 'It is a picture of London few people know: a searingly honest attempt to take a look at a smouldering part of the world we live in and which, most of the time, we try to ignore.'[7] But Sapphire's colour turns out to be a red herring. The detectives follow a false trail which leads past the students and nurses of the International Club and the playboy son of a black bishop to Tulip's Club, and from there to the bedside of a jovial racketeer, Horace Big Cigar.[8] Despite hostility and contempt for Sapphire as a girl who rejected her black roots once she found she could pass as white, the casual, spontaneous violence of these denizens of the black demi-monde stops short of murder, and the culprit is finally discovered in the white lower middle-class family of Sapphire's fiancé David Harris (Paul Massie). By getting pregnant and expecting David to marry her, Sapphire threatened the social aspirations of this ferociously respectable family. But for Mildred, the unhappily married daughter of the family (Yvonne Mitchell), this is merely a cover for hysterical sexual jealousy.

Mildred's murderous desire could have been provoked by some blatantly sexual white woman (Diana Dors, Joan Collins, even Sylvia Syms), but the link between irrational race hatred and sexual repression is reinforced by the film's almost obsessive interest in Sapphire's sexuality and its relationship to her colour. 'Red taffeta under a brown skirt,' muses Supt. Hazard, puzzled by Sapphire's dual identity. 'Yes, that's the black beneath the white all right,' his racially prejudiced deputy replies. And though Hazard reproves him for such simplistic assumptions, it is the contrast between the flamboyant sexuality of the blacks (with the exception of Sapphire's brother, a drably respectable family doctor) and the stifling repression of the whites (at least of the Harris family) that gives the film a disturbing resonance which belies its surface message about the need for tolerance and understanding.

Dearden and Relph returned to the race theme three years later in *All Night Long*, a transposition of the *Othello* story to the London jazz scene, but it is a stylised, allegorical film and the true successor to *Sapphire* is their next collaboration with Janet Green, *Victim*, released in August 1961. The formula is similar to that of *Sapphire* – a young man's suicide provokes a police investigation which leads to what Raymond Durgnat calls 'a Cook's Tour round homosexual London'.[9] This time, though, the police play a subsidiary role and the burden of investigation falls on Melvin Farr, a successful barrister played by Dirk Bogarde. Despite appearing in some memorably disreputable roles – a nineteenth-century racing spiv in *Esther Waters*, a psychopathic juvenile gunman in *The Blue Lamp*, a murderous con-man in *Cast a Dark Shadow*, a leather-clad Mexican bandit in *The Singer Not the Song* – Bogarde was still very much a matinée idol, and it was thought he was taking quite a risk in portraying Farr as homosexually inclined.

The Wolfenden Report of 1957 had recommended the decriminalisation of homosexuality; but it was another ten years before legislation was passed, and during this interim period a number of films dealt with homosexuality in a mildly sympathetic way. *The Trials of Oscar Wilde* was the most persuasive, but it was set in the past and Wilde as an artist could be considered a special case. *Serious Charge* (1959, d.

Terence Young), by contrast, is set in a Home Counties dormitory town and concerns an up-to-date vicar (Anthony Quayle) and a bunch of troublesome teenagers. The 'serious charge' – that the vicar has sexually molested one of the teenagers – is without foundation, but the film still works effectively as a denunciation of bigotry and intolerance.

Victim uses the same formula as *Sapphire*, combining elements of a whodunit (who is the blackmailer who has driven 'Boy' Barrett to suicide and is terrorising the rest of the homosexual community?), with the exposition of a social problem (the injustice of a law which, by making homosexuality a criminal offence, operates as a 'blackmailer's charter'). As in *Sapphire*, we are introduced to a section of society, hitherto ignored by the cinema, against which prejudice is shown to be unreasonable. And once again, the most guilty party proves to be an unhappy, sexually repressed woman. This time, however, little explanation is provided for her hatred of homosexuals, and unlike Mildred, who is helped and protected by her family, Miss Benham (Margaret Diamond) is a loner, her only helper (Derren Nesbitt) an irrationally violent motorcycling leather boy.

Psychological subtlety is reserved for the relationship between Melvin Farr and his wife (Sylvia Syms), one of those repressed middle-class marriages which haunt British cinema. Here, though, the cause of unhappiness is not the woman's failure to be content with her lot or her inability to have children, but the man's latent homosexuality. Thus there is a disturbing reversal of roles. In earlier films like *Brief Encounter*, *The Passionate Friends* or *Mandy*, the women have desires which their conventional husbands are unable to satisfy. In *Victim*, Laura Farr forces her husband to confess that it is his guilt-ridden love for Barrett which is the problem. This would seem to obliterate the rationale of their marriage. But Laura insists on standing by her husband, and Farr, grateful for her sympathy and friendship, implies that he will be more appreciative of her once he has undergone the ordeal of exposing the blackmailers – and his own homosexual tendencies. This is all very stiff upper-lip, but as Andy Medhurst, in a sympathetic analysis of the film, points out, Farr's acknowledgment of his passion, and of the destructive effects of denying it, constitute an 'indictment of repression' which makes the film deeply moving despite its miserable message that homosexuality is a curse that has to be lived with.[10]

Victim was made after *Room at the Top* and the first three Woodfall films had been released, but visually it is more akin to earlier Dearden and Relph films like *The Captive Heart* (1945) and *Frieda* (1947) than to the Kitchen Sink films. Art director Alex Vetchinsky and photographer Otto Heller had both done their best work on 1940s films which might be termed atmospherically realistic (Vetchinsky on *Waterloo Road* and *The October Man*, Heller on *Temptation Harbour* and *Queen*

41

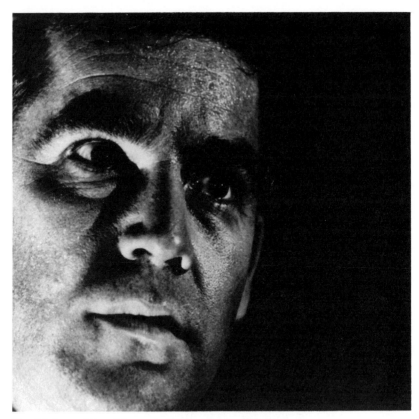

Harris's long night of the soul: Michael Craig, *Life for Ruth*

of Spades), and their last film with Dearden and Relph, *Life for Ruth*, marks a culmination of that tradition. Their function is by no means a neutral or passive one: Heller's lighting and Vetchinsky's production design focus attention, point to detail, create atmosphere and help the film to penetrate to a deeper level of realism than mere surface reflection.

Like *Sapphire* and *Victim*, *Life for Ruth* was scripted by Janet Green and John McCormick, but the 'social problem' – religious bigotry causing the death of a young girl – is by no means as black and white an issue as the race prejudice in *Sapphire* and the persecution of homosexuals in *Victim*. John Harris (Michael Craig) refuses to allow the blood transfusion which will save his daughter's life; but he has already risked his own life by rescuing her (and another child) from the sea. Moreover, while he is a man of deep emotions and deep convictions, the doctor (Patrick McGoohan), whose humanitarian feelings are so outraged by what he sees as the unnecessary death of a child that he has Harris prosecuted under the Prevention of Cruelty to Children Act, is callow and arrogant.

With the social issue less clear-cut, the film falls back into familiar Dearden and Relph concerns about communities (Harris finds himself ostracised by the people he grew up with) and the problems of a marriage crumbling under pressure (Harris's wife – played by Janet Munro – leaves him after Ruth's death but returns to stand by him when she realises he is alone against the world). A police inspector, who might be seen as representing Dearden and Relph's voice of moderation, cautions the doctor that 'religion's a tricky business: everybody feels, nobody thinks'. But the combination of the bleak Durham coastline in winter, Heller's shadowy lighting of interiors, and the intense performances of Michael Craig and Janet Munro creates an atmosphere where religion seems an essential part of reality. In the ghostly, silent hospital where Ruth lies still and heavily bandaged, the doctor's plea that Harris should abandon his religious beliefs and save his daughter's life seems like the smooth-talking plausibility of the devil. At the end, after Harris's long night of the soul, when he returns to the place where he plucked his daughter from the sea only to lose her again and whispers an agonised 'Ruth' into the wind, one experiences a sense of the mystery of life which transcends the cosy notion of a benevolent God waiting in Heaven to receive his good children.

Life for Ruth was poorly received by most critics and failed to repeat the box-office success of *Sapphire* and *Victim*. Dearden and Relph then went on to make *The Mind Benders* – an interesting, if unconvincing, film about a marriage (Dirk Bogarde and Mary Ure) brought to the brink of destruction by a rash experiment in brainwashing – and *A Place to Go*, with Rita Tushingham and Mike Sarne as a young working-class couple struggling to keep on the straight and narrow in Bethnal Green. Neither was commercially very successful and Dearden and Relph abandoned realism and social problems in favour of a glossy cosmopolitanism.[11]

The View from the Shop Floor
Though Dearden and Relph tackled controversial subjects in a bold and serious way, the subjects they chose were able to command the support of a broad consensus of liberal opinion. They pointedly steered clear of themes like industrial relations and politics which might disrupt such a consensus. John and Roy Boulting had made a serious film about a politician – *Fame is the Spur* – back in 1948, and dabbled with the threat of nuclear destruction in *Seven Days to Noon*. But in the mid-50s they discovered that they could be more successful with comedy and began a serious of cheeky satires – *Private's Progress*, *Brothers in Law*, *Carlton-Browne of the FO*, *Lucky Jim* – which were irreverently critical of British institutions. By the end of the decade the series seemed to have run its course, but the Boultings seized on

topical concern about 'wild cat' strikes to make a film about industrial relations: *I'm All Right Jack*.

Comedies about work were rare and tended to be set in the North (*Sing as We Go, Penny Pool, Demobbed, The Man in the White Suit*). *I'm All Right Jack* belongs to the prosperous South-East where, the film's narrator tells us, 'Industry, with tremendous opportunities for the young man, industry, spurred by the march of science in all directions, was working at high pressure to supply those vital needs for which the people had hungered for so long.' What industry actually produces, however, is 'Detto the new black whitener', 'NumYum the chewy chocolate bar' and, at a factory where Stanley Windrush (Ian Carmichael) finally lands a job, missiles for corrupt foreign powers.

Stanley is a wise fool whose naivety and 'stupidity' prevent him from accepting the crazy conventions of management who produce useless products and trick people into buying them, and workers whose belligerent mistrust of their employers causes them to work as slowly as possible. He is paired most effectively with a Communist shop steward, Fred Kite (Peter Sellers), whose hard-boiled approach to industrial relations is undermined by a childlike faith in man's inherent good nature and a complete inability to look after himself. Both men are manipulated by roguish entrepreneurs (Dennis Price and Richard Attenborough), Stanley into becoming a blackleg and a media hero, Fred into becoming an unpopular demagogue deserted by his wife.

The film provoked (still provokes) a degree of left-wing hostility for showing factory workers as lazy clods who sleep with their vests on. But there is a grudging appreciation of their truculent cynicism and the caricatures are affectionate rather than malicious. More important, *I'm All Right Jack* has an impressively comprehensive view of society which though superficially nostalgic (the film begins and ends in an idyllic rural naturist park and industry is shown as corrupt and mindless) taps the ambivalence that most working people feel towards their work – a mixture of resentment, stoicism and affection.

The Boultings, like many of the film-makers who made their names in the 40s, did not move too far from the middle ground of the Labour Party. The group responsible for *The Angry Silence* – Bryan Forbes, Richard Attenborough, Michael Craig, Guy Green – were younger and more right-wing.[12] Defending *The Angry Silence*, Forbes claimed: 'The one, tiny little point I was trying to make is simply put in words of one syllable. It was that *everybody has the right to be different* and that any attack on this right must be resisted by thinking people.'[13] As in most of Forbes's scripts (*I Was Monty's Double, The League of Gentlemen*), an acute ear for natural dialogue is combined with a *Boy's Own* view of the world which leads psychologically well-rounded characters into irritatingly artificial situations.

Forbes and the other leading personnel deferred their salaries in order to keep the film's budget below £100,000, and the whole film has that intensity and conviction that comes from a team working on something they believe in. Factory worker Tom Curtis (Attenborough) refuses to join his mates when a pointless unofficial strike is called, and is sent to Coventry when the dispute is ended. A number of sequences – the highly charged moment when Tom tries to smash through the wall of silence built round him in the works canteen, Tom's Italian wife's furious, tearful attack on their lodger for obeying union instructions not to talk to his friend and landlord – are intensely convincing, despite having little to do with the realities of industrial life.

As a cameraman in the 40s, Guy Green contributed subtly atmospheric photography to the films of David Lean. As a director, he eschewed Lean's fastidious delicacy in favour of a cruder, more deliberate style.[14] This has its advantages in infusing *The Angry Silence* with a melodramatic frenzy which makes it difficult to stay uninvolved. But it accentuates rather than resolves Forbes's uneasy blending of realist domestic drama and wild fantasies about Teddy Boys, Communists and the horrors of factory life. In the face of all the sanctimonious praise heaped on the film – the *Daily Mail* called it 'a savage study of mob violence and mob stupidity', the *Daily Express* claimed it was 'a story that will shock you and shame you' – it is tempting to attack the film's pessimistic view of working-class solidarity. Sheeplike workers who strike over nothing, Teddy Boys as union thugs, shop stewards firmly under the thumb of outside agitators, blacklegs frightened into joining a strike by having their windows smashed and their children terrorised, have little foundation in fact. But the issues are mediated through two interesting central characters.

Attenborough's Tom Curtis is different from his mates with his foreign wife and his insistence on doing things his own way, but still enough of one of the lads to be a staunch trade unionist and a valued member of the football team. Raymond Durgnat, trying to explain the film's popularity among working-class audiences (the Ipswich workers whose factory was used for the film initially declared themselves betrayed, but when shown the film voiced their approval), points out that despite being one against hundreds, Tom Curtis is the 'typical working man' with whom audiences identify: 'The hero's prominence, and one's identification with him, make him the working-class norm, after all. From this point-of-view it's important that the factory owners are relatively blameless at the beginning and that the strike is manipulated from outside – for otherwise his individualism becomes simply the creepy egoism of a scab.'[15] As Tom tries to explain to his harassed, bemused wife (Pier Angeli), 'I'm the union as much as they are.' The film is structured around Curtis, but from the vantage point of today

Michael Craig's Joe Wallace, the easy-going, empty-headed womaniser who lodges with Tom and his wife and feels understandably embarassed about sharing the home of a man he is not supposed to talk to, is the more sympathetic of the two. He is less nuanced, less complex than Attenborough's Curtis – a lumbering presence rather than a psychologically rounded personality – but as a British equivalent to the Brando of *On the Waterfront*, with vacancy taking the place of angst-ridden dumbness, Craig's character is intriguing.

In 1959 Dearden and Relph joined forces with Forbes, Attenborough and Jack Hawkins to set up Allied Film Makers as a producers' co-operative loosely associated with the Rank Organisation (which had realised that films made by independent producers tended to be more popular than their own in-house productions). Allied began with a popular caper film, *The League of Gentlemen*, written by Forbes for Dearden and Relph, which they followed with a less popular Kenneth More comedy, *The Man in the Moon*. The next four films – Dearden and Relph's *Victim* and *Life for Ruth* and Forbes's *Whistle Down the Wind* and *Seance on a Wet Afternoon* – are much more serious and ambitious.

Whistle Down the Wind, based on a story by Mary Hayley Bell, was envisaged as a star vehicle for her daughter Hayley Mills, who had made her debut in Lee Thompson's *Tiger Bay* as a Cardiff street urchin abducted by a young murderer.[16] *Whistle Down the Wind* casts her in a similar role as a poor farmer's daughter who mistakes an escaped convict for the born-again Jesus Christ. With Hayley Mills flanked by ordinary non-acting children and a solid set of character actors (Bernard Lee, Norman Bird, Alan Bates) sympathetically directed by Forbes, the film works well as an exploration of a children's fantasy world, and the setting among the bleak hill farms of north Lancashire prevents it from lapsing into fey whimsicality. Though no great stylist, Forbes turned out to be an excellent director of actors, and the five small-scale realist films he made in the 60s (*Whistle Down the Wind*, *Seance on a Wet Afternoon*, *The L-Shaped Room*, *The Whisperers* and *The Raging Moon*) stand up much better than his ill-conceived big-budget films (*The Wrong Box*, *Deadfall* and *The Madwoman of Chaillot*). As Brian Baxter points out in his perceptive if indulgent assessment, Forbes is at his best 'expressing a lyricism of the grubby everyday rather than of the heroic, a refusal to inflate a situation into any wider significance than the audience itself cares to infer, and a determined avoidance of anything that might be thought sentimental.'[17] Although *Victim* and *Whistle Down the Wind* were commercially successful, *Life for Ruth* and *Seance on a Wet Afternoon* did much less well and Allied Film Makers faded away after 1964.[18]

Allied was modelled on the Bryanston Corporation, formed by Michael Balcon and other independent producers earlier in 1959 to make films for British Lion. Balcon claimed that

> many of the best independent producers and producing teams in the country were attracted to it – Basil Dearden and Michael Relph, Ronald Neame and Albert Fennell, George Brown, Monja Danischewsky, Aubrey Baring, Kenneth and Gerald Shipman, the brothers Dent, Colin Lesslie, Charles Frend, Norman Priggen, Michael Truman, John Davis (not to be confused with the chairman and managing director of the Rank Organisation), Hal Mason and myself. Later we were joined by Woodfall Films, the company Tony Richardson and John Osborne had formed.[19]

Bryanston was responsible for twenty first features and twelve featurettes between 1959 and 1964, not all of which were old-fashioned remnants of the Ealing tradition. Charles Crichton's *The Battle of the Sexes* (1960) is his best comedy since *The Lavender Hill Mob* in 1951, and like Pennington-Richards's *Ladies Who Do* (1963) it slyly undermines the image of an affluent, progressive society without lapsing into nostalgic whimsy. Alexander Mackendrick's *Sammy Going South*, unfashionable though it appeared to be in 1964, now looks one of the best films of the decade. And despite Balcon's preference for policeman-as-hero films, Bryanston backed two good crime films which look at life from the criminal's point of view, Cliff Owen's *A Prize of Arms* and Ken Hughes's *The Small World of Sammy Lee*. Most of Bryanston's other productions, however – Charles Frend's *Cone of Silence* (funny business among airline pilots), Leslie Norman's *Spare the Rod* (Max Bygraves taking on the kids of a rough East End school), Lewis Gilbert's *Light Up the Sky* (Tommy Steele and Benny Hill in a wartime searchlight battery), even Charles Crichton's *The Boy Who Stole a Million* (*Hue and Cry* meets *Bicycle Thieves* in the slums of Valencia) – look well-meaning but rather tired and timid, and it is the Woodfall films produced under the Bryanston umbrella which stand out as serious studies of contemporary life.

Flame in the Streets
Gainsborough, which in the 40s had acted as a more commercial alternative to Ealing, seemed to bear more fruitful progeny. Sydney, Muriel and Betty Box, who ran the studio from 1945 to 1950, had initiated a cycle of social problem films which substituted a combination of mild sensationalism and a concern for social justice for the moral earnestness which permeated Ealing. Films such as *When the Bough Breaks*, *Good Time Girl* and *The Boys in Brown* were successful enough to tempt other producers to try the same formula, and 50s British cinema is enlivened by enterprising low-budget shockers like *Cosh Boy* (directed by Lewis Gilbert for the Woolfs), *The Flesh is Weak* (directed by

Don Chaffey for Raymond Stross) and *Passport to Shame* (directed by Alvin Rakoff for British Lion). Muriel Box herself directed a number of interesting low-budget social problem films in the early 60s (*Subway in the Sky*, *Too Young to Love*, *The Rattle of a Simple Man*). But the most significant heirs to the Gainsborough tradition are the writer Ted Willis, the producer/director team of Betty Box and Ralph Thomas, and the writer/producer/director Val Guest.

Ted Willis served his apprenticeship in the Communist-oriented Unity Theatre before joining Gainsborough as a scriptwriter in 1946. He collaborated with the Boxes in the cosy populism of *Holiday Camp* and the Huggett family films and created the character of George Dixon for *The Blue Lamp* (though the script was written by T. E. B. Clarke and the film made at Ealing). In the 50s he wrote a series of scripts and plays which dealt explicitly with the problems of ordinary people: *Woman in a Dressing Gown* (1957), *The Young and the Guilty* (1958), *No Trees in the Street* (1959).[20] His best film, *Flame in the Streets* (1961), which compares interestingly with Dearden and Relph's *Sapphire*, was directed by Roy Baker, who despite having made a number of impressive films – *The October Man*, *Passage Home*, *Tiger in the Smoke*, *A Night to Remember*, *The Singer Not the Song* – has attracted a minimum of critical attention.[21]

Flame in the Streets originated in a stage play, *Hot Summer Night*, which Willis wrote in 1958 and adapted for television the following year as part of ABC's Armchair Theatre, which also provided an outlet for playwrights like Harold Pinter, Clive Exton and Alun Owen. The plays were made with tiny budgets, used only two or three sets and were necessarily dependent on good scripts and acting. Willis's play fitted the format very well.[22] On a hot summer evening Jacko Palmer, a trade union official, returns to his humble home in Wapping, confronts a problem with his subordinates who are reluctant to endorse the promotion of a black man to a chargehand position, and then discovers that his only daughter, who has risen out of the working class to become a teacher, wants to marry a black man. Jacko is not very pleased but is loath to jettison his liberal principles. 'I can't support one man in the factory and bar another one from my own home,' he says, and he is prepared to go along with his daughter's decision. But for his wife Nell it is a more serious matter. Having fought against poverty and squalor all her life and endured an unsatisfactory marriage to a bullyingly inconsiderate husband for the sake of her daughter, she is not prepared to see her end up 'in one room with a horde of black children'. Thus the race theme, though important, is subsumed under a general family crisis. Early in the play Jacko's old dad tells him, 'You don't convince people, you 'oller at them until they give in for the sake of a bit of peace.' When people start to 'oller back at him, his egocentric world is shattered. Sonny Lincoln, the black boyfriend, refuses to listen to Jacko because, he complains, he speaks to him as an inferior, unaware that Jacko acts in the same belligerent, domineering way with everybody. And Nell, desperate that she has sacrificed her life for nothing, turns on Jacko with the same furious hatred she has expressed for the blacks.

Instead of trying to reproduce the small-scale virtues of the television play, Baker and Willis work a thorough transformation. *Flame in the Streets* is shot in CinemaScope and Technicolor and the time and setting changed. The action takes place not on a hot summer night, but on 5 November, then – with bonfires on every other street corner – a great occasion for communal celebration. As in *Look Back in Anger* and *The Entertainer*, events reported in the play are shown in the film; but whereas in the Osborne/Richardson films this makes for an untidy mishmash of film and theatre, here the changes work to move a domestic drama into the social sphere. We see the squalid surroundings the blacks have to live in, and the relationship between the daughter, Kathie, and her black boyfriend is made to seem more exotic by the very fact that the film is made in colour.[23]

As striking is the change effected by casting John Mills in place of John Slater as Jacko. Slater's Jacko is a modern, full-time union official whizzing from conference to negotiating table to television studio, his Wapping home merely a badge to prove his honorary membership of the working class. Mills is a craftsman, still at work in a Notting Hill furniture factory, who fits his union activity into his spare time. Thus he is much more closely involved in the everyday politics of the workplace: he himself has to persuade the workers to accept the black chargehand rather than delegating the task to his subordinates. He is more old-fashioned than Slater's Jacko and his bigotry and blindness more formidable and deeply rooted. This necessarily changes his relationship with his wife, and the changes are reinforced by the different emphases put on Nell's character by Ruth Dunning in the television version and Brenda de Banzie in the film. Ruth Dunning's Nell is a dignified working-class matron with a temper and a personality and a sexual relationship, albeit an unsatisfactory one, with her husband; she is the dominant force in *Hot Summer Night*, overwhelmingly sympathetic despite her racism. Brenda de Banzie (who played Archie Rice's long-suffering wife in *The Entertainer*) is something different. Several reviewers complained that Brenda de Banzie was too middle-class for the part, but anyone with experience of 50s working-class life will recognise that exaggerated refinement which some women used to adopt as a barrier against the surrounding squalor. (Annie Walker, one-time landlady of the pub in *Coronation Street*, is a later example.) The collapse of her primness and formality into hysterical abuse in her attack on Kathie for wanting to sleep with a 'nigger' and on Jacko for taking her for granted speaks as much about

Flame in the Streets: Jacko Palmer (John Mills), a trade unionist closely involved in the everyday politics of the workplace

sexual repression as it does about the harshness of working-class life, and the heightening of melodramatic tension in the home is paralleled by the introduction of leather-jacketed, motorbike-riding young hooligans, who push people around and almost succeed in burning Gomez, the black chargehand, on the bonfire. They are less real characters than folk devils, embodiments of everything which is worthless and evil (a gang of Teddy Boys in *Sapphire* perform the same function with less relevance to the plot). Here they act as an external catalyst, jolting Jacko into a realisation of where his true loyalties lie.

Like most of Willis's work, *Flame in the Streets* suffers from being pedantically well-meaning, but in contrast to the patrician aloofness of Dearden and Relph, Willis gets much closer to his working-class protagonists. Such characters as Jacko Palmer – a skilled craftsman in a furniture factory and a strong unionist – appear much less frequently in British films than their lower middle-class equivalents like Bernard Miles's Mr Harris (a signwriter with his own small business) in *Sapphire*. As in *Sapphire*, the plot allows for an exploration of an 'unknown London' – the racially mixed area of Notting Hill – and an examination of the prejudice and sexual frustration lying beneath the civilised veneer of respectable white society. In this respect Jacko's family comes out of it rather better than the Harrises. Whereas David Harris is shamefacedly prepared to forgive and forget that the attractive white girl he loves has black blood, Kathie Palmer is fascinated by her black boyfriend's air of exoticism. She accepts her father's teachings at face value and sees no reason why other people's prejudices should come between her and the man she loves. Jacko is exposed less as a bigot than as a man who, living his life according to the union rule book, has lost his capacity for dealing with personal, emotional issues. (As his wily old dad – played by Wilfred Brambell – tells him, 'You can't put this on the agenda as "Any other business".')

Brenda de Banzie's Nell seems as rabidly prejudiced as Mildred Harris. She openly accuses her daughter of a perverse sexuality in preferring a black man: 'I'm ashamed of you. When I think of you and *that* man sharing the same bed . . . It's filthy, disgusting, it makes my stomach turn over and I want to be sick.' But at least she is able to find a voice for her hatred. And to Jacko's bewildered embarrassment she uncovers its cause in her own unhappy marriage. Goaded out of her stoical endurance, she turns on him: 'We've been married for twenty-four years and what've we got? A table, chairs, a bed, a telephone. What else? . . . You had no time for her [i.e. Kathie's] life or mine. When you came home you came as a visitor. You even turned my front room into an office.' Jacko protests that he loves her and he has never looked at another woman, but Nell's discontent is with the entire taken-for-granted status of a working-class wife: 'You even made love to me as if you were taking a quick drink.'

Inevitably in the shift of emphasis from the particular to the general, there is a heavier reliance on simplification and stereotyping, but this is a price worth paying. In *Hot Summer Night*, where virtually all the action takes place in the Palmer home and the conflict is essentially within the family, resolution comes through a simple act of realism and generosity. Jacko, his eyes opened to the needs and desires of his wife and daughter, makes amends for his past blindness by promising that he and Nell will move out of the poky little house which his wife hates, thus leaving it empty for Kathie and her black husband. In *Flame in the Streets*, where issues and events are exposed more to the real world (the location shooting in Notting Hill and Alex Vetchinsky's superbly detailed sets give a very solid sense of place), such a solution would be facile; and matters are more ambiguously resolved with the two couples, battered by the emotional turmoil they have been through, making tentative efforts to find a common ground.

Willis is as easy to criticise as Dearden for providing facile solutions to complex problems, but *Flame in the Streets*, like *Sapphire*, has a dignity and seriousness which is very appealing.[24] And just as the moral earnestness of Janet Green's script for *Sapphire* is offset by Dearden's penchant for shock effects and melodramatic devices, Willis's tendency towards bathos is mitigated by Roy Baker's quiet, patient direction, which allows his actors time to create characters whose limited articulacy gives justification and meaning to the clichés through which they express themselves. Despite superficial similarities between *Sapphire* and *Flame in the Streets*, Willis is essentially a naturalist trying to capture the rhythms of everyday life (enthusiastically endorsing Paddy Chayefsky's interest in 'the miracle of the ordinary'), whereas Dearden and Relph – in their best work at least – tend to combine a restrained concern for doomed romances (for much of *Sapphire* we are led to believe that David Harris has murdered his pregnant fiancée) with an interest in how groups – from the prisoner-of-war camp of *The Captive Heart* to the black sub-culture of *Sapphire* – and closed communities work. *Flame in the Streets* is Willis's best attempt at dealing with contemporary issues and was treated kindly by the critics, but it was not a box-office success and Willis retreated to his old standby, the television series *Dixon of Dock Green*, while Baker moved on to the very different television world of *The Avengers*.[25]

The Future Britain

Betty Box and Ralph Thomas are best known for the 'Doctor' series they made for the Rank Organisation, beginning with *Doctor in the House* in 1954. When they began making films which looked more seriously at society, they were sneered at by the critics for what was assumed to be an opportunistic jump on to the band-wagon of social realism. This was hardly fair since Betty Box, like Ted Willis an ex-member of the Communist Party, had produced *When the Bough Breaks* and *The Boys in Brown* as well as the taut political thriller *The Clouded Yellow* (directed by Ralph Thomas from a script by Eric Ambler and Janet Green). Their *No Love for Johnnie* (1961) was the first film since *Fame is the Spur* in 1948 to take political life as its central theme.[26]

There are similarities between *No Love for Johnnie* and *Room at the Top* in that they both show an ambitious working-class man involved with various women in the course of his struggle for power and material success. The novel on which the film was based had been written by an up-and-coming Labour MP, Wilfred Fienburgh, in 1958 and published the following year, by which time he had been killed in a car crash. It was seized on by the Tory press as an exposé of corruption and spiritual bankruptcy in the Labour Party, but it could more reasonably be interpreted as a personal lament for the loss of idealism by a man who had come to see politics as a dirty business.

A middle-aged Labour MP, Johnnie Byrne, is disappointed in his expectations of a government post when his party is returned to power in the later 50s and is simultaneously deserted by his wife. He joins a left-wing 'ginger group' but puts more of his energy into a love affair with a girl only half his age. He sacrifices his opportunity to embarrass the government and establish himself as an alternative leader within the party to make love to the girl. But she leaves him, convinced that

No Love for Johnnie: Johnnie Byrne (Peter Finch), one of the new generation of ambitious, image-conscious Labour politicians

the age gap between them is unbridgeable and that his career will make impossible the sort of cosy domestic life she wants. Dejected and demoralised, Johnnie is on the point of patching things up with his wife when the Prime Minister offers him a minor post in the Government, pointing out to him that he had not been offered anything earlier because his wife, a leading light in the Communist Party, made him a security risk. He jettisons his reconciliation plans and contentedly resumes his dreams of political power.

Nicholas Phipps and Mordecai Richler's adaptation changes very little of this main story, and by cutting the flashbacks to Johnnie's past they emphasise the sense of events happening during a short time span, a turning point in a man's life, albeit one which leads him back to the path he was on before. The film is weakest in its depiction of parliamentary life: the studio-built House of Commons never really comes alive, and with the exception of Paul Rogers, the character actors brought in to represent the Labour Party are disappointingly one-dimensional. Peter Finch's Johnnie Byrne, on the other hand, seems to offer an accurate insight into the new generation of ambitious, image-conscious Labour politicians who were to come to power three years later.

Reviewers complained that Finch had softened Johnnie's character and blunted the irony of the story, but it is the film's main achievement that it transforms Johnnie from a self-pitying charlatan into a semi-tragic figure whose mid-life crisis reveals an appalling vulnerability under the polished exterior. In the book, the women he is involved with are weak stereotypes – his wife a thin-lipped, frigid, left-wing activist, the woman with whom he is tempted to have an affair a blowsy nonentity, the girl he falls in love with a pretty receptacle for his passion. As played by Rosalie Crutchley, Billie Whitelaw and Mary Peach (ironically the dull ordinary girl with an invalid mother passed over by Joe Lampton in *Room at the Top*), they are well-rounded individuals attracted to Johnnie but aware of his defects and unwilling to fit in with his whims and fantasies. Thus his crisis of political confidence is compounded by a confusion of sexual identity – the only time he makes love successfully is when he should be challenging the Prime Minister in Parliament – which is explored but not resolved. The film's sophistication, which was entirely missed at the time, might have attracted more attention if it had been released two years later when the Profumo scandal dominated the headlines, but in 1961 reviews were generally hostile and box-office reception lukewarm.

Box/Thomas turned for their next film, *The Wild and the Willing*, to the commercially more lucrative but artistically more treacherous territory of rebellious youth. Their film attracted critical derision (though large audiences) and no one has deemed to take it seriously since. This is unfair but understandable. *No Love for Johnnie* is a simple, powerful story very well told; *The Wild and the Willing* is a bundle of clichés – rowdy students, an embittered professor and his 'nymphomaniac' wife, a rag stunt that ends in tragedy. However, the film makes good use of its locations (Lincoln – one of the few cathedral towns to miss out in the post-war university boom), and it does deal interestingly with the clash of cultural identities faced by working-class students at university.[27]

Harry (Ian McShane) is a working-class lad able to mix with the toffs because he's good at rugby (and because he's brighter than they are). He is annoyingly well-balanced and sure of himself but he becomes increasingly sympathetic as his interest shifts from Josie, his beautiful but dull student girlfriend (Samantha Eggar) to the wife of his tutor, Professor Chown (Paul Rogers). Chown is an ill-conceived amalgam of the cuckolded schoolmaster of Terence Rattigan's *The Browning*

Version and the influential Cambridge scholar F. R. Leavis. He despises Harry as an uncouth barbarian, but is honest enough to acknowledge his intellectual originality and is less concerned with his wife's infidelity as such than that her sexual demands will interfere with Harry's academic progress. Virginia Maskell looks too beautiful and too intelligent to be married to this cold fish or to be seeking solace among the even less prepossessing students, but she manages to convey a fey, restless femininity which explains her power over men if not her interest in them. McShane's best moments are with her, his appreciation of her, his willingness to go beyond a simple affair, to have a loving relationship, capturing a gentleness and decency which is the reverse of working-class *machismo*.

Unlike *No Love for Johnnie*, where the love relationship dominates the film, here it is overshadowed by a plot centred upon Harry's student friends. His room-mate, Phil (John Hurt), has a passion for Josie's room-mate, Sarah (Catherine Woodville), who despite appearances to the contrary is also working-class. As Phil is small and insignificant, bad at games and not much of a drinker, and his idea of giving a girl a good time is taking her to see *Birth of a Nation*, it is not surprising that Sarah prefers the captain of the rugby team. When Harry, made reckless by Mrs Chown's refusal to leave her dead marriage for him, decides to plant a chamber pot on the college clock tower, he reluctantly allows Phil to accompany him so as to prove his manhood. The inevitable happens, allowing Phil to die a tragic death, Professor Chown to act decently by defending Harry – unsuccessfully – against expulsion, and Harry to cut loose from Mrs Chown and his student pals and go out into the world. As with the 'Doctor' films, everything is neatly rounded off, but the bolder, braver film which Box/Thomas might have made remained unrealised.

Val Guest's career began at Gainsborough long before the Boxes arrived. He collaborated on the scripts of Will Hay comedies like *Oh Mr Porter* and *Where's That Fire?* and made his debut as a director with Arthur Askey's *Miss London Ltd* in 1943. Between 1955 and 1965 his films cover a wide range of subjects – science-fiction, war films, crime thrillers, a musical, disaster films, social commentary – but Guest imbues them with a middle-brow populism similar to that propagated by the *Daily Express* in its heyday.[28] Two films he made in the early 60s – *The Day the Earth Caught Fire* and *80,000 Suspects* – deserve particular attention.

Guest co-scripted *The Day the Earth Caught Fire* with Wolf Mankowitz, with whom he had already collaborated on *Expresso Bongo* (1959). Released in 1961, at a time when the most talented British directors were absorbed in themes of everyday life, its subject matter was refreshingly outrageous. America and the USSR simultaneously carry out nuclear test explosions which tilt the earth off its axis and shift it on to a collision course with the sun. This is kept secret from the public, but a *Daily Express* reporter (Edward Judd) discovers the truth and determines to tell the world about its probable fate.

The film was made as an independent production for British Lion and suffers from a budget that would not stretch to colour (though parts of the film were tinted yellow) or to any but the most rudimentary special effects. Guest makes up for this by using the *Daily Express* building (its splendid art deco front concealing the usual messy Fleet Street editorial floor and grimy printing presses) and its long-standing editor, Arthur Christiansen, to give a sharp edge of authenticity to the film. The relationship between the three principals – Judd (at that time ranked alongside Finney as a promising young actor), Janet Munro, and Leo McKern – is not developed to any depth, but it is a witty, enjoyable film, a worthy successor to Guest's *Quatermass* films in the 1950s.

80,000 Suspects (1963) is less spectacular, but like Guest's two crime thrillers, *Hell is a City* (1960) and *Jigsaw* (1962), it was made largely on location in an English provincial town and superbly photographed by Arthur Grant. The 80,000 suspects are the inhabitants of Bath, who are threatened by a smallpox epidemic. The script was based on Elleston Trevor's *The Pillars of Midnight*, written in 1957, but a real smallpox outbreak occurred in Bradford early in 1962 and the film had a

Married love revitalised by the fear of death: Claire Bloom and Richard Johnson, *80,000 Suspects*

56

grisly topical relevance. Guest skilfully combines an almost documentary interest in the attempts to control the epidemic – long queues of people waiting to be vaccinated in the snowy night, Christiansen appearing once again as a crusading editor – with a highly wrought domestic melodrama about a doctor (Richard Johnson) and his problems with his disillusioned wife Julie (Claire Bloom) and ex-mistress Ruth (Guest's wife Yolande Donlan), which are resolved with predictable but satisfying force while the epidemic rages.[29]

Whereas Dearden and Relph often rely on enlightened policemen and other voices of authority to represent their point of view, Guest tends to choose a genial, middle-aged, idiosyncratic individualist – Leo McKern's veteran reporter in *The Day the Earth Caught Fire*, Cyril Cusack's inquisitive Catholic priest in *80,000 Suspects*. They set a much more human, fallible, compromising tone to his films, and this is reinforced by odd little cameos – Norman Bird and his besieged family in *80,000 Suspects*, for example – of characters who are troubled less by inner crises than by the material problems of living in a world where accidents and disasters are part of the natural order. In contrast to Dearden and Relph's characters, whose repressed intensity indicates an anxiety and distrust of the world, Guest's protagonists, even when threatened by various unpleasant forms of extinction, seem to retain their belief in a benign universe where most people are basically decent and friendly. Ruth dies a horrible death, but it seems like a solution rather than a punishment; and Julie wakes from her brush with death to find her problems have evaporated with her fever.

John Hill comes to the conclusion that the social problem films 'for all their raising of problems, ended up confirming rather than querying a consensual view of the world. This was the result not only of what they did, or rather didn't, show, but of how such problems were then used to reconfirm a particular set of attitudes and assumptions.'[30] This might be harsh, but it is a useful check on the assumption that because the films are socially concerned they are necessarily progressive. What Hill misses, though, is the fascination these films exert now. Time having exposed their ideological assumptions and prejudices, their fictions become less important than the reality of the attitudes they embody, turning them into cultural artefacts. Lawrence Alloway argues that early silent films are fascinating 'rather as documents, as relics, than as on-going works of art. They are more like the bones of a saint in the crypt than the painted altarpiece of his martyrdom in the chapel.'[31] The aesthetic qualities of 60s social problem films should not be disregarded so easily, but here too it is the aura of social significance, the glimpse they offer into a past society, which makes them valuable.

3

CRITICAL DEBATES

The risk for film criticism is that the canon of individual authorship, applied to an expendable art form, will simply lead to the insulation of criticism within a kind of hobbies-corner specialism. Then the criticism of pop films might become technical and esoteric, like the cult of Hi Fi, or like surfing in the United States. In point of fact, what is needed is a criticism of movies as a pop art which can have a critical currency beyond that of footnotes and preposterous learning. (Lawrence Alloway, *Encounter*, 1964)[1]

Stand Up! Stand Up!

Between June 1959 and June 1960 *Films and Filming* invited twelve prominent critics to express their views on the nature and importance of film criticism. With the exception of Jympson Harman, understandably groggy after forty years and nine thousand reviews for the London *Evening News*, their articles are intelligent and amusing, explaining the problems of confined space, the need to be entertaining, to be fair, to retain some sort of enthusiasm; but what they say about film consists largely of platitudes. Four years later, a follow-up survey found that two of the original contributors had died and five more had retired.[2] With a new type of cinema breaking through and the old guard of the critical establishment being put out to grass, there was a sense of ferment in film criticism.

Before the war middle-class intellectuals found it difficult to be anything other than patronising or dismissive of a popular form of entertainment like the cinema. Serious writers like John Grierson and Paul Rotha were critical of the commercial exploitation of what they thought of as a vitally important medium, and had little time for the mainstream narrative film. In the 1940s, when the artistic and intellectual ethos of the documentary movement seemed to permeate the industry, there was an upsurge of critical enthusiasm for British films which appeared to be setting the world an example in the creation of a socially responsible, realist, quality cinema. Dilys Powell wrote optimistically that 'a certain sharpening of public taste is to be observed. Themes which would once have been thought too serious or too controversial for the ordinary spectator are now accepted as a matter of course.'[3] But if it was so – and there are grounds for suspecting that audiences sat through *Desert Victory* and *Western Approaches* because they were hungry for news of how the war was being fought, and that their emotional preference was for florid fantasies like *Dangerous Moonlight*, *Madonna of the Seven Moons* and *The Seventh Veil* – the fashion for realism hardly survived the war. To the disgust of the critics, the film industry of the post-war period devoted itself to producing low-life melodramas and exotic costume pictures, and in disillusion they turned to foreign films (in particular Italian Neo-Realism) and encouraged middle-class cinemagoers with an interest in 'the art of the film' to turn away from the mainstream cinema.[4]

Critical condemnation of the vulgar vitality of late 1940s cinema struck a chord with the conservative businessmen who moved in to prominent positions of power in the industry at the end of the decade, and there was a move away from 'sordid' and 'unsavoury' subjects. But instead of the serious explorations of contemporary life demanded by the critics, film production in the 1950s was dominated by inoffensive comedies and patriotic war films.[5] In this climate several publishing ventures set up in the previous decade failed to survive: both the *Documentary Newsletter* and the *Penguin Film Review* were moribund by 1950. *Sequence*, begun by Gavin Lambert and Lindsay Anderson, petered out in 1952, but Lambert and another ex-*Sequence* editor, Penelope Houston, were soon editing the British Film Institute magazine *Sight and Sound*, and transformed it into a glossy, sophisticated film journal. Lambert and Houston's hearts were in the international development of art cinema, but they retained an appalled fascination with the state of the British film industry. Symposiums were held to discuss whether it was still alive, a series of articles was published on the decline of British documentary ('The Sulky Fire'), and John Grierson was given a regular column to berate the younger generation of film-makers and critics for their lack of inspiration and idealism. Ironically it was a letter from a reader, John Russell Taylor (later film critic of *The Times*), complaining of the bias *Sight and Sound* writers showed for 'committed, humanist films', which unexpectedly sparked off a real critical debate.[6]

Sartre's stress on the need for *engagement* had aroused interest in left-wing circles in the mid-50s, but Jimmy Porter was not alone in complaining that 'there aren't any good brave causes left', and all that the two writers singled out by Taylor (Lindsay Anderson in 'Panorama at Cannes' and Walter Lassally in 'The Cynical Audience') were guilty

of was the mildly patronising humanism which *Sight and Sound* inherited from critics like Dilys Powell, William Whitebait, Richard
Winnington and Roger Manvell. In his reply, 'Stand Up! Stand Up!',
Anderson took up a much more radical stance, insisting, as Sartre had,
that neutrality was not an option, that 'there is no such thing as
uncommitted criticism, any more than there is such a thing as insignificant art.'[7]

Appearing in the autumn of 1956, between the first production of
Look Back in Anger and the Suez crisis, 'Stand Up! Stand Up!' aroused
considerable controversy; and when the 'new left', angry over Suez,
scornful of the old-style Communism which had sent tanks into Buda-
pest, began its own journal, the *Universities and Left Review*, Anderson's article was reprinted as 'Commitment in Film Criticism'.[8] Three
years later a group of *ULR* contributors combined with students from
the London School of Film Technique to launch a 'committed' film
journal, *Definition*. It lasted for only three issues, but in its concern
with the way in which film might foster a radical, critical, even subversive view of society, with the way in which the internal world of
the film interacted with its audience and with other aspects of culture
and society, *Definition* started left-wing criticism along the tortuous
path which would eventually lead to psychoanalysis, semiotics and
Marxism. Auteurism, the other main strand of critical thought, tended
towards the opposite direction: to a concentration on detailed analysis
of the film itself in relation not to society but to other films, and in
particular to other films made by the same director.

Continental Influences
In 'Stand Up! Stand Up!, Anderson had quickly by-passed John Russell Taylor's criticism and concentrated his attack on the trivialising
attitude of British film culture represented by an exhibition to com-
memorate 'Sixty Years of Cinema' and 'the old English Philistinism' of
the *Observer*'s film critic, C. A. Lejeune. He failed to realise that
Taylor's insistence on aesthetic rather than moral judgment, far from
stemming from the 'let's keep politics or anything else serious out of
this' school epitomised by Lejeune, was a harbinger of the passionate
enthusiasms of auteurism. Back in 1954, in a review of the state of
current French critical writing, Anderson had noted that otherwise
interesting and exciting film journals like *Cahiers du Cinéma* and *Positif*
vitiated their appreciation of serious film artists like Buñuel and Renoir
by their 'perverse cultivation of the meretricious' in their adulation of
commercial film-makers like Howard Hawks, Otto Preminger and
Alfred Hitchcock.[9] In fact, the French critical theories and practices,
though popularly boiled down to the 'auteur theory', were more important than an enthusiasm for particular directors. André Bazin, the
guiding light behind *Cahiers du Cinéma*, was responsible for a series of

essays which substantially demolished the basic tenets which had sustained film theory for its first fifty years: that montage was the crucial creative element in film-making, that film was essentially a visual medium and thus sound was an irrelevance, that film art depended on the director/artist reinterpreting in an expressive way the camera's ability to reproduce the real world.[10] Bazin's ideas provided a theoretical justification for the preference many young French intellectuals felt for Hollywood films – particularly gangster films, thrillers, comedies and Westerns – which had hitherto largely been considered beneath critical contempt.

In the view of orthodox film theory, Hollywood was the enemy of art, a factory, a machine, which sucked in European talent (Fritz Lang and Alfred Hitchcock were the classic examples) and destroyed it. Exception was made for John Ford after *The Informer*, and enthusiasm was expressed for bright talents like Orson Welles, Elia Kazan, Nicholas Ray and Fred Zinnemann. But it was an enthusiasm which was easily extinguished, and *Cahiers'* championing of Samuel Fuller, Frank Tashlin, Raoul Walsh, Budd Boetticher, Anthony Mann, even Hitchcock and Hawks, was considered outlandish and extravagant. Only when critics like Godard, Truffaut, Chabrol, Rohmer and Rivette became prize-winning film-makers in the late 1950s did *Sight and Sound* begin to take 'the French Line' seriously. By this time, however, Britain had its own school of auteurists.[11]

In April 1960, Ian Cameron, Mark Shivas and Victor Perkins took over the film section of the student arts magazine *Oxford Opinion* and launched a vigorous assault on the critical establishment of which *Sight and Sound* was now seen as a bastion. Echoing John Russell Taylor's letter four years earlier, Cameron condemned *Sight and Sound* for 'the pallid philanthropy that has always provided its criteria for evaluation', and Mark Shivas challenged the convention that only a handful of Hollywood directors (those with social consciences) needed to be taken seriously, arguing that 'The distinction between commerce and art, the insistence on the cinema as solely an intellectual medium rather than as a visual and sensual one, has resulted in a number of directors and countless films being entirely disregarded.' Such arguments might have been ignored had they not been accompanied by outspoken onslaughts on the critics themselves. Victor Perkins complained that 'any fool can blather about positive affirmations. But in an art as new as the cinema it demands intellect, perception, and sheer hard work to get to grips with aesthetic questions. And these are gifts which our critics too obviously lack.' Ian Cameron asserted that in Britain, 'Criticism is thought of as a job for the unskilled or at best semi-skilled, a refuge for failed film directors and superannuated law reporters, a relaxation for literary critics and lady novelists ...'[12] Such comments provoked equally intemperate replies. Peter John Dyer, for example, the editor of the *Monthly Film Bulletin*, was obviously not amused:

> The enthusiasm of such critics may seem invaluable to the cause of cinema; celluloid may be coming out of their ears. But I wouldn't trust them with an inch of space in any magazine of mine. I wouldn't employ them because of their judgment, or rather their lack of it; and because it follows that they will enjoy neither influence nor staying power.[13]

Though these new critics were excluded from the pages of *Sight and Sound* and the *Monthly Film Bulletin*, small film journals like *Screen Education* and *Film* (the journal of the Federation of British Film Societies) eagerly participated in the debate, publishing polemical articles by Ian Cameron of *Oxford Opinion*, Dai Vaughan and Philip Riley of *Definition*, and mavericks like Ian Jarvie and Raymond Durgnat.

In January 1961, *Film* tried to act as honest broker between the warring camps and arranged a public debate.[14] The auteurists screened Samuel Fuller's *Pick Up on South Street*, which predictably made few converts among the left-wing contingent but at least assured a lively debate. Few of the established critics made the effort to attend, but Penelope Houston, now editor of *Sight and Sound*, wrote a considered response to the new criticism. She conceded that new blood might be necessary and that it might be found in the *Oxford Opinion* writers, but she disliked their breathy enthusiasm:

> Reviewing a film in terms of half a dozen striking shots, and of what their emotional impact and technical brilliance meant to you, is like walking in a fog without a torch. The mist of images swirls around, landmarks are obscured, without realising it one progresses in a series of circles. Cinema is about the human situation, not about 'spatial relationships'.[15]

The new generation, with its demand for 'kicks', for 'films which stab at the nerves and the emotions', is contrasted with Houston's own, which grew up quickly against a background of war and post-war austerity. She defends Lindsay Anderson and re-assesses the 'commitment' debate but, wary of moving into the 'sphere of the cultural gauleiters', settles for a liberalism which embodies an 'allegiance to principles but a certain flexibility of mind about assumptions'.[16] This was hardly likely to satisfy critics from left or right. Alan Lovell had already attacked the 'complacent liberalism' of *Sight and Sound* in the second issue of *Definition*, and the next issue carried an editorial reviewing the whole debate and a powerful reiteration of the left-wing position by Paddy Whannel.

Popular Art
The divergence in attitude and outlook between auteurists and committed critics was reflected in their attitude to the 'New British Cinema'. *Definition* and its supporters, as one might expect given the influence of Lindsay Anderson, were generally favourable. Paddy Whannel wrote approvingly on *Room at the Top*, Stuart Hall on *Look Back in Anger*, Boleslaw Sulik on *Saturday Night and Sunday Morning*, Alan Lovell on *Saturday Night and Sunday Morning* and *The Loneliness of the Long Distance Runner*.[17] By contrast, when the auteurists launched *Movie* in June 1962, they did so with a vociferous attack on British cinema old and new. According to Victor Perkins:

> Five years ago the ineptitude of British films was generally acknowledged. The stiff upper lip movie was a standard target for critical scorn. But now the British cinema has come to grips with Reality. We have had a break-through, a renaissance, a New Wave. . . . All we can see is a change of attitude, which disguises the fact that the British cinema is as dead as before. Perhaps it was never alive. Our films have improved, if at all, only in their intentions. We are still unable to find evidence of artistic sensibilities in working order. There is as much genuine personality in *Room at the Top*, method in *A Kind of Loving* and style in *A Taste of Honey* as there is wit in *An Alligator Named Daisy*, intelligence in *Above Us the Waves* and ambition in *Ramsbottom Rides Again*.[18]

This polemical insistence on the inferiority of British cinema had some justification when critical significance was granted the Kitchen Sink films and denied the films of Preminger, Hitchcock, Hawks, Minnelli and Sirk. And though the *Movie* critics' advocacy of a classical Hollywood style (which was already in the throes of disintegration) made them unsympathetic to the erratic informalities of 'New British Cinema', other directors afforded little attention elsewhere were treated sympathetically in the pages of *Movie*. Richardson and Schlesinger were beyond the pale, but Victor Perkins, temporarily at least, championed Seth Holt and Clive Donner, Ian Cameron wrote perceptively about Alexander Mackendrick, and Robin Wood brilliantly about Michael Reeves.[19]

In France, auteurism was used as a weapon to smash the old guard of French directors and make way for a 'new wave' of cinema. Between 1958 and 1963 over a hundred young directors – many of them former critics – made their first feature film.[20] French intellectuals made use of a mythic image of America to free themselves from the conventions of their own culture:

From Miles Davis to Marlon Brando, William Faulkner to comic

63

strips, American culture offers many Frenchmen the vision of a new world, poetic, violent and free. It offers a positive, if hopelessly idealised, counter-image to the ordered, academic, bourgeois tradition that stretches from *La Princesse de Clèves* to René Clair.[21]

The *Movie* writers had ambitions to make films themselves, but they found it much more difficult to break into film production than their French counterparts. Mark Shivas became a producer, but mainly for television films and series; Paul Mayersberg broke through into scriptwriting after making a significant contribution to Roger Corman's *The Tomb of Ligeia*, and later provided original and intellectually demanding scripts for Nicolas Roeg's *The Man Who Fell to Earth* and *Eureka*. But although Ian Cameron's bold graphic design and the vigorous, polemical writing of Robin Wood and Victor Perkins influenced the development of film culture in Britain, *Movie*'s impact on film production was minimal.

The alliance between film-makers and 'committed' critics on *Definition* proved shortlived, and there was an increasing emphasis on education and theory rather than actual film-making. One might have expected the 'committed' writers to show a wider interest in British films, but the old left-wing suspicion of mass culture imposed strict limits on their tolerance of a cinema which, once the brief Kitchen Sink interlude was over, seemed to have exchanged timid conformism for empty-headed trendiness. Anderson's call for a film criticism which took into consideration the role of film in society found a resonance in Richard Hoggart's *The Uses of Literacy* (published in 1957) and Raymond Williams's *Culture and Society* (1958). Neither book was concerned with film – except in so far as Hoggart deplored it as an aspect of that 'shiny barbarism' which was eroding working-class culture – but they shifted the debate about British culture from the increasingly remote organic communities which F. R. Leavis saw as alone capable of significant art, to the practical reality of life in an industrial society, and focused attention on the role of the mass media.

Like Anderson, who condemned the degraded leisure habits of the working class in *O Dreamland!* but showed admiration and affection for the workers of Covent Garden in *Every Day Except Christmas*, both Hoggart and Williams wrote warmly about a working-class culture which had hitherto been ignored and was now being eroded by the mass media. But whereas Anderson was an upper middle-class Scot attracted to working-class culture as an antidote to the small-minded hypocrisy of English middle-class life, Hoggart had been brought up in a Leeds slum and Williams in a Welsh mining village, and they held more complex, less idealised views about working-class life. The contrast between the true values of working-class culture and the false values of mass culture was still very much in evidence in *The Uses of*

Literacy and *Culture and Society*, but Williams had every sympathy with working-class people wanting to acquire 'bourgeois' comforts and amenities, and Hoggart was wary of simplistic contrasts:

> It is easier, because they have an antique music hall flavour, to admit some of the strengths in working-men's club singing than to see the signs of life in skiffle and teddy-boy clothes. These elements may not amount to a great deal but they can show a kind of independence, vitality and choice. And even as one says this one realizes that such a widening of view only increases the need for sharp distinctions. Instances of vitality are usually taken over quickly by the mass-media, wrapped in cellophane, and then presented as the real thing. It's important not to confuse a more flexible view with cultural slumming or with a highbrow's anti-highbrow nostalgia.[22]

By the mid-60s the study of popular culture had acquired academic respectability. Hoggart was able to set up the Centre for Contemporary Cultural Studies as a department of the University of Birmingham, and in schools there was an expansion in film education.

Prior to the early 60s 'film appreciation' had been a major spin-off from the 'film-as-art' movement. Encouraged by the BFI Education Department under Paddy Whannel and Alan Lovell, film education was taken over and expanded by protagonists of the 'committed' school. By the end of the decade committed critics like Whannel and Lovell had adopted auteurism as a useful strategy for studying the cinema, but by combining it with the new disciplines of structuralism and semiotics they maintained the gulf between themselves and the old-style auteurists like Cameron and Perkins.[23] Through the journal *Screen* and the activities of the BFI Education Department, this new school of avowedly Marxist film criticism achieved an impressive dominance over the higher reaches of British film culture. (*Sight and Sound* continued to occupy the middle ground but at the cost of losing touch with film theory.) There were soon to be divisions and bifurcations in the new orthodoxy, but most serious writers on film were influenced by the new currents.[24]

Left-wing critics were profoundly ambivalent in their attitude to popular culture. Paddy Whannel and Stuart Hall's book *The Popular Arts*, published in 1964, attempts to find 'that "holding centre" between, on the one hand, the cheapjack slackness and sensationalism which is all that's worst in show-business, and, on the other, the mixture of panic, fear and snobbery which, by and large, has been the educational world's chief contribution to the debate.'[25] But for the little band of intellectuals who were willing to embrace popular culture wholeheartedly its lukewarm tolerance was not enough. In a cruel review Raymond Durgnat concluded:

I hope that the book, respectworthy and suggestive as it is, has no influence on the mass media whatsoever, because, despite its many good qualities, it's still too bound to the assumptions and tone of the grammar school sixth form. The authors probably think of themselves as Marxists cleverly appealing to bourgeois moral earnestness, but to my mind they're cultural Gaitskellites, or Grimondites, whose assumptions may work on the right, but they certainly confuse the left. Give it to your Tory headmaster, order a copy for your school library – but for yourself, go and see *The Servant*, or *Spartacus*, or *Rebel Without a Cause*, again.[26]

Durgnat was something of a lone wolf among British film critics, but his enthusiasms were familiar enough to the Independent Group which first began to meet at the Institute of Contemporary Arts in the early 1950s. It was made up of a diverse bunch of artists, sculptors and critics who were dissatisfied with the stuffy exclusiveness of the art establishment and sought inspiration in

the despised aesthetics of a society geared for profit and turn-over, and in particular with the mass-produced dream which had evolved to help sell the ever-growing flood of objects: the lumpen fantasy world of long-limbed compliant girls, fast cars, penthouses, streamlined violence and neon lights reflected in private swimming pools.[27]

The radicalism of Pop Art, a term first used by Independent Group critic Lawrence Alloway, is now regarded with some scepticism, so it is worth stressing just how important a break it was with traditional art practices. As Richard Hamilton put it:

In much the same way that the invention of photography cut away for itself a chunk of art's prerogative – the pictorial recording of visual facts – trimming the scope of messages which Fine Art felt to lie within its true competence – so has popular culture abstracted from Fine Art its role of mythmaker. ... It is the *Playboy* 'Playmate-of-the-Month' pull-out pin-up which provides us with the closest contemporary equivalent of the odalisque in painting. Automobile body stylists have absorbed the symbolism of the space age more successfully than any artists. Social comment is left to TV and comic strip. Epic has become synonymous with a certain kind of film and the heroic archetype is now buried deep in movie lore. If the artist is not to lose much of his ancient purpose he may have to plunder the popular arts to recover the imagery which is his rightful inheritance.[28]

Hamilton's argument that 'mass production and the mass media made

66

possible a far greater number of individual choices than under a pre-industrial or craft economy' was unfavourably received at the National Union of Teachers Conference on 'Popular Culture and Personal Responsibility' in 1960, and when the conference papers were published (as *Discrimination and Popular Culture*) Hamilton's contribution was not included.[29]

The mainstream of film and cultural studies also remained resistant to such affirmative approaches, but between 1959 and 1969 Lawrence Alloway did publish a number of articles about film, ranging from a short piece on horror films (a refreshing contrast to Derek Hill's lumbering survey in *Sight and Sound*), to a book-length essay on the films of 'Violent America' to accompany a season of films he organised at the Museum of Modern Art in New York in 1969.[30] Apart from the piece on Hammer's horror films, his articles concentrate on Hollywood films; but in contrast to the *Movie* writers, whose search for traditional forms of artistic complexity quickly passes Britain by, Alloway's principles can be applied as well to British as to American films.[31]

Alloway's starting point is that film, as a mass art, is different from but not inferior to or less important than high art. Faced with 'continually changing alliances of talent rather than with simple pyramids of personal authority', auteurism is less useful than a study of the cinema based on iconography and genre. Taking up points made by Walter Benjamin in his essay 'The Work of Art in the Age of Mechanical Reproduction', Alloway stressed how film has changed the very nature of art, how reproducibility has destroyed the value of aesthetic contemplation, how the 'aura' around a work of art which gave it a religious value has disappeared with its uniqueness, and that the balance between what Benjamin distinguishes as the cult value and the exhibition value of a work of art has irrevocably shifted in favour of the latter. Benjamin, writing in Fascist Germany in the 1930s, was understandably gloomy about the use to which film could be put. Alloway could afford to be optimistic, arguing that:

> Mass production techniques, applied to accurately repeatable words, pictures and music, have resulted in an expendable multitude of signs and symbols. To approach this exploding field with Renaissance-based ideas of the uniqueness of art is crippling. Acceptance of the mass media entails a shift in our notion of what culture is.[32]

He also takes from Benjamin the idea that film offers a unique insight into human behaviour, habits, fashions, presumptions, obsessions; that 'The cinema, as a combined technological recording art, is riddled with links to areas of behaviour that are highly fugitive: social styles, ways of moving, sexual signals.'[33] *Movie*, perceptive enough occasionally to acknowledge the value of positions other than their own, published Alloway's 'Iconography in the Movies', but his vigorous populism had less in common with *Movie*'s approach than with that of the short-lived journal *Motion*. [34]

Motion first appeared in the summer of 1961. While claiming to be left-wing, it did so from a very different position from the 'committed' critics of *Definition*. Ian Johnston remained editor of the journal for all its six issues, but the composition of the editorial board changed dramatically. Cambridge auteurists Charles Barr and Peter Cowie came and went as well as the less easily classifiable Allen Eyles, but the dominant influence at the end was Raymond Durgnat. Though he too had studied English at Cambridge, Durgnat's heart was closer to Bugs Bunny than to F. R. Leavis. In an illuminating article entitled 'The Mass Media – A Highbrow Illiteracy' (written after the death of *Motion* in a journal called *Views*), Durgnat stated his position clearly:

> Those intellectuals of my generation who interested themselves in jazz, in the cinema, in science fiction, in American comics, did not 'capitulate' to the 'pressures' of the mass media; on the contrary. We deliberately chose them – or rather intuitively responded to them – both as artistic pleasures unsullied by the assumptions of our schoolmasters, and for their 'subversive' vulgar view of human nature. [35]

This was part of a more general phenomenon: there is an almost identical passage in George Melly's *Revolt into Style*, and the 21 year-old Ray Gosling's semi-autobiographical *Sum Total*, published in 1962, is wracked by a central conflict between the values of the grammar school sixth form and the exciting life out there in the city among the Teds and the juke-boxes. [36] By the mid-60s books like Peter Laurie's *The Teenage Revolution*, Nik Cohn's *Today There Are No Gentlemen* and Jeff Nuttall's *Bomb Culture* show a fierce if divided loyalty to popular culture.

Durgnat's most serious statement of principles comes in two articles he wrote for the last issue of *Motion* in 1963, 'Puritans Anonymous' and 'Standing Up for Jesus'. Durgnat sees puritanism lurking behind 'all those philosophies that aspire, not, like Aristotle's, to a judicious balance of selfishness and altruism, of baseness and liftiness, but like Plato's, to an actual *eradication* of "unworthy" impulses, however deeply they plunge into the soul.' [37] In 'Standing Up for Jesus' he asserts that the mainstream tradition of art and art criticism since Matthew Arnold espoused a 'high moral purpose' which lives on, debilitated but still tenacious in the pages of *Sight and Sound*. Thus Anderson's 'commitment' is to a middle-class puritanism that has no sympathy or understanding of popular working-class culture, and 'what masquerades as vaguely leftish goodness is really middle-class fear of the brutal and licentious proletariat.'[38] Exposing the artificiality of the division between left and right, he criticises the narrowness of *Definition*'s approach and points out that the films of Nicholas Ray, Samuel Fuller and other favourites of the auteurists 'are worth noticing carefully not only because of their plastic language but because of their concern with man in society.' The committed critics, 'Just because of their intellectual fundamentalism . . . are constantly attacking, despising, ignoring film-makers who in some ways at least are on their own side.'[39]

In France, the journal *Positif* combined Durgnat's robust support for left-wing humanist directors like Huston, Brooks, Penn, Kazan, with a similar interest in

> the horror movie and the 'fantastic' in general (Sternberg and Corman, for example), in certain kinds of crazy comedy (especially Tashlin and Jerry Lewis) and in eroticism and the star phenomenon (particularly women stars like Marilyn Monroe, Kim Novak, Louise Brooks, but also, for instance, Brigitte Bardot) . . .[40]

In Britain, Durgnat, the one major critic to pay serious attention to British cinema throughout the decade, was increasingly marginalised from the mainstream of film studies. His articles in *Films and Filming* and the American *Film Comment* and his marvellous book *A Mirror for England* were largely ignored by his fellow critics in Britain, and his seminal article on Michael Powell was sneaked into *Movie* under another name.[41] At the end of the decade Alan Lovell wrote an interesting, exploratory essay on British cinema for the BFI Education Department. It is symptomatic of the neglect into which the study of British cinema had fallen that he called it 'British Cinema – The Unknown Cinema'.[42]

4

ART AND COMMERCE

Perhaps the most important function of class was the multiplication of immediate social signs, so that the individual was supported by a human context. 'Mass-culture' in a society moving towards classlessness and atomised by its technical gadgets is a fumbling attempt (constantly distorted by the financial considerations inseparable from mass-production) to create synthetically the contacts, rituals, and symbols which will serve as a projection of the individual's life and allow him to commune with society as a whole. (John Weightman, 1960)[1]

Art Cinema?

An interest in the art of the cinema had developed in the 1920s with the establishment of the Film Society and the film journal *Close Up*, and in the 1930s there was sufficient interest to sustain small West End cinemas like the Shaftesbury Avenue Pavilion and the Academy in Oxford Street. British highbrow film culture looked to Europe for inspiration, and though the British Documentary Movement was regarded favourably in progressive circles, the mainstream commercial industry was dismissed as a pale imitation of the Hollywood 'film factory'. During the war there was great intellectual enthusiasm for what Dilys Powell called 'the movement towards documentary truth in the entertainment film'.[2] But in the late 1940s attention shifted back to the burgeoning international art cinema. Intellectual interest in films was fostered by evangelists like Dr Roger Manvell, and in response the film society movement flourished. In 1939 there were eighteen societies, in 1946 there were forty-eight, in 1955 two hundred and thirty, in 1971 seven hundred and fifty.[3]

As cinema attendance was eroded by television, several of the independent cinemas and small circuits turned from showing films which had already played at the bigger cinemas to a mixture of sex films, art films, exotic epics and horror films, together with re-runs of popular British and American classics. Distributors like Gala, Miracle, Eros, Films de France and Cross Channel imported anything from *Hiroshima Mon Amour* to *Around the World With Nothing On*, a cultural mix which was frowned upon by *Sight and Sound*:

> The audience for the latest nudist film or tour of the European striptease joints is not the audience for Godard or Antonioni. Yet there is neither enough sensationalism nor enough quality to sustain the average cinema; and the result is an unholy alliance, a policy which results in the optimistic selling of *Une Femme Mariée* as '24 Hours in the Life of an Adulteress' or the pretence that films like *Mondo Cane* are art as well as sensation. Cinemas, like dogs, get a bad name. A potential audience is lost because it would rather go without than join the sad, raincoated queues in their forever frustrated search for screen pornography.[4]

But films which appealed exclusively to an art-house audience could expect only meagre returns in the British market – Godard's *A Bout de Souffle* took less from the 130 British cinemas it was booked in to than *From Russia With Love* took in a week in a single cinema – and British films with artistic pretensions needed to reach a much wider audience if they were to be financially viable.[5]

Tony Richardson's *Tom Jones* and John Schlesinger's *Billy Liar!*, both released in May 1963, marked a turning away from working-class realism towards the zany optimism which signalled the arrival of the 'Swinging Sixties', but this was less discernible at the time than the turn towards 'art'. Robert Vas, in a laudatory article entitled 'Arrivals and Departures', hailed *This Sporting Life* as both a summing up of the Kitchen Sink tradition and the first of a new kind of seriously artistic film:

> And now, when we in Britain seem finally to have an audience, producers, actors and writers for this new realism, the appearance of the first really major work is necessarily an arrival as much as a departure. It builds on the achievements of the last seven years, unifies patterns and points towards directions still unenvisaged.[6]

Things were not to develop in quite the way that Vas, or Anderson, hoped, but *This Sporting Life* did seem to provoke British film-makers into making artistically ambitious films. One could group together Joseph Losey's *Eve* and *The Servant*, Wolf Rilla's *The World Ten Times Over*, Peter Brook's *Lord of the Flies*, Clive Donner's *The Caretaker*, all released in 1963; Karel Reisz's *Night Must Fall*, Jack Clayton's *The*

Pumpkin Eater, Bryan Forbes's *Seance on a Wet Afternoon*, Losey's *King and Country*, and Kevin Brownlow and Andrew Mollo's *It Happened Here* (1964); Sidney Lumet's *The Hill*, Anthony Simmons's *Four in the Morning*, Roman Polanski's *Repulsion*, James Ivory's *Shakespeare Wallah*, and John Schlesinger's *Darling* (1965); Reisz's *Morgan*, Polanski's *Cul de Sac*, Truffaut's *Fahrenheit 451*, Richardson's *Mademoiselle*, Forbes's *The Whisperers*, Anderson's *The White Bus*, and possibly Losey's *Modesty Blaise* (1966); Antonioni's *Blow Up*, Richard Lester's *How I Won the War*, Losey's *Accident*, Richardson's *The Sailor from Gibraltar*, Don Levy's *Herostratus*, Albert Finney's *Charlie Bubbles*, Peter Watkins's *Privilege*, Joseph Strick's *Ulysses*, and Jack Clayton's *Our Mother's House* (1967); Richardson's *The Charge of the Light Brigade*, Anthony Page's film of Osborne's *Inadmissible Evidence*, Peter Brook's *Tell Me Lies*, Peter Medak's *Negatives*, Anderson's *If. . . .*, Losey's *Boom!* and *Secret Ceremony*, and, in intention if not achievement, Guy Green's *The Magus* and Jack Cardiff's *Girl on a Motorcycle* (1968); Reisz's *Isadora*, Ken Russell's *Women in Love*, Lester's *The Bed Sitting Room*, Richardson's *Laughter in the Dark*, and possibly Richard Attenborough's *Oh What a Lovely War* and Anthony Newley's *Can Heironymus Merkin Ever Forget Mercy Humppe and Find True Happiness?* (1969); William Friedkin's *The Birthday Party*, Godard's *Sympathy With the Devil*, Maurice Hatton's *Praise Marx and Pass the Ammunition*, Christopher Miles's *The Virgin and the Gypsy*, John Boorman's *Leo the Last*, Losey's *The Go-Between* and *Figures in a Landscape*, Russell's *The Music Lovers*, and Nicolas Roeg and Donald Cammell's *Performance* (1970).[7] It would be wrong, however, to assume that because they have serious intentions, big subjects and themes and devices designed to appeal to an intellectual audience, they are necessarily the best that British cinema had to offer. Paul Mayersberg, in a radio talk he called 'The Art That Never Was', declared:

> the great stumbling block of Anglo-Saxon film criticism has been the attempt to separate commerce from art in what is a mass medium. There is, of course, no distinction to be made and no need to look for, let alone define, the dividing line between them. Two courses are open to the critic. He can look upon film as art, the way many French critics do, equal in status and potential to the art forms of music, poetry and painting, or he can look upon film, without shame or a sense of inferiority, as the mass medium it is. . . . I think the second, the mass medium approach, is the most useful in that it takes into account the actual processes of film-making, the commercial interests that are inevitably bound up with the production of film, the non-aesthetic elements of movies such as the appeal of the stars and the iconographical significance of the stories, subjects and characters.[8]

72

This chapter juxtaposes films which strive towards art with films which at the time they were released were viewed as purely commercial, though the divisions between 'art' and 'commerce' are not always clear-cut.

'Is it the chromosomes, do you think? Or is it England?'
Night Must Fall, Karel Reisz's belated follow-up to *Saturday Night and Sunday Morning*, is based on a pre-war play by Emlyn Williams, as too is Joseph Losey's first important British film, *Time Without Pity* (1957). Losey uses gloomy lighting and intense performances to turn a stage melodrama into an English *film noir*. Reisz and the television playwright Clive Exton update *Night Must Fall* to the 60s and attempt a psychological reinterpretation. Penelope Houston complained that 'one feels that a great deal of theoretical rather than practical intelligence went into the problem of how to reconstruct an old warhorse of stage melodrama to make it work in the modern anti-narrative idiom.'[9] But Reisz's film is *more* melodramatic than Richard Thorpe's 1937 version, where Danny (Robert Montgomery), the psychopathic murderer who keeps the head of one of his victims in a hat-box, is marked more by his disregard of class barriers than by conventional signs of madness. In this earlier version there is little suspense, the heroine (Rosalind Russell) suspects Danny from the start, and the threat from madness and disorder is sensibly repulsed.[10]

Albert Finney's Danny is more explicitly sexually disturbed: coldly manipulative with younger women and dangerously excited by their mothers. With his slicked-back hair, staring eyes and manic little gestures, he dominates the film, but he seems to operate in an artificial world. In Emlyn Williams's play, set in the rigidly class-divided society of the 30s, Danny can be seen as a representative of the poor and oppressed who wreaks awful vengeance on those who have patronised and cheated him. In Reisz's film, society has changed too much for this to be believable. Servants are hard to come by and think themselves as good as their masters, and Mona Washbourne's Mrs Bramson is less a rich old monster who deserves to be slain than a silly woman for whom murder is a horribly disproportionate punishment.

Reisz's updating also damages the relationship between Danny and Olivia, which is central to the 1937 version (indeed the whole film can be seen as Olivia's sexual fantasy). Rosalind Russell's Olivia is a true heroine – depressed, unfulfilled, romantic – a Jane Eyre figure who yearns for excitement and adventure so much that she remains attracted to Danny even when she knows he is a murderer. At the end of the film she returns to the house not to save her aunt – who exploits and bullies her – but because she needs to discover for herself that Danny really is 'loathsome, horrible', incapable of caring for anyone but himself and not the bold adventurer she has longed for to carry her off to a life of passion and romance. Reisz's Olivia (Susan Hampshire) is a bored, pampered rich girl and her relationship with Danny is one of those love-hate relationships across the class barriers which are such a persistent motif in British films of the 60s, from *Look Back in Anger* at the beginning of the period to *The Reckoning* at the end. The best parts of the film do concern Olivia and Danny: the opening juxtaposition of Olivia's early morning meanderings with Danny's efforts to dispose of the body of his latest victim; the end where she returns to the house, finds her mother murdered and confronts her helplessly mad lover. But the relationship is dealt with so elliptically – Reisz cuts from Danny about to rape Olivia to them playing happily together on his motorscooter – that there is little sense of a real bond between them.[11]

The film was not a commercial success, and attracted a certain amount of hostility from the fans of Albert Finney, who had become internationally famous as the boisterous innocent Tom Jones by the time *Night Must Fall* came out. If Finney had played the lead role in Reisz's next film, *Morgan* – a role it is difficult to imagine anyone other than David Warner playing but for which Finney was eminently suitable – *Night Must Fall* might have been retrospectively recognised as an interesting experiment sandwiched between two of the most successful films made in Britain in the 60s.

Morgan began life in 1962 as a television play, *A Suitable Case for Treatment* by David Mercer, about a working-class writer whose existential crisis leads to mild schizophrenia and a break-up with his upper middle-class wife. But in 1963 Mercer discovered the writings of R. D. Laing (*The Divided Self*, 1960, and *The Self and Others*, 1961) and his screenplay for *Morgan* was heavily influenced by Laing's argument that madness is a rational response to intolerable pressures put on nonconforming individuals by their families and society, ideas which were to fuse with psychotropic drugs and Herbert Marcuse's concept of 'repressive tolerance' to give a philosophical grounding to the 'alternative culture' of the late 60s.[12] As Barry Curtis points out: 'In 1962 Morgan returns to the working class . . . in 1966 he goes creatively and defiantly mad.'[13] With the substitution of David Warner for Ian Hendry, who had played the older and more conventional character of *A Suitable Case for Treatment*, *Morgan* was finely tuned to attract a young, radical audience.

David Warner's Morgan Delt represented a new sort of 60s man. In contrast to the aggressively masculine heroes of the early 60s films, Morgan carries his masculinity as a vulnerable, battered banner: a natural man unfit to live in the urban jungle. He dreams constantly of a return to the real jungle where man, gorilla-like, can swing through the trees, scare off rivals with a show of bravado, and physically carry off the mate of his choice, but he is not without friends and resources in the wilderness of the city. His rich wife (Vanessa Redgrave) is divorcing him because he is impossible to live with, but she still loves and admires him; his old mum (Irene Handl) doesn't understand him, but she nourishes and comforts him where she can; and Wally (Arthur Mullard), the old wrestler who acts as a surrogate father, shares with Morgan a nostalgia for simple animal pleasures.

If *Night Must Fall* shows madness as egocentricity run riot, *Morgan* shows it as endearingly outrageous. When Morgan kidnaps Leonie it is a sad, funny, doomed attempt to prove that the need for warmth and affection is more important than the need for a rational, well-ordered life. His madness harms only himself and even self-destruction is shown as merely a stage on the path towards tranquillity and wisdom. Other 60s representations of morbid obsessions and madness – Michael Powell's *Peeping Tom* (1959), Jack Clayton's *The Innocents* (1961), Roman Polanski's *Repulsion* (1965), Bryan Forbes's *Seance on a Wet Afternoon* (1964), William Wyler's *The Collector* (1965) and Roy Boulting's *Twisted Nerve* (1968) – were less benign.

Seance on a Wet Afternoon is based on a clever but not particularly distinguished short novel by a young Australian writer, Mark Mac-Shane, about a medium whose plan to demonstrate her gifts to the world go disastrously wrong. *The Collector* is an adaptation of an ambitious novel by John Fowles about a young man whose sudden and unexpected wealth gives him the opportunity to live out an obsessional fantasy. Both films deal with similar subjects. Myra Savage, the medium, and her husband kidnap a child whose whereabouts they plan to reveal to prove the effectiveness of her psychic power; Freddie Clegg, the Collector, kidnaps a pretty art student as a means of persuading her to fall in love with him.

Forbes had enjoyed considerable commercial success with his previous two films, *Whistle Down the Wind* and *The L-Shaped Room*, but he found it difficult to finance and cast *Seance on a Wet Afternoon*. Simone Signoret, who might have brought humanity to Myra's character, Shelley Winters who might have brought humour, and Anne Bancroft who might have brought dignity, all turned down the role. As played by the American stage actress Kim Stanley, she is – like Danny in *Night Must Fall* – an irrational psychopath whose plight arouses little interest; and her victim, a spoilt little girl, is comparable to Mrs Bramson, irritating but undeserving of her awful fate. Kim Stanley's laboured Method acting (encouraged by Forbes's invention of a still-born baby to act as her spirit guide), Nanette Newman's fluttering hysteria, and Richard Attenborough's grotesque make-up reinforce the sense of artificiality.

William Wyler had directed his first film in 1925 and forty years later his career was drawing to a close. *The Collector* is slow and ponderous, and Wyler eschews the stylistic innovations adopted by

75

more fashion-conscious directors. John Russell Taylor reported sarcastically that 'all disturbing advance suggestions that Wyler had gone New Wave with *The Collector* prove happily unfounded.'[14] And James Woolf commented disparagingly on Wyler's old-fashioned methods: 'When Wyler moves the camera it's like launching a ship, you can hear the engines churning, you feel like cheering and breaking a bottle of champagne.'[15] Despite this and the fact that *The Collector* is a big-budget Technicolor film shot partly in Columbia's Hollywood studios, it seems more deeply rooted in 60s British society than *Night Must Fall* and *Seance on a Wet Afternoon*. Wyler may be old-fashioned but he is extraordinarily sure-footed, moving his grim story forward with an inexorable drive and guiding Terence Stamp and Samantha Eggar into rivetingly convincing performances.

Fowles's novel is in two parts, comprised of Clegg's account of the kidnapping and the secret diary kept by his victim, Miranda Grey, during her incarceration. Miranda's narrative is more flaccidly written than Clegg's but it fulfils two useful functions: the Miranda of Clegg's narrative is an idealised fantasy figure, while the diary reveals the 'real' Miranda; the conflict between beauty and ugliness, between the life-affirming artist and the death-loving collector, is – as one might expect – dwelt on more fully by Miranda than by Clegg.

In the finished film Miranda's account is missing, exorcised by the need to reduce the film's length from four hours to a commercially more viable two hours. All that remains of Kenneth More's substantial role as Miranda's artistic mentor is a brief back-of-the-head shot in a pub. The point of view of the film, then, would seem to be that of Clegg, and as he is played by Terence Stamp (described after *Billy Budd* as 'the most beautiful man in the world') one might expect the film to collude in Clegg's fantasies – love triumphing against impossible odds being a common enough theme in the cinema. It is greatly to Wyler's credit that from the moment Miranda regains consciousness in her well-furnished prison, we know that there is no possibility of a happy end. Samantha Eggar's Miranda might look like a picture-book Sleeping Beauty, but she has no desire to wake up in some man's fantasy world, and there will never be any question of her returning his 'love'.

Danny in *Night Must Fall* and Myra in *Seance on a Wet Afternoon*, though sporadically frightening, are essentially pathetic figures, too sick to know what they are doing, reduced at the end of the film to incoherent madness. Clegg in *The Collector* is far more formidable, far closer to normality. In the novel he is physically unattractive and irredeemably blighted by small-minded bigotry.[16] Stamp is able to make him more interesting, conveying ugliness and spiritual deformity by mannerism and gesture – a peculiar way of holding his head to one side, a stiffness in his movements, an over-formality in his way of

The triumph of evil: Terence Stamp, Samantha Eggar in *The Collector*

speaking – showing how beauty can be crippled and distorted by neurosis and malice. The sense of Beauty and the Beast which pervades the novel is absent from the film (as are the references to *The Tempest*), replaced by resounding echoes of class tension. The 60s – with increased affluence, the expansion of university education, and the development of a pop music-based youth culture – saw a big increase in contact between young middle-class and working-class men and women. Relationships which would have been quite exceptional before the war became much more commonplace. But, particularly when they were between working-class men and middle-class women, they generated considerable anxiety.[17] Like Joe Lampton, Freddie Clegg is a clerk in the Borough Treasurer's Office (in the film this becomes a bank), and like Joe he sets his heart on a middle-class 'grade one' girl who seems to move in a privileged world from which he is excluded. Joe uses charm, good looks and his sense of his own worth to win Susan. Clegg has none of Joe's advantages, but with the unexpected windfall of a football pools win he has the financial resources to attempt to live out his fantasies.

Despite the extensive cuts made to the planned version of the film, Wyler still manages to give both Miranda and Clegg enough space to emerge as likeable characters. Both make efforts to please the other, but nothing can grow in the barren climate of fear which Clegg's actions have set as the framework for their relationship. Miranda, wrenched from a life which had purpose and momentum, problems and pleasures, is slow to concede even friendliness, and Clegg is right to recognise that his ignorance and inferiority, his inability to make sense of the things Miranda thinks important, would prove a fatal handicap in the real world. When all has ended in disaster he comforts himself with the thought that 'My only mistake was aiming too high. I ought to have seen I could never get what I wanted from someone like Miranda with all her lah-di-dah ideas and clever tricks. I ought to have got someone who would respect me more, someone ordinary.' And with the same fastidious care we have seen him exercise in capturing butterflies, he begins stalking another victim. He is no madder than he was at the beginning of the film; but from being an extreme version of the working-class hero seeking to break through class barriers to win the girl of his dreams, he has changed into a fantasy-ridden monster on a par with the Moors Murderers.

Night Must Fall was made for MGM, *The Collector* for Columbia, and both were considered 'prestige' productions. *Peeping Tom* and *Repulsion* were made for companies (Anglo-Amalgamated and Compton-Tekli) which generally made films for the bottom end of the market and must have seemed to their producers if not to their directors to combine a certain amount of artistic prestige with an exploitable degree of sex and violence. Nat Cohen's acumen in backing offbeat projects which turned out to be commercially as well as artistically successful (*A Kind of Loving*, *Billy Liar!*, *Darling*, *Nothing But the Best*, *Poor Cow*, *The Go-Between*) is remarkable. But *Peeping Tom* was sandwiched between two other Eastmancolor horror films – Arthur Crabtree's *Horrors of the Black Museum* and Sidney Hayers's *Circus of Horrors* – and must have looked safe enough despite its peculiar subject matter. Similarly *Repulsion*, though in a different category to Compton-Tekli's more straightforward exploitation films (such as *Saturday Night Out* and *The Yellow Teddy Bears*), was seen to have a commercial potential lacking in *Cul de Sac*, the script which Polanski first presented to them (and which to their credit they allowed him to make as a follow-up to *Repulsion*). Both *Peeping Tom* and *Repulsion* were well-reviewed in the trade press and were commercially successful, but they provoked very different reactions from the critics. *Repulsion*, as the first British film of a foreign director who had won prizes at international festivals, was treated with respect, despite reservations in some quarters about whether it was really necessary to deal with such nasty and distressing subjects. *Peeping Tom* suffered the worst torrent of abuse any film had had to suffer since *No Orchids for Miss Blandish* in 1948.[18]

It is impossible to forgive the prurience and blindness with which the critics (with the exception of Ian Johnson in *Motion* and Jean-Paul Török in *Positif*) condemned what is undoubtedly a masterpiece, but even now *Peeping Tom* is a very disturbing film, only acceptable perhaps because Michael Powell is acknowledged as a film-maker of great integrity as well as dazzling ability. Its setting – late 50s London – is reminiscent of *Sapphire*, and duffle-coated Carl Boehm is as solitary and introverted as duffle-coated Paul Massie: both conceal their passion beneath a bland exterior.[19] But in *Sapphire*, for all the disturbance caused by eruptions of violent sexuality, the liberal, enlightened authorities – Nigel Patrick's quizzical, rational Superintendent Hazard, the doctor who puts down Inspector Learoyd for his racist assumptions, Earl Cameron's stoically dignified black doctor – are firmly in control. In *Peeping Tom*, the voice of sanity is a blind, bitter, whisky-swigging, middle-aged woman (Maxine Audley), who in the face of evil and madness can only stumble back to her room muttering, 'All this filming isn't healthy'.[20]

Repulsion is a young man's film with energy and inventiveness making up for occasional crudities caused by limited resources and lack of experience. Its story, written quickly by Polanski and his regular collaborator Gerard Brach, is less complex than that of *Peeping Tom* and is significant only by virtue of Polanski's direction. Carol (Catherine Deneuve), a young foreigner, drifts into madness when her elder sister goes away for a few days leaving her alone in a big, gloomy, London flat. Two visitors, one a well-intentioned would-be boyfriend (John Fraser), the other a slimy lecherous landlord (Patrick Wymark), are murdered by her when they try to penetrate her private world.

Polanski's creation of an environment of madness is comparable to Jack Clayton's in *The Innocents*. An adaptation of Henry James's *The Turn of the Screw*, Clayton's film is marvellously effective in its use of atmospherics, but our involvement is limited by the ambiguity over whether it is the children or their governess who is mad and evil. It is difficult to know whether to feel sympathy for Miss Giddens as a victim of her own obsessions, horror at her sexual repression turning her into a murderous monster, or awe and admiration as she confronts what she thinks is the evil embedded in the seemingly innocent children. *Repulsion* loads its emotional weighting more decisively. Carol is mad and her victims are, in the first case innocent, in the second not entirely blameworthy, but we enter into her world so completely that the murders seem like just a revenge on men who have turned her into a frightened, irrational animal. By seeming threatening, obtrusive, interfering, and because they mirror the malaise by which she is afflicted, they deserve what they get.

The sexual fear and disgust which sets off Miss Giddens's imagination is perceived as an evil supernatural force. In *Repulsion*, it is more earthbound – the noise of love-making in the next room, the toothbrush and soiled vest of her sister's lover, the decaying old ladies whom Carol tends in the beauty parlour, the skinned rabbit which comes to seem like an aborted foetus, the relentless, predatory lechery of all the men she encounters (even the patient, gentlemanly Fraser) – and sets up a contrast between female fragility and male sexual aggression. In *Peeping Tom*, things are less straightforward. Mark is virginal, passive, unassertive, and his relationship with Helen (Anna Massey) is almost childlike. Helen's relationship with her fellow-lodger would seem to imply that she is not a sexual innocent, but her asexual clothes and frank manner are in marked contrast to the blatant sexuality of Mark's victims – a prostitute, a dancer, a pin-up model. Mark's inability to conform to 'normal' masculinity leads him to psychopathic violence. The price Carol pays for refusing to behave like a 'normal' woman is to be plagued by fears of sexual assault.

Women's Problems
Jack Clayton's *The Pumpkin Eater*, a film about the mid-life crisis of a middle-class woman, received lengthy and in several quarters sympathetic critical treatment. But for *Sight and Sound*'s editor, Penelope Houston, it was altogether too modish:

> Clayton inaugurated the whole British back-to-the-provinces movement with *Room at the Top*; and in *The Pumpkin Eater* I suspect that he is showing the same freakish instinct for the mood of the times. Probably with no more deliberate intention on his part, he would seem here to be ratifying the British cinema's *entente* with Europe.[21]

Houston's accusation that Clayton was unduly influenced by Antonioni and that *Pumpkin Eater* is a shallow copy of a European art film now seems misplaced. The film, despite the casting of Anne Bancroft in the central role, looks quintessentially British, and Clayton has proved to be the least fashionable of directors. He refused to repeat the success of *Room at the Top* with another Kitchen Sink subject and instead chose to make *The Innocents* for 20th Century-Fox. *The Pumpkin Eater*, though it reunited him with Romulus, turns its back on poverty and the working class. Its heroine is troubled by the malaise of affluence which causes her children to be tidied away in nurseries and boarding schools and drives her to a nervous breakdown in Harrods. (Clayton's next film, *Our Mother's House*, released during the 'Summer of Love' in July 1967, was an almost perversely unfashionable story of five children attempting to conceal from the world their mother's death.)

Penelope Mortimer's novel, which unfolds as a series of imaginary missives from the protagonist, Jo, to a schoolfriend, is at times trite and one-dimensional. Jo's parents, friends, even her husband, are seen only through her eyes and are hardly more than ciphers. In the film Maggie Smith, Yootha Joyce, Richard Johnson, Cedric Hardwicke, Rosalind Atkinson and Peter Finch give them solid substance and make Jo's crisis more real and less neurotic. And Harold Pinter's script retains the content of the novel but gives it a spiky and disturbing edge. Two incidents – the plea for help from a desperately unhappy middle-aged woman who has seen Jo's photograph in a glossy magazine and assumes her life must be perfect; and Jo's visit from an itinerant prophet, the 'New King of Israel' – which in the book are little more than whimsical details, are used by Pinter to capture that opening out on to a world of pain and sorrow which occurs when one is jolted out of the rut of routine existence. Clayton is able to reconstruct Jo's life from the empty shell of her dreams. Her grief, her suffering, rather than her psychotherapy cause her to heal herself. The ending, where Jo is woken by the voices of her husband and children advancing on the old windmill she has retreated to, is moving not because it is a 'happy end' but because it embodies a matter-of-factness about life going on, that losses and compromises and betrayals are something one has to live with.

In its adoption of a woman's view of the world, *The Pumpkin Eater* was similar to *The L-Shaped Room* (1962), a Romulus film which Clayton had backed out of, leaving the scriptwriter, Bryan Forbes, to direct. The film was seen by the critics as a ragbag of Kitchen Sink clichés, though in retrospect, with its naive heroine, its gallery of eccentrics and its setting in a London lodging house, it has more in common with Dickens than with Sillitoe, Braine or Osborne.[22] Its London is still divided into bedsits serviced by corner cafés where cod and chips, bread and butter and tea can still be had for two shillings, but the theme of a middle-class girl finding unaccustomed warmth and contentment among the underprivileged looks forward to *Up the Junction*. It is a long film imbued with a cosy pathos, but adventurous casting prevents it being any sort of routine sob story. Leslie Caron is unexpectedly poignant as Jane, the middle-class girl who finds that discarding her virginity has brought the new problem of pregnancy, and Tom Bell is remarkable as Toby, the failed writer who teaches her about love but retreats when he thinks he will have to abandon his ambitions as a writer to support a wife carrying another man's child.

In Lynne Reid Banks's novel, the romance between Jane and Toby is seriously blown off course but manages to sail through to a happy ending, with the heroine given financial independence through the convenient death of her favourite aunt, and Toby, after thrashing the father of Jane's child, realising how important she is to him. Bryan Forbes boldly casts sentimentality to the winds. Jane has no kindly aunt to bale her out, and Tom Bell's Toby – a much more unreliable and explosive mixture than the cuddly Jewish writer of the novel – is left to nurse his neurosis as Jane makes the sensible choice of returning with her baby to her parents on the Continent. This inconclusive ending works (the film was a big box-office success) partly because the magnetic screen relationship built up between Tom Bell and Leslie Caron seems strong enough to survive without a resolution, but partly because their relationship is displaced from the centre of the narrative. Toby's sulks, coinciding with Christmas and the birth of the baby, give the women of the house – three magnificent eccentrics played by Pat Phoenix, Avis Bunnage and Cicely Courtneidge – the opportunity to occupy the centre of the stage. With pre-feminist solidarity they nudge Jane out of her self-pity and bring her attention back to the value and significance of bringing a child into the world.

One of the things missing from *The L-Shaped Room* – understandable in a film already two-and-a-half hours long – is Jane's relationship with her father. In the novel her mother dies giving birth to her, and she has a close but antagonistic relationship with her father who misunderstands or disapproves of virtually everything she does. He is so disgusted by her pregnancy that he turns her out of the house (though there is an eventual reconciliation). This relationship is transposed almost intact to Wolf Rilla's *The World Ten Times Over* (1963). Rilla, the son of the German actor Walter Rilla, was a competent director treading the same sort of path as Guy Hamilton, John Guillermin, Terence Young and Lewis Gilbert, and one might have expected that he too would eventually move on to directing James Bond films or American disaster movies. But in 1963 he switched from solid, mainstream entertainment (*Village of the Damned*, *Piccadilly Third Stop*) to a much more risqué subject: the sex lives of two ill-adjusted nightclub hostesses. *The World Ten Times Over* seems to have damaged Rilla's career even more effectively than *Peeping Tom* did Powell's, and though he is no undiscovered auteur, *The World Ten Times Over* is an impressive and adventurous film.

In a twenty-four hour period the two girls, Billa (Sylvia Syms) and Ginnie (June Ritchie), dismiss their menfolk from their lives and determine to bring up Billa's as yet unborn baby together. Billa's day with her father, a small-town schoolteacher (William Hartnell) who has come up to London for an Old Vic matinée of *Coriolanus* and a lecture on 'Juvenile Delinquency and the Teacher's Role in Preventing It', is nicely handled, but the core of the film is Ginnie's lightning

82

romance with Bob (Edward Judd), the rich son of a property developer who wants to leave his wife for her in order to prove that he has a will of his own. The day they spend together, which is intercut with Billa trying to break the news of her pregnancy to her father, is full of what were to become the clichés of the 'Swinging London' film – riding in open-topped sports cars, running through parks, doing 'mad' things like agreeing to fly off for exotic foreign holidays, being irresponsible and carefree and reckless and spontaneous, but troubled by memories of a lost innocence which can never be recaptured. Ginnie sums it up in the speech which gives the film its title: 'When I was a child I used to dig holes in the sand. I used to dig these holes large enough to sit in and then I'd sit in them so that I couldn't see anybody and nobody could see me. And I thought the most marvellous things. Oh, nothing was impossible then. And I was Queen of the World, ten times over. Until they spoiled it all by fetching me home to supper or bed or something.' June Ritchie, the stolid, puddingy Ingrid of *A Kind of Loving*, gives a brilliant performance as the first fully-fledged 60s woman: impulsive, quixotic, game for anything.[23] The world seems to be her oyster, but the shadows very rapidly close in. She is able to lead her rich boyfriend by the nose, but she can't avoid his world of tacky modern bars and glass office towers where her energy and exuberance count for nothing and the only place for her is as a glorified whore.

Jo Armitage's dislocation, her alienation from society, is personal and temporary; at the end of *The Pumpkin Eater* she returns to the bosom of her family, who love her and need her. Ginnie is more fundamentally alienated, not because she is psychologically disturbed, but because society allows her no proper outlet for her talents and aspirations. She represents that section of discontented young people who later in the decade became the driving force of the Underground and the Women's Movement. It is her energy which dominates the film, and her difficulty in coming to terms with a hypocritical and contradictory society which justifies the harsh treatment dealt out to the two men. Both of them are severely put upon. Billa's dad is mocked and humiliated by the nightclub girls until he casts away his liberal tolerance and reveals a blinkered bigotry which explains why he can be of no help to his daughter. Bob, after sacrificing his marriage and offending his powerful father, is left deserted and confused. Both of them are basically good men, but they are self-obsessed and, like the Collector, their fantasies are dangerous to the women they profess to love.

With the honourable exception of Thomas Wiseman in the *Sunday Express* and Alexander Walker in the London *Evening Standard*, critical reaction to Rilla's bold experiment was hostile. The *Monthly Film Bulletin* dismissed it as a 'glum and modish essay', *The Times* wrote of 'heavy garlands of high-toned women's magazine dialogue', the *New*

The World Ten Times Over: Billa (Sylvia Syms) and Ginnie (June Ritchie) give up on men and find solace in each other

Statesman of 'slick artificiality'.[24] *The World Ten Times Over* drifted into the hazy no-man's-land between art films and sex films (it was retitled *Pussy Cat Alley* for distribution in America). Ironically, then, in its gloomy but perceptive treatment of the difficulty of relationships between men and women *The World Ten Times Over* shares its seriousness, its sadness, with Anthony Simmons's *Four in the Morning*, which attracted few commercial bookings but won the loyal support of the film society movement.

Simmons's career closely parallels that of Lindsay Anderson. Both men made documentaries about working-class life (Simmons's *Sunday by the Sea*, 1953, and *Bow Bells*, 1954; Anderson's *O Dreamland* and *Every Day Except Christmas*) in which they strove for a form of poetic realism. Both found it difficult to function in the mainstream of the industry, though Simmons co-produced Joseph Losey's *Time Without Pity* (1957) and directed a low-budget farce, *Your Money or Your Wife* (1959). *Four in the Morning* was made on a shoestring budget, half of which came from the National Film Finance Corporation, half from the film-makers' own resources. It began life as an atmospheric documentary about London's river, but with the encouragement of the NFFC Simmons expanded it by intercutting the original documentary story about the river police fishing a girl's body from the Thames in the early hours of the morning and seeking to discover her identity, with

84

two fictional stories about young couples (Ann Lynn and Brian Phelan, Judi Dench and Norman Rothwell) reaching crisis points in their relationships.

It is a sad film, ending with the young mother walking out on her husband and the two lovers travelling away from each other in opposite directions in the underground as commuters streaming over London Bridge signal the start of another ordinary day. And again it is suffering, angst-ridden women who are the central characters. Ann Lynn's nightclub singer could have worked in the same club as Ginnie and Billa of *The World Ten Times Over*, and the bedsit she will return to alone is probably an L-shaped room. Brian Phelan, her vacillating admirer, is a down-market version of Edward Judd's Bob in the Rilla film and blood brother to Tom Bell's defensive, insecure Toby in *The L-Shaped Room*. Like Ginnie and Bob, this couple – we never get to know their names – seem to have the freedom of the city, jumping into a speedboat, picking up fruit from Covent Garden market, desperately trying to be carefree and spontaneous and ending up alienated and apart. Judi Dench's young wife might have been a schoolfriend of Billa's or Lynne Reid Banks's Jane, and her bitterness at being left to look after her squalling baby while her husband goes out drinking seems to justify the decision of the other two women to bring their babies up without depending on men for support.

Links between *Four in the Morning*, *The World Ten Times Over* (both of which benefit enormously from the location photography of Larry Pizer) and *The L-Shaped Room* are easy enough to make. The view of a semi-low-life London is consistent through all three films, though there is little overlap between their settings. *Four in the Morning* focuses on the river with a brief excursion inland to Covent Garden; *The L-Shaped Room* is set among the run-down mansions and greasy cafés of Notting Hill; *The World Ten Times Over* concentrates on the West End and Soho, though it also ventures into the brash new world of car parks and tower blocks. *The Pumpkin Eater* is more glossy, its setting the up-market London of Harrods and St John's Wood. But in mood and atmosphere it shares an elegiac quality with the other three films, and all these women are tempted by suicide as an escape from a confusing, hostile, unpredictable world.

Low-budget Experiments
The World Ten Times Over and *Four in the Morning* were inexpensive films compared to *The Pumpkin Eater* and *The L-Shaped Room* (both budgeted at approximately £350,000), but their budgets were gargantuan compared to those of *It Happened Here* (£7,000) and *Herostratus* (£10,000).[25] Kevin Brownlow began shooting *It Happened Here* in 1956, hoping that once he had shot a few scenes he would be able to attract financial backers. The mainstream industry remained indiffer-

ent if not hostile, but with the help of Andrew Mollo, a sixteen-year-old expert on military uniforms, he persevered and, after squeezing £3,000 out of Woodfall, he completed the film in 1963. On such a tiny budget Brownlow and Mollo's subject – life in Britain under a Nazi occupation – was madly ambitious. But like Peter Watkins's television films *Culloden* (1964) and *The War Game* (1966), it gains a documentary realism from its grainy black-and-white photography and erratic structure, and its vision of England in wartime seems more authentic than that achieved in lavishly budgeted films like *The Eagle Has Landed* or *Yanks*.

A woman is evacuated from her West Country village, but not before witnessing her neighbours mown down by trigger-happy partisans. In London she reluctantly joins the Immediate Action Organisation, the semi-military Fascist nursing corps. But she doesn't settle in well and is disciplined when a doctor friend is arrested for sheltering a wounded partisan. Her punishment seems paradoxically mild: to be sent to a small country hospital in idyllic surroundings. After administering 'pain-killing' injections to a batch of labour-camp workers brought in suffering from T.B., she realises too late that the hospital is a death station for disposing of those people not capable of useful work for the state. A violent confrontation with her superiors leads to her arrest, but the train taking her away is blown up by the advancing partisans and she is taken prisoner. Though her sympathies are now distinctly anti-Nazi, the partisans are shown to be as callous and brutal as their opponents.

The film's 'neutrality' attracted considerable hostility (though to their credit several critics vehemently defended the film), and a sequence in which Fascist collaborators – played by active members of the National Front – argued with the heroine about the need to exterminate the Jews was cut by the film's distributors, United Artists. The criticism is unfair but understandable. After the conventional British or American war film, *It Happened Here* is quite shocking in refusing its audience the pleasure of a good side to identify with (when unarmed collaborationist prisoners are massacred, it seems even more arbitrary and unjust than the atrocities committed by the Nazis), but Brownlow's anti-Fascism is honest and open enough for the film to maintain its scrupulous fairness and still come down on the side of resistance rather than collaboration.

Brownlow and Mollo were film enthusiasts who combined working in the industry (Brownlow mainly on documentaries, Mollo for Woodfall) with an adolescent dream – they were only teenagers when they began making *It Happened Here* – which proved so rich and fruitful that it grew up with them to become a major film. Don Levy, director of *Herostratus*, was one of the first post-graduate students taught by Thorold Dickinson at the Slade School of Art. Brownlow and Mollo's film is experimental only in the way it was produced. Indeed, part of the film's achievement is how cleverly it constructs the surface realism aimed at in war films. (Brownlow's imitation newsreel and Mollo's costumes are impressively authentic, and Mollo was recruited by David Lean to achieve the same sort of accuracy in *Doctor Zhivago*.) *Herostratus* attempted to break completely with mainstream cinema, though it retains a narrative of sorts.

An angst-ridden young man (Michael Gothard) decides to let an advertising agency turn his suicide into a publicity stunt. But a night of love (with Gabriella Licudi) makes him see life differently and, going a day early to the office block from which he is supposed to jump, he gets involved in a tussle and accidentally pushes another man to his death. Some of Levy's images are remarkable – the devastated flat, a doll with an eyepatch swinging gently from the ceiling, Levy's wife in black leather and umbrella prowling the streets of St Pancras – and the film's eccentricity makes it memorable. But it is seriously flawed by technical deficiencies, and if sympathy is to be extended it has to be for Levy's intentions (comprehensively mapped out in his guide to how to watch the film), not for his achievements. The actors huff and puff over their roles with awful deliberation, their words muffled by poor sound recording, and the montage sequences are coded in a private language which, even following Levy's instructions, it is difficult to decipher.[26]

Herostratus was a startling precursor of the avant-garde cinema which sprung up in Britain in the late 60s and which, whether in the form of the fine art experimentation of the London Film-Makers Co-op or the agit-prop activism of Liberation Films, Cinema Action and the Berwick Street Film-makers Collective, rejected the very structure of the mainstream film industry and looked for their models to the American underground or the Russian film-makers of the 1920s rather than to European art cinema. These politically vigorous varieties of art cinema were to become increasingly dominant in the next decade. A handful of directors struggled through the 60s making low-budget, semi-commercial features – Barney Platts-Mills with *Bronco Bullfrog* (1970) and *Private Road* (1971), two pleasingly modest explorations of the lives of confused post-hippy teenagers, Maurice Hatton with *Praise Marx and Pass the Ammunition* (1970), a wonderfully authentic evocation of late-60s radical politics – but they found it difficult to survive among the declining opportunities of the 1970s.[27]

Joseph Losey

Joseph Losey was one of the very few directors working in Britain during the 60s who received serious, indeed comprehensive, critical attention. He came to Britain in the early 1950s, having been named as a Communist to the House of Representatives Unamerican Activities

Committee while filming in Italy and seeing little point in returning to Hollywood. His early career in the British film industry was by no means untroubled: Anglo-Amalgamated only allowed him to make *The Sleeping Tiger* when he agreed that the producer, Victor Hanbury, be given the director's credit, and Hammer succumbed to American pressure and removed him from *X The Unknown*. In the late 50s his work was enthusiastically taken up by a group of young French critics, and before long *Sight and Sound* was taking him seriously.[28] His credentials as an auteur were impeccable: he had done interesting work in the theatre as a disciple of Brecht, he had made a couple of good Hollywood films, he had fought against anti-Communist hysteria and B-movie producers to maintain his personal and artistic integrity, and above all he was not British. In the 60s he was unique in his ability to command the support of disparate critical schools. For *Movie*, Losey was the one 'British' director who could undoubtedly be classed as an auteur, for *Sight and Sound* he was a committed artist with a progressive view of the world, for Raymond Durgnat he was an adventurous experimenter continually pressing against the boundaries of popular culture.

Losey's genre films – *The Sleeping Tiger* (1954), *The Intimate Stranger* (1955), *Time Without Pity* (1957), *The Gypsy and the Gentleman* (1957), *Blind Date* (1959), *The Criminal* (1960), *The Damned* (1961) – are certainly interesting, though in retrospect so are similar films made by Val Guest, John Guillermin, Roy Baker, Clive Donner and Wolf Rilla. His art films – *Eve* (1962), *The Servant* (1963), *King and Country* (1964), *Modesty Blaise* (1966), *Accident* (1967), *Boom!* (1968), *Secret Ceremony* (1968), *Figures in a Landscape* (1970) and *The Go-Between* (1970) – which were treated with a critical indulgence which contrasts with the severity meted out to their British counterparts, have stood the test of time less well.

Eve (a Franco-Italian production with English dialogue) comes much closer than Clayton's *The Pumpkin Eater* or Reisz's *Night Must Fall* to being a European art film. Losey regarded it as his most personal film:

> ... the shame, the heterosexual/homosexual aspects, the marriage destructiveness, the beauty destroyed, the impurity, the blasphemy, the destruction of icons, the bells, all these things – they all sort of just splurged out at that point. It was almost an orgasm, and it was probably correct to say of the film that it was self-indulgent.[29]

The combination of James Hadley Chase's pulp-fiction story about a Welsh writer, Tyvian, ensnared by a *femme fatale* in Venice, with Losey's anguished intellectual obsessions holds a bizarre fascination which post-production tinkering (the film was recut by its producers and Losey's soundtrack filled with Billie Holiday songs was jettisoned) doesn't entirely dispel. There are superbly effective sequences – Eve's arrival at Tyvian's riverside mansion, Tyvian's descent into drunken despair – and the casting of Stanley Baker opposite Jeanne Moreau and Virna Lisi is daring if not wholly successful. But it remains a film of fragments which the obsessive love affair between Tyvian and Eve fails to unite.

The Servant is a cold, clever film which leaves an indelible impression. Like Robert Siodmak's *The Rough and the Smooth*, made in Britain in 1959, it is an adaptation of a story by Robin Maugham and it is instructive to compare the two films. Despite Ken Adam's sets, Otto Heller's lighting and Siodmak's inventive direction, *The Rough and the Smooth* lacks the visual coherence of *The Servant*. To set against this, Siodmak's attitude to the bizarre story is judicious and sophisticated. Mike Thompson (Tony Britton), an upper middle-class archaeologist on the verge of marriage to a newspaper heiress (Natasha Parry), is seduced by an unscrupulous German tart (Nadja Tiller) who drags him into a network of unsavoury relationships which very nearly destroy him. Resisting the opportunities for misogyny, voyeurism and sadism inherent in Maugham's story, Siodmak responds with a mid-European tolerance which allows us to sympathise both with the girl and with her male dupes.

Robert Siodmak's European sophistication, William Bendix, Nadja Tiller, Tony Britton in one of the triangular relationships in *The Rough and the Smooth*

89

In *The Servant*, Losey uses Richard MacDonald's production design and Douglas Slocombe's photography to create a distinct setting for the action. Underneath this brilliant surface, though, there are serious flaws. Harold Pinter's script strains for effect and makes nonsense of an already weak story. Tony (James Fox) is virtually the same character as Mike in *The Rough and the Smooth* (Mike is raising money for an expedition to find Noah's Ark, Tony to build cities in the Amazonian jungle), but whereas Mike is humanised by his ordeal and becomes as sympathetic as it is possible for an upper middle-class dilettante to become, Tony's transformation is from arrogant idiot to pathetic idiot. Barrett (Dirk Bogarde), who fulfils the same destructive role as Ila (Nadja Tiller), is a more complex character, but as the film drags on his complexity begins to appear perversely contradictory. He starts out as a class warrior subverting his foppish master, enters into a period of homosexual symbiosis where class relations are forgotten, and finally emerges as the thoroughly evil leader of a coven of witches which has ensnared his former master. This is just about plausible as a reworking of the Faust legend, with Barrett as a Mephistopheles who buys Tony's soul with good cooking, hot water bottles and impeccable taste in curtains. But it is difficult now to see anything more than fortunate timing and a vague air of decadence linking this muddled upper middle-class nightmare to the real-life scandals of the Profumo Affair which boosted its box-office potential.[30]

King and Country is less complex and ambitious than *Eve* and *The Servant*. A brief anecdote about the court martial of a First World War soldier (Tom Courtenay) who, after four years of the madness of trench warfare, decides he has had enough and begins walking home, it was originally intended for television and, despite flattering reviews in the *Spectator*, *Sight and Sound* and the *Monthly Film Bulletin*, compares unfavourably with contemporary television productions such as Tony Richardson and John Osborne's *A Subject of Scandal and Concern* (1960), Stuart Burge's adaptation of John Arden's *Serjeant Musgrave's Dance* (1962), and Harold Pinter's *A Night Out* (directed by Philip Saville in 1960).[31] *Accident*, Losey's second collaboration with Pinter, is a well observed, visually attractive film with a delicate middle-class sensibility. Stanley Baker repeats the role he played in *Eve* of a middle-aged womaniser making a fool of himself over a woman who doesn't love him, and Dirk Bogarde appears in his favourite 60s guise as a male menopausal Oxford don (cf. *The Mind Benders* and *Sebastian*). Both men give cleverly nuanced performances and the film is shot through with moments of beauty and perception. *Accident* is the best of the Pinter/Losey collaborations, but it teeters on the brink of becoming precious and ridiculous and hardly seems to justify the claims made for it by some critics as a masterpiece of British cinema.[32]

Boom! and *Secret Ceremony*, two expensive little films Losey made with Elizabeth Taylor, are less substantial but more likeable than *Accident*. Both are exercises in style, where bizarre settings and obscure stories cast a veil over banal and clichéd ideas, but *Secret Ceremony*'s abstract melodramatics have a genuinely haunting effect and *Boom!* has a baroque magnificence (thanks to Losey's collaborators, designer Richard MacDonald and cinematographer Douglas Slocombe) which Richard Burton and Elizabeth Taylor exploit to the full. Public reaction was lukewarm, and in critical and commercial terms Losey's most successful film was *The Go-Between* (1970), a disappointingly conventional Pinter adaptation of an L. P. Hartley story about a twelve-year-old boy's traumatic introduction to sexual and class transgressions during a holiday in an Edwardian country house.[33]

Authorship and Industry

From the early years of the war until the late 1940s, British cinema produced a rich diversity of films which makes the period something of a golden age. Most of the directors involved failed to maintain an intensity and originality in their work amidst the conformism and cultural stagnation of the 50s, and the films they survived to make in the 60s have been accorded little attention. In the case of some of the most prestigious directors of the 40s, like Anthony Asquith and Carol Reed, this is understandable. After making the grimly effective *Orders to Kill* in 1958, Asquith spent his last years making increasingly banal prestige productions like *The VIPs* (1963) and *The Yellow Rolls Royce* (1964). Carol Reed fell even more deeply into the pit of vacuous internationalism, following up *Our Man in Havana* (1959) with *The Running Man* (1963), a muddled and indulgent film starring Laurence Harvey, Alan Bates and Lee Remick, and a very long Renaissance biopic (about Michelangelo), *The Agony and the Ecstasy* (1965), before redeeming himself with the solid professionalism of the musical *Oliver!* for John Woolf.[34] David Lean, the other high promise of the 40s, seemed to go from strength to strength. *The Bridge on the River Kwai* (1957) was followed by *Lawrence of Arabia* (1963) and *Doctor Zhivago* (1966), and it was not until the failure of *Ryan's Daughter* (1970) that his career foundered. Alain Silver and James Ursini in their book *David Lean and His Films* write intelligent thematic analyses of these ambitious but ponderous films, but more interest tends to be generated in how Lean makes his films than in what they are about.[35] No doubt the cinema would be a poorer place without such grandiloquent epics, but it is difficult to create any sort of useful context in which to discuss them. The two directors from this earlier generation who might now be regarded as truly significant film-makers – Michael Powell and Alexander Mackendrick – continued to make films which combined accomplished professionalism with thematic complexity, but their efforts were mostly disparaged by the critical establishment and their position in the industry became increasingly untenable.

Philip Kemp writes that Mackendrick, 'whose technique, accomplished and inventive though it is, never obtrudes itself into the narrative', has fared less well with contemporary critics than Michael Powell, 'whose imagery [is] so evidently packed with hermetic tropes, as to signal immediately that things are going on beneath the surface, inviting excavation'.[36] In the 60s the opposite was true. The British auteurist critics abhorred directors who transgressed the rules of classical Hollywood with obtrusive devices and flashy effects, and in their 'Histogram of Talent' lumped Powell alongside Jack Lee Thompson, Basil Dearden, John Guillermin and Jack Cardiff as 'competent or ambitious' directors whose claims to be taken seriously could be safely ignored. As far as *Sight and Sound* and its allies were concerned, Powell, with his penchant for frivolity and technical virtuosity, had always been suspect, and after *Peeping Tom* he was written off. Mackendrick might have expected to fare better. His work at Ealing – *Whisky Galore*, *The Man in the White Suit*, *Mandy*, *The Maggie* and *The Ladykillers* – was enduringly popular and Mackendrick himself was serious, articulate and approachable.[37] Perhaps because they were big-budget, Technicolor, CinemaScope films, the two films he made in Britain in the 60s – *Sammy Going South* and *A High Wind in Jamaica* – were treated much more favourably by *Movie* and its allies than by the orthodox critics.

Unusually for a British director, uniquely for an Ealing director, Mackendrick had gone on to make a good American film, *The Sweet Smell of Success* (1957). On his next two ventures, *The Doctor's Dilemma* and *The Guns of Navarone*, disagreements with the producers led to him being replaced by another director. By 1963 he was back in England with his old mentor Sir Michael Balcon. Ealing had achieved its biggest commercial success not with one of the famous comedies but with a virtually forgotten film about the setting up of a game reserve in East Africa, *Where No Vultures Fly* (d. Harry Watt, 1951). Consequently Balcon was enthusiastic about Mackendrick's *Sammy Going South*, the story of a ten-year-old boy's progress from Port Said to Durban after his parents are killed in a British air-raid, and persuaded his colleagues at Bryanston to back it as their first venture into big-budget film-making in preference to Woodfall's *Tom Jones*. His judgment was wildly wrong. *Tom Jones* – backed by United Artists – went on to become one of the most profitable films of the decade, while *Sammy Going South*'s modest popularity proved insufficient to recoup its costs and discouraged Bryanston from any further ambitious projects. The critical consensus was that the film was old-fashioned. Harold Macmillan had made his speech about the 'Wind of Change' sweeping through Africa in 1960, and in the new climate of African independence films about big game hunters and the exciting life led by white settlers (*Harry Black and the Tiger* and *Nor the Moon by Night*, for example), which had been popular in the 50s, now seemed out of tune with the times.[38] Mackendrick was condemned for failing to come to grips with the real Africa, for using the resources of CinemaScope and Technicolor to make a glorified travelogue.

In fact Mackendrick skirts the dangers inherent in his subject matter – a ten-year-old hero, exotic wildlife, picturesque scenery – with great perspicacity. His cameraman, Erwin Hillier, is seduced by flamboyant sunsets on the White Nile but they are not inconsistent with the strange colour effects he creates in his studio desert. Sammy's odyssey does not have the grand sweep of *Lawrence of Arabia*, but it is heroic in a sense that Lawrence's is not. Sammy makes his journey because he sees no alternative, and the world he passes through is harsh and dangerous – his parents are buried under the rubble of his home, the Syrian trader who protects him is blinded by a red-hot stone, the sanctuary he finds with Edward G. Robinson is razed to the ground by the police – but not actively malevolent, and the Africans display a kindly indifference to Sammy's fate. One can be heroic, as Sammy is when he shoots the leopard, simply by being steadfast and sincere. In the grown-up world where Lawrence fights his battles, being a hero involves decisions costing thousands of lives and has a dehumanising effect on the hero.

A High Wind in Jamaica (1965) was financed by 20th Century-Fox and Mackendrick seems to have had a battle to keep control of the project: according to Philip Kemp, half an hour was cut from the director's version before the film was released. It is remarkable, then, how close Mackendrick gets to the essence of Richard Hughes's novel. Hughes wrote the novel in 1929, and Mackendrick had tried to persuade Balcon to let him make it at Ealing, but Fox had acquired the rights and refused to relinquish them. The story concerns a band of children who, making the long voyage home from Jamaica to England, are inadvertently kidnapped by pirates. Unexpectedly, the pirates act in an honourable and unbloodthirsty way, but when they are captured, evidence given by the children leads to them being hanged.

Hughes's novel is not at all Disney-like, its heroine, Emily, being the exact opposite of the lovable moppets played by Shirley Temple or Hayley Mills and her relationship with the shambling, unhappy pirate captain disturbingly convoluted. The film is inevitably softer. Having refused to sentimentalise the children, Mackendrick accepted the need to attract stars to play the only two important adult roles – the pirate captain and his mate – and Anthony Quinn and James Coburn are jovially good-natured in contrast to the world-weary pirates of the book, gloomily aware they are an unprofitable anachronism in the fast approaching age of steam ships. However, Mackendrick is a director who accepts the need for compromise and works hard to make good his losses. Quinn's Captain Chavez jabbers away to his crew in Spanish (which his German original was unable to) and, if he is more like a kindly uncle than the ambivalent father-figure of the book, he makes the story more human, more optimistic, more down-to-earth. Emily's betrayal in the book implies a sexual rejection which is so ambiguously dealt with that one is left to draw the conclusion that either there is something deeply treacherous in the female psyche or Emily herself is a little minx. In the film both parties are blameless: Chavez is less deeply disturbed by the children than his crew are, and Emily's betrayal is accidental.

In compensation for the loss of Emily's obscure internal mental processes, Mackendrick amplifies the other marvellous achievement of the book: the sense of two worlds colliding as the children invade the austere male preserve of the pirate ship. The affinity the children have for Caribbean superstition, which had shocked their mother into sending them away in the first place, horrifies the pirates, who are more prone than they are to irrational fears. This culminates in a sequence where the boys accidentally twist round the ship's figurehead while the girls carry out a mock religious ceremony, with little Laura throwing her long hair over her face to impersonate a duppy, a Jamaican ghost which wears its head back to front.[39]

During the long years when Mackendrick was frustrated in his desire to make *A High Wind in Jamaica* he twice attempted to 'steal' the idea of the book in scripts dealing with English children disrupting the lives of violent but likeable primitives – during the Salvatore Giuliano bandit uprising in Sicily and during the Zapata revolution in Mexico. Neither project came to fruition, but one can see *Sammy Going South* as virtually a trial run for *A High Wind in Jamaica*. Both films begin with a catastrophe – the British air-raid on Port Said which kills Sammy's parents, the 'high wind' which destroys the children's home – that disrupts what had been a happy colonial existence. Both films have ten-year-old protagonists who form a close relationship with an ageing rogue – Emily with Chavez, Sammy with Edward G. Robinson's Cocky Wainwright. In both films, seemingly vulnerable and innocent children exploit the sentimental attitudes of the adults they encounter and cause their downfall. But *Sammy Going South* is essentially a film about the passage from boyhood to manhood. The more perceptive adults make sacrifices which help Sammy in the transition from his child's world to the world of adults. Orlando Martin's grizzled Moslem elder forgoes the gratitude due him for protecting the boy; Zena Walker, his legitimate guardian, her right to control him; Edward G. Robinson, the illegitimate wealth he has built up as a game poacher.[40] In *A High Wind in Jamaica* there is only disastrous misper-

Children's fantasies, real pirates. Anthony Quinn, *A High Wind in Jamaica*

ception between children and adults. The parents fail utterly to understand the deeds, desires and feelings of their children, banishing them
from the idyllic island because they think they need the civilising
influence of an English boarding school and misinterpreting their experiences with the pirates to suit their own prejudices. The pirates are
more uneasily aware of the gulf between their own perception of events
and that of the little guests they unwillingly entertain, but they too are
unable to penetrate and comprehend the children's world and are sent
to their death on the misleading evidence of the children who have
come to love and admire them.

The idea of innocence that destroys, innocence as savagery – which
was dealt with more pedantically in Peter Brook's *Lord of the Flies* –
puts *Sammy Going South* and *A High Wind in Jamaica* in a different

95

category to other British films which deal with children, such as Jack Lee Thompson's *Tiger Bay* or Bryan Forbes's *Whistle Down the Wind*. Both these films are excellent in their way, but they are held back by an attitude to children which is fundamentally sentimental. The only contemporary film which shares Mackendrick's respect for children as complex human beings is Clayton's *Our Mother's House* (1967); but, interesting though the film is, its cold neutrality seems to substitute suburban reticence for the conflict of rationality and superstition, magic and squalor, which permeates Mackendrick's films.

The exploration of a marvellous and mysterious universe had been the special characteristic of Michael Powell and Emeric Pressburger's films of the 1940s, particularly *A Matter of Life and Death*, *Black Narcissus* and *The Red Shoes*. But even Powell and Pressburger failed to maintain their impetus through the stagnant waters of the 50s. In 1960, by which time they had ceased to work in collaboration, Powell made *Peeping Tom*, in which man's darker instincts – held firmly in check in the earlier films – appeared outrageously dominant. The film disgusted the critics and severely damaged Powell's reputation, and his next film, *The Queen's Guards* (1961), a patriotic celebration of the British army, seemed almost an act of atonement. Unfortunately it pleased nobody: at a time when writers like Simon Raven and Andrew Sinclair were writing revealing inside stories of army stupidity and unpleasantness, Powell shows the Grenadier Guards as brave and honest.[41] The public, only just freed from the boredom of National Service, were not impressed, perhaps sharing the view of the haulage contractor whose daughter wants to marry the hero that the Guards are 'the most snobby outfit on the face of the earth'; and Powell's later admirers have found this paean of praise to the upper-class military caste difficult to assimilate.

Contemporary critics were evenly divided: the reviewers of the *Daily Worker*, the *Daily Herald*, the *Guardian*, the *Financial Times*, the *Observer*, the *Spectator*, *Tribune* and the *Monthly Film Bulletin* condemned the film unreservedly; Dilys Powell of the *Sunday Times* joined the potential officers and gentlemen of *The Times*, the *Daily Telegraph*, the *Sunday Telegraph*, the *Sunday Express* and the *Evening Standard* in finding considerable virtue in the film. The most perceptive criticism came from Quentin Crewe in the *Daily Mail*:

> The interesting thing is that one comes out of it pondering problems which most people haven't considered since 1945. Ostrich-like in a haze of Welfare State bonhomie, the majority today think of the aristocracy as humorous relics of an unreal past. But this film presents the aristocratic principle as something to be reckoned with. We are invited to look at the esoteric methods by which an elite corps is built up and then decide whether or not we admire it.[42]

Ironically, those values that in 1961 were thought by progressive critics to be so out of date as to make the film laughable seem to be by no means irrelevant now. It would be difficult to 'go slumming' in the heart of Docklands, and reverence for the Royal family has waned since its younger members became media figures, but one can quite imagine Powell's guardsmen serving in Northern Ireland or leading the attack at Goose Green.

Characters whom one ought to find obnoxious – John Fellowes (Daniel Massey) is a toffee-nosed prig with an egocentric military bore for a father and a battily refined mother, and his friend Henry Wynne Walton (Robert Stephens) is a debonair cad – become almost endearing. It is not that Powell sentimentalises: even when John pays homage at his brother's grave, the elaborately carved headstone among the forest of wooden crosses acts as a reminder that he lies surrounded by soldiers who died less memorable but more honourable deaths. But he allows his characters to expose their weaknesses, to make themselves human. Henry enjoys old Fellowes' ramblings but he also takes a sly pleasure in John's obvious boredom and embarrassment; the old man sadly acknowledges that he has drunk too much and talked too much; John is ridiculously angry when the beautiful girl (Elizabeth Shepherd) he doesn't really love slips from him to Henry. The script is shakily constructed, but it serves Powell well enough and three things in particular stand out.

The British cinema of the 60s sees more than its fair share of tourist's London, and one might expect a film which sets its action around the Trooping of the Colour ceremony to be unbearably mawkish. In fact Powell – partly because of the skill with which he integrates newsreel footage of the Queen and the actual ceremony, partly because of his obvious affection and respect for his subject – succeeds in revitalising the pageantry, making it meaningful and moving. John's home life, despite being haunted by the mysterious death of an elder brother who more properly belongs to a nineteenth-century melodrama, captures the rigidity and pathos of the stiff upper lip tradition. His father (Raymond Massey), a cripple who swings through the exclusive but cluttered flat on what he calls his trolley bus system, and his long-suffering dignified mother, insistent that her eldest son is still alive, have a sad, faded dignity which makes them sympathetic. Powell gives his guards officers an enviably attractive life, and unlike most 60s heroes they are untroubled by doubts about the value of what they are doing. But he is too wry and intelligent to be swept into simple jingoism. The raid which John and Henry lead against the Middle Eastern rebels serves its purpose in proving that they are more than tin soldiers, but as John has damaged his back and Henry's armoured cars are late, it is left to a working-class Colour Sergeant to lead the successful charge, and the prisoner they had hoped to rescue has been shot.

'Operation successful, patient died, what?', barks the commanding officer philosophically.

Powell never made another feature film in Britain (though he did occasional television work, produced David Greene's *Sebastian* and directed *The Boy Who Turned Yellow* for the Children's Film Foundation). His last two films were made in Australia, which in the 1960s had only a rudimentary film industry. *The Queen's Guards* shares the upper-class point of view of Powell's quota quickies (and misses the mid-European sophistication which Emeric Pressburger contributes to *The Life and Death of Colonel Blimp*). *They're a Weird Mob* (1966) returns to the community values of Powell and Pressburger's 1940s films, particularly *A Canterbury Tale* and *I Know Where I'm Going*, though its setting is the ugly suburban sprawl of Sydney rather than the British countryside.

It is a gauche, untidy film, dismissed by the *Monthly Film Bulletin* as 'a routine women's magazine romance' and by the *Guardian* as a 'pretty gross farce'. But the more open-minded critic of *The Times* found it 'strangely compelling even at its most awful', and though it is the least likely of Powell's films to be regarded as Art, it has a freshness of vision, an ability to challenge and change assumptions denied more pretentious and prestigious works.[43] Powell's exploration of male values is handled with wit and accuracy and little of the romanticism that seeps into the films of John Ford, Howard Hawks or Raoul Walsh. A raucous song, 'It's a Man's Country', dominates the soundtrack but Powell's men are a peculiar mixture of toughness and laziness, ambition and inadequacy. Nino (Walter Chiari), the hero, is continually humiliated and insulted when he fails to understand the conventions of Australian society, but he responds with dignity and is rewarded with friendship and material well-being. The process is one of shedding pretensions and formalities, not one of initiation into a group. Powell's enthusiasm for manly activities, which made him sympathetic to the upper-crust soldiers of *The Queen's Guards*, makes him just as interested in the trench-digging, brick-stacking, concrete-laying activities of his Sydney labourers. And as with his soldiers, there is a quirky tolerance of imperfection rather than a celebration of a masculine ethos.

Not all Australians were enamoured of Powell's view of their country. Sylvia Lawson in the *Nation* commented:

So far as dialogue, story, and the whole slapdash approach to character and society are concerned, it's the sort of film that could only have been allowed to happen in a country without an industry. If, during the past ten years or so, we had been experiencing the scrutiny of our own film makers, it's unlikely that at this point we would be embracing a work that shows an immigrant labourer – exjourno though he is – buying *that* block of land after about three months' residence: it looks like twenty thousand dollars' worth. Nor one that finished with an all-mates-together beer party – and then (zoom out) that aerial shot of the Harbour that belongs nowhere but in a cigarette ad., and clearly implies that all this beer, matiness and marrying the boss's daughter, is what's generally going on inside the place.[44]

But as with the Pinewood Himalayas of *Black Narcissus*, Powell is concerned less with land values than with spiritual redemption.

By 1968, when *Age of Consent* was released, Raymond Durgnat had already begun the process by which Michael Powell was recognised as Britain's foremost director.[45] But to the industry and the critical establishment he had become a half-forgotten figure, and the fact that he was making films in Australia seemed a legitimate excuse to treat him with amused condescension. The story – about a middle-aged artist (James Mason) who finds a half-wild teenage girl on the island he has retreated to and falls in love with her – has an obvious resemblance to *Lolita*, but in contrast to the massive coverage granted that film, *Age of Consent* attracted a minimum of critical comment. *Sight and Sound* did not bother to review the film, but Penelope Houston contributed a ninety-word review to the *Spectator*, summing up with blithe condescension: 'Nature girl (Helen Mirren) keeps taking her clothes off. Mr Mason intelligently rambles, and a sagacious dog named Lonsdale is worth his weight in bones.'[46] Viewing them now, there is little question which is the superior film. *Lolita*, Kubrick's first British film, is over-long and uncertainly poised between comedy and tragedy. The disturbing sexual obsession with permeates Nabokov's novel is mostly absent, James Mason acting throughout like a possessive, over-indulgent father to Lolita. The supposed awfulness of mid-American middle-class society, so sensitively explored by Douglas Sirk in *There's Always Tomorrow* and *All That Heaven Allows*, here, in the environs of Borehamwood, seems utterly unauthentic, and it falls to Peter Sellers with his party-piece impersonations to provide the film with high points.

Age of Consent initially appears to be less ambitious. Mason's Brad Morahan is an artist, representative only of himself. And after a quick jump from New York to Queensland, society is confined to a tiny offshore island populated by two women and a girl. But this is enough for Brad to recover his inspiration and for Powell to create – with the startling photography of Hannes Staudinger – a magic universe. In contrast to the smutty cynicism of Humbert Humbert's relationship with Lolita, that between Brad and Cora is one of liking and respect. Cora is as self-seeking, as manipulative and materialistic as Lolita, but whereas Lolita is a parasite, Cora is a worker, eager to support herself

The exploration of a marvellous and mysterious universe. James Mason, Helen Mirren in *Age of Consent*

and physically strong enough to defend herself (as she proves to the handsome young ferryman who tries to force his attentions on her). Powell later expressed his dissatisfaction with the quality of the paintings Brad produces, but in the film this doesn't seem important. It is not the individual pictures which matter but the general ambience. The paintings and sculptures Brad fills his shack with seem to reflect both his personality and the beauty of Cora and the island. The film is by no means an exquisitely harmonious work of art. The semi-slapstick scenes between Jack MacGowran and Antonia Katsaros seem clumsily over-boisterous; but as disruptions of Brad and Cora's idyll this is appropriate enough, and the final vision is as impressive as that of the best Powell and Pressburger films of the 1940s.[47]

Despite Paul Mayersberg and Ian Cameron's championing of Alexander Mackendrick, *Movie* was never able to muster much enthusiasm for the exploration of British cinema, and from the opposite camp Alan Lovell dismissed the idea that Britain was ever capable of an art cinema beyond the British Documentary Movement, concluding that: 'Stranded between two kinds of cinema [Hollywood's unabashed commercialism and Europe's artistic seriousness], the British entertainment cinema has never established a character of its own. It has been a cinema founded on unconscious compromises that have repressed it and prevented it from developing.'[48] Possibly only Powell and Mackendrick transcend the barrier between art and entertainment, Hollywood and Europe, and it is easy to argue that Britain's art cinema is weaker than that of France and Italy and its commercial films lack the breadth and vitality of Hollywood. But from this artistically broken-backed industry emerge groups of films which for all their imperfections, their dearly bought concessions either to art or to commerce, constitute a cinema which is a significant and valuable part of the culture they spring from.

5

WHEN DINOSAURS RULED THE EARTH

As the neon died and the glittering chandeliers in the foyer gathered dust, the 'Super Cinema', domed and gilded or chromiumed and tiled, lush carpeted and enveloped in the scented ooze of the Mighty Wurlitzer, joined its predecessor, the Gin Palace, in the vast and curious lumber room of Britain's social history. The Common Man had no longer an acute need of one-and-ninepenceworth of vicarious luxury. With the aid of his new house, his car, the H.P., his wife's magazines, and his do-it-yourself kit, he could build an only slightly less colourful – and much more satisfying – world for himself at home. (Harry Hopkins, *The New Look*, 1963)[1]

The Decline of the Cinema

The cinema industry grew at a tremendous rate in the inter-war years: the huge, elaborate, luxurious picture palaces built in the 1920s and 30s offered a refuge from overcrowded, underheated homes and the films themselves a brief respite from grim reality. High unemployment made it easy to recruit the army of low-paid cleaners, usherettes, doormen and projectionists needed to maintain and run these 'dream palaces'. But in the 1950s, with rising wages and full employment, it was difficult to preserve the old regime. The *Kinematograph Weekly*'s 'Company of Showmen' soldiered on, sending their ageing doormen to parade the streets in bizarre costumes, arranging elaborate foyer displays and tie-ins with local shopkeepers, but the old enthusiasm had gone. Cinema admissions reached a peak of 1,635 million in 1946 and the next ten years saw a gradual decline. By 1956 the figure was down to 1,101 millions and over 500 cinemas had closed their doors. In the next five years, as television changed from a middle-class luxury to a working-class necessity, the decline became precipitous. Between 1957 and 1963 the number of cinemas halved and admissions fell from 915 to 357 millions.[2] The government reluctantly acknowledged that cinema exhibition was in a state of crisis, and after 1957 began to reduce the heavy Entertainments Tax levied on cinema seats. In 1960 it was abolished altogether, but as audiences continued to drift away, cinema owners had to raise rather than lower prices to keep their heads above water.

Attempts to stem the decline by introducing elements which the small screen lacked – colour, widescreen, 3D – were initiated in America but inevitably affected the British film industry. By the end of 1955 more than half the cinemas in Britain (with nearly three-quarters of the seating capacity) had adapted to showing widescreen films. In most cases, however, this was merely a matter of fitting projectors with anamorphic lenses and changing the shape of the screen (if it wasn't practical to widen it the top and bottom could always be masked off). The more elaborate changes needed to show films with stereophonic soundtracks were resisted by Rank as well as the smaller exhibitors, and 20th Century-Fox, which insisted on restricting its CinemaScope films to cinemas with stereo facilities, had to organise its own circuit from the well-run and up-market cinemas of the Essoldo and Granada chains. In the long run, however, Fox acknowledged the futility of forcing change on over-cautious British exhibitors and patched up its quarrel with Rank.[3]

The indigenous British response to change was typically negative. In 1957 ABC Television's acquisition of twenty-five Alexander Korda films and the BBC's of one hundred RKO films threatened to boost the number of films shown on television – already considered dangerously high at around five a week – and the industry took concerted action. In February 1958 it was announced that a Film Industry Defence Organisation (FIDO) had been set up and that 'if any producer or distributor enters into a contract after today's date to allow any cinema feature film, either British or imported, to be shown on TV in the United Kingdom, exhibitors will not book any films from that producer or distributor.'[4] The exhibitors had agreed (reluctantly) that a farthing levy be imposed on all cinema tickets sold in order to provide a fund to buy up the television rights of British films. But the problem of when films could be safely yielded up to television – after all, some of the Korda films were over twenty years old – was never solved. There were additional complications in that interconnections between the film and television industries were becoming increasingly common. Rank was involved in Southern Television, ABPC in Rediffusion, the Woolf brothers in Anglia, the Bernsteins – who owned the Granada cinema chain – in Granada Television. By 1960 FIDO was beginning to look like a watchdog with no bite and very little bark, and the industry settled for an agreement that no film of box-office significance be shown on television until five years after its cinema release.

The first victims of the decline in audiences had been the smallest, oldest cinemas which pursued a precarious existence showing films which had seen better days in more prestigious cinemas. But by the mid-50s the big circuits were afflicted too. In 1956 the Rank Organisation, which controlled Odeon and Gaumont, closed forty-nine of its cinemas.[5] In October 1958 John Davis, the Rank Chairman, announced that due to the shortage of films the two circuits, which hitherto had exercised considerable autonomy, would be merged.[6] For the Rank Organisation this was a logical solution to its problems: the merged circuit (most of the Odeons, with around eighty of the best of the Gaumont cinemas) could rely on its monopoly position to remain profitable, and the surplus cinemas – many of them decaying properties in prime town centre sites – could be sold off just as a property boom was getting under way. But the shift from a three-circuit to a two-circuit system did not just affect the cinemas owned by Rank.

Despite its fierce entrepreneurial spirit, cinema exhibition in Britain was a mass of rules and regulations, most of them derived from the principle of 'exclusivity' which underpinned the industry. Since the early years of the century when the public began to show preferences for particular films and particular film characters, it became important for cinemas to exclude their rivals from showing the same film. Once the practice of hiring films rather than buying them outright became the norm, distributors saw advantages for themselves in allowing the larger and more prestigious cinemas a temporary local monopoly in the first showing of their films before passing them on to the smaller, less profitable cinemas.

In *The Decline of the Cinema*, economist John Spraos describes how 'The typical cycle of a film is to start in the largest cinemas, have a second run, after an interval, in the next largest, then return for a third run in the next size and so on down to the smallest cinemas.'[7] The system of 'barring', whereby one cinema was able to prevent other cinemas in its vicinity from showing the same film, was complicated into an elaborate hierarchy by the development of the circuit system. The three large circuits – ABC, Gaumont and Odeon – which came to dominate the industry in the 1930s, had strong links with the distributors so that, for example, all 20th Century-Fox films went out on the Gaumont circuit and all Warner Brothers films on the ABC circuit. Large though the circuits were, they were underrepresented in some areas of the country, and to offer the distributor a better deal, cinemas owned by independents and smaller circuits were incorporated into the release pattern. Circuit cinemas tended to be larger and more modern than those owned by the independents, but where a non-circuit cinema was noticeably superior to the local Odeon, Gaumont or ABC it was sometimes included in the first release at the expense of the circuit cinemas.

104

The merger of the Odeon and Gaumont releases meant that independent cinemas which had participated in the Gaumont or Odeon releases tended to be squeezed out. Davis tried to appease his critics by announcing that the rump of the old Gaumont circuit would be allowed to combine with other cinemas to form a National circuit, but this was never a very healthy concern.[8] By 1961 exhibitors were complaining that they were being saddled with the rejects of the more powerful circuits, and a report by the Cinematograph Films Council revealed that the average return for a film released on the National circuit was only £35–40,000 compared to £80,000 for films shown in ABC cinemas and £90,000 for those which reached the Odeons.[9] The shortage of product which had been the main reason for merging the two circuits meant that the National circuit was starved of films, distributors preferring to queue up to get their films into the ABCs and Odeons rather than accept the miserable rewards a National circuit release could offer. By 1963 it had virtually disintegrated, and the growing disenchantment of the smaller circuits and independents manifested itself in an increasing tendency to break away from the standard release pattern and programme their cinemas with popular classics, foreign sex and art films, and the 'X' films which the circuits were reluctant to show.[10]

In 1964, Ian Cameron complained of the inadequate response made by cinema owners to dramatically changed conditions:

> It is an industry of old men and nowhere is its age more apparent than among exhibitors. Most of them are old men running old cinemas, which could often have been modernised in the palmy days when business showed a healthy profit. But then there was no need to do more than running repairs and the occasional paint job. Four-fifths of the country's cinemas fell in with the automatic booking pattern of the circuits, and running a cinema was a pleasant way of making a living. It was no training at all for the rigours of running a cinema in the sixties.[11]

But it was as much a matter of mistaken initiatives as apathetic inertia. Keith Robertson points out that John Davis's managerial revolution in the Rank Organisation profoundly affected how its cinemas were run. Increased centralisation meant 'dividing the country into regions, imposing booking patterns, in other words taking away power altogether from the local chap'.[12] Greater opportunity for promotion with the company's hierarchy hardly compensated for the loss of local control and tended to mean that talented and enterprising cinema managers quickly moved on to more lucrative fields. And because of the barring system, attempts to exploit the market by giving extended runs to popular films in the first-run cinemas meant that smaller exhibitors were not only denied the chance of profiting from their popularity, but forced to wait even longer than usual for the other films that their more prestigious rivals had the right to show first. As one exasperated Yorkshire showman complained in 1961: 'At the time of writing, *Ben Hur* and *The Guns of Navarone* have played concurrently for four weeks at two of Bradford's three first run cinemas, and by doing so they have stopped the flow of eight films to all the cinemas normally barred by them, covering an area of 50 square miles.'[13]

The reduction of the release pattern from three streams to two also affected the power balance between the circuits and the producers and distributors. In explaining his reasons for the merger, Davis had pointed out that 'The falling supply of product has put the producer ... in the position that he could dictate to which theatre or group of theatres an important film should go', and that 'the distributor has been able to dictate his terms as to where his product would play, often with the threat that if we did not agree to his proposition he would take it to ABC.'[14] After 1959 it was the exhibitor – or rather the two big circuit bookers – who could dictate terms. Paramount broke its twenty-five year association with Rank rather than allow its Dean Martin/Shirley Maclaine comedy *All in a Night's Work* to be consigned to the indignity of a National release.[15] But the American companies, tied in with one or other of the major circuits and making a decreasing number of films, were relatively secure. British producers, particularly those grouped around the independent distribution company British Lion, were more vulnerable and found that their films were being squeezed out in favour of films backed by Rank or ABC's own production interests.

For an independent British film producer a delayed or inadequate release (on the remnants of the National circuit, for example) could spell disaster, and there was a vociferous outcry against the unfair tactics of Rank and ABC's bookers. In October 1963 David Kingsley, the managing director of British Lion, complained that a number of British films were stuck in the pipeline because Rank and ABC were giving preference to films they had a financial interest in. The circuits countered by claiming that these 'martyred' films were being passed over because they were dull and old-fashioned and the public didn't want to see them. The charge had a very slight foundation in truth, but it obscured the fact that the films included Sidney J. Furie's excellent, topical *The Leather Boys* (which proved commercially very successful when it was released), Peter Brook's *Lord of the Flies*, Clive Donner's *The Caretaker*, and at least two sharp comedies, C. M. Pennington-Richards's *Ladies Who Do* and Roy Baker's *Two Left Feet*.[16]

Complaints about Rank and ABC's domination of the industry led Edward Heath, then President of the Board of Trade, to refer the 'Supply of Films to the British Cinema' to the Monopolies Commis-

106

sion. Their report, finally delivered in October 1966, proved to be a clear and incisive indictment of the monopoly influence exerted by the two big corporations. The Commission decided there were two alternatives: to institute radical change, which to be effective would involve dismantling the Rank and ABC circuits; or to ask the duopoly to restrain their excesses and put their own house in order. In view of the delicate state of the cinema exhibition industry and a reluctance to involve the government too messily in its affairs, the Commission recommended the latter course.[17] Rank and ABC continued to prove themselves poor stewards of the nation's cinemas. Their modernisation programmes were always too little and too late – twinning and tripling of cinemas did not get properly under way until the 1970s – and the spiral of decline continued through the next two decades. In 1970 admissions were down to 193 millions and the number of cinemas had been reduced to 1,492; by 1980, the figure was 96 millions and there were only 942 cinemas. Because of the sub-division of cinemas there were still 1,562 screens in 1980, but the days when cinema was the overwhelmingly dominant form of public entertainment were over.[18]

The Producers

Britain had no real equivalent to the Hollywood system whereby a single company owned studios and handled the distribution and exhibition of the films made there. Rank and ABPC were vertically integrated companies, but only for short periods did they attempt ambitious production programmes.[19] The most important films of the 30s had been made by the independent producer Alexander Korda, the most important films of the 40s by independent production companies like Powell and Pressburger's The Archers and Filippo del Giudice's Two Cities, using Rank's money but subject only to the most distant control. Rank had attempted to mould these companies into a close and cohesive group in the late 40s, but it was only after disastrous losses, severe haemorrhages of talent and the closure of several studios that production was concentrated at Pinewood, and there the studio ethos left much to be desired. Frederic Raphael, who began his career at Pinewood as a scriptwriter, looked back with almost pathological loathing:

> Who will ever forget those days at Iver when, cloistered in the fumed oak dining-room (reminiscent of a golf club where no one ever paid his subscription), frightened producers blenched at the mere idea of any film which contained the smallest tincture of reality? 'Nothing genuine added' had to be the label on every confection. As at Byzantium, there was no choice between *proskynesis* and summary execution: the strongest went to the wall; the servile lived to wilt again another day. Feasting their limp guests on rigid

107

gammon and clotted potatoes, the cowed courtiers proposed unspeakable projects and dreamed less of fame or wealth (though both were pious hopes) than of a named slot in the car park.[20]

In the 50s around fifteen films a year were made by Rank contract directors and producers at Pinewood, but most of them were unexcitingly formulaic and the backbone of the production programme was provided by vehicles for Norman Wisdom. By the end of the decade Rank and ABPC were both relying increasingly on independent producers. Writing in 1966, Terence Kelly proclaimed:

> Gone are the days when Mr Rank had his stables of stars, starlets and directors to fill the Odeon and Gaumont screens. Today the group concentrates an annual investment of around £5 million into a small number of pictures. A handful of these come from British film-makers or stars, some of them people long associated with Rank. The big investments – apart from the new scheme with the NFFC – have involved backing the independent producer of international epics by guaranteeing him a minimum return on distribution in specified countries. Thus it supported Samuel Bronston's *El Cid*, *55 Days at Peking*, *The Fall of the Roman Empire* and *The Magnificent Showman*.[21]

By the end of the decade even these stabs at big-budget production had ceased, and Rank's main contribution to film production was the *Carry On* series taken over from Anglo-Amalgamated in 1967.

Independent producers divided into small but not unprestigious concerns like the Woolf brothers' Romulus, Carl Foreman's Open Road, and Irving Allen and Cubby Broccoli's Warwick, which generally made their films in collaboration with the big American distributors; and the companies which had established themselves by making 'B' films, the most important of which were Hammer and Anglo-Amalgamated.[22] Hammer was set up in the immediate post-war period (though its roots go back to the 1930s), and it pursued a precarious existence making very low-budget adaptations of radio series like *Dick Barton – Special Agent* and *PC 49*. In the 50s the company thrived in a small way, doing a deal with American producer Robert Lippert whereby they would import minor Hollywood stars for their films and thus make them acceptable for distribution – if only as 'B' movies – in the American market. Modest ambitions and tiny budgets ensured that no masterpieces were turned out, but Hammer had the advantage of having two talented directors working for them – Terence Fisher and Val Guest – and from the mid-50s onwards, as Guest's Quatermass films were followed by Fisher's Frankenstein and Dracula, Hammer began to enjoy an unprecedented international success.

Anglo-Amalgamated, founded in the early 1950s by two Jewish businessmen, Stuart Levy and Nat Cohen, took over the tiny Merton Park studios in Wimbledon which Sydney Box had used as a head-quarters for documentary film-making in the war years. Like Hammer, they relied on a staple diet of low-budget crime films and comedies, but whereas Hammer moved into science-fiction and subsequently into horror, Anglo made the field of crime its own with its long-running *Scotland Yard*, *Scales of Justice* and Edgar Wallace series – drab, low-key little films which, better than any documentary, chart the progress from austerity to tacky affluence. Anglo was also sufficiently astute to back the first British teenage film, *The Tommy Steele Story*, and its successors, and to initiate the *Carry On* cycle. As the market for second features shrank, Anglo turned its attention to more ambitious projects, backing Michael Powell's *Peeping Tom*, bringing over Roger Corman to make *The Masque of the Red Death* and *The Tomb of Ligeia*, and teaming up with Joseph Janni and John Schlesinger for *A Kind of Loving*, *Billy Liar!*, *Darling* and *Far from the Madding Crowd*. In 1969 the company was swallowed up by ABPC/EMI, but Cohen continued to exercise considerable influence over the British film industry.[23]

Michael Balcon represented the culturally respectable end of British cinema, and his Bryanston Corporation, set up in April 1959, was responsible for a very different range of films from those offered by Hammer and Anglo-Amalgamated. Balcon's record at Ealing had been an impressive one, but by the mid-50s the studio's success rate was declining and Rank, which had provided a generous distribution deal since 1945, withdrew its support. In fairness to Ealing's shareholders, who had seen little in the way of profits for several years, Balcon agreed to the sale of the studio to the BBC, and after deals to preserve Ealing's identity with ABPC and MGM failed to work out satisfactorily, the company was wound up and Bryanston was set up as a consortium of independent producers. According to Balcon:

The strength of the idea lay in that as a co-operative of reputable film-makers we were able to facilitate the financing of productions more easily than if the members had been operating as individuals. The financial method was that known as a 'revolving credit' with the bank. This meant that if we put up, say, £200,000 for a production our credit was good for three times that amount, the bank recovering its money from the first proceeds of the film and the credit or loan continuing – or revolving – accordingly. When a subject was approved we gave the producers a guarantee of seventy per cent of the budget and the producers found the balance from private sources and/or the NFFC.[24]

The National Film Finance Corporation, set up by the government to make loans to film-makers in 1949, had proved remarkably successful. Apart from a £3 million loan made to British Lion which it had been saddled with from birth, the NFFC lost an average of £127,000 a year on the £40 million it invested in 438 feature films during its first ten years. During the same period the industry paid back to the government approximately £300 million in Entertainments Tax.[25] Nevertheless, even a small subsidy was viewed with suspicion for an industry where high salaries and big profits were common. An NFFC report explained that:

> The paradox of the situation is that even a film which is a commercial failure and which never approaches profitability nevertheless provides substantial profits for a variety of people. The production costs include the remuneration of artists, producers, directors, technicians, authors and others which by ordinary standards are often extremely high. These payments are made whether the film is successful or not and the loss not infrequently falls on the Corporation as the provider of the end money.[26]

'End money' was the final thirty per cent which would be paid – if the film was profitable – after the distributor had taken back his seventy per cent 'front money'. In the 50s, with a large, if declining, domestic market, most medium-budget films could be relied upon to make at least modest profits, but as cinemas continued to close, films had to look increasingly towards an international market in which the risks, if also the rewards, were much greater. It was a world which British Lion, the distribution company which handled the films of Bryanston and other independent producers, was ill-equipped to cope with.

British Lion
British Lion was a distribution company which also owned large studios at Shepperton. The company had originally been set up in 1930 with the object of making films from the novels of Edgar Wallace (who was on the board of directors and actively involved in the company). Caught out by the coming of the talkies, and the unexpected death of Wallace in 1932, the company was only saved by a distribution deal with Republic, whose Roy Rogers and Gene Autry Westerns proved to have a durable popularity singularly lacking in British 'B' films. In 1946 the company was taken over by Alexander Korda and completely transformed. Such was Korda's charisma and prestige that he was able to attract Britain's top film-makers – Carol Reed, David Lean, Michael Powell, Frank Launder and Sidney Gilliat, the Boulting brothers – and a large chunk of government money. Unfortunately, despite the success of films like *The Third Man* and *The Happiest Days of Your*

Life, British Lion's production programme failed to make a profit, and when Korda died in 1956 his debts to the government were still unpaid. David Kingsley, the former head of the NFFC, was appointed managing director in January 1958 and two teams of film-makers – John and Roy Boulting and Frank Launder and Sidney Gilliat – who had begun to supply British Lion with a steady stream of popular comedies, were made directors of the company. Their films – *Private's Progress, Brothers in Law, Lucky Jim, Blue Murder at St Trinians, Carlton-Browne of the FO, The Bridal Path, Left, Right and Centre, I'm All Right Jack, A French Mistress, Only Two Can Play* and *Heavens Above!* – provided British Lion with a solidly commercial backbone which helped it to carry out its appointed task as the distributor of independently produced (and thus more risky) films with no guaranteed place on the big circuits.

At the end of 1963 the government decided that British Lion was now healthy enough to return to the private sector. The affair was badly mishandled, however, and provoked the opposition of the existing board of directors, who resented not being given sufficient time to organise a management buy-out, as well as widespread anxiety among independent producers who were already worried by the log-jam of films waiting to get on to one or other of the big circuits. In the event it was Michael Balcon who gained control of the newly independent British Lion, leading an uneasy coalition of the old management team, the vanguard of the New Wave (Tony Richardson, John Osborne, John Schlesinger and Joseph Janni), Brian Epstein, and the American art cinema distributor Walter Reade, to victory over a rival consortium led by Sydney Box and Ted Willis.[27]

Balcon hoped that he might succeed in making British Lion the focus of the most creative elements in the industry, as it had been for a brief period in the late 40s, but the Boultings and Launder and Gilliat preferred a more cautious approach. The seven films made between January 1964 when Balcon assumed control and October 1967 when he resigned make up a commercially sensible film programme, using Hayley Mills in two films – *The Family Way* and *Twisted Nerve* – which broke with her Pollyanna image but made the most of her resilient innocence, and balancing risky experiments like *Morgan* and the unfortunate *Girl on a Motorcycle* with safe comedies like *Joey Boy, The Great St Trinian's Train Robbery* and *Till Death Us Do Part*. Balcon had expected rather more, and no doubt found it galling to watch American companies like United Artists and Paramount make more adventurous use of British talent. But the independent producers who had flocked to British Lion in the early 60s had either disappeared – Bryanston itself was dormant after backing Michael Winner's *The System* in 1964 and was sold to Associated Rediffusion in January 1965 – or had turned to the Americans.[28] While British Lion, with only limited financial resources, was forced to stick to the traditional practice of offering a guarantee for 70 per cent of a film's budget, leaving the producer with the difficult task of raising the other 30 per cent 'end money', the American distributors were prepared to put up 100 per cent of the money.

The Americans are Coming

American investment in British films had, throughout the 50s and early 60s, been in films like *The African Queen*, *Cockleshell Heroes* and *Mogambo*, which owed more to Hollywood than to Britain. United Artists' decision to back three films – *Dr No*, *Tom Jones* and *A Hard Day's Night* – was to have a revolutionary effect on the British film industry. After a slow start Ian Fleming's James Bond novels had been phenomenally successful, and it seems remarkable now that the only attempt to film them had been a low-budget American television adaptation of *Casino Royale*. In 1962 'Cubby' Broccoli, co-founder with Irving Allen of Warwick Films, a vigorous independent production company, and Harry Saltzman, Osborne and Richardson's partner at Woodfall, decided separately and then together that Bond was worth a serious effort.

Broccoli and Saltzman wanted to make a series of Bond films, but this raised the problem of how to cast their James Bond. Distributors were unwilling to back them without an established star, but established stars were unwilling to commit themselves to more than one film. Fortunately an unprecedented number of talented young actors emerged in the early 60s. Albert Finney, Tom Courtenay, Alan Bates and Terence Stamp had established rather different images from that associated with James Bond by 1962, but Richard Harris, Peter O'Toole, Richard Johnson and Paul Scofield were not as yet major presences in films. The producers decided to take more of a gamble by casting Sean Connery, an actor whose film career had been restricted to playing second fiddle to leprechauns and musclemen in *Darby O'Gill and the Little People* and *Tarzan's Greatest Adventure* and to interesting but unprestigious crime films like *Hell Drivers* and *The Frightened City*. They decided that the Bond films, with their exotic settings and exciting action, would turn him into a star if he was right for the part. It was a half-truth that led them to underestimate just how valuable an asset Connery was with his cool classlessness and his slight Scottish burr. But as a gamble it paid off spectacularly.[29]

Fleming was surprisingly popular with some of the 50s Angry Young Men: Philip Larkin and Kingsley Amis defended his work and John Braine shared his interest in status symbols and brand names.[30] The *machismo*, the snobbery, the ambition which the heroes of *Lucky Jim* or *Hurry on Down* or *Look Back in Anger* or *Room at the Top* struggle with are lazily embraced in the James Bond novels. Broccoli and Saltzman's films go further, adding a lush but only half-serious sensuality. Ironically, in the same way that the critic Paul Johnson had fulminated against the novels for their vulgarised dream of upper-middle class life, Amis condemned the films for simplifying and cheapening their fantasies and failing to respond to their genuine exoticism. This sort of pro-Fleming criticism of the Bond films and 'the Batman from Blades', as Larkin labels Connery, underestimates Broccoli and Saltzman's achievement. Skilfully they display the attractions of a material life richer and more adventurous than Joe Lampton could ever have dreamed of – cars that fly and swim and have customised flame-throwers, endless supplies of cool drinks, sleek women, strange and exciting locations. In the new Britain, classlessness was to mean that everybody had a share in upper-class luxury as well as in working-class jollity and gutsiness.

Tom Jones offered escapism of a different kind. Costume pictures in the 50s divided between the macabre gothic horror films associated with Hammer and swashbuckling adventure yarns – *Ivanhoe*, *Quentin Durward*, *Rob Roy*, *Kidnapped* – made for Disney and MGM. There was nothing remarkable about United Artists backing Woodfall's *Tom Jones* when Bryanston refused to put up enough money for it to be made in colour rather than black and white. But the resulting film was totally unlike the Hollywood/England swashbuckling epic. *Tom Jones*, adapted by John Osborne from Henry Fielding's eighteenth-century novel, drew on a film tradition of easy-going eroticism where characters take advantage of historical distance to display unrestrained sexual passion (*The Private Life of Henry VIII*, *Nell Gwyn*, *The Man in Grey*, *Caravan*, *The Wicked Lady*). Tom Jones (Albert Finney), despite his precarious position in life as a foundling disowned by the kindly squire who has brought him up, is untroubled by the *angst* and ambition afflicting modern heroes, and his healthy sexual appetite is more than matched by that of the women (Diane Cilento, Susannah York, Jennifer Jayne, Joan Greenwood) he comes into contact with. Osborne, Richardson, Lassally and Finney's joyful enthusiasm in their escape from the kitchen sink gave the film a vitality which swept it to popular success in America (where it grossed more than any 60s British film except *Goldfinger*, *Thunderball* and *To Sir, With Love*) as well as in Britain.

When United Artists producer Walter Shenson looked for a director who could handle a film about the Beatles, his eye fell on Richard Lester. An American who had made an early start as a television director, Lester had come to Britain in the mid-50s and struck up a friendship with two of the Goons, Spike Milligan and Peter Sellers, with whom he made a peculiarly surreal television comedy series, *A Show Called Fred*, for the BBC. In 1960 they teamed up again for *The Running Jumping and Standing Still Film*. It was little more than a home movie and only eleven minutes long, but on the strength of it Lester went on to direct *It's Trad Dad* for Amicus and *The Mouse on the Moon* for Shenson.

It's Trad Dad pitches two jazz-crazy teenagers against a grumpy world of adults, but Lester's exuberance was hampered by two very wooden principals, Helen Shapiro and Craig Douglas, and a script cobbled together by his producer Milton Subotsky. *A Hard Day's Night*, scripted by the young Liverpool playwright Alun Owen, is less frenetic but more insolent in its picture of the four good-natured Beatles trying to live out their lives in a world restricted by idiotic and outdated prohibitions: where you're not allowed to listen to your transistor radio on the train, where you can't run through the fields without being accused of trespassing, where you're being continually asked hostile, puerile questions. Lester presents this world with a detached, quizzical surrealism which matches the Beatles' stoical Liverpool humour and adds up to a tougher, more elegant version of the absurdism of the Goons. Decked out with the first fruits of Lennon and McCartney's song-writing talents, the film was a justifiable success and gave substance to the British claim to be in the vanguard of a new, dynamic, youthful culture.[31]

Adaptations of a series of bestselling spy thrillers, a bawdy costume drama, a youth-oriented film exploiting the international success of a British pop group – none of United Artists' ventures was particularly risky. But the impact of the Bond films, *Tom Jones* and *A Hard Day's Night* on the US market changed attitudes towards Britain, fostering a belief that London, rather than Paris or Rome or Hollywood, was the most exciting place in the world to make a film.

6

BRAVE NEW WORLD

The way I look at it is that the whole world's changing out here, and I'm moving with it because I like the way it's changing all the way. Oh, you don't see it in the papers, but you wait five, ten, fifteen years' time when you come back. You won't know this little old island. Perhaps I won't either. But I know I'm loving every minute of this changing, seeing a whole way of life come through, seeing a world change right in front of my eyes and knowing I'm part of it, caught right in the middle, helping to change it all and being changed by it all at the same time. (Ray Gosling, *Queen*, 1961)[1]

Sex and Affluence

Harold Macmillan's assertion that 'some of our people have never had it so good' had some foundation in fact. Wages rose by 72 per cent between 1951 and 1963 while prices rose by only 45 per cent.[2] Unemployment was minimal and the spread of consumer goods – televisions, refrigerators, washing machines, record players – seemed to indicate that poverty too would soon be a thing of the past. Christopher Booker describes the onset of the 'affluent society' in the late 50s:

The jingles and slogans of commercial television had saturated the consciousness of the nation, even coming to replace age-old nursery rhymes in children's games. Deep freeze had arrived and TV Instant Dinners and Fish Fingers and Fabulous Pink Camay. And with so many bright new packages on the shelves, so many new gadgets to be bought, so much new magic in the dreary air of industrial Britain, there was a feeling of modernity and adventure that would never be won so easily again. For never again would so many English families be buying their first car, installing their first refrigerator, taking their first continental holiday. Never again could such ubiquitous novelty be found as in that dawn of the age of affluence.[3]

But the economy was less healthy than it seemed. In 1958 Andrew Shonfield, the economics editor of the *Observer*, wrote a damning indictment of British economic policy, contrasting the low rate of growth of Britain's economy with that of its European counterparts and pointing out that high government expenditure on defence, coupled with inefficient management and an obstructive work-force, meant that Britain was liable to fall further and further behind.[4]

A pre-election boom helped Macmillan to lead the Tories to a third consecutive term of office, but by 1962 things were starting to go wrong.[5] Eric Lubbock overturned a Tory majority of 14,000 to win Orpington for the Liberals in March, and in July, after more by-election reverses, the Prime Minister sacked seven members of his Cabinet and replaced them with younger men. This proved a mixed blessing: Selwyn Lloyd, the ex-Chancellor of the Exchequer, was thought to have been unfairly sacrificed, and one of the new appointments, Henry Brooke, proved to be a peculiarly accident-prone Home Secretary.[6] In September, the Vassall spy case brought calls for Lord Carrington, the First Lord of the Admiralty, to resign; and in February the following year, rumours began to circulate about high-life orgies. They focused increasingly on the involvement of War Minister John Profumo with Christine Keeler, an aspiring model who was also associating with black racketeers and a Russian naval attaché. Christopher Booker recalled that: 'a boundless fantasy emerged, in which not only every member of the Government but the entire upper class of England seemed to have been caught up in an orgy of model girls, perversions and fancy dress sexual frolics.'[7] The unedifying picture of a decrepit, lecherous and devious Establishment was reinforced by the hounding to death of society osteopath Stephen Ward (who had introduced Keeler to Profumo) and the undignified scramble for the leadership of the Conservative Party when Macmillan resigned in October 1963.

Worries about society were not confined to the shenanigans of the rich and powerful. Richard Hoggart's regret at the erosion of working-class culture by the disciples of 'shiny barbarism' found wide support on the left, and Arnold Wesker's campaign to involve the Labour Party and the trade unions in helping to bring 'real' art to the masses was remarkably successful in its early stages.[8] The encroachments of 'mass culture' concerned Conservative intellectuals too. Irving Kristol, editor of *Encounter*, warned the CIA-funded Berlin Congress for Cultural Freedom in 1960:

... we are on the defensive against 'mass culture' which is what 'popular culture' has become. Whereas 'popular culture' was the culture of a class (the uneducated), 'mass culture' is a culture shared to a greater or lesser degree by everyone. We all watch the same TV shows, read the same advertisements, see the same movies. As a result of the increase in popular wealth, popular taste now has a coercive power such as civilisation has never before witnessed. By its sheer massive presence, 'mass culture' tends to crowd culture of any other kind to the margins of society.[9]

In the same vein, the Pilkington Committee on the future of broadcasting (which was dominated by Richard Hoggart) issued a report in 1962 which condemned commercial television for its debasing triviality and recommended that the BBC be given a second channel as a means of raising the cultural standards of the nation.[10]

The Angry Silence, Flame in the Streets, Sapphire, Victim and most of the other social problem films were too busy with their particular abuses to mount a detailed critique of society as a whole. But a group of films made between 1962 and 1965 – *Term of Trial, Live Now – Pay Later, The Comedy Man, Nothing But the Best, The Beauty Jungle, Darling* – does have some relevance here. *Term of Trial* is bleakly pessimistic about the new trends, while *Nothing But the Best* mockingly celebrates them, but all six films are centrally concerned with life in an 'affluent society'.[11]

Term of Trial, like *Serious Charge* (1959) and *Spare the Rod* (1961) earlier and *To Sir, With Love* (1966) and *Three into Two Won't Go* (1969) later, explores the pitfalls confronting middle-aged men when dealing with sexually precocious teenagers. The story, from a novel by James Barlow, is small-scale and pessimistic, in its obsession with drunkenness and petty humiliation more reminiscent of Patrick Hamilton than the droll humour of the Movement writers or the working-class realism of Alan Sillitoe and Stan Barstow. Graham Weir, a schoolmaster in a drab inner city Secondary Modern School, turns to drink to cope with his malicious, lazy pupils, his wretchedly discontented wife and his spiteful, narrow-minded colleagues. He becomes friendly with one of the few bright children in the school, a pretty fifteen-year-old, but rejects her when she tries to turn the friendship into a sexual affair. Taking a confused revenge, she accuses him of having molested her; but in the resulting trial, Graham, a pacifist who is constantly haunted by fear of his own cowardice, at last stands up for himself and the girl admits that she has lied.

The film, directed by Peter Glenville for Romulus, with its heavyweight acting from Laurence Olivier and Simone Signoret, puts greater emphasis on the ills of society than it does on Graham's inadequacies.[12] Thus his speech to the court is less a vindication of his innocence than a last stand against the 'shiny barbarism' of the new culture. 'Exquisite irony,' Graham tells his persecutors,

> that I should be condemned by a society that presumes itself more moral than I, a society endlessly titillating itself with dirty books and newspapers and advertising and television and the work of cynical and indifferent minds. I must be condemned by them for walking round with a child in a foreign city, I must be condemned for smacking her lightly to lessen her pain at the end of her pathetic infatuation. What I felt for her, was the love of an unworthy man for a quality – innocence, tenderness, love – the thing God gives us before the filth of the world begins to cover it up. But it was love, not the filth you mean. Sex was not in my mind for that child when she was in that hotel bedroom and it was never, never in my most secret intentions towards her.

Before going into the courtroom, Graham walks round town and is constantly assaulted by images of cultural decay: teenagers dance listlessly to a juke-box, guilty-looking youths peer at a newsagent's window full of sexy books and magazines, a black man and some scruffy student types hang around the doorway of a record shop, and the local cinema, next door to a gun shop, shows *The Ape's Revenge*. There is an element of prurient middle-class distaste for youth culture here, but Graham is no moral rearmament crusader. Raymond Durgnat argues that his refusal to sexually consummate the relationship

Images of cultural decay? *Term of Trial*

with Shirley 'betokens his confusion about teenagers. He can't understand that older schoolchildren are, biologically, adults.'[13] But Graham has a healthy sexual interest in his wife, and he acts in a kind and responsible way towards the infatuated girl. By contrast the schoolboys led by Terence Stamp are a sneering, leering, smuttily voyeuristic lot and the teachers are not much better.

There is certainly a generation clash: Graham is still in a *Brief Encounter* world of intense but restrained emotions; Shirley, anxious to explore her sexual potential, is ready for the 'Swinging Sixties'. But naive though he may be, Graham is perceptive enough to see that she is using him as an escape route to a fantasy life which has no connection with the drab reality he can offer. The ending is ironic, with Graham lying to his wife, pretending that he really did seduce the girl, realising she needs to believe this in order to think him enough of a man to be worth staying with. But this is a generous gesture rather than an admission of defeat. As with *Morgan*, there is a tacit understanding that it is society rather than Graham who is sick.

Live Now – Pay Later (1963, d. Jay Lewis) and *The Comedy Man* (1963, d. Alvin Rakoff) are much less prestigious productions, but they both have a good humour which makes them very likeable. *Live Now – Pay Later*, based on a television play by Jack Trevor Story, is a black comedy centred round a high-pressure salesman who, unlike Arthur Miller's semi-tragic figure, enjoys what he does and almost believes in it. The novel has the tart, humorously bitter quality which characterises the best of the Movement writings. But Story's perspective is more plebeian, unashamedly lower-middle class. In a key sequence, Albert the salesman is arrested for murder on the evidence of a pretentious middle-class woman who immediately arouses the hostility of the police ('There wasn't a man on the force in the town who had passed his eleven plus or its equivalent'), and in a show of class solidarity they ostentatiously take Albert's side and refuse to press charges.[14]

The film files down Story's rougher edges (the British censor ensured that Treasure – June Ritchie – has a baby, not an abortion, and vetoed references to 'sods', 'bumpsville', 'farting around' and Albert's fascination with all women 'from the age of consent to the age of collapse'), but it retains his ambivalent attitude towards the affluent society.[15] Durgnat points out that

> Against the hero's conspicuous consumption the film asserts a moral norm altogether different to that of *Term of Trial*. Family happiness is attained by a wife with five children, one of whom is another man's, and by her old-fashioned hubby who works as a railway porter but more than compensates for his small wage and tubby figure by solid, old-fashioned kindness.[16]

119

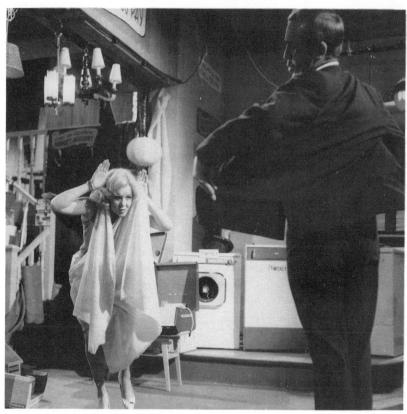

Albert (Ian Hendry) and Treasure (June Ritchie) 'farting around' among the rewards of affluence. *Live Now, Pay Later*

But, as in *Sparrows Can't Sing* (1963) and *Alfie* (1966), the kindly husband who represents the moral norm is less attractive than the immoral but charismatic hero. Albert, brilliantly played by Ian Hendry, and his empty-headed female customers are shown to be irrationally obsessed by material goods, but they are treated with a degree of affection. The film's more savage satire is reserved for the local golf club set – unscrupulous businessmen and corrupt local politicians – who are the traditional target of populist films as far back as Gainsborough's *Vote for Huggett* (1949) and Victor Saville's *South Riding* (1938).

Ian Hendry was very much part of the new generation of actors. He made his debut in *Room at the Top* and interspersed roles such as Morgan Delt in the television play *A Suitable Case for Treatment* and the confused, idealistic Doctor Lewellin in *Children of the Damned*, with others like Albert in *Live Now – Pay Later* and Don Mackenzie in *The Beauty Jungle*, where he utilises his sleazy charm to get his way with the world.

120

Kenneth More, Hendry's counterpart in *The Comedy Man*, had been the epitome of middle-class wholesomeness in 50s films, but in 1960 he fell out with Sir John Davis (over Rank's refusal to allow him to play in *Guns of Navarone*) and subsequently found it difficult to get good parts in British films.[17] When he left his wife for Angela Douglas (with whom he worked on Clive Donner's *Some People*), he found himself virtually ostracised by the film industry until his success in the BBC's adaptation of *The Forsyte Saga* made his undiminished talent and popularity impossible to ignore. Thus *The Comedy Man*, a low-budget film about the disappointments and compromises of life as an actor, was a peculiarly appropriate subject for him, and the autobiographical element is emphasised by the fact that Angela Douglas plays a star-struck but ambitious young actress.

More is 'Chick' Byrd, a fading middle-aged actor who is sacked from his job in a provincial repertory company for sleeping with the pro-ducer's wife, and comes to London to find that the opportunities just aren't there any more. In desperation he bends his principles, appears in a television commercial for 'Honeybreath' sweets, and finds himself a well-paid celebrity. Success brings him few emotional rewards, how-ever: his faithful ex-mistress (Billie Whitelaw) departs for the flinty integrity of Wolverhampton rep., his best friend (Edmond Purdom) returns from Hollywood a glossy sham, and his young lover (Angela Douglas) flirts unscrupulously with the agent (Dennis Price) who rep-resents everything that is corrupt and cynical about the theatrical world. Rakoff is not the most sensitive of directors, but he has the grace to stand off from easy moralising and there is an almost frighten-ing conviction about the acting – Cecil Parker as a derelict old gentle-man-player, Dennis Price as the ineffably supercilious theatrical agent with a baroque waistcoat and a waspish tongue, and above all More, trying to maintain dignity and honour when circumstances demand servility and dissemblance, allowing his seemingly unassailable opti-mism to crumble into anxiety and self-doubt.

Like *Live Now – Pay Later* (and *Darling*), *The Comedy Man* is an odd mixture of social criticism and satirical humour (More and Pur-dom ironing their shirts in their appallingly seedy bed-sit is almost a parody of the opening of *Look Back in Anger*), and like them its attitude to the affluent society is uncertain.[18] If Chick finally decides to be 'a first-rate failure rather than a second-rate success', turning his back on the spurious wealth and fame won by 'Mr Honeybreath' (while Ian Hendry in *Live Now – Pay Later* and *The Beauty Jungle* continues to pursue his empty dreams), he does so without bitterness. And his break with the young women who had seemed to offer an easy path through the affluent jungle is made without rancour, in marked contrast to Robert's sadistic rejection of Diana at the end of *Darling*.

121

Chick's conviction that honesty, integrity and consideration for others still matter is entirely absent from *Nothing But the Best*, directed by Clive Donner for Anglo-Amalgamated and released a month before *The Comedy Man* in October 1963. As with *Live Now – Pay Later*, its origins lay in a television play, *The Best of Everything* (1961), but partly because of Donner's style and his insistence on making the film in colour, partly because of Frederic Raphael's relentlessly topical script and the incorporation of Millicent Martin, William Rushton and Bernard Levin from the television satire show *That Was the Week That Was*, *Nothing But the Best* qualifies as the first of the 'Swinging London' films.[19] In essence it is a parody of *Room at the Top*, a savage, irreverent reworking for the boom-time society which had taken off since *Room at the Top* had been written: an echo of a time when 'A-type ladies in E-type Jags' were the goal of every bright young man.[20] Significantly its hero (Alan Bates) works for an estate agent, and as in *Billy Liar!* the film is set against a background of building sites and demolition. Jimmy Brewster climbs to the top without *angst* or guilt or tragic sacrifice; he doesn't sell his working-class soul, he steals one with a better pedigree. Donner (unlike John Schlesinger in *Darling*) does nothing to mitigate the sharp metallic nastiness of Raphael's script; and, helped by Nicolas Roeg's photography, the film captures a world where image is everything.

Nothing But the Best was not a great commercial success but it now appears one of the seminal films of the decade, its central contrast between Alan Bates's enterprising, unscrupulous lower-middle class clerk on the way to the top and Denholm Elliot's fey, upper-class degenerate serving almost as a metaphor for what was happening in political life as the Tory Party's popularity crumbled under the impact of the Profumo Affair and their new leader, the fourteenth Earl of Home, proved less than a match for Labour's cocky, image-conscious Harold Wilson.

Live Now – Pay Later and *The Comedy Man* were modest low-budget films, and *Nothing But the Best* and *Darling* risky productions made for a company generally content to make 'B' films. *The Beauty Jungle* (1964) was a big-budget CinemaScope film directly funded by Rank, though with Val Guest as director and Arthur Grant as lighting cameraman it was a much less bland production than those normally associated with Rank. Ian Hendry's Don Mackenzie, a bored but ambitious reporter on a provincial newspaper, sees an opportunity to break into the big time as the manager of a Bristol typist, Shirley Freeman, who shows a surprising facility for winning prizes at beauty contests. He succeeds, but to his chagrin finds that he is in love with her and she doesn't reciprocate his feelings; furthermore, she has learnt to be even more unscrupulous and ambitious than he is. Janette Scott, who plays Shirley, vies with Nanette Newman for the title of

Jackie White, Jacqueline Jones, Janette Scott, unsugary beauty queens. *The Beauty Jungle*

Nice Girl of early 60s British cinema; but whereas Newman's sugary surface conceals a sugary centre, Scott's conceals an iron determination which is exploited here to make her beauty queen an unexpectedly formidable heroine.

As in *Hell is a City*, *Jigsaw* and *80,000 Suspects*, Arthur Grant's location photography (of Bristol and the various tacky venues of the beauty contests) and Guest's quirky character actors (Norman Bird, Ronald Fraser and Peter Ashmore) combine to create a peculiarly evocative early 60s ambience against which Shirley's rise and fall is played out. As one expects with a Val Guest film, clichéd situations outgrow their predictable expectations. Don's moment of truth comes when he realises that Shirley isn't actually going to bar him from her bed, but that she is allowing him in out of pity and gratitude rather than love. And Shirley's high point of happiness – finding herself alone with the film star (Edmund Purdom) she idolised as a teenager – droops sadly when she realises he is impotent, or gay, or just totally uninterested in sex.

Shirley introduces herself as 'an ordinary, happy little typist', and the achievement of *The Beauty Jungle* is to show just how ruthless and ambitious and unscrupulous ordinary people can be, given the chance. Nevertheless, she is essentially an old-fashioned girl with a clearly focused sense of right and wrong, and at the end of the film one expects her to go back, wiser and a bit richer, to the sort of life she sprang from (which is, after all, what most beauty queens do). Julie Christie's Diana Scott in John Schlesinger's *Darling* (1965) is a 'new woman'. She leaves her husband for an older man (Dirk Bogarde) who leaves his wife and children for her, but she refuses to settle down with him and in pursuit of her career has a loveless affair with a powerful advertising executive (Laurence Harvey), and finally marries a rich, old Italian Count (José Luis de Villalonga).

Julie Christie, commenting on the scarcity of positive images of women in 60s cinema, argues that

> Here was a woman who didn't want to get married, didn't want to have children like those other kitchen-sink heroines; no, Darling wanted to have *everything*. Of course at the time, this was seen as greedy promiscuity and she had to be punished for it. But there was an element of possibility for women, of a new way of living, which is why the film was such a success.[21]

Diana's life might be empty, superficial and ultimately sad, but it still seems more fun than working in Woolworths. She is manipulative, but transparently so, ambitious and selfish but by no means as inhuman and unscrupulous as many of the people who surround her, such as the vampirish Harvey and the cold, rigid, utterly self-centred count. In *Darling*, what is new is less Diana's ambition (which would not be inappropriate for a 50s model or an 1890s chorus girl) than the carefree fecklessness that Julie Christie brings to the part. Retreating to her middle-class home after an abortion, her restless, spontaneous character seems infinitely preferable to the bored, petty-minded conservatism of her parents and an elder sister who is so ossified into middle-age that she could be her mother. And Diana does *try* to be good. After the stresses and strains of two stormy sexual relationships, she develops a platonic friendship with a gay photographer (Roland Curram). On holiday together they live as brother and sister, and it is he who destroys their idyll by sneaking off for a nocturnal rendezvous with a young scooter-boy.[22]

The bias of sympathy in Frederic Raphael's script seems to lie with Robert (Dirk Bogarde), the enlightened middle-class television reporter who leaves his cosy Hampstead marriage for a precarious relationship with Diana and bitterly spurns her at the end when she decides to come back to him. But Robert virtually disappears from the film once Diana leaves him, and though Bogarde is a good enough actor to convince us that his life has been casually destroyed, we have not actually seen him suffering. On the other hand we are fully aware of the grinding emptiness of the world he is forcing Diana to return to, and his rejection of her seems petulant, almost sadistic.

Diana is a Joe Lampton figure, crucified by her own success. Like him, she pursues the goals which society sets her and once she gets them she doesn't want them. But in contrast to Joe, who encourages a young girl he is interested in for her money to fall in love with him and whose failure to admit his mistake brings about the death of the woman he loves, Diana harms only herself. She ends the film rich and famous but covered with a patina of artificiality which is destructive less because it shuts out what might have been in her relationship with Robert than because it destroys her potential for honesty and vitality. As Schlesinger put it: 'What this film is about is the loneliness that Diana's kind of life must lead to. The emotional coldness that descends upon her in the end is the real danger.'[23]

Teenage Dreams

Full employment and rising wages benefited young people as they did everyone else, but the fact that they tended to spend their money on a narrow range of goods and services – records, clothes, make-up, entertainment – meant not only that teenagers were a very visible manifestation of the new affluence, but that their tastes and preferences were of significant economic importance.[24] Youth cults had existed before among the small elite who went into higher education (still only 4 per cent in 1960 compared with 16 per cent in 1975), and among the unrespectable poor where stylishly dressed street gangs like the Napoo and the Bowler Hats had a long and notorious history.[25] But it was not until the 1950s that 'teenagers' emerged as a coherent category transcending class and covering a wide spectrum of young people.

Such economic changes had important cultural effects. Mary Quant, who left art school in 1955 to set up a boutique for the fashion-conscious bohemians of Chelsea, found that by the early 60s her clothes were attracting a mass market. Barbara Hulanicki, launching a modest catalogue postal service for cheap, simple clothes, found herself inundated with orders and by 1964 was able to open Biba as a boutique to cater for the growing number of 'classless' young women. Even more remarkable was the revolution in men's clothes. When John Stephen opened his first clothes shop in Carnaby Street, most of the customers for his stylish, colourful clothes were homosexuals and foreign tourists. By the end of 1959 he was reaching a new clientele of Mods.[26]

Fifties youth culture had been dominated by Teddy Boys, who with their flashy clothes and their penchant for violence can be seen as a last flowering of the semi-criminal working-class youth cults. Mods were different. Most of the pioneers were lower-middle class grammar school boys, and they wanted to look distinctive but at the same time neat and respectable. Their attention to detail, the studied use of colours and styles which defied conventions, owed more to homosexual

125

dress than it did to the ostentatious flamboyance of Teddy Boys and spivs. Teds – and the leather-clad Rockers who succeeded them – remained a cult; Mods – despite the Bank Holiday battles of 1964 and the newspaper hysteria over 'sawdust caesars' and 'rats who only hunt in packs' – transformed men's fashion and were an essential element of the new 'pop' culture.[27]

The Kitchen Sink films and the social problem films of the late 50s and early 60s were certainly aware of social change and the development of youth culture, but they tended to be wary of it. Joe Lampton is condemned to a life of affluent misery because he hasn't the strength to 'be himself' and reject society's shallow materialism in favour of a wholesome, authentic life with Alice. Arthur Seaton is a working-class hard man determined to have a good time and not get ground down, a descendant of the pre-war working-class heroes of Jim Phelan, James Hanley and George Garrett and with substantially the same embattled view of the world. Both *Look Back in Anger* and *The Entertainer* are permeated with a nostalgia for a turn-of-the-century golden age and are distinctly hostile to the 'shiny barbarism' of modern society. *A Taste of Honey* dwells lovingly on Salford's grimy industrial landscape and looks with a baleful eye (reminiscent of Lindsay Anderson's *O Dreamland!*) at a seaside amusement arcade, but it retains Shelagh Delaney's indulgent sympathy for her fey, irresponsible heroine and her proto-Mod admirer. And in *The Loneliness of the Long Distance Runner* Sillitoe's allegory about the writer's need to distance himself from the society he observes becomes a celebration of anarchic teenage rebellion against the stultifying conformism of British society.

A Kind of Loving and *Billy Liar!* are more ambivalent. Vic Brown and Billy Fisher, for all their discontents, remain tied to their families and seem uncertain what they do want from society. But Schlesinger's underlying empathy with his young protagonists is clear enough. In a revealing sequence which parodies the stereotypes of more conservative films, Billy, desperate to get into a dance hall to see Liz (Julie Christie), finds that both his unwanted fiancées are waiting for him to take them in. His troubles are compounded by the arrival of a gang of rough-looking lads on motorbikes, but far from being intimidated by them, Billy borrows a helmet and a leather jacket and passes in with them unnoticed. Such empathy with young people is much rarer in the social problem films of Dearden and Relph, Ted Willis, Bryan Forbes and Richard Attenborough. In *The Angry Silence* and *Flame in the Streets*, Rockers and Teddy Boys are surly, ignorant bullies with no redeeming features, and *Violent Playground*, which Dearden and Relph made in 1957, seems to regard rock and roll as a primitive malevolent force.

Social problem films aimed at lowbrow audiences and young people themselves are much less hostile to the new youth-oriented culture.[28]

126

They tended to be made by small companies and independent producers, and were often dismissed as exploitation films because of their
explicit interest in sex. But films like Muriel Box's *Too Young to Love*
(1959), Edmond T. Greville's *Beat Girl* (1960), Leslie Norman's *Mix
Me a Person* (1961, written by Jack Trevor Story and, like *Beat Girl*,
making good use of Adam Faith), Robert Hartford-Davis's *The Yellow
Teddy Bears* (1963), Michael Winner's *The System* (1964) and Gerry
O'Hara's *The Pleasure Girls* (1965), for all their crudities and simplifi-
cations, are refreshingly tolerant and sympathetic towards the
problems of their young protagonists.

Two of the most interesting of these films, *The Boys* (1962) and *The
Leather Boys* (1963), were directed by Sidney Furie, a young Canadian
who came to Britain in 1960 and who was also responsible for two Cliff
Richard musicals, *The Young Ones* (1961) and *Wonderful Life* (1964).[29]
The Boys is a solidly conventional courtroom drama with Richard
Todd prosecuting and Robert Morley defending four teenage boys
(Dudley Sutton, Tony Garnett, Jess Conrad and Ronald Lacey)
accused of murder. The prosecution witnesses – a bus conductor, two
teenage girls, a lavatory attendant, an upper-middle class motorist –
paint a picture of four hooligans on the rampage. But when the boys
themselves tell their story a different picture emerges. We learn of
their poverty-stricken background, their dull jobs, their struggle to
snatch a little pleasure and excitement from a world which regards
everything they do with a stern eye of disapproval. With its intermin-
able interrogations and repetitive flashbacks the film tends to drag on,
but this is easily forgiven for the unpatronising view it presents of
British working-class life and the sympathy it extends to these not
particularly attractive victims of society. By the end of the film Robert
Morley is able to sum up a position which the audience, if not the
court, would endorse:

> I could say that any four boys, given the circumstances which
> involved my clients, might have done this dreadful, senseless thing,
> that any four boys consistently condemned by social and economic
> background, by their fellow citizens, by their very appearance, took
> the inevitable next step: indulged in petty robbery; that this was a
> petty crime, and that the killing was as foreign to their nature as the
> killing of a bird or a cat. I could say that these were no more than
> boys trying to have an evening out.

In fact, there is a further twist to the film which reveals that Stan
(Dudley Sutton), the most fully developed of the boys, is capable of
killing birds, cats and elderly nightwatchmen, but by this time they
have come to seem complex, idiosyncratic characters rather than either
victims of society or threatening hooligans.

The Leather Boys: Pete (Dudley Sutton) and Reg (Colin Campbell) at the seaside

In an interview on the set of *The Boys*, Furie said that he was interested 'in moving away from the teenage themes to, say, a film dealing with the problems of young married people'.[30] If *The Boys* is an unusually progressive social problem film, *The Leather Boys* (1963) is an unexpected addition to the Kitchen Sink cycle. As the title implies, the main protagonists of the film are young motorbike enthusiasts, though there is no hint of the Mod/Rocker violence which was to upset middle-aged sensibilities the following year, and the 'leather boys' are shown to be cheerful, hard-working, working-class kids whose violence is restricted to the risks they take with their own lives. In the 1930s and 40s the motorbike had been the poor man's car, and in Britain it never became the symbol of generational conflict it was in America. Biker cults certainly existed by the mid-50s, but unlike their American counterparts the emphasis was less on drink, drugs and outrage than on the speed and appearance of the bikes themselves. Rockers tended to channel their aggression into marathon tests of endurance (such as the return trip to Edinburgh in *The Leather Boys*), or dare-devil races along the M1. Peter Laurie, in investigating the 'teenage revolution' in 1965, found them 'cheerful, romantic, reckless souls, with a dark Saxon relish for pointless self-destruction'. Furie sets much of the film's action at the Ace Café, a 'sprawling seedy petrol station café near the London terminus of the M1', but he remained

128

true to his original intentions and the film is less about bikers as such than about the problems of young married people.[31]

Reg (Colin Campbell) appears initially to be a loud-mouthed tearaway, but he is soon shown to be a steady, ordinary sort of lad, the one member of his family prepared to put himself out to save his granny (Gladys Henson) from the Old Folks Home she dreads. The real problem is Dot, his schoolgirl bride (Rita Tushingham). They marry, have a honeymoon at Butlins, and set up home together, but as she is young, feckless and materialistic, things soon start to go wrong. In a witty sequence summing up the problem, Dot comes out of the hairdressers, goes into one shop to buy sweets, another to buy *True Romance*, gives money to some kids wanting 'a penny for the guy', buys some baked beans, and comes home to find Reg angry that the flat is in a mess and there is no tea. Soon he is seeking solace with his fellow bikers and in particular with the daring, eccentric Pete (Dudley Sutton, who had made his debut as one of *The Boys*). Pete agrees to take up lodgings with Reg's granny (thus enabling her to stay in her own home), and is joined by Reg when he walks out on Dot. Sharing everything, including the bed, they become very close friends. It is obvious to us, though not to Reg, that Pete is gay; but as their relationship remains non-sexual, Furie is able to show it as deep and genuine without interference from the censors.

Unfortunately, industry hostility led to the film being shelved, and it was only after a vigorous campaign by its supporters in the media that *The Leather Boys* got a circuit release. It proved to be commercially successful and most critics praised its treatment of homosexuality, but Thomas Wiseman in the *Sunday Express* made the interesting point that 'The implication of this film seems to me to be brutally antifeminine: that what makes men turn to men is women.'[32] This is plausible but disingenuous. Reg, the central character, is a dull, conventional boy overshadowed by his charismatic wife and boyfriend. Though they hate each other, Dot and Pete are both wild and impulsive. Dot's troubles with Reg begin when she turns up, almost unrecognisable, with dyed blonde hair, and her chance of a reconciliation with him is wrecked when he finds her in bed with someone else. Pete's sexuality is necessarily suppressed, but his vitality is attested to by spontaneous acts of generosity – moving in with Reg's granny at the drop of a hat, chucking in his job to sail away with Reg without a backwards glance. What makes the film remarkable is its refusal to impose facile, artificial solutions on the problems of the young. Reg is left with nowhere to go at the end of the film because there *is* nowhere for him to go until he wakes up to the changes that are going on around him.

The Boys and *The Leather Boys* were both made on the fringes of the film industry, *The Boys* by Kenneth Rive's Gala company, which had prospered by importing foreign art and sex films (from *Il Generale Della Rovere* to *Fire in the Flesh* and *The Tigress of Bengal*), *The Leather Boys* by Raymond Stross, an unusually colourful British producer responsible for a number of controversial films (*The Flesh is Weak*, *A Question of Adultery*, *A Terrible Beauty*, *The Mark*, *The Very Edge*, *Ninety Degrees in the Shade*, *The Fox*, *I Want What I Want* – most of which made good use of his wife Anne Heywood's talents).[33] *The Party's Over* was made for Rank and directed by Guy Hamilton, who had begun his career as Carol Reed's assistant on *The Fallen Idol* and *The Third Man*. However, scenes of inadvertent necrophilia proved too sensational for the Corporation's respectable image and the film was shelved. When it was finally released in 1965, two years after it had been completed, Hamilton, who by this time had established an international reputation as the director of *Goldfinger*, considered his film so mutilated that he removed his name from it.[34]

A prologue warns that *The Party's Over* 'is the story of some young people who chose to become – for want of a better word – beatniks. It's not an attack on beatniks. The film has been made to show the loneliness and the unhappiness and the eventual tragedy that can come from a life lived without love for anyone or for anything. Living only for kicks is not enough.' But censorship cuts mean that one has to read the original plot synopsis to discover why the film is shocking. It is ostensibly about Melina (Louise Sorel), a rich, spoilt American girl whose *ennui* leads to two grisly deaths, but the centre of interest shifts to two couples – Moise (Oliver Reed) and Libby (Ann Lynn) and Carson (Clifford David) and Nina (Catherine Woodville). Moise is a wild, malevolent womaniser who is fascinated by Melina because she despises him. Libby is a world-weary white blues singer who mournfully puts up with Moise's contemptuous treatment of her because she assumes that underneath he must love her and need her. Carson is Melina's fiancé, despatched to London by her oil tycoon father (Eddie Albert) to fetch her back to Texas. In his search for her in the bohemian ghettos of Chelsea he is made a fool of but eventually befriended by Nina, an upper-middle class English girl who is beginning to tire of the adolescent nihilism of her friends. Her move back into the mainstream is paralleled by Carson's shedding of his quiescent conformism. Strengthened by his deepening relationship with Nina, he extracts the truth from Moise about Melina's death and abandons his carefully planned career in the oil industry to follow Nina back to her Cotswolds home.

The story (by Marc Behm, who wrote the story for *Help!*) is unnecessarily melodramatic, but Guy Hamilton's direction is capable enough and the young actors are excellent. With its echoes of Left Bank trendiness and air of pseudo-decadence it is easy to see why critics and audiences were alienated by the film. But these quaintly

Moise (Oliver Reed): 'Me, I'm just a dead fly in the soup at the tycoon's banquet.' *The Party's Over*

fashionable beatniks are fascinating, and historical distance gives a period charm to dialogue such as Moise's introductory line – 'Me, I'm just a dead fly in the soup at the tycoon's banquet', and Carson's parting shot – 'I'd like to find a place called Stow-on-the-Wold. Does it really exist?'

While *The Party's Over* was condemned for sensationalism, Clive Donner's *Some People* (1962), about teenagers becoming involved in the Duke of Edinburgh's Award Scheme, arouses suspicions of fatuous worthiness. In fact, thanks to Donner's use of his unusual Bristol locations, a simple but intelligent script by John Eldridge, and the enthusiastic playing of Kenneth More and the young cast, the film has an attractive freshness and vitality.

Three factory workers, Johnnie (Ray Brooks), Bill (David Andrews) and Bert (David Hemmings), at a loose end after being banned from riding their motorbikes, are ejected from their local youth club and wander into a church where they begin fooling around with the organ.

131

This appals the vicar, but the organist and choir-master (Kenneth More) shows some sympathy and allows them to use the church hall to rehearse their band. His pretty daughter Anne (Annika Wills) and some members of the choir soon join in, and there is an interesting fusion between the working-class and middle-class teenagers as they find they have musical tastes and abilities in common. A romance develops between Anne and Johnnie, but she persists with her plans to go to university and refuses to commit herself to him. Bert enthusiastically, Johnnie with some reservations, participate in the Award Scheme, but Bill rebels against what he sees as middle-class patronage and eventually leads in a gang of toughs to smash up the church hall.

Some People is weighted heavily in favour of conformism, but Donner's attitude is worlds away from Ted Willis and Dearden and Relph. The three grounded bikers are rebellious but nonetheless hard-working and respectable, and their rejection of youth club culture, which, as Peter Laurie puts it, 'fitted into the incredibly English world of doing good in sensible shoes and baggy skirts', is endorsed by the film.[35] If Bill is still beyond the pale as a working-class rebel, Johnnie is no gutless conformist. With his blank, pale face, greasy black hair and pugnacious stance, Ray Brooks is as good a representative of working-class youth as Albert Finney and Tom Courtenay and more indicative of the future than either of them. Donner's films are notable for their absence of nostalgia (even his historical epic *Alfred the Great* is

Donner's working-class families: Ray Brooks, Harry H. Corbett in *Some People*

132

distinctly modern) and their use of colour and unusual locations. His working-class homes, here and in *Here We Go Round the Mulberry Bush*, are cheerful, cluttered places where people read and write despite the noise from the ubiquitous television, and the clash between the generations is less one of mutual hostility than of mutual incomprehension. In *Some People* Johnnie, after being kindly but firmly shown the door by Anne, wanders aimlessly through Bristol until he reaches a pub where, to his embarrassment, he finds his father (Harry H. Corbett) drinking at the bar. His tongue loosened by alcohol, he explains a working-class father's dilemma: 'You know, Johnnie, it's funny, you gets married, you has children and you brings 'em up, and half the time they're ruddy strangers to you, complete ruddy strangers.' The rift is healed to some extent when Johnnie agrees to play the pub piano, giving his father something to be proud of and at the same time refertilising his own working-class roots, enabling him to leave the pub more secure and resolved about his place in the world.

Partly because easy options like marrying a middle-class girl are closed to him, Johnnie steers an uncertain path between Bill's paranoid mistrust ('They get you young and defenceless and they hang on. Conform and be happy. "Yes, sir." "No, sir." And "God Save the Queen, sir."') and Bert's contented absorption into craftsmanship. His pensive reconciliation with Bill and his insistence that his relationship with Anne has been valuable ('She taught me a lot – and not what you're thinking either') strikes a nice balance between realism and the eupeptic optimism of the Cliff Richard musicals.[36]

Pop Culture
After the success of *Rock Around the Clock* and the emergence of British rock and roll stars, British film producers were quick to realise there was a new market to tap. Hardly had 'Rock With the Caveman' entered the hit parade than Anglo-Amalgamated began filming *The Tommy Steele Story* (1957), and it was quickly followed by *The Duke Wore Jeans*, and *Tommy the Toreador*.[37] These musicals, aimed directly at the teenage market, tended to be inanely conformist and their main virtue lay in the professionalism with which once threatening teenage idols are transformed into lovable young men only too happy to be integrated into adult society. In *Tommy the Toreador* (1959, d. John Paddy Carstairs), for example, Steele plays a young sailor adrift in Spain who, following in the comic footsteps of George Formby and Norman Wisdom, is tricked into becoming a bullfighter. There is a short and poorly integrated scene where Tommy meets a crowd of British teenagers in a Spanish nightclub and sets the joint rocking, but more typical of the film is the 'Where's the Birdie?' sequence, a good old-fashioned music hall number which Steele performs with great aplomb alongside comedy stalwarts Bernard Cribbins and Sid James.

Soho musical. Maisie (Sylvia Syms) and Johnny (Laurence Harvey), *Expresso Bongo*

Similar vehicles were found for other pop stars like Terry Dene (*The Golden Disc*) and Billy Fury (*I've Gotta Horse*), though Adam Faith developed a more complex screen persona in *Beat Girl*, *Never Let Go* and *Mix Me a Person*. But it was Cliff Richard who became the first big British teenage success on film. After appearing in a minor role as a potential juvenile delinquent in *Serious Charge*, he was cast as 'Bongo Herbert' in Val Guest and Wolf Mankowitz's *Expresso Bongo*, a musical which cheekily parodied the rapid ascent of Tommy Steele from coffee-bar singer to pop idol. The first half of the film is a fascinating evocation of Soho in the 50s, with Laurence Harvey excelling himself as Johnny Jackson, a smooth-talking Jewish drummer-turned-agent. But once the story shifts to the rise of Bongo Herbert, crude parody takes over and what might have been a British answer to Mackendrick's *The Sweet Smell of Success* disintegrates into an Ealing-like homily on the virtues of being small and unsuccessful.

Three musicals were then created around Cliff Richard: *The Young Ones* (1961), *Summer Holiday* (1962) and *Wonderful Life* (1964).[38] Despite Richard's limitations as an actor they are lively, inventive, enjoyable films, their young directors Sidney Furie and Peter Yates being more in tune with their subject than the Hollywood veterans entrusted with Elvis Presley's musicals. All three films have at their centre a clash between youth and age. In *The Young Ones*, Cliff Richard comes into conflict with his property developer father (Robert Morley), who plans to demolish a scruffy youth club. In *Summer Holiday*, he and his pals, on holiday in Europe in an expropriated London Transport bus, rescue a young American heiress from the clutches of her possessive mother. In *Wonderful Life*, Cliff and the gang take over from the ageing star of a film musical and turn it into a lively success. In each of the films there is a set-piece confrontation where Cliff argues that young people are healthy and responsible and better at doing things than their hidebound elders, but what is threatened is a very mild revolution. When things look like getting out of hand – as in *The Young Ones* when the rougher element in the club kidnap his father – Cliff shows himself to be firmly on the side of law and order.

Rock and roll seemed destined to be a short-lived phenomenon in Britain. Singers like Tommy Steele, Cliff Richard, Billy Fury, Adam Faith and Marty Wilde remained popular but came to rely on pop ballads and tuneful melodies. Nik Cohn describes 1960 as 'the worst year that pop has been through. Everyone had gone to the moon. Elvis had been penned off in the army and came back to appal us with ballads. Little Richard had got religion. Chuck Berry was in jail, Buddy Holly was dead. Very soon, Eddie Cochran was killed in his car crash. It was a wholesale plague, a wipe-out.'[39] The vacuum was unexpectedly filled by Trad Jazz, with figures like Chris Barber, Kenny Ball and Acker Bilk suddenly thrust from beer cellar obscurity into the limelight. A handful of films celebrated the phenomenon – *Jazzboat*, *Band of Thieves* and, most remarkably, Richard Lester's first feature film *It's Trad Dad* (1962), which takes a more radical stance on the clash between the generations than the Cliff Richard musicals. Adults (with the exception of some of the performers) are presented as grumbling killjoys determined to frustrate any attempt the young people make to have a good time, and even the DJs (Pete Murray, Alan Freeman and David Jacobs, magnanimously playing themselves) are shown as vain, self-seeking parasites.

The Trad Jazz boom proved short-lived and rock and roll had struck deeper roots than it seemed. In a countrified version popularised by

Lonnie Donegan and called skiffle, it had proliferated in innumerable amateur pop groups who soon began to look to black American music to expand their repertoire. In 1963 it burst to the surface again with the Beatles' insistent Liverpudlian chant 'Love Me Do'. This was a genuinely new sound, original and innovative enough to launch a wave of British pop groups.[40] If in retrospect many of them were not as good as they seemed, their choice of obscure American material more sophisticated than their ability to reproduce it, they opened doors which were never to be completely closed again. Peter Laurie, in describing this teenage revolution, captures the apocalyptic spirit of the 60s:

> The transition from a people among whom there is a small enclave who have culture and a large majority who have not, to one in which culture is the property and opportunity of all, presents a situation very like that in South Africa. In England we have a cultural apartheid; in the centre the embattled arrogants in control of money and power: and surging round them a great sea of unfettered vigour which threatens to roll over all that is old, dull and pretentious and extinguish it.[41]

Such was the popularity of the Beatles by 1964 that if *A Hard Day's Night* had been made as tamely and conventionally as most youth musicals it would still have been a success. What Richard Lester did was to invent a style which helped to carry the group forward to another stage of development rather than pushing them into the arms of traditional show business.[42] Lester's borrowings from the techniques of television commercials and the new photography of David Bailey, Terence Donovan and Anthony Armstrong-Jones were woven into a neatly appropriate backcloth against which the Beatles exercised their musical talents and their offbeat charm. His stylistic innovations were much more apparent in *The Knack*, an adaptation of a play by Ann Jellicoe first performed in 1961 and not a million miles away in attitudes and style from Shelagh Delaney's *A Taste of Honey*.

The three principals – Ray Brooks, Michael Crawford and Rita Tushingham – had all made their marks in serious, realist films; here, by contrast, they are enveloped in a crazy exuberance.[43] From the initial sequence, where a long queue of blonde, mini-skirted girls wait patiently for the peremptory attention of Tolen (Brooks), the boy with the 'knack', one might suppose the film to be a male chauvinist fantasy about the opportunities opened up by the new climate of permissiveness. In fact, the real hero is Colin, a shy, weedy schoolteacher (Crawford) who, against all expectations, wins the love of the innocent but canny country girl Nancy (Tushingham), who comes to London looking for adventure. Her naivety works as a charm against which Tolen's evil magic is harmless. He is able to unlock the gates of her sexual

136

The confidence of youth: John Boorman, Barbara Ferris, Dave Clark on location at Smithfield meat market. *Catch Us If You Can*

feelings in a way that Colin can't, but he is barred from entering, and when he has served his purpose Nancy discards him, deflating his ego as effectively as she deflates the tyres of his glossy white motorbike. Once she realises her own sexual potency, Nancy is capable of rescuing Colin, and as in *It's Trad Dad*, the combination of two young people full of genuine affection and enthusiasm for the world is shown to be strong enough to overcome all the obstacles set up by capricious, selfish but essentially impotent adults.[44]

Similar themes are explored in another pop group vehicle, *Catch Us If You Can*, which was unfavourably compared to Lester's films when it was released in 1965. The group here, the Dave Clark Five, have little of the charisma and less of the musical ability of the Beatles and make very dull heroes, but there are compensations. John Boorman's restlessly inventive direction prevents the film from sagging into cliché, and Peter Nichols's inconsequential but witty script is fleshed out with the quirky characterisations of Barbara Ferris (a fairy princess with a croaky working-class voice) as the heroine, Yootha Joyce and Robin Bailey as an anguished, ill-matched middle-aged couple, and Ronald Lacey (the youngest of *The Boys*) as the leader of a band of Salisbury Plain beatniks. The film takes the form of a characteristic Boorman trek through the West Country in search of an elusive Holy Grail, but what is more relevant here is the way in which it deals with the revolt of its young people against the affluent society.

Both Dinah (Barbara Ferris) and Steve (Dave Clark) are heavily

137

involved in the mechanics of the commercial world, she as a model whose face smiles out from hoardings, magazines and television screen as 'the Meat Girl', he as a stuntman working on television commercials. They tire of the inanity of the commercial they are working on at Smithfield market and run off together, but they make their escape in an E-type Jaguar, and when they run into the beatniks on Salisbury Plain they find their long hair and scruffy clothes intimidatingly alien ('King Normal', their leader labels Steve in disgust). What they run away to, a tiny island off the Devon coast, turns out to be decaying and derelict ('It smells of dead holidays,' Dinah complains). When the tide goes out, they find it is not an island after all and there is not even a stretch of water to protect them from the horde of pressmen and photographers who have caught up with them. Their romance ends with the failure of their quest: she adapts herself once more to smile at the camera, he goes off to pursue his career as a stuntman.[45]

In so far as it shows young people being manipulated by the media, the film's view of the world tallies with J. B. Priestley's notion of 'admass' and Richard Hoggart's 'shiny barbarism'. But while attacking the oppressive, manipulative aspects of the new culture, *Catch Us If You Can*, like the Lester films, is basically optimistic. The young protagonists revel in their affluence and the transitory freedom it offers, and the films are imbued with a sense of adventure, of new and exciting worlds to explore. In *The Knack*, Rita Tushingham comes to London grasping her *Honey* magazine, full of optimism and misconceptions, and is not totally disappointed. In *Catch Us If You Can*, Dinah and Steve show each other their favourite 'secret places' in London: Steve a swimming pool where they go skin-diving, Dinah an orange grove. But the films have an aura of wistfulness, of melancholy, expressing a doubt whether – even with the challenges and opportunities open to young people in this interlude of full employment and expansion in education – one really can have a good time and not have to pay an awful price for it.

7

SWINGING LONDON

This spring, as never before in modern times, London is switched on. Ancient elegance and new opulence are all tangled up in a dazzling blur of op and pop. The city is alive with birds (girls) and beatles, buzzing with minicars and telly stars, pulsing with half a dozen separate veins of excitement. The guards now change at Buckingham Palace to a Lennon and McCartney tune, and Prince Charles is firmly in the long-hair set. (Piri Halasz, *Time*, 1966)[1]

London Life

It was not until April 1966 that *Time* magazine discovered 'the swinging city', but London had shaken off the vestiges of wartime austerity a decade earlier when Mary Quant set up her first boutique in the King's Road, John Stephen began turning the environs of Carnaby Street into a centre for male fashion, and the Soho Fairs provided a public focus for beatniks and ravers to celebrate their opting out from the conventions of polite society.[2] Of course, the great majority of London's population was not swinging, and until the early 70s most of London remained a city of bedsits and corner shops, greasy cafés and council housing estates. But changes were occurring which did have a fundamental effect on society and the environment.

Post-war reconstruction had favoured the creation of new towns like Harlow and Stevenage to relieve London's overcrowding. It was hoped that the population in the conurbation could be reduced by up to a million. Indeed the 50s did see a massive exodus of Londoners, but this was counterbalanced by the inflow of people from other parts of the country and, more visibly, of Commonwealth immigrants. London was becoming a younger and more cosmopolitan place. Manufacturing industry was moving out, discouraged by traffic congestion and the Clean Air Act of 1956 which had put an end to London's killer smogs, but work in the building trades and in offices was plentiful. As London

139

became a cleaner and more pleasant place to live in, young middle-class people – those who wanted to avoid the safe suburban lifestyle of their parents, those who missed the working-class communities from which they had escaped, those who simply wanted to avoid a long trek into work every day – began to move into inner London suburbs like Camden Town and Islington, where shabby Georgian and Victorian houses could be bought cheaply. To the efforts of these pioneers of gentrification must be added those of property developers who, in co-operation with local authority planning departments, set about clearing great tracts of land for comprehensive redevelopment.[3] Their ambitious schemes resulted in the careless destruction of much that was valuable and the erection of eyesores which still blot the landscape, but they contributed to the sense of rapid change which was to reach its apotheosis in the 60s.

Piri Halasz's article in *Time* was important in crystalising an image, but it was a belated acknowledgment of a phenomenon which had already been celebrated the previous summer in articles like the *Daily Telegraph* colour supplement's 'London – The Most Exciting City', in David Bailey's *Box of Pin-Ups* (thirty-six photographs of people, from Lord Snowdon to Ron and Reggie Kray, who epitomised the 'glamour' of London in the mid-60s), and the launch of a 'Swinging London' weekly magazine, *London Life*. Ironically, in April 1966, while *Time* told the world about 'London: The Swinging City', attention in Britain was focused on the horrors revealed in the trial of the Moors Murderers, Ian Brady and Myra Hindley, rather than on Carnaby Street and the King's Road, and there were indications that, with the newly re-elected Labour government plagued by economic difficulties and industrial unrest, the optimistic climate was beginning to change.[4] Significantly, the handful of films which might be regarded as genuine Swinging London films – *Nothing But the Best*, *The Knack*, *Morgan*, *Georgy Girl*, *Kaleidoscope*, *Alfie* – had already been made and in most cases released by the spring of 1966. Except for affectionate parodies like *The Jokers* (1966, d. Michael Winner) and *Smashing Time* (1967, d. Desmond Davis), subsequent films tended to be ambivalent or indifferent. Films as different as Antonioni's *Blow Up* (1967), Michael Winner's *I'll Never Forget What's 'Is Name* (1967) and David Greene's *Sebastian* and *The Strange Affair* (both 1968) show a middle-aged suspicion of Swinging London, while John Osborne's *Inadmissible Evidence* (1968, d. Anthony Page) denounces hedonistic young people and their permissive society even more bitterly than *Term of Trial*.

Surprisingly, American directors made little use of the concept of Swinging London. Otto Preminger in *Bunny Lake is Missing* (1965), Sidney Lumet in *The Deadly Affair* (1966), Stanley Donen in *Arabesque* (1966) tend to concentrate on an older, less fashion-conscious London. When Preminger ventures into the Carnaby Street area of

Soho it is to visit an antique dolls' hospital run by elderly eccentric Finlay Currie. Lumet sets his story around the suburban homes of his three central characters with occasional excursions into slumland and a Hitchcockian climax at the Aldwych Theatre. *Arabesque* does have an interlude where Gregory Peck is tipped out on to a busy road under the influence of a hallucinogenic drug, but he wakes up safely back among the dreaming spires of Oxford, and Donen, like Hitchcock in his 30s film *Sabotage*, sets his most exciting scene in London Zoo's reptile house.

James Clavell's *To Sir, With Love* (1966) takes us through a traditional cheery East End to a run-down school where Sidney Poitier faces the same problems with apathetic or sadistic colleagues, insolent youths and sexy young girls as Max Bygraves in *Spare the Rod* and Laurence Olivier in *Term of Trial*. But in this likeable but unimpeachably conformist film – which took more money at the American box-office than any other British film in the 60s except *Goldfinger* and *Thunderball* – Poitier converts the rock-and-rolling louts and provocative dolly birds (Judy Geeson, Lulu, Adrienne Posta) into 'young ladies and gentlemen'.[5] Fielder Cook's *Prudence and the Pill* (1968), with Judy Geeson and a plot built round adultery and birth control, might be mistaken for a comic examination of the permissive society, but it turns out to be a frothily sexless upper-middle class farce, with nearly fifty-year-old Deborah Kerr and nearly sixty-year-old David Niven as its protagonists. Jack Smight's *Kaleidoscope* (1966), which is riddled with zooms and dissolves and has a heroine (Susannah York) who owns a boutique in Hampstead and designs 'kinky clothes for baby-faced Chelsea girls who like to show off their pretty little knees', comes much closer to what a Swinging London film should be. But even here, playboy Warren Beatty spends much of his time in Continental casinos, and we don't see much more of London than the familiar tourist sights.

The Permissive Society
Writing about the importance of fashion for the young, Peter Laurie dismisses fears that this was another manifestation of the advance of 'admass':

> Considered in the larger context, this process is not as dreadful as it may seem. It is only the sudden change from a society with perhaps a hundred thousand makers of taste and players of the fashion game among a wilderness of millions who were too ignorant, poor and out of touch to care; to one in which there are five million players.[7]

The same applied to sex. Attitudes which had been confined to a leisured elite and a bohemian fringe became more widespread. But it is

141

Susannah York, designing 'kinky clothes for baby-faced Chelsea girls'.
Kaleidoscope

easy to exaggerate the change. A safe oral contraceptive pill was available by the late 50s but it did not come into widespread use in Britain
until ten years later. A survey carried out in 1970 found that only 19
per cent of married couples under forty-five used the pill, and the idea
that most single girls were sexually promiscuous had little foundation
in fact. Geoffrey Gorer's study of *Sex and Marriage in England Today*,
published in 1971, found that 63 per cent of women (and 26 per cent of
men) were virgins at the time they married.[8] Liberalising legislation
was passed in the late 60s, with the Abortion Act, the Sexual Offences
Act (legalising sexual relations between consenting males over twenty-
one) and the NHS (Family Planning) Act in 1967, followed by the
Divorce Law Amendment Act in 1969. But as Elizabeth Wilson
observed later in a perceptive examination of the 'permissive' sexual
climate of the 60s, 'there was a compulsion to be sexual' but 'by an

impossible sleight of hand, sexuality was both to expand and flower in liberated fashion *and* to be organised within marriage.'[9] Such contradictions manifested themselves in films which attempted to deal with Swinging London and its supposedly permissive morality.

Alfie (1966, d. Lewis Gilbert) and *Georgy Girl* (1966, d. Silvio Narizzano), like *The Knack* and *Morgan*, were based on pre-Swinging London sources, and their attitude towards the new permissive climate is sometimes confused. Margaret Forster's novel *Georgy Girl*, though it was not published until 1965, is an old-fashioned story of how a plain but good-hearted girl takes over her pretty flatmate's husband (temporarily) and baby (permanently) and finds a kind of happiness with an ageing admirer. Lynn Redgrave does wonders with Georgy, passing herself off convincingly as big, plain and clumsy but showing an energy and resourcefulness which makes her appeal to men understandable. Josh, the vacillating husband, is transformed by Alan Bates from shaggy bohemian to madcap Mod, and Charlotte Rampling effectively embodies the flatmate Meredith, a Christine Keeler-like figure despite her prowess with the violin. Meredith's attitude to relationships and babies is displayed as callous and selfish, but her defiance of the conventions of marriage and motherhood gives the film a shocking frisson which is not quite snuffed out by the disapproval with which she is viewed. Morality remains firmly with Georgy, but she is not without a devious streak herself – shrewdly manipulating her father's millionaire employer to provide a father for the baby when Josh proves inadequate.

Georgy Girl was the last Swinging London Film to be made in black and white (from 1966 onwards virtually all British feature films except modestly budgeted art films like *Ulysses* and *The Private Right* were made in colour), and its view of London – the Edgware Road, a scruffy flat in Maida Vale, a children's playground, even the early evening chase through the West End and the trip down the river – makes the city look hardly more swinging than *A Kind of Loving*'s Stockport or *Billy Liar!*'s Bradford. *Alfie*, made in colour and with a cool jazz score from Sonny Rollins, might seem more modish, but except for the device of Alfie talking directly to the audience, Lewis Gilbert's direction is solidly old-fashioned.

Alfie began life as a 1962 radio play (*Alfie Elkins and his Little Life*) by Bill Naughton, who adapted it for the stage and wrote the screenplay for the film. It was set in the 50s and recounted the amorous exploits of 'a working-class Don Juan'.[10] Alfie Elkins belongs to the semi-criminal world of spivs and wide-boys which dated from the war years rather than the Swinging Sixties. His characteristics – an almost psychopathic vulgarity which links women, clothes and cars as commodities to be flaunted to prove to the world that he has achieved success without the privileges of birth or education – could be tenta-

143

'A rat is a rat . . .': Alfie (Michael Caine) and Annie (Jane Asher) in *Alfie*

tively identified with the working-class actors, photographers and pop stars who were supposed to inhabit Swinging London. But Michael Caine (who was born Maurice Micklewhite in the Elephant and Castle area of London) takes Alfie into the 60s without losing his traditional working-class roots. As Isabel Quigly hautily pointed out:

> Vain, easy-going, autocratic, physically fastidious, cowardly, undo-mestic, irresistible, he is the sort of man once thought totally un-English but now being fished out of the proletarian pond where Englishness of the traditional sort never flourished. Like the new bright clothes on the new bright boys, he suggests a subterranean national character rising to surprise even the locals.[11]

Critical attempts to dismiss Alfie – 'Come off it lads. A rat is a rat, and hanging a blue ribbon on the beast doesn't turn him into a prize Pomeranian' – don't quite ring true.[12] Michael Caine captures the vulnerability, the inadvertent generosity, of Naughton's character-type as well as his less admirable qualities. Complaints that Alfie's habit of talking to the camera is a clumsy theatrical device might be true in a general sense, but here it disconcertingly prevents us from distancing ourselves from Alfie's blind egocentricity. His attitude to women is less misogyny than a failure to communicate on anything but the most basic level. That he should break off from his love-making to tell us about the object of his attentions is evidence less of contempt than of his inability, which we share, to penetrate the self-enclosed world in which his women live. Alfie plays according to the rules that assume women to be helpless, brainless and inherently inferior – 'She, it, what does it matter, they're all birds' – but he fools only himself. After making all the right moves but losing his 'peace of mind', he ends up confused rather than repentant and there is something genuinely plaintive about his final 'So what's the answer? That's what I keep asking myself. What's it all about?'

Smashing Time (1967, d. Desmond Davis) is generally taken as marking the turn from freshness and originality in films about Swinging London to the clichéd tackiness which marked its decline. Desmond Davis had worked as camera operator on *A Taste of Honey*, *The Loneliness of the Long Distance Runner* and *Tom Jones*. His first film as director was an adaptation of Edna O'Brien's *The Girl With Green Eyes*, made for Woodfall in 1964 with Lynn Redgrave and Rita Tushingham. After two less successful attempts at lyrical realism, *The Uncle* (1964) and *I Was Happy Here* (1965), he teamed up again with Redgrave and Tushingham for *Smashing Time*, and earned the disapproval of Alexander Walker for making 'a film whose crude exploitation of them once more as innocents-at-large in the big city was to show how coarse and knowing the freshness of the cinema had turned once Britain was "swinging" and the movies had to swing with it.'[13] This is unfair. *The Girl With Green Eyes* is a sort of coda to the Kitchen Sink cycle, a modest, gentle, mildly humorous black-and-white tale of innocence and naivety untraumatically coming to terms with the wicked world. *Smashing Time*, with its two heroines coming down from the north to sample the delights of Carnaby Street, comes close to being a slapstick farce. As such (particularly when compared to most late-60s comedies), it works very well. George Melly, who wrote the script, was sufficiently in tune with Swinging London to create accurate caricatures like Michael York's working-class photographer, Anna Quayle's trendy aristocrat who calls her boutique – to the consternation of pragmatic northerner Tushingham – Too Much, and, intruding from the still black-and-white world of television, Peter Jones's *Candid Camera* linkman 'bringing happiness and glamour into simple ordinary people's drab little lives'.

Davis's Woodfall training stands him in good stead, and there is an attention to detail in the script, casting and art direction which is rare in British comedy. Irene Handl's second-hand clothes shop lady uses one of her chihuahuas as a prop; Murray Melvin, the proto-Mod of *A Taste of Honey*, reappears as a velveteened dandy; Brenda (Tushingham) is taken up for radical chic photography ('Gauche' foundation cream, 'Direct Action – the perfume with the provocative aura'); a Tretchikoff painting presides over the shabby flat where she and

145

Yvonne (Redgrave) briefly find a home. The girls might be obsessed with Carnaby Street, but much of the action takes place in the seedier bits of Camden Town and the film has a solid sense of geography to underpin its fantasies. Most of the critics thought that five set-piece slapstick sequences (sauce/paint/insect repellent spraying in Arthur Mullard's greasy café; art gallery private view with Bruce Lacey's robots on the rampage; pie-throwing in a King's Road restaurant; bedroom farce ending in Tushingham, Redgrave, Ian Carmichael and David Lodge in a collapsed bed under a collapsed ceiling, the Post Office Tower spinning so fast that it becomes a fairground Wall of Death with its trendy diners splayed against the wall) was a bit too much, and Alexander Walker was prissily concerned about who was going to clear up all the mess.[14] But looking back over twenty years later, such visual exuberance seems unusual and admirable, the riot of Pop Art colour a refreshingly bold addition to the adventurous but still monochrome London of *Morgan* and *The Knack*.

Georgy Girl, *Alfie* and *Smashing Time* all look for thrills in the big city but end up endorsing homely virtues like sincerity, loyalty, friendship. This is as true of Clive Donner's *Here We Go Round the Mulberry Bush* (1967), one of the few films to look unpatronisingly at young people and their attitude to sex. Donner, with *Nothing But the Best* and *What's New Pussycat?* (1965), was as much responsible as Richard Lester for introducing stylish eclecticism to British films and, apart from an austere adaptation of Harold Pinter's *The Caretaker*, he insisted on working in colour. But unlike the surrealist-influenced Lester, Donner remained, even at his most zany and outrageous, a realist. *Here We Go Round the Mulberry Bush*, despite its psychedelic titles, its Stevie Winwood music, its fantasy sequences, occupies the same moral universe as *Some People*. Donner shot the film in Stevenage new town, the first fruit of post-war planning, in a deliberate attempt to escape Swinging London.[15]

Jamie (Barry Evans) is more obsessed with sex than Johnnie is in *Some People*, but that has as much to do with his class position as the changing permissive climate. Jamie's father might be absorbed in his football pools, and his mother goes round with curlers in her hair, but in their modern suburban home few elements of traditional working-class culture survive, and far from being alienated and isolated, Jamie moves easily between the remnants of the working class whose lives still revolve round the fish and chip shop and the public school party-hopping set. Jamie ought to belong to Geoffrey Gorer's group of working-class grammar school boys 'likely to have undergone a good deal of mockery and self-questioning for their studious abstention from the pursuit of money and pleasure which their mates envy from the age of fifteen', and consequently driven to emphasise their manliness 'by frequent copulation or attempts thereat'. But in the ten years since

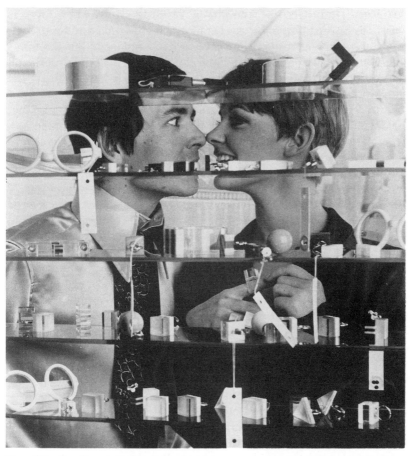

One of the few films to look unpatronisingly at young people and their attitudes to sex: Barry Evans, Angela Scoular in *Here We Go Round the Mulberry Bush*

Gorer described the perils of hypergamy, things had changed, at least in the democratic uniformity of the new towns. With an abundance of holiday jobs, the expectation of going to a university as a right rather than a privilege, and the proximity of girls much less coy about sex than they would have been a decade earlier, life seems much easier for an upwards-aspiring grammar school boy than it had been for Joe Lampton and Vic Brown a few years earlier.

The urgency of Jamie's quest for someone to rid him of his virginity (made more insistent by the fact that his younger brother already seems to have lost his) leaves little time for subtlety in his attitude to women. The five girls he tries his luck with are (in turn) dumb, manipulative, artificial, silly and unscrupulous, and are hardly given more of an independent identity than *Alfie*'s women. Once he has succeeded in gaining sexual experience he feels able to approach and

147

bed Mary (Judy Geeson), the girl he really likes, but she proves as willing to discard him as he was his first sexual partner and his dreams of a steady, loving relationship have to be abandoned. But the film's sympathies are with Jamie, who now gets down to his school work and passes his exams while the philandering Mary fails hers. Thus at the end, while she seems stuck in a suburban treadmill, he looks forward to university and a proper relationship with Mary's hard-working, serious-but-still-attractive friend Claire, who is going to the same university. But as Donner explained: 'The film is intended, of course, to be at times a subjective fantasy: it is subjective completely, even in the parts that are not fantasy. The fact that the boy speaks in the first person all the way through seems to me to make it absolutely clear.'[16] Thus the film is often cruel and unfair, but in allowing us to see the world through the eyes of a gauche, spotty-faced suburban schoolboy, Donner makes *Here We Go Round the Mulberry Bush* as accurate and valuable a guide to the excitements and disappointments of adolescence as *Some People*.

Michelangelo Antonioni's *Blow Up* explores an unease about the nature of Swinging London society – in particular its immersion in fantasy – rather than the opportunities for sexual fulfilment opened up by the permissive society. Robin Wood argues that it is a film 'constructed like a poem of thematically related images, about the way in which perceptions can be tampered with, undermined, and finally broken down.'[17] This might well have been Antonioni's intention, and it comes through in some memorable sequences: the transition Thomas makes at the beginning from down-and-out to Rolls Royce-driving whizz-kid, the scenes in the park, with its chill secretive beauty, and in the dark-room where Thomas laboriously reveals to himself the murder he has witnessed without seeing. But the burden of representing Swinging London – the David Bailey-like hero, the guitar smashing, the casual sex, the dope-smoking party, the mime troupe with which the film begins and ends – combines with the faster rhythm of cutting imposed on the film by editor Frank Clarke to disrupt the mysterious quality which makes *L'Avventura*, *La Notte*, *L'Eclisse* and *Deserto Rosso* enigmatically complex films.

Michael Winner's *I'll Never Forget What's 'Is Name* is also sceptical about the values of Swinging London. Oliver Reed is not very convincingly cast as a man who has sold his soul to advertising and wants to make a return to intellectual integrity, but despite its occasional crudities the film has a vivid, nightmarish quality which makes it interesting. Andrew Quint (Reed) is first seen wielding an axe, with which he proceeds to chop up his desk, and his increasingly desperate attempts to break out of the gilded coffin which his success has created around him are accompanied by dreams of a traumatic childhood and attempts to relive his past. He rejoins the little magazine he worked for before

148

being sucked into the advertising world, he goes to a school reunion, he visits his Cambridge tutor, but always over his shoulder lurks Orson Welles's monstrous father figure. Finally he returns and makes a commercial out of the gory fantasies which haunt his life only to find, amid the enthusiastic applause of the National Film Theatre audience, that he has been awarded first prize at the Festival of Creative Advertising. Winner cheats unscrupulously, killing off his heroine in a car crash and allowing Andrew to use footage of her death which *he* couldn't possibly have shot. As Penelope Gilliatt pointed out, 'The film doesn't really hate the sophisticated boredom it depicts at all; it finds the atmosphere alluring, and takes the hero's melodramatic spasm of repentance seriously.'[18] But it remains Winner's most personal and ambitious film.[19]

Life at the Bottom

Anti-Swinging London films begin as early as 1965 with *Life at the Top* (d. Ted Kotcheff), a sequel to *Room at the Top*. Joe Lampton finally plucks up courage to leave Susan and follow tough television reporter Honor Blackman down to London, only to find that his lack of educational qualifications makes it easy to keep him outside the charmed circle he thought he had entered, and that he is inadequate and out of place among his girlfriend's BBC colleagues ('Full of love and Oxfam they are, full of humanity, but introduce a stranger, a non-club member into their midst and they'll insult him just for the hell of it'). Joe retreats to Warnley and Susan (who has grown up to become Jean Simmons); and the pull to the South was by no means irresistible. Yvonne and Brenda take London by storm and have their smashing time, but they use their return tickets to escape back up north. In *Mrs Brown You've Got a Lovely Daughter* (1968, d. Saul Swimmer) the pop group Herman and the Hermits spend the first three-and-a-half reels in scruffy but friendly Manchester. And when they do move south they find to their disgust that London is full of flower children in plastic dresses and red cloaks, and 'there are more [pop] groups than there are coppers'.

Joe's difficulties in coping with London sophistication have to be set against Michael Marler's success in *The Reckoning* (1969, d. Jack Gold). Marler (Nicol Williamson) is a working-class Liverpool Irishman who has made it into the world of big business more by bloody-minded intransigence than sly charm and wins a posh wife and a house in Virginia Water. But Williamson's Marler, like Michael Caine's Harry Palmer in *The Ipcress File* and its successors, comes on the scene when, with a Labour government in power, a working-class background could be passed off as fashionable. With the middle classes moving into the Darkest England of inner city suburbs, the reality of poverty and class division was rediscovered and two of the most

149

successful films of 1967/8, Peter Collinson's *Up the Junction* and Ken Loach's *Poor Cow*, turned away from Swinging London towards a working-class realism reminiscent of the northern Kitchen Sink films of the early 60s.[20] *Up the Junction* began as a series of autobiographical articles in *New Society* written by Nell Dunn, about a young middle-class woman who takes a factory job in Battersea and discovers working-class life. In 1965 it was made into a television play directed by Ken Loach which outraged conservative moralists by depicting without condemning a casual attitude to sex and violence and a painfully explicit abortion scene. Loach, a committed left-wing film-maker, went on to make *Cathy Come Home* the following year, leaving the commercial potential of *Up the Junction* to be exploited by Peter Collinson.

Collinson had made the transition from television to feature films with *The Penthouse* (1967), a dubious but compelling variation on the much used tale of a couple trapped by malevolent intruders. His version of *Up the Junction* (1967) retains Loach's uncensorious attitude to working-class sexuality but drops his explicit social criticism; and the fragile sisterly comradeship which had been Nell Dunn's central concern is shoved aside to make way for a love-across-the-class-barriers plot involving the middle-class heroine with a working-class Mod who is confused but fascinated by her attraction to a life he sees as irredeemably sordid.

Suzy Kendall's Polly is an upper-middle class Chelsea girl who leaves her parents' big house and posh car and crosses the bridge to garish, vulgar, colourful Battersea.[21] This working-class netherworld is definitely not swinging, but with its scruffy little factories, boisterous pubs and vulgar but cheerful people it seems enchantingly real to her compared to the stuffiness and formality of life on the other side of the river. The working-class girls (Adrienne Posta, Maureen Lipman) are one-dimensional enough to be caricatures, but so full of fight that their anarchic energy sears through the film. Polly is insipid and wrong-footed but, unlike her equivalent in the TV version, she's no passive observer. She is the one who has to convert the relationship with Peter (Dennis Waterman) into something physical, and her values – that money and appearance don't mean much, that there's a lot in the working-class way of life which should not be discarded – are sympathetically considered. But she is balanced against Dennis Waterman's restless, ambitious, working-class malcontent, who is pushed into criminality by his need to impress her. Polly's cruel put-down of his *Room at the Top* ambitions – 'I don't want to be a parasite and I certainly don't want to marry one' – is made to seem arrogantly sanctimonious when it becomes apparent that it is he who will pay for her lesson in life's complexities and unfairness.

While Collinson was making *Up the Junction*, Ken Loach was work-

Working-class heroine: Carol White in *Poor Cow*

ing on a similar Nell Dunn-scripted story, *Poor Cow* (1967), as his first
feature film. It is a paradoxically unsentimental film, showing the
poverty, the stunted lives, the lack of opportunity which remained
unchanged by the rocketing fortunes of a handful of working-class
photographers and footballers, actors and models. Like Loach's television plays *Up the Junction* and *Cathy Come Home*, the film was
centred on a young woman played by Carol White and combined
cinéma vérité documentary techniques with dramatic reconstruction.
For the *Monthly Film Bulletin* it was 'an incongruous mixture of realism and romanticism', and even Pauline Kael looked down her nose at
a film which dealt with its central character 'in terms of the sensuality
and happiness possible within her degraded life.'[22] Time and feminism
have been kind to the film, and its Godardian borrowings – titles
dividing the film into episodes, the use of direct address to camera –
give *Poor Cow* a distance from its subject which Loach's subsequent

151

feature films lack. Carol White's Joy is allowed to be sentimental, fey, unreliable, promiscuous, foolish, and the film comes close to banality at times. The sequence where Carol White and Terence Stamp make love under a waterfall looks like a shampoo commercial, but the sentimentality is the character's, not the film's, and makes sense as a nostalgically recalled moment of happiness in Joy's grim life.

At one point Joy tells us, 'All you need is a man and a baby and a couple of nice rooms to live in.' In reality she wants much more, but that basic right to health, happiness and prosperity, which is held tantalisingly beyond her grasp, permeates the film, imbuing it with an idealistic faith in humanity and society reminiscent of the films of Frank Capra and Frank Borzage. Combined with Brian Probyn's warm colour photography and Donovan's songs, this gives *Poor Cow* a back-streets romanticism, a neo-realist populism, rarely seen in British films.

Love in the City

A surprising number of films at this time centred on the problems of being a woman in Britain in the late 60s. If *Poor Cow* showed life to be often grim for a working-class girl, the leisured life of a Chelsea art student shown in Mike Sarne's *Joanna* (1968) also had its ups and downs. Swinging London films are often handicapped by the worthlessness of their characters. Genevieve Waite's Joanna, with her little-girl voice and her gawky charm, failed to win over most of the critics, and coy eyebrows were raised in American reviews about the film's unquestioning acceptance of a sexual relationship between a white magistrate's daughter and a black nightclub owner.[23] Joanna is ostensibly part of the Chelsea Set (indeed, Sarne's comments on the film make it sound like a remake of *The Party's Over*), but the non-English cast (Waite, a South African, Donald Sutherland, Christian Doermer, Calvin Lockhart, Glenna Forster-Jones) save it from the parochial indulgence one might have expected.[24]

Joanna, her head stuffed with fantasies and nightmares, is a refreshingly different heroine, her promiscuity implying neither a desperate need of men nor an out-of-control sexuality. When Cas, her art lecturer (Christian Doermer), remarks, 'I think the only thing women's emancipation has meant is the freedom to get laid', he seems to be passing judgment less on her sleeping around than on the restless seeking after thrills which prevents her making any proper commitment to life, work or art. Unlike Julie Christie's Diana, Joanna is not ambitious or unscrupulous, and she ends the film happily 'committed' to a handsome, cultivated African (Calvin Lockhart) who has been found guilty of murder and sent down for ten years.

The concept of Swinging London was constantly under attack, but it could still be argued that London really *was* an exciting place to be.

'The world of artists and criminals and the idle, aimless society which makes up the metropolitan scene.' Christian Doermer, Genevieve Waite, *Joanna*

An article in *Town* magazine, for example, introducing 'London's Other Underground', asserted:

> Today, creative people in New York and Paris look with envy at London. The stale, over-worked myth of Swinging London, that PR man's dream, has been exploded. Peer at London a little more closely and you will see a new reality – London as a focal city for permissive experiments in literature, art, film, theatre, music and any of those in permutation with each other.[25]

Joanna captures some of this excitement. It is ludicrously portentous at times, with Donald Sutherland's stricken English lord stuttering out moral homilies while watching the Moroccan sun go down or dying in a grainy black-and-white hospital ward. But this is more than redeemed by Sarne's original and interesting conception of life in London in the late 60s, and his sense in allowing Walter Lassally an unprecedented degree of freedom in experimenting with photographic styles to bring this world to life. Visually the film is unparalleled in making London look like a beautiful city.[26]

Joanna was mercilessly attacked by the critics, and there were no further attempts to celebrate London as a swinging city. Most late-60s films which dealt with romance did so with a mixture of sentimentality and tart realism.[27] Kevin Billington's *Interlude* (1968) relied on a plot, about a girl falling in love with a married orchestral conductor, which won praise and blame as a sort of *Brief Encounter* for the 60s. Billington makes good use of locations – the back corridors and poky studios of the BBC, the untidy editorial floor of the *Evening Standard*, the vast empty spaces of the Albert Hall auditorium – and the peripheral characters, particularly John Cleese's PR man with ambitions to be a satirist and Donald Sutherland's adulterous 'tower of weakness', are likeably idiosyncratic. But the film stands or falls on the relationship between Stefan (Oskar Werner), the famous conductor, and Sally (Barbara Ferris), the *Evening Standard* reporter who revitalises his atrophied emotional life.[28]

The relationship between a materially rich, emotionally impover-ished middle-aged man and a spontaneous, vulnerable, sexually willing

Divided loyalties: Oskar Werner dines with his mistress (Barbara Ferris) and his wife (Virginia Maskell) in *Interlude*

young woman is a common theme in 60s British cinema. (Six films released in 1969 – *Three into Two Won't Go*, d. Peter Hall; *All the Right Noises*, d. Gerry O'Hara; *Twinky*, d. Richard Donner; *One Brief Summer*, d. John Mackenzie; *Age of Consent*, d. Michael Powell; and the Norman Wisdom comedy, *What's Good for the Goose*, d. Menaham Golan – have this as their main subject.) Beneath the clichés – the all-too-brief holiday by the sea, the confrontation with the long-suffering wife, the chance meeting years after the affair is over – *Interlude* is refreshingly unsentimental. Virginia Maskell (who had committed suicide by the time the film was released) puts in a fine performance as Stefan's upper-middle class wife, emotionally winded by the prospect of her husband leaving her for a Cockney guttersnipe who drives a red Mini and doesn't know her Berlioz from her Bartok. But her plight becomes increasingly irrelevant. Sally and Stefan try to do the decent thing by her, but when it comes to deciding whether to stay together they both ignore her feelings and concentrate on whether they could make a life together. Stefan recognises that the emotional warmth he gains from Sally is worth more than the cold respectability of his marriage. But it is Sally who decides their fate. Her truculently pragmatic 'Why should I share your life when I used to have one of my own?' picks up on the marginalisation of her identity we have witnessed throughout the film as she sinks under her famous lover's shadow, and asserts the need for independence and respect within a relationship.

A Touch of Love (1969, directed by Waris Hussein from Margaret Drabble's novel *The Millstone*) and Desmond Davis's *A Nice Girl Like Me* (1969) also centre on independently-minded women, but concentrate more on their problems with babies than on the romantic entanglements which brought them into being. *A Touch of Love* lurches between light comedy and gloomy melodrama, but its unromantic picture of the trials and tribulations of pregnancy – the long waits in dingy clinics and crowded surgeries, the indignity of intimate examinations, the indifference to pain and discomfort of harassed, poorly paid hospital staff – is nicely realised. By contrast, in *A Nice Girl Like Me* babies are produced with bewildering ease and the film's lyrical, soft-focus view of life is at times irritatingly coy.[29] However, the romance between gruff Harry Andrews and flighty but warm-hearted Barbara Ferris is well-handled, and the supporting cast (Fabia Drake, Gladys Cooper, Joyce Carey, James Villiers, even the grubby, badly behaved babies) bring the film to life.[30]

Both films eschew conventional views of Swinging London. In *A Touch of Love*, Rosamund (Sandy Dennis) lives in her absent parents' flat in a red-brick block off the Marylebone Road, middle-class but not even slightly swinging, and within walking distance of the British Museum Reading Room where she is working on her Ph.D thesis. The

155

pubs are full of BBC people (the unwitting father of the baby is a television announcer), but they are an unfashionable-looking lot and only the proximity of Regent's Park and the Post Office Tower poking its way into the background remind us of that other, trendier, London. Candida (Barbara Ferris) in *A Nice Girl Like Me* leaves her maiden aunt's country cottage to have her first baby in her dead father's house along the Embankment, but for all Manny Wynn's lush photography there is no danger of her joining the Chelsea Set. Davis, enterprisingly if not wholly successfully, moves from the slapstick of *Smashing Time* to a brave attempt at screwball comedy, concentrating on the confusions, discomforts and misapprehensions generated by his ruled-by-emotion heroine, who collects another two children before humiliating and rejecting the glass-eyed suitor (James Villiers) who could retrieve her for polite society, and settling for old but good-with-animals-and-children Harry Andrews.

The Sense of an Ending
If 1967 was the 'summer of love', 1968 was the year of expected revolution. Jeff Nuttall in the preface to *Bomb Culture* apocalyptically declared that 'the plain and obvious fact is that between the autumn of '67 when I completed this manuscript, and the summer of '68 when I am writing this preface, young people under various pretexts made war on their elders, and their elders made war on them. The war continues.'[31] In fact, the demonstrations and sit-ins proved to be echoes of events occurring elsewhere and the shockwaves of America's disastrous war in Vietnam. But a handful of British films were touched by the whiff of revolution.

Peter Watkins had made a brilliant, controversial film for the BBC, *Culloden* (1964), using television investigative methods of presentation to probe an important historical event – the pitched battle which ended Bonnie Prince Charlie's attempt on the English throne. It was a technique pioneered in the American TV series *You Are There* in the 1950s, but the limitations of television studio technology inevitably lent an air of make-believe to the procedures. Watkins, using a huge cast of non-actors, and *cinéma vérité* techniques, was able to create a world which looked shockingly real. A year later he tried the same technique to explore a Britain of the not too distant future suffering the ravages of nuclear war. *The War Game* (1965) was considered by the BBC governors too disturbing for a television audience and the film was shelved (though allowed a limited theatrical release through the British Film Institute) until 1985. Watkins, understandably, resigned from the BBC in protest. *Privilege* was his first feature film and again looks to the near future when a pop star, Steven Shorter (Paul Jones, who had been the lead singer with the Manfred Mann band), is manipulated into being the tool of a repressive government.

156

Most critics were derisive (only Nina Hibbin in the *Morning Star* was unreservedly favourable), and admittedly on a first viewing *Privilege* does seem amateurish, poorly timed and simplistic. But once one's expectations have been suspended and one stops looking for the cathartic shocks of *Culloden* and *The War Game*, it is possible to see Watkins's film as refreshingly original. Paul Jones and Jean Shrimpton act like petulant three-year-olds – Steven's most successful blow against the system is at a dinner party where he sulkily blackmails everyone into drinking hot chocolate rather than wine with their oysters – but Watkins does distance himself from this glum couple and the film is crammed with bizarrely effective caricatures. Max Bacon's greedy, grasping, oddly human record company executive is as impressive in his way as Meir Tzelniker's less schmaltzy equivalent in *Expresso Bongo*. And Steven's hangers-on are a convincingly repulsive bunch, from the non-stop pattering American PR man to the little bodyguard, 'five foot eleven inches in uplift boots', who bounces on Jean Shrimpton's bed in the forlorn hope that she'll join him.

The combination of Watkins's own experience at the BBC (where his status changed rapidly from golden boy to outcast) and the increasingly apocalyptic spirit of the late 60s works to make the film seem hysterical and not always convincing. The ending, where the public, having meekly accepted Steven's conversion from licensed rebel to ultra-conformist, turn on him angrily when he stutters out his demand to be treated as a person, seems to endorse his manager's view of them as 'stunted little creatures with primitive emotions' which have to be harnessed for their own good.[32] But the attack on born-again Christianity (celebrated two years later in Mary Whitehouse and Malcolm Muggeridge's Festival of Light), with a bevy of bishops encouraging a pop group in monks' cowls to grind their way through 'Onward Christian Soldiers', has a bite which makes most 60s satire look like pillow-fighting. As the film's sole supporter in the national press suggested: 'Perhaps the real reason for the blind-spot reaction is that unlike most prophetic fantasies ... it doesn't perform the trendy trick of pin-pricking the Establishment. It bashes away at it with wounding blows, and there are some who prefer not to look.'[33]

Poor critical reception meant that Rank executives, who found the film offensive, needed little excuse for giving it only a limited release.[34] Memorial Enterprises, the company set up by Albert Finney and Michael Medwin which had initiated *Privilege* for Universal, needed considerable courage to persevere with Lindsay Anderson's equally controversial *If....* (1968), but fortunately George Ornstein, by the late 60s Paramount's production chief in London, had sufficient faith in Anderson's ability as a director to back the film. Anderson was keen to point out that *If....* was not just about public schools, describing it as 'a metaphor, if you like, of life in Britain today – the image of the school as a reflection of a certain British tradition.'[35] If one accepts this, the film's view is a bleak one. Whatever virtues the public school ethos once embodied, here it is in a state of advanced decay. The housemaster (Arthur Lowe) is bumblingly ineffectual, the headmaster (Peter Jeffrey) more interested in business management than Greek grammar, and real power is in the hands of a triumvirate of prefects, forerunners of the 'young fogies' of Thatcherism. They are opposed by proto-revolutionary Mick Travers (Malcolm McDowell), but the violence he is provoked into using by their mindless authoritarianism is indiscriminate and seemingly futile.

David Robinson reported while *If. . . .*was being made that 'despite the passages of slow motion, the satire, the fantasy, it is predictable that the film will have little relation to the current school of modish, geary, swinging post-TV cinema.'[36] Anderson's use of colour and black and white seems to obey a not always comprehensible logic, but nobody could accuse him of following someone else's trend. *If. . . .* is as bravely idiosyncratic as any other Anderson film, but Mick Travers – enigmatic but passionate, scruffy but glamorous – was a perfect symbol for the aspiring revolutionaries of 1968, just as David Warner's Morgan Delt had been in 1966 for future hippies, and as with *Morgan*, the film was an unexpected box-office success.

From its opening titles it is apparent that *The Breaking of Bumbo* (1970) is one of David Puttnam and Alan Parker's despised 'red London bus movies' (though it was never released in the cinema). As well as the ubiquitous red buses, the film's plot seems improbable and its views of Swinging London grinding to a halt amid student demonstrators and bottle-throwing skinheads shoddily unconvincing. It comes as a surprise, then, to discover that it is based on a good novel written ten years earlier by the film's director, Andrew Sinclair. Some of the dialogue survives the transfer from book to film, and Richard Warwick (McDowell's second-in-command in *If. . . .*) is an amiable enough Bumbo. The main problem, apart from Sinclair's uncertain direction, is that Bumbo is a 1950s figure (in the novel he is a guards officer who tries to start a mutiny in protest over Suez), and the idea of transposing him to a late-60s London of demonstrations, sit-ins and student revolutionaries, ingenious though it might have looked on paper, simply doesn't work. In 1956 Bumbo was a precursor of those upper-middle class young men whose lives were changed by the revelation that assumptions and institutions they had been brought up to think sacred could be questioned, even laughed at. In 1968 he merely looks like a not very bright Hooray Henry torn between the arrogant exclusiveness of life as a guards officer and the decadent temptations of Swinging London. What might have been a powerful liberal riposte to the celebration of traditional values in Michael Powell's *The Queen's Guards* proves to be embarrassingly inconsequential.

158

Revolutionary politics: *Praise Marx and Pass the Ammunition*

Radical politics are explored from a more plebeian point of view in Maurice Hatton's *Praise Marx and Pass the Ammunition* (1970). John Thaw's Dom is a full-time Trotskyist activist dedicated to permanent revolution, though his world is confined to tiny left-wing splinter groups and the peripheries of industrial disputes. Thaw had been one of the Borstal boys in *The Loneliness of the Long Distance Runner* and went on to play likeable tricksters in 'B' films like *Five to One* (1963, d. Gordon Flemyng) and *Dead Man's Chest* (1965, d. Patrick Dromgoole) before finding fame alongside Dennis Waterman in the television series *The Sweeney*. In essence, Dom is Colin Smith grown up and crossed with Morgan Delt to become a happily self-deluded class warrior, less concerned with storming the citadels of capitalism than with capturing the daughters of the bourgeoisie for political re-education in his bed.

Dom's hunting ground is the seedy, run-down London of the late 60s which is also displayed, cheerfully, in Dick Clement's *Otley* (1968), whimsically in John Boorman's *Leo the Last*, and luridly in Donald Cammell and Nicolas Roeg's *Performance* (1969), where it is a saturnalia presided over by sadistic gangsters and decadent pop stars. With the rise of television-trained directors like Kevin Billington, Waris Hussein, Jack Gold, John Mackenzie – as well as Loach, Collinson, Boorman and Schlesinger – there was a movement towards greater realism and more solidly substantial subjects. But alongside this there were excursions into fantasy, into private interior worlds, evident in

Performance but also in Losey's *Secret Ceremony* (1967), Albert Finney's *Charlie Bubbles* (1967), Peter Medak's *Negatives* (1969) and comedies like *Work is a Four-Letter Word* (1967, d. Peter Hall) and *The Bliss of Mrs Blossom* (1968, d. Joe McGrath). In 1969 Eric Rhode went so far as to claim that:

> The dominant note of films in the 1960s has been their exploitation of fantasy – not the sort of fantasy that underlies thought and behaviour but the kind of fantasy that denies the truths of perception and feeling. As in commercials, this kind of fantasy is intended to induce a state of ease. We have seen the First World War turned into a superior musical and the Crimean conflict reduced to phantasmagoria. James Bond and Alf Garnett have been our national heroes and swinging London our cloud-cuckoo land. . . . There has been a steady evacuation of social content and social meaning: brightness and caricature dance in a void.[37]

Such jeremiads were not uncommon from British film critics in the 60s, and on a wider social level the theme was amplified in Christopher Booker's extraordinary book *The Neophiliacs*, which sees the period from the mid-50s to the late-60s as dominated by a collective nightmarish fantasy. In life the difference between fantasy and reality is crucial even if it is something which has to be constantly negotiated. In film the difference is merely one of convention, and for a brief period in the 60s even the most basic conventions (not looking at the camera, correctly exposing the film, telling stories with beginnings, middles and ends) came under siege. The fear of hedonistic excess which pervades Booker's account finds an equivalent in Rhode's distrust of stylistic experimentation. But in Britain the 'distortion' of reality in mainstream cinema now seems moderate and undisturbing, and the critical diatribes as irrational as seventeenth-century religious broadsheets.

When Eric Rhode complains about a fantasy-ridden cinema, he directs his attack at films which present a view of contemporary life he thinks of as misleading and unauthentic. Fantasy films which deliberately delve into an unreal world, in particular Hammer's horror films, were considered beneath contempt by Rhode and most of his fellow critics.

8

OTHER WORLDS

In Britain, horror has developed into a new film genre, with its own conventions and its own styles. There is much talk of 'Free Cinema'. But with its power of suggestion, its fits of madness, its invitation to travel in a land of dark wonders and erotic fantasy, isn't the real Free Cinema the free cinema of the British horror film? (Jean-Paul Török, *Positif*, 1961)[1]

Frankenstein Has Risen from the Grave

In 1973, ironically the last year in which British horror films could claim an international audience, Dave Pirie's *A Heritage of Horror* was published. Pirie argued that 'on commercial, historical and artistic grounds the horror genre, as it has been developed in this country by Hammer and its rivals, remains the only staple cinematic myth which Britain can claim as its own and which relates to it in the same way as the Western relates to America.'[2] Pirie's book was the first, and still the most important, attempt to give serious consideration to Hammer's horror films. Hammer was founded as a distribution company in the 1930s by Enrique Carreras and Will Hinds (whose stage name was Will Hammer). In the late 1940s the company turned to film production, enterprisingly adapting popular radio series like *Dick Barton* and *PC 49* and importing minor Hollywood stars to make its films acceptable in the American market. Starting at a time when many studios were still requisitioned and the price of the remaining space was very high, Hammer found it cheaper to take over a large country house – austerity reached even the very rich in the 40s – and in 1951 settled at Down Place, Bray in Buckinghamshire, where it remained for the next fifteen years. In 1955 the company adapted BBC television's highly successful science-fiction series, *The Quatermass Experiment*. Lawrence Alloway, in a short but perceptive article in *Encounter*, pointed out that 'Almost all so-called "science fiction" films are in fact monster films, with their

161

roots in Mary Shelley and Bram Stoker, not in 20th-century tech-nology (which is the core of modern science fiction).'[3] It was a conclu-sion that James Carreras, Hammer's commercially astute managing director, had already come to, and after making two *Quatermass* sequels he turned back to Mary Shelley's Gothic tale, *Frankenstein*.

The Curse of Frankenstein (1957) was made for around £65,000 and grossed around £300,000 in Britain, £500,000 in Japan and more than £1 million in America.[4] Thus it was hardly surprising that it should launch a whole cycle of Gothic horror films. What is surprising is the success with which Hammer managed to sustain this cycle over a period of fifteen years. Hammer – like Gainsborough, Ealing and Merton Park – was a small studio where the same technicians, direc-tors, even actors, worked regularly and closely together, and the colla-borative nature of their films is apparent. The contributions of com-poser James Bernard, writers Jimmy Sangster and Anthony Hinds, editor James Needs, cinematographers Jack Asher and Arthur Grant and production designer Bernard Robinson were crucial to the success of Hammer's films, but it is difficult to imagine the cycle being as interesting and consistent over such a period without Terence Fisher.[5]

Fisher is by no means as inventive and creative a director as Powell or Mackendrick, but he has a distinct style and a clearly thought out view of the world. He had served a thorough apprenticeship as an editor and co-directed two of the best of the late Gainsborough films, *So Long at the Fair* and *The Astonished Heart*, before beginning his long association with Hammer. Some of the low-budget films he made in the 50s, such as *The Four-Sided Triangle* and *The Stolen Face*, are interesting, but his status as a major director rests on the seventeen horror films he made between 1957 and 1972.[6]

In view of the 'sensational' subject matter of these films it is hardly surprising that Fisher has suffered more than any other important British director from the short-sighted dilettantism of British film culture. While French critics expressed their gratitude at his skill and intelligence in reviving the old myths of horror, in Britain he was dismissed as either a vulgar desecrator of the Universal classics who sacrificed atmosphere and subtlety for grossness and gore or – contra-dictorily – as a banal and colourless director whose lack of imagination meant he was ill-qualified to handle supernatural themes. Such lack of judgment is perhaps only to be expected from the watered-down Bloomsbury ethos of the critical establishment, but it is ironic that, as Dave Pirie puts it, a director whose films 'unlike [those of] almost any other director working in the British commercial cinema . . . appear to embody a recognisable and coherent *Weltanschauung*' should have mer-ited only derogatory comment in *Movie* and that there is no book-length study of his work.[7]

Fisher's Gothic films are less exotic than their UFA and Universal

Cushing's Frankenstein: a severe rationalist rather than a wild-eyed romantic.
The Curse of Frankenstein

predecessors. Peter Cushing's Baron Frankenstein is an Enlighten-
ment scholar, a severe rationalist rather than a wild-eyed romantic,
while Christopher Lee's Count Dracula has more in common with the
sadistic aristocrats played by James Mason in the Gainsborough melodramas than he does with puffy, evil-eyed Bela Lugosi. Fantastic
shadows, bizarre settings, melodramatic exaggeration are replaced by
urbanity and restraint only occasionally disrupted by shocking images
of bodies pierced by wooden stakes, mouths dripping blood, naked
brains, severed limbs. Fisher's technique is almost pedantically disciplined. As he explained:

163

Most of what I learned filmwise was in the cutting rooms. That gives
you a great sense of the pattern of the film, the overall rhythm. This
dramatic rhythm is the basis of technique, of style. For example,
I've always involved the monster in the frame, placed him in the
decor. I've never used the conventional style, where you keep harp-
ing on reaction shots and cutting away from him. I believe in building things up naturally, but I've never *isolated* the monster from the
world around, or tried to avoid showing him.'[8]

The Curse of Frankenstein is characterised by mordant realism and dark
humour rather than macabre symbolism and expressionist excess.
Frankenstein operates on his corpses quickly and efficiently in a well-
worn, blood-stained dinner jacket, and the moment when the spark of
life enters the monster – the climax of James Whale's *Frankenstein* –
happens almost casually in Fisher's film, when Frankenstein is out of
the room. Cushing's Frankenstein, sexually active and almost Bond-
like in his casual use (and disposal) of women, sets a tone altogether
new to the horror film and to British cinema.

The ethos of realism which was to be so important to the British new
Wave is unexpectedly evident at Hammer. Bernard Robinson's production design is suitably atmospheric, but his sets are essentially solid
and realistic. His castles and graveyards are eerie enough, but there is
no trace of the cobwebs, spiders, rats, owls and toads which figured so
prominently in traditional horror films. The threatening shadows and
disorienting camera angles which are the legacy of the German expressionist films of the 1930s were disowned by Hammer. Colour imposed
a different set of values. Floyd Crosby, Roger Corman's cameraman on
his Edgar Allan Poe films, bathes his characters in coloured light and
obscures the semi-abstract sets in mists and shadows, but Hammer's
cameramen were more cautious. Jack Asher's photography in *The
Curse of Frankenstein* is restrained and muted, with only the guillotine
silhouetted against a purple sky at the end to indicate his penchant for
colour effects.[9] In subsequent films – mostly shot on more expensive
and less garish Technicolor – Asher allowed himself a freer rein, and
though never disrupting the underplayed realism of Fisher's *mise en
scène* his Gothic films are enriched by visually striking sequences: the
Count descending the castle staircase to make his sinister yet perfectly
naturalistic entrance in *Dracula*; Freda Jackson clawing at the earth to
help an undead corpse rise from its grave in *The Brides of Dracula*; the
slime-encrusted Mummy disappearing into a sea of green and purple
and blue and orange mud in *The Mummy*; the cruel reds and blacks of
the fire-, torch- and candle-lit prologue to *The Hound of the Baskervilles*.

Arthur Grant, who took over from Asher as Hammer's regular
cameraman in 1961, was best known for his black and white location

photography on Group 3 films like *The Brave Don't Cry*, *Background* and *The End of the Road* and his evocations of Manchester, Brighton and Bath in Val Guest's *Hell is a City*, *Jigsaw* and *80,000 Suspects*. His Gothic films marked a return to a more natural use of colour. *The Curse of the Werewolf*, for example, despite Richard Wordsworth's only half-human beggar, Anthony Dawson's decaying lord and Oliver Reed's anguished werewolf, has a brightness and clarity which matches well with Anthony Hinds's fairytale-like script.

Of Hammer's two main scriptwriters, Jimmy Sangster (*The Curse of Frankenstein*, *Dracula*, *The Revenge of Frankenstein*, *The Mummy*, *The Man Who Could Cheat Death*, *The Terror of the Tongs*, *Devil Ship Pirates*) creates plots which are almost too neatly well-rounded, with the dovetailing of detail leaving little time for the messiness of human relationships. *The Curse of Frankenstein* begins with Frankenstein in the death cell desperately trying to convince a priest of the truth of his tale; it ends with the monster disappearing into a vat of acid and Frankenstein's friend and fiancée colluding to deny that it ever existed. *The Revenge of Frankenstein* begins with Frankenstein escaping the guillotine and setting up practice in Carlsbruck as Dr Stein; it ends with Frankenstein, his brain now housed in a new body – in effect becoming his own monster – setting up in London as Dr Franck. Sangster's *Dracula* has little of the epic sweep of Bram Stoker's novel with its range of narrators and its movement from the Carpathians to Whitby and Sussex, and it is determinedly unmystical. Van Helsing uses crucifixes and garlic flowers as tangible weapons, not as symbols, records his notes on a phonograph (it is Dr Seward who does this in the book), and explains to Michael Gough that the idea that vampires can turn into bats or wolves is 'a common misapprehension'. In a brilliant sequence Sangster wrote to dispense with the elaborate business of Carfax and the adjacent lunatic asylum, Mina (Melissa Stribling), the very image of a respectable Victorian housewife, is summoned to an undertaker's and seduced by Dracula. She is found out when her husband and Van Helsing try to make her wear a crucifix, but what they fail to realise is that she has secreted Dracula's coffin in the wine cellar. That night Mina receives her vampire lover in her bedroom while her husband and Van Helsing patrol the grounds outside.

By the time of *The Brides of Dracula* (1960) Sangster's enthusiasm for Gothic horror was obviously flagging, and two other writers, Peter Bryan and Edward Percy, were brought in to help out. In contrast to the reckless confidence of Van Helsing's pronouncements on vampire lore in *Dracula*, here there are dull pedantic passages of exposition about the habits of vampires which then turn out to be contradictory. What saves the film is its magnificent climax which – except for the surprise of Van Helsing getting (and surviving) a full-blooded vampire bite – owes little to the script and everything to Robinson's atmospheric but realistic sets, Asher's photography (particularly the hissing vampire girls in their white death robes), Malcolm Williamson's score (with its intimations of a religious ceremony), and Fisher's direction.

Under the influence of Hitchcock's *Psycho*, Sangster turned to writing intricately plotted thrillers and his Gothic mantle was assumed by 'John Elder', a pseudonym used by Anthony Hinds, who had followed his father into the company. Hinds's scripts are looser and less contrived but more sentimental in their insistence on including a love relationship. The young couples he introduces into his scripts are sometimes insipid, but they add a human dimension lacking in the cold sardonic world evoked in Sangster's scripts. In *The Curse of the Werewolf* (1962), for example (based very loosely on Guy Endore's *The Werewolf of Paris*), the love affair between Léon (Oliver Reed) and Cristina (Catherine Feller) is essential to the plot. The whore who tries to introduce Léon to sex without love changes the shy, mild-mannered young man into a murderous animal, while Cristina, by her selfless devotion, is able to prevent his transformation even at the height of the full moon. In *The Kiss of the Vampire* the very smugness of the relationship of its honeymooning couple, Gerald and Marianne Harcourt (Edward de Souza and Jennifer Daniel), makes more intriguing Marianne's seduction into a family of sophisticated vampires who reject Gerald as an uncouth boor. In *The Phantom of the Opera* and *The Evil of Frankenstein* pathetic monsters (Herbert Lom/Kiwi Kingston) find some sort of solace in the kindness of a vulnerable girl (Heather Sears/ Katy Wilde), and in Hinds's best script – *Frankenstein Created Woman* – the situation is reversed, with Frankenstein's handsome young assistant in love with the deformed girl whom Frankenstein subsequently recreates as a beautiful man-killing monster.

The Tempestuous Loveliness of Terror

Hammer's films were treated with contempt by most film critics. The severed limbs, the callous amorality of the Frankenstein films, the frailty of human bodies, the surfacing sexuality of the vampire films, must have been disturbing to a generation brought up on *The Baby and the Battleship* and *Doctor in the House*, and the critics tried to preserve the cosy ethos espoused by such films by keeping horror films beyond the pale.

Derek Hill's article 'The Face of Horror', written for *Sight and Sound* in 1960, neatly sums up the prevailing prejudices. Hill sees horror films as a symptom of a sick society which in a vicious spiral reinforce that sickness. Accordingly, 'Every horror film cycle has coincided with economic depression or war. Now we have the biggest, ugliest threat of them all, and a bigger, uglier horror boom than ever before.'[10] The attempt to link what is happening in society to the themes and motifs of contemporary films (undertaken by Siegfried

Kracauer in *From Caligari to Hitler* and Robin Wood in *American Nightmare*) is laudable enough, but from Hill's opening sentence – 'Only a sick society could bear the hoardings, let alone the films' – it is apparent that he has little useful to say about films or society.

The other main argument deployed by Hill is that Hammer and the other British horror film-makers break all the rules which a 'proper' horror film should obey:

> The power of suggestion, the greatest tool of the vintage horror film, was abandoned. Instead, the screen began to concentrate on revolting close ups. ... Instead of attempting mood, tension or shock, the new Frankenstein productions rely almost entirely on a percentage of shots of repugnant clinical detail. There is little to frighten in *The Curse of Frankenstein* or *The Revenge of Frankenstein*, but plenty to disgust.[11]

The argument that horror should be a matter of hints and suggestions had respectable antecedents, having been used by Burke and Coleridge to differentiate between good and bad Romantic literature. Coleridge, for example, wrote of the later Gothic novels:

> Situations of torment, and images of naked horror, are easily conceived; and a writer in whose works they abound deserves our gratitude almost equally with him who should drag us by way of sport through a military hospital, or force us to sit at the dissection table of a natural philosopher. ... Figures that shock the imagination, and narratives that mangle the feelings, rarely discover *genius*, and always betray a low and vulgar taste.[12]

Pirie quotes Mario Praz and Devendra Varma to re-evaluate the once-despised *Schauer-Romantik* school of literature, with its celebration of 'the grotesque power of something ghastly too vividly imprinted on the mind and the sense'.[13] Lawrence Alloway in his 'Monster Films' article – a well-argued riposte to Hill – expresses the exasperated impatience of the horror film enthusiast:

> It is pointless to expect classic forms of suspense to be built up by hints and implications while the monster is delayed, as in literary ghost stories. The reason for making and witnessing monster films is the visibility of the monster, the damage to persons and property, the suggestion of rape as the monster carries off the girl. Unlike the discreet forms of ghost story, shock, astonishment, fear, are the product of the monster parade. ... The emphasis in these films is on the body as a package, which can be opened. What we find fills us with awe and horror. Death both repels and rouses, and monster

films exploit the ambiguities of repulsion and curiosity. . . . These films are an imagery, both fantastic and highly conventional, of what happens to flesh, of the fate of being a body.[14]

Hammer was unconcerned by the attacks of the critics as long as box-office receipts remained high. After the phenomenal success of *The Curse of Frankenstein*, American companies willingly entered into distribution deals with Hammer for their future projects.[15] Universal, which had threatened legal action over *The Curse of Frankenstein*, backed Hammer's remake of *Dracula* and, when it proved even more popular than *The Curse of Frankenstein*, offered Hammer the remake rights to all their 1930s horror films. Ironically, *The Mummy*, *The Old Dark House*, *The Man Who Could Cheat Death*, *The Two Faces of Dr Jekyll* and *The Curse of the Werewolf* proved only modestly successful, and the last in this series of films, an expensive remake of the old and much filmed melodrama *The Phantom of the Opera* (1962), proved a costly flop.

In earlier versions the Phantom, whatever the wrongs done to him, was mad, bad and vicious. In Fisher's film he is dangerous only in his desire to protect his secret existence and, despite his horrific appearance, which we barely glimpse, is still sensitive enough to be moved to tears by the heroine singing. Critics who had condemned Hammer for its supposed emphasis on gruesome horror were lukewarm in supporting this reinterpretation of the old melodrama as a romantic love story, and cinemagoers who had come to see a horror film were disappointed by its lack of thrills. The harmonious relationship which Fisher had established with Hammer was disrupted by the film's box-office failure, and while Fisher went to Germany to make *Sherlock Holmes und das Halsband des Todes*, new directors were brought in to make the next two ventures into horror.

Despite the failure of *The Phantom of the Opera*, the quality of Hammer's Gothic films remained remarkably constant until the end of the decade, and Don Sharp's *The Kiss of the Vampire* (1962) and Freddie Francis's *The Evil of Frankenstein* (1963) very much fall within the parameters Fisher had set. In Francis's film the main weakness is the monster itself, which Hammer unwisely based on the original Karloff monster of the 30s. As the creation of Cushing's neat, rationalist Frankenstein its expressionist excesses look totally out of place, and this has led the film to be dismissed even by perceptive critics like Pirie. But where one might have expected a degeneration into crudity there is, at worst, misplaced pathos. In contrast to the dull but calculating women of the Sangster films, Anthony Hinds creates a heroine (Katy Wilde) who is a sympathetic female 'monster'. Unfortunately her role is largely decorative, but there is an eerily effective sequence wherein Frankenstein finds her jabbering happily to his long-lost crea-

Society of vampires: Isobel Black, Jennifer Daniel, Jacqueline Wallis in *The Kiss of the Vampire*

ture, who has been miraculously preserved in the ice. Frankenstein himself is less compelling but more sympathetic than in the earlier films. Set against the greed and stupidity of everyone around him ('Anything they don't understand, anything that doesn't conform with their stupid little pattern they destroy!'), his unhealthy obsession pales into insignificance and he assumes an almost godlike guise as the persecuted man of science.

The Brides of Dracula had succeeded reasonably well in pitting Van Helsing against a minor disciple of Dracula, Baron Meinster (David Peel). *The Kiss of the Vampire* boldly dispensed with both Dracula and Van Helsing, teaming a young and rather inadequate hero with an older, wiser but by no means infallible vampire-hunter. Don Sharp's style, with its fluid camera and frequent dissolves, is more like Roger Corman's than Terence Fisher's, and he is helped by James Bernard's uncharacteristically lush and melodramatic score. But where Corman's films have a baroque richness about them, *The Kiss of the Vampire* is cold and bleak. The hero (Edward de Souza) and his young wife lodge in an almost deserted hotel presided over by Peter Madden, most gaunt and gloomy of Hammer's character actors, and the vampire-hunter, Professor Zimmer (Clifford Evans), is a brandy-soaked depressive whose tattered clothes and wild eye immediately offend the hero's English sensibilities ('Don't worry, darling, he's been drinking,' he tells his wife when Zimmer tries to warn them of their peril). The

169

vampires, by contrast, are impeccably civilised, morbid aesthetes rather than monsters, and their destruction at the end by a horde of bats carries the thrill of a vengeful popular uprising.

When Fisher returned to Hammer, he seems to have done so very much on his own terms. His next film for the studio, *The Gorgon* (1964; photographed by Michael Reed and scripted by John Gilling), was in the same vein as *The Curse of the Werewolf* and *The Phantom of the Opera*, dealing with mystery and romance rather than horror. It is obvious early on in the film that there is some link between the Gorgon and Dr Namaroff's assistant Carla (Barbara Shelley), but it takes three male investigators to discover exactly what it is and by that time one of them (Michael Goodliffe) has been turned to stone, another (Richard Pasco) has fallen in love with Carla and refuses to believe the truth, and it is left to the third (Christopher Lee) to bring matters to a close. The woebegone appearance of the Gorgon herself is disappointing, but the turning-to-stone sequences – which rely as much on the performances of Michael Goodliffe and Richard Pasco as on make-up – are very effective. Perhaps because of the conflicting interests of Gilling and Fisher, the love triangle between Barbara Shelley, Richard Pasco and Cushing's Dr Namaroff (as subtle as any of his Frankenstein character-isations in balancing good and evil) is never allowed to develop the necessary depth and intensity, but it is an intriguing, complex film.[16]

Fisher's next film, *Dracula – Prince of Darkness* (1965), returned Christopher Lee to his Dracula role, but the story – by Anthony Hinds but based on a script written by Sangster in the late 50s – continues the strategy adopted in *The Kiss of the Vampire* of pairing a relatively colourless juvenile lead with a vampire-hunting character actor.[17] Un-fortunately, whereas Edward de Souza's smudgy charmlessness provided a useful foil to the icily civilised vampires and the disreputable Professor Zimmer, Francis Matthews's Charles Kent and Andrew Keir's Abbot Sandor are depressingly one-dimensional. Worse, Dracula is reduced from the omnipowerful embodiment of evil he had been in 1958 to a hissing nuisance, a jack-in-the-box who pushes aside his own disciple in an undignified scramble for a victim's blood, and makes an ignominious exit through a hole in the ice of his castle's moat. He is overshadowed by his own accomplices: Klove (Philip Latham), his butler who, with the efficiency of a malevolent Jeeves, cuts the throat of one of the bumbling English gentlemen who unwisely accept the late Count's hospitality and uses the blood to bring his master back to life; and Barbara Shelley's Helen, whose transform-ation from pinched, straitlaced English gentlewoman to ravening, voluptuous sex fiend is remarkable. Pirie argues strongly for accepting the film as an allegory of sexual repression, and the staking of Helen by Father Sandor and his monks is the most disturbing sequence in any of Fisher's films, but it is a difficult film to like.

1965 was Hammer's peak year as far as Gothic horror was concerned, with four films – *Dracula – Prince of Darkness, Rasputin, The Plague of the Zombies*, and *The Reptile* – produced in quick succession. Hammer's horror films had been so popular in the late 50s because they had seemed to bring excitement and colour into a dull, conformist society. By the mid-60s, in the wake of the 'new wave' and the 'youth revolution', things had changed. What had once been repressed and unspoken could now be represented openly. Films like *Alfie* and *Blow Up* made Fisher's fairytale world look increasingly tame. *Dracula – Prince of Darkness* went some way to accommodate the new climate with its throat-cutting ceremony and the staking/raping of Barbara Shelley. But the forces of good represented by Father Sandor are complacently confident in the face of the puny threat represented by Dracula, and the film's moral outlook is conservatively conventional. Don Sharp's *Rasputin* similarly seems to fall between two stools: presenting Rasputin as a sexually voracious nineteenth-century hippy but diverting sympathy from his unscrupulous vitality to the corrupt and stupid courtiers who murder him. John Gilling's sinister, moody films, *The Plague of the Zombies* and *The Reptile*, are more traditional but more satisfying.

The script for *The Plague of the Zombies* was written by Peter Bryan, who had also scripted Fisher's version of *The Hound of the Baskervilles*, and there are marked similarities between the two films. In both stories an eminent Victorian gentleman is asked to go to a remote and wild part of Western England to investigate deaths which seem to have some sort of supernatural cause. Pirie argues that Terence Fisher 'uses Conan Doyle's plot to establish a stylish dialectic between Holmes's nominally rational Victorian milieu and the dark fabulous cruelty behind the Baskerville legend.'[18] But the supernatural in *The Hound of the Baskervilles* is merely a trick, and the film ends with order and rationality restored. *The Plague of the Zombies* is more complex. Aristocratic viciousness is still at the root of the problem – Diane Clare is hunted down by red-coated horsemen, just as the peasant girl is in the prologue to *The Hound of the Baskervilles* – but here it combines with evil supernatural forces. Clive Hamilton (John Carson), the local squire, has returned from the West Indies with a knowledge of voodoo, which he uses to create zombies out of the Cornish villagers who are unwilling to work in his tin mine. Into the besieged, paranoid little community comes Sir James Forbes (André Morell, who had played Watson in *The Hound of the Baskervilles*), carrying with him the full weight of scientific rationality (even his pretty daughter – Diane Clare – is practical and independently minded). He is a comfortable, competent figure and his ultimate victory over the forces of darkness is even less in question than that of Sherlock Holmes. But whereas Holmes has to contend only with a madly embittered girl, the align-

171

Aristocratic viciousness: Diane Clare and the huntsmen, *The Plague of the Zombies*

ment of occult power, aristocratic ruthlessness and capitalist exploitation (the huntsmen double up as cruel, whip-yielding overseers in the mine) that Sir James finds himself up against is rather more formidable.

The Reptile is potentially as interesting as *The Plague of the Zombies*. It takes up a theme used in very early British horror films like *The Vampire* (1913) and *Heba the Snake Woman* (1915), of a woman whose involvement in mystic practices in the East results in her transformation into a dangerous snake. But here the action is staged in a mist-shrouded Cornwall where the Snake Woman is vulnerable to the cold and has to be carefully nurtured.[19] The cast is excellent: Noel Willman (who had played the morbidly sensitive Dr Ravna in *The Kiss of the Vampire*) as the Snake Woman's guilt-ridden father (it is his rather than her occult meddling which has caused her transformation); tough, pock-marked Ray Barrett and long-faced, mournfully beautiful Jennifer Daniel (who had been seduced by Dr Ravna in *Kiss of the Vampire*) as the newly-weds whose idyllic rural retreat turns into a nightmare of death and disaster; and Jacqueline Pearce, most sensual of Hammer heroines, as the Snake Woman. Unfortunately Hinds's script is hackneyed and poorly put together, and the rushed denouement – with Marne Maitland's sinister Oriental disposed of in a bubbling sulphur pool and the Snake Woman expiring from a gust of cold wind – has little of the cathartic impact of *Plague of the Zombies*.

John Gilling's record as a director is more patchy than Fisher's, and it is difficult to discern much of a pattern in his films. But in his first film for Hammer, *The Shadow of the Cat* (1961), he had demonstrated his ability to sustain atmosphere and create suspense, and his swash-bucklers – *The Bandit of Zhobe, Fury at Smugglers' Bay, The Pirates of Blood River, The Scarlet Blade, The Brigand of Kandahar* – show a strong, coherent sense of narrative. Pirie concludes that 'both *The Plague of the Zombies* and *The Reptile* are among the most deeply pessimistic films that Hammer have ever made. There is no sense of relief at the climax of either … and, though fire has purged the community of evil, a sense of shock prevails and the gloom remains unrelieved.'[20] The two films are certainly uncompromising – in neither case is any concession made to a happy end – but Gilling's heroes (André Morell, Ray Barrett) are too robust to get downhearted and, as in the films of Val Guest, disaster heightens rather than deadens the human spirit.

In *The Plague of the Zombies* and *The Reptile*, however, there is an additional element. The bizarre imagery captured by Arthur Grant's photography shows the forces of darkness as alluringly attractive. The transformation of Mrs Tompson (Jacqueline Pearce) from peaceful corpse to glaring-eyed zombie, Dr Tompson's green-tinged dream where the zombies rise from their graves, Dr Franklyn disgustedly beating at the nightgown and shrivelled skin left by his daughter when she hibernates for the winter, provide a contemporary equivalent to 'the tempestuous loveliness of terror' that Shelley found in a painting of the Medusa in the Uffizi Gallery: '… pleasure and pain are com-bined in one single impression. The very objects which should induce a shudder – the livid face of the severed head, the squirming mass of vipers, the rigidity of death, the sinister light, the repulsive animals, the lizard, the bat – all these give rise to a new sense of beauty, a beauty imperilled and contaminated, a new thrill.'[21]

The Last Days of Hammer
1965 was the last year Hammer's activities were concentrated on Bray. *Dracula – Prince of Darkness, Rasputin* and the two Gilling films were modestly successful but they had nothing like the impact of the early Hammer horrors, and with the 'Swinging London' scene erupting, the attention of the American companies was attracted to more fashionable and prestigious film-makers than Hammer. In 1966 James Carreras made a deal with ABPC, which agreed to provide financial backing for Hammer's films and distribution through Warner-Pathé, the company they jointly owned with Warner Brothers, in return for Hammer aban-doning Bray and making use of ABPC's under-utilised studio resources at Elstree. Apart from John Gilling's hurried and under-budgeted *The Mummy's Shroud*, the last Hammer film to be made at Bray was

Fisher's *Frankenstein Created Woman*. It was a project which had been announced in the early 60s as a vehicle for Brigitte Bardot and, adequate though Susan Denberg is, one can still regret the absence of Bardot from this dark fairytale of sexual revenge.

Like *The Evil of Frankenstein*, the film was scripted by Anthony Hinds, but *Frankenstein Created Woman* dispenses with the lumbering monster which had been the least satisfactory element of the earlier film and develops the role of the deformed, disfigured girl. The main action is tragic, but the submerged humour present in all Hammer's Frankenstein films is allowed nearer the surface. We first see Frankenstein as a deep-frozen corpse, and when he is miraculously revived he is a sharper, lighter, less obsessive character than we have come to expect. Teamed with St Trinian's veteran Thorley Walters (who had played Watson to Christopher Lee's Holmes in Fisher's *Sherlock Holmes und das Halsband des Todes*), he seems more like the wryly eccentric Victorian detective than the Faust-like figure of the earlier films. As in *The Evil of Frankenstein*, there is a faithful assistant, Hans (played here by Robert Morris in place of Sandor Eles), but here he is given more to do. Sent for champagne to celebrate the success of Frankenstein's experiment, he becomes embroiled in a fight with three upper-class wastrels and is framed for the murder of the innkeeper whose deformed daughter he loves. After a brief trial he is guillotined, and Christina (Susan Denberg), the innkeeper's daughter, is so overcome with grief that she drowns herself.

As Paul Willemen points out:

> The movie is structured as a pattern of symmetrical inversions and echoes. The first half starts with the double ritual of horror as a father is guillotined before the eyes of his son and then the son's decapitation is witnessed by his lover, while the second half, contained between Christina's two suicides by drowning, is punctuated by two rituals of pleasure as she seduces and gruesomely kills Hans's tormentors. These flamboyant explosions of violence mingled with pleasure and death are bound together by the Baron's calm but relentless experimentation.[22]

Frankenstein acts like a despotic but benevolent godfather. He speaks up for Hans at his trial but welcomes the opportunity of using his soul – which he has established stays in the body for an hour after death – to further his experiments. His action in bringing Christina back to life and curing her deformity ('a bone too short perhaps, a blood clot near the brain, nothing you can't put right') seems unambiguously beneficial to humanity, but it fails to take into consideration the emotional factor. The new Christina is physically a flawless beauty, but her sweet and forgiving nature is now ruled by the soul of her lover, which burns with a desire for revenge. In a series of eerie encounters Christina entices the men who had mocked her in her previous incarnation and caused the death of her father and her lover, and murders them at the moment they are about to make love to her. Her task done, this most perfect of Frankenstein's creations insists on throwing herself into a ravine.

Fisher followed *Frankenstein Created Woman* with *The Devil Rides Out*, and was preparing to shoot *Dracula Has Risen from the Grave* when he broke his leg and Freddie Francis was asked to step in. Pirie compares the film unfavourably with *Dracula – Prince of Darkness*, and there is certainly little of the thematic complexity which Pirie draws out from the Fisher film. Francis is less diffident, more voyeuristic than Fisher, and some of the best scenes – the dead girl swinging from the church bell in the film's prologue, Barbara Ewing and Veronica Carlson's fearful, voluptuous encounters with Dracula – have a macabre erotic beauty. Hinds's tendency towards loosely plotted scripts is accentuated by Francis's uncertainty over which direction he wants the film to go in, but the visual imagery assumes a life of its own.[23] Francis was an extremely talented cameraman as well as being a director, and here, in the only film he made with Arthur Grant, he uses colour in an abstract, experimental way untypical of Hammer's films. Dracula's coffin and his castle door are fringed with blue and yellow light, the cellar which serves as his refuge has a lurid lime-green tinge, and Maria's bedroom, once Dracula enters, is suffused by a warm yellow glow which gives an extraordinary sensuality to their love-making.

The fact that Francis is treated with even less respect than Fisher has meant that *Dracula Has Risen from the Grave* has never been given the attention it deserves, and misinterpretations of the film show a nervous anxiety to defuse its erotic power. The prologue is wilfully misunderstood: jokes are made about the old woman's coffin which Dracula appropriates, and Zena (Barbara Ewing), whose death is shockingly savage, is said to die 'with an expression of triumphant and satisfied lust frozen on her face'.[24] In terms of emotional intensity and visual beauty, though, *Dracula Has Risen from the Grave* is the only one of Hammer's numerous vampire films to rival Fisher's first *Dracula*.

Hammer made its last film at Bray in 1967 and finally sold its interests in the studio in 1971.[25] The visual quality of *Dracula Has Risen from the Grave* and Fisher's *Frankenstein Must Be Destroyed*, both of which were made at Elstree, showed that Hammer's success was not necessarily tied to its tiny country-house studio, but both films had the enormous advantage of Arthur Grant's photography and Bernard Robinson's production design. After *Frankenstein Must Be Destroyed* Robinson gave up with Hammer (he died in 1970), and Grant (who survived him by only two years) was never able to achieve the same spectacular results with other art directors.[26] Taken as a group, the Hammer films made between 1968 and 1973 (after which the company made only sporadic ventures into film production) look distinctly unimpressive when measured against those made at Bray. But Hammer did not give up without a fight its pre-eminent position as a producer of horror films. Concentrating where it had been most successful in the past, Hammer made four Dracula films between 1969 and 1973 (*Taste the Blood of Dracula*, *The Scars of Dracula*, *Dracula A.D. 1972*, and *The Satanic Rites of Dracula*); three Frankensteins (Fisher's *Frankenstein Must Be Destroyed* and *Frankenstein and the Monster from Hell* and Sangster's *The Horror of Frankenstein*); a last attempt at the Mummy legend (*Blood from the Mummy's Tomb*); clever variations on the Jekyll and Hyde and Jack the Ripper stories (*Doctor Jekyll and Sister Hyde* and *Hands of the Ripper*); and a number of assorted vampire films (*The Vampire Lovers* and its successors *Lust for a Vampire* and *Twins of Evil* and the much more interesting *Vampire Circus* and *Captain Kronos – Vampire Hunter*).

Of the new directors recruited by Hammer, Roy Baker showed himself to be ill-suited to the genre; indeed, many of the accusations levelled at Fisher about uninspired and pedestrian direction can be applied with more justice to Baker, who in other areas of film-making has shown himself a talented director. The crassness of his approach in *The Scars of Dracula* is unfortunately equalled by that displayed by Jimmy Sangster in *The Horror of Frankenstein* and *Lust for a Vampire* and Alan Gibson in *Dracula A.D. 1972* and *The Satanic Rites of Dracula*. The only directors who look at all at home in the genre are Robert Young, with his (in parts at least) thrilling and innovative *Vampire Circus* (1973), and Peter Sasdy, who made a promising debut in 1969 with *Taste the Blood of Dracula*

Sasdy adopts a more realistic, clinical approach to Victorian society than Fisher, with an emphasis on psychology rather than myth. *Taste the Blood of Dracula*, like all the later Dracula films, is afflicted by a host of ineffectual juveniles, but here at least Sasdy is able to pit them against their corrupt patriarchal elders, involving Count Dracula in a Victorian generation clash which makes for interesting if in the end inconclusive insights into the sexual repression which structured Victorian society. Arthur Grant gives the film a certain visual continuity with *Dracula Has Risen from the Grave* – the predominant yellows of the brothel sequences, the reds of the Café Royal, the night photography in gardens, woods and graveyards – but in Sasdy's more solid Victorian world he finds less scope for experiment. Sasdy followed up *Taste the Blood of Dracula* with two interesting films – *Countess Dracula*, and *Hands of the Ripper* – but, like many of the seemingly promising directors of the late 60s, he drifted into mediocrity.

Hammer's policy of employing young directors meant that neither

Fisher nor Francis made another Dracula film. *Dracula Has Risen from the Grave* was commercially very successful, but it was the last film Francis made for Hammer and his subsequent career has been disappointing. He continued to direct horror films in the 70s, but only *The Creeping Flesh* proved of much interest and the commercial and artistic failure of *The Ghoul* and *The Legend of the Werewolf*, which Francis directed for his son's company, Tyburn, signalled the end of British horror as a major force. Fisher made only three more films after *Frankenstein Created Women* – *The Devil Rides Out, Frankenstein Must Be Destroyed* and *Frankenstein and the Monster from Hell* – but they were well up to the standard of his earlier work.

Frankenstein Must Be Destroyed (1968) was written by Hammer assistant director Bert Batt, but there are familiar Fisher/Hinds juxtapositions: between the comfortable respectability of the lodging house Frankenstein moves in to and the stark cruelty of the nearby lunatic asylum; between the suave, cruel Frankenstein (who goes so far as to rape his reluctant assistant's fiancée) and the sad-eyed, wholly human monster. The first half of the film has its satisfactions – the series of dramatic events which set Frankenstein on his travels again, Thorley Walters's irascibly quirky police investigator, the confrontation between Frankenstein and the dull gentlemen he ousts from Veronica Carlson's sumptuous lodging house – but it is only with the sequence where a water main bursts and reanimates a body Frankenstein has buried in the garden (another visual *tour de force* from Arthur Grant) that the film really takes off. The insipid hero and heroine (Simon Ward and Veronica Carlson), whose lives are casually ruined by Frankenstein, are pushed to one side as the anguished relationship between the monster (Freddie Jones) and his wife (Maxine Audley) is developed.

The operation which provides a new body for the demented but easily cured brain of Frankenstein's incarcerated colleague Dr Brandt – unbloody but almost unwatchably excruciating – results in the creation of Hammer's most sympathetic monster. The anguished relationship between the monster and his wife is beautifully conceived and emotionally very powerful. In the asylum Brandt is reduced to a catatonic state which makes him completely unresponsive to his wife's presence. After being kidnapped and operated on by Frankenstein, he is speechless and heavily bandaged, but he is able to comfort his wife by making tentative signals which indicate that not only is he alive when she thought him dead, but he is sane enough to recognise her and want to communicate with her. For a brief period it appears that Frankenstein has returned to the almost philanthropic figure of *Frankenstein Created Woman*, rescuing Brandt, curing him of his dementia, reuniting him with his wife. But impatient of the messiness of human relationships, he whisks him away. Frankenstein's desire for know-

Frankenstein's sad-eyed, wholly human monster (Freddie Jones): *Frankenstein Must Be Destroyed*

ledge is made to seem small-minded and insignificant compared to Brandt's need for love, and the film's climax assumes a rich, tragic intensity. Brandt escapes and makes his way home. Capable of speech but aware of the shock his new body might cause his wife, he leaves a note by her bedside and when she wakes, speaks to her from behind a screen, only to find that she is horrified and refuses to believe this pathetic creature's claims to be her husband. Knowing that Frankenstein will eventually track him down, the embittered monster, with nothing left to live for, waits for his saviour/tormentor and, determined to destroy both himself and Frankenstein, carries him into the blazing ruin of what was once his home.

After *Frankenstein Must Be Destroyed*, Fisher was to have directed *Lust for a Vampire*, a sequel to Roy Baker's *The Vampire Lovers*, which, with its bare breasts and lesbian vampire, had inaugurated a more explicit attitude to sex than had been evident in any of Fisher's films. Just before shooting began he again broke his leg, and Jimmy Sangster was brought in to direct the film. It is interesting to speculate whether Fisher would have managed to overcome the obstacles of a weak script, an unusually indifferent cast and an insensitive score and whether, like Sangster, he would have relied on the lush eroticism which is the film's only redeeming feature. By the time he began his next – and last – assignment, *Frankenstein and the Monster from Hell* (1974), Hammer had retreated from its 'permissive' policy, and in Anthony Hinds's

178

script the only sexual element is the flawed heroine confined to the lunatic asylum after rape has robbed her of the power of speech.

As in *The Revenge of Frankenstein*, the baron's humane care of his patients has to be set against his tendency to make use of parts of their bodies for his experiments; as in *Frankenstein Must Be Destroyed*, Frankenstein operates on the criminally insane, but now he himself is an inmate of the asylum, and though judicious use of blackmail means that his privileges include his own laboratory, almost all the film takes place within the asylum and it is unremittingly grim. Frankenstein, now looking like an old man, is more human, more kindly than in *Frankenstein Must Be Destroyed*. But his experiments look futile: the monster combines the brain of a sensitive mathematician and violinist with a body resembling that of a deformed gorilla. And when, after the monster has been torn apart by the other inmates, Fisher pulls back his camera to show Frankenstein through the asylum's barred windows talking cheerily about the need to start immediately on a new creation, our sympathies are with his appalled disciple. The film has a complexity and a sophistication which is light years away from the other late Hammer productions such as *The Horror of Frankenstein* or *The Scars of Dracula*, but it is nonetheless sad that Fisher's career should end with such a chillingly sombre film. His death in September 1980 went almost unnoticed in Britain. Harry Ringel had written a fitting epitaph seven years earlier: 'Like his Frankenstein, he has worked resolutely, without critical encouragement, under the most compromising circumstances. His mistakes noisily roam the countryside; his best films deaden within a cultural vacuum.'[27]

Dave Pirie argues that the stunted growth of the Surrealist movement in Britain made it possible for a submerged, unconscious Surrealism to emerge in Hammer's (in particular Fisher's) horror films. Unfortunately, except for Raymond Durgnat and Lawrence Alloway, who shared some of the concerns and interests of the Surrealists of *Positif* and *Midi-Minuit Fantastique*, British critics were too insular to discern the quality of 'methodical and unselfconscious eccentricity' which permeated British horror films.[28]

Science fiction

Science fiction, which had been an important genre in the 1950s, became a poor relation of horror in the 60s, and the few big-budget science fiction films made then now appear shrunken and insignificant. Now that the dope clouds have lifted, Kubrick's *2001: A Space Odyssey* (1968) no longer seems the breakthrough, the revelation it was thought to be, its one undeniably brilliant moment, the computer HAL sadly singing 'Daisy' as the terminals of his brain are disconnected, swamped by a mass of dated special effects. Similarly, Truffaut's humanism in *Fahrenheit 451* (1966) has to overcome the

179

handicap of scrappy modernist sets and a rickety conceptual framework. The very idea of firemen acting as secret police-like oppressors seems peculiarly un-British and only the sentimental, almost absurd, scenes – Oskar Werner outraging the sensibilities of his wife's friends by reading them passages from *David Copperfield*; the old lady quoting Bishop Latimer as she goes up in flames with her books; the Book People, forlorn upholders of civilised values, wandering round the damp woods memorising their chosen volumes – bring the film to life. It is not that Kubrick's or Truffaut's films are contemptible, merely that they share the flaws and incoherencies of other science fiction films made on incomparably smaller budgets.

Terence Fisher's three science fiction films – *The Earth Dies Screaming* (1964), *Island of Terror* (1965) and *Night of the Big Heat* (1967) – were routine assignments which had more in common with his 50s 'B' films than his Gothic horrors. *The Earth Dies Screaming* is by far the best, a neat, clever little film (it is only 64 minutes long) with a good cast (Dennis Price, Thorley Walters, Vanda Godsell, the husband and wife American 'B' film stars Virginia Field and Willard Parker) and an excellent score by Elizabeth Lutyens. The story, about a disparate group of survivors of an alien gas attack, recalls Steve Sekely's adaptation of John Wyndham's *The Day of the Triffids* (1962), but Fisher's film is incomparably better made. The title sequence, with cars and trains and planes crashing and commuters toppling over at railway stations, clears the way for an evocation of quiet rural England worthy of Jennings or Cavalcanti, the incongruity of robots and zombies patrolling the streets of the small country town where most of the action is set giving the film a disturbing resonance.

Island of Terror and *Night of the Big Heat* are less interesting and Fisher never quite overcomes the obstacle of their inadequate scripts, but both films have redeeming features. *Island of Terror*'s electric swan-like monsters, which suck the bones out of a body to leave sheep, cows and men as bags of barely identifiable jelly, have a macabre charm, true descendants of late 50s/early 60s monsters like the Trollenberg Terror and Behemoth the Sea Monster. And the inanity of the romance between the juvenile leads (Edward Judd and Carole Gray) has to be set against Peter Cushing's cruelly pragmatic response to the aliens' threat: to inject the island's cows with Strontium 90 and feed them to the monsters. *Night of the Big Heat*, set on an offshore island which in the midst of the British winter experiences an alien-induced heatwave, is more plausible than *Island of Terror*, but, despite the startling opening sequence where the titles smash through the screen of a scanner in a research station, the alien invasion is little more than a backdrop against which Patrick Allen has to make a choice between two women: voraciously sexual Jane Merrow and primly self-possessed Sarah Lawson. Fisher and his actors do their best, and Alex Vetchinsky's art direction ensures that everyone is suitably drenched in sweat, but the story obstinately refuses to take off and neither the passionate triangle nor the alien threat really convinces.

The most important theme of 50s science fiction – that of intelligent aliens visiting the earth – lingered on creatively in a number of low-budget films. MGM's *Village of the Damned* (1960, d. Wolf Rilla) and its successor, *Children of the Damned* (1963, d. Anton M. Leader), both use children in a peculiarly disturbing way as carriers of the alien threat. In *Village of the Damned* (based on John Wyndham's *The Midwich Cuckoos*) twelve women give birth simultaneously to coldly precocious children who become increasingly threatening as they grow older. Rilla maintains a fine ambiguity, encouraging our sympathy for the children against the panicky hostility of the adult world, but making it apparent that their superior intelligence is directed towards evil ends. The young protagonists of *Children of the Damned* are inclined to use their gifts to benefit humanity, but their ruthlessness when crossed is still daunting. Two trigger-happy policemen who shoot the children's dog are made to turn their guns on each other; high-level talks between the children and their respective governments (they are from Russia, China, America, Africa and India as well as from Britain) end in bloody mayhem when the children angrily reject plans to harness their power for destructive purposes. Unfortunately, the film doesn't quite have the courage of its pacifist convictions, and it is a clumsy private's dropped screwdriver rather than the Commander-in-Chief's order which triggers the military retaliation that finally puts paid to the threat and the promise the children represent.

Butchers' *The Night Caller* (1965, d. John Gilling) and Anglo-Amalgamated's *Invasion* (1966, d. Alan Bridges) are more lightweight but more exciting, and both are very stylishly shot. Gilling uses traditional elements – a scaly hand, a glowing sphere, sinister night photography – to create suspense, but he is by no means tied by 'B' film conventions. The heroine and potential love interest (Patricia Haines) is unexpectedly dispatched two-thirds of the way through and the alien, who is neither wholly good nor wholly bad, escapes back to Ganymede with his forty willing Bikini Girl captives. *Invasion* is more self-consciously modern and realistic. Edward Judd is a harassed National Health doctor and his sidekick (Valerie Gearon) smokes heavily and has a Vidal Sassoon haircut.[29] Alan Bridges, better known for directing television plays like David Mercer's *Let's Murder Vivaldi* and Dennis Potter's *Traitor*, is stylistically much more pretentious and unconventional than Gilling, and his talents are well suited to this odd little story of an inter-alien incident – a prisoner escapes while being transported to a penal colony – disrupting the mundane reality of hospital life. There are plot flaws, but the characters – including the demure but deadly devil girls from Lystria – are fascinating, and Bridges maintains

181

a nice sense of ordinary people reluctantly, almost indignantly, involved in unusual events.

The best of this modest but attractive group of films is *Unearthly Stranger* (1963), directed by John Krish for Independent Artists. From its desperate beginning, with John Neville running up an endless spiral staircase and gasping out his story into a tape recorder, to its eerily effective end, with the two scientists' dawning realisation that their audience of reassuringly familiar charladies are malevolent aliens, it is a marvellously atmospheric and inventive film. Reg Wyer's subtly disorienting photography and Patrick Newell's slimy, sweet-eating security man contribute to the film's success, but what makes it particularly unusual is the convincing relationship between the scientist hero (John Neville) and a female alien, a theme not explored again so fruitfully until Ridley Scott's *Blade Runner*. Neville's stubbornness in refusing to acknowledge the signs that he has married an alien (she sleeps with her eyes open, has no pulse, doesn't blink, can pull hot dishes out of the oven without burning her hands) is complicated by a reluctance to allow his most intimate relationship to be subjected to scientific scrutiny. One can sympathise with his resentment when his colleague asks, 'Would you allow me to come to your home, and in

Demure but deadly devil-girl from Lystria: Yoko Tani, *Invasion*

182

The pain of being non-human: Gabriella Licudi, John Neville, *Unearthly Stranger*

your presence, anaesthetise your wife so that we can see, once and for all, whether she's a real human being or an illusion.' For her part, the alien wife, the unearthly stranger (Gabriella Licudi), is placed in an impossible dilemma. Having realised the value of human emotions like love and pity, she no longer wants to go through with the destructive plans of her fellow aliens, but her replicant's body is not meant for a fully human existence. Children and animals shy away from her despite her glowing beauty, tears scar her face, and when her husband reassures her ('I told you they couldn't harm us, I told you, if we love each other they'll leave us alone'), he finds his arms empty, his wife dissolved.

Hammer's ventures into science fiction began back in 1952 with films like *The Four Sided Triangle* and *Spaceways*, but after the success of *The Curse of Frankenstein* the future was abandoned for the Gothic mysteries of the past. When the company tried to diversify away from horror it was towards dark, sardonic swashbucklers – John Gilling's *The Pirates of Blood River* (1962), *The Scarlet Blade* (1963), and *The Brigand of Kandahar* (1965), Peter Graham Scott's *Captain Clegg* (1962; infinitely more powerful than Disney's version of the same story, *Doctor Syn*), and Don Sharp's *Devil Ship Pirates* (1964); and exotic adventure pictures like *She* (1965, d. Robert Day), *The Vengeance of She* (1967, d. Cliff Owen) and *The Lost Continent* (1968, d.

183

Michael Carreras). The Hammer primitive epics – *One Million Years BC* (1966, d. Don Chaffey), *Slave Girls* (1966, d. Michael Carreras), *The Viking Queen* (1966, d. Don Chaffey), *When Dinosaurs Ruled the Earth* (1969, d. Val Guest) and *Creatures the World Forgot* (1970, d. Don Chaffey) – are bizarre mixtures of elements from the nudist film, the Italian peplum epic and the African wildlife saga, but they deserve to be mentioned because like horror and science fiction they create a totally imaginary world.

One Million Years BC was a remake of a 1940 Hal Roach picture, with Ray Harryhausen's animated monsters replacing the magnified lizards of the original and Raquel Welch proving herself an unlikely but charismatic heroine. Without using dialogue, the permutations on the prehistoric formula were limited, and *The Viking Queen* and *Slave Girls* returned to more conventional peplum subject matter. But they failed to create anything like the impact of *One Million Years BC*, and in 1969 Hammer brought in the sophisticated science fiction writer J. G. Ballard to script a successor, *When Dinosaurs Ruled the Earth*. According to Dave Pirie, much of Ballard's original treatment was rejected, and though the idea of centring the film round the upheavals caused by the separation of the moon from the earth remains, as much energy is devoted to Victoria Vetri's Disneyish relationship with a friendly dinosaur and its mother.[30]

Creatures the World Forgot is the least well-regarded but most interesting of Hammer's journeys into the ancient past. Michael Carreras, whose expensive mistakes (*The Lost Continent, Moon Zero Two*) have to be measured against his constant willingness to experiment, here dispenses not only with dialogue but with dinosaurs (which of course had ceased to exist long before man evolved), and relies on surprisingly aggressive gnus and wildebeests to make life difficult for his quarrelsome cavemen. As a three-generation family saga culminating in a Cain and Abel feud between flaxen-haired Tony Bonner and dark, scowling Robert John, the film seems more slow-moving than its predecessors, and there are moments when these stone age primitives look uncomfortably like a tribe of hippies on their way to the Isle of Wight. But with the help of Rosalie Crutchley and Marcia Fox's sorceresses, this is by far the most successful of Hammer's films in capturing a morning-of-the-world savagery.

Despite the popularity of the first two *Quatermass* films, it was not until 1967 that Hammer decided to film the third and most impressive of Nigel Kneale's serials, *Quatermass and the Pit*. Sympathetic performances from Barbara Shelley, Andrew Keir and James Donald and competent direction by Roy Baker make it a likeable film, but Bernard Robinson's production design and Arthur Grant's photography seem to lose their impact in the unfamiliar spaciousness of MGM's Borehamwood studio. It was not a commercial success, but Hammer neverthe-

184

less persevered with Michael Carreras's ambitious 'space western' *Moon Zero Two* (1969). Again Baker's direction is workmanlike and there are attractive cameo performances by Adrienne Corri, Warren Mitchell and Dudley Foster, but the film's achievements in no way match up to its ambitions and it flopped badly.

Joseph Losey's *The Damned*, made for Hammer in 1961, was shelved by its distributor, Columbia, until 1963. It is a flawed film – as much because of Losey's failure to integrate his three plot strands as because of changes insisted upon by Hammer – but it is still one of the most complex and interesting of British science fiction films. Like *Village of the Damned* and *Children of the Damned*, Losey's film features a group of exceptional children, but the similarities are misleading. These children are not the product of an alien invasion but of a government scheme. In a network of caves which form a natural underground bunker, the children grow up isolated from contact with all human beings except the black-clad figures who sneak in at night to leave their food and collect their laundry. All communication with the outside world is through a television screen from which a kindly civil servant educates and instructs them. They are being exposed to larger and larger doses of radiation as a form of vaccine to enable them to survive a radioactive world in the aftermath of nuclear war.

Losey intertwines this grim little parable with two other strands. The civil servant, Bernard (Alexander Knox), leases his cottage on the cliff above the children's cave to a sculptress, Freya (Viveca Lindfors), with whom at some time in the past he has had an amorous relationship. She stands for individualism, humanism, acceptance of the world, he, despite being sensitive and considerate, for a cold rationality which, like Frankenstein's, is ultimately anti-human. One might have expected Losey (who with Evan Jones completely rewrote the script Hammer presented to him) to develop their unlikely relationship. But, drawing a dubious parallel between the government's institutionalised violence and the reckless, motiveless violence of a gang of young hoodlums, he makes the film's central relationship that between Simon, a well-meaning American insurance broker (Macdonald Carey), and Joan, the gang-leader's neurotic sister (Shirley Ann Field). This is useful for the mechanics of the plot – running away from the vengeful gang, Joan and Simon stumble into the children's world and help them escape – but the concentration on these two relatively insipid characters distracts attention from the more interesting aspects of the film. Nevertheless, Arthur Grant's night photography and Elizabeth Frink's sculptures give the film a haunting quality, and the ending, with the briefly liberated children rounded up, Freya brutally dispatched by Bernard to ensure the project is kept secret, and Simon and Joan drifting out to sea dying of radiation sickness, is impressively uncompromising.[32]

Hammer's Competitors

Though Hammer dominated the British (indeed the international) horror scene, other companies were not slow to see the profits to be made from horror films. In the late 50s John Croydon and Robert Day made two films starring Boris Karloff, *Corridors of Blood* and *Grip of the Strangler*; and Monty Berman and Robert Baker produced a cycle of gruesome melodramas – *Blood of the Vampire*, *The Siege of Sidney Street*, *Jack the Ripper* and *The Flesh and the Fiends*. With the exception of the uninspiring recreations of the Ripper and Sidney Street stories, they are thrilling little films, but made in black and white and remaining within the old expressionist tradition they had little of the impact of Hammer's Gothic horrors.[33] By the early 60s Baker and Berman, Day and Croydon had moved on to other pastures, but another exploitation company, Compton-Tekli, which had been responsible for sex/problem films like *The Yellow Teddybears* (1963), made occasional ventures into horror, most notably with Roman Polanski's *Repulsion*. *The Black Torment* (1964) and *Corruption* (1967) were clumsily directed by Robert Hartford-Davis and failed to realise the potential of their interesting casts and stories, but James Hill's *A Study in Terror* (1966), which sets Sherlock Holmes on the trail of Jack the Ripper, is more significant. Pirie dismisses the film as ugly and banal, the *Aurum Encyclopedia of Horror* labels it inept, but Desmond Dickinson's photography gives the film a lively visual attractiveness and the Wilkie Collins-like plot remains coherent despite its complexities. The violence is undeniably decorative, and the Whitechapel whores with their soft, dolly bird faces and their sexy, expensive costumes look as if they have just left a Chelsea fancy dress party. But this fits well with the mannered performance of John Neville as Holmes, the cleverly intricate plot, and Alex Vetchinsky's subtly stylised sets. It is a very 60s version of the Ripper legend, witty, cruel and colourful, but one that has not yet been bettered.[34]

Gene Gutowski, who had produced *Repulsion*, *Cul de Sac* and *A Study in Terror*, managed to get MGM and American mini-major Filmways to back Polanski's next film, *Dance of the Vampires*. Unfortunately Hollywood, and in particular executive producer Martin Ransohoff, proved to be less sensitive and intelligent than Soho sleaze merchants Compton-Tekli in their appreciation of what Polanski was trying to do. With breathtaking inanity the film was retitled *The Fearless Vampire Hunters or Pardon Me But Your Teeth Are in My Neck*, and fifteen minutes were chopped out. Fortunately, most of Polanski's version has survived. Paul Willemen makes the point that 'the generally accepted wisdom that horror shall either be played straight or become a comedy is false since both jokes and anxiety are rooted in the same soil of unconscious desires and combine to generate the sense of the uncanny', and claims that *Dance of the Vampires* 'is one of the very few perfectly achieved examples of the uncanny, delicately poised between the familiar and the weird'.[35] Thus sequences such as that in which Count Von Krolock descends amidst a flurry of snowflakes on to Sarah in her bath, and the minuet performed by the decaying vampires which breaks into an undignified chase when Professor Abronsius and Alfred are exposed by their image in the ballroom mirror, provoke thrilled but troubled laughter.

Attempts at parody – Hammer's *The Ugly Duckling* (1959, d. Lance Comfort), *The Horror of Frankenstein* (1970, d. Jimmy Sangster), Baker and Berman's *What a Carve Up* (1961, d. Pat Jackson), even *Carry On Screaming* (1967, d. Gerald Thomas) – tend to be silly rather than frightening. *Dance of the Vampires* manages to be funny and chilling, with the help of Krzystof Komeda's score and Douglas Slocombe's photography, capturing that 'tempestuous loveliness of terror' which is the essence of horror.

Anglo-Amalgamated, which had shared the bottom end of the market with Hammer in the 50s, ventured into horror in the early 60s with its so-called 'piercing cycle' – *Horrors of the Black Museum*, *Circus of Horrors* and *Peeping Tom* – and collaborated with American International Pictures (AIP) on two Edgar Allan Poe films made in England by Roger Corman in 1964, *The Masque of the Red Death* and *The Tomb of Ligeia*. The best of Corman's American Poe films – *The Fall of the House of Usher* and *The Pit and the Pendulum* – were visually much more baroque than their Hammer contemporaries, and Vincent Price's ponderous, melodramatic style is totally different from Cushing's wry realism. *The Masque of the Red Death*, photographed by Nicolas Roeg, is almost a parody of the earlier Poe films, with swirling mists, abstract colours and a ludicrously portentous story. Predictably, while most Hammer films were dismissed as trash, the critics were happy to take this empty, confused piece of film-making seriously. But if *The Masque of the Red Death* is sub-Cecil B. de Mille, *The Tomb of Ligeia*, photographed by Arthur Grant, is altogether different. With the exception of Michael Reeves's *Witchfinder General* (which also makes good use of Vincent Price), it is the only British horror film to equal the intensity and vision of the best of the Hammer films. In a complete break with Corman's other Poe films (and with most of Hammer's horror films), *The Tomb of Ligeia* uses real locations. According to Corman:

> In order to make it somewhat interesting for me, I broke all of my rules. For instance, I had never wanted to shoot in real situations. I felt we were dealing with the world beyond the conscious, a closed, somewhat artificial world, so I tried to shoot everything in studios. Everything was constructed, and maybe built a little off scale. ... But with *The Tomb of Ligeia* I said, 'Okay, I'm gonna show reality.' We went into the English countryside and photographed a fox hunt,

a wedding at a very pretty English church, a sixteenth-century monastery in ruins, to be used as the exterior of the house. It was very, very interesting. As a result *Ligeia* had a very different look from the other Poe films, because it was the first and only time the sun ever shone in one of them – I did it just to see what would happen when I broke the rules.[36]

This might have been disastrous, but Grant is one of the few great cinematographers to be equally at home in the studio and on location, and he knits it all together to create a uniquely mysterious atmosphere. The film also benefits from a sophisticated script by Robert Towne (with some uncredited help from Paul Mayersberg). In place of the simplistic contrast between devil-worshipping debauchee Prospero and god-fearing virgin Francesca in *The Masque of the Red Death*, Price's Verden Fell is an attractive mixture of metaphysical scruples and morbid obsessions, who has good reasons for questioning whether his first wife Ligeia rests quietly in her grave.

Like Hitchcock's *Rebecca*, *The Tomb of Ligeia* deals with the deep-seated fears provoked by the marriage of a young woman to an older man, but in Corman's film the emotional turmoil caused by the discovery of his dark secrets is shifted from the psychology of the man/wife relationship to a surreal imagery of dreams and symbols. Fell is morbid, sinister; he wears dark glasses not to hide some disfigurement but because he is abnormally sensitive ('I live at night, my vision is painfully acute'). Rowena (Elizabeth Shepherd) is a headstrong, healthy, outdoor girl, and this union of dark and light initially appears to benefit both of them. But their marriage is foredoomed. In a key sequence, Corman cuts between Rowena following the cat which appears to act as Ligeia's familiar down cobwebby passages and up the stairs of a crumbling bell-tower while Fell, walking in the grounds with the young man who has introduced him to Rowena, attempts to explain how Ligeia still haunts him: 'As her body progressively wasted she seemed to turn to the very stones of the abbey for renewed strength, as if she could sustain that burning desire for life . . . in a sense Ligeia became the abbey.' The bells ring and Rowena is on the point of falling to her death when Verden rescues her. 'You're safe now, my darling, you're safe now with me,' he tells her, and after a few seconds' silence the bells ring again as the scene dissolves to their wedding. Once they return from their honeymoon, Ligeia and the house begin to destroy their happiness, Fell drifts into misanthropic madness, Rowena fades away, her days disturbed by eerie events like the discovery of hair not her own in her hairbrush, her nights disturbed by bizarre dreams. Peter John Dyer in the *Monthly Film Bulletin* complained about the 'loss of narrative clarity which featured so strongly in *Masque of the Red Death*', but it is less that the film is

The Tomb of Ligeia: Rowena (Elizabeth Shepherd) haunted by her predecessor
Ligeia

incoherent than that its structure is that of an overwhelmingly rich and
complex dream.[37]

Interesting though its excursions are, Anglo never attempted to
specialise in horror and Hammer's only real competitor was Amicus, a
company run by two Americans, Max J. Rosenberg and Milton
Subotsky. It was Subotsky who, before he even came to Britain, suggested to Hammer that they should remake *Frankenstein*, but he was
never involved in the production of the film which transformed Hammer's fortunes and his own first venture into horror was a modestly
budgeted black and white film called *City of the Dead* (1960).
Subotsky's claim that it is 'one of the best horror films of all time' is
something of an exaggeration. Christopher Lee is ill at ease as an
American professor who is also a three-hundred year-old witch, and
the ostensible star of the film is the epitome of 50s blandness, dance-
band singer Denis Lotis.[38] Despite Subotsky's concern for story structure, the framework of *City of the Dead* is extremely rickety, with Lee
sending off his prettiest (but surely not his brightest?) student to do
research on witchcraft in Whitewood, a 'city' which seems to consist of
a spooky hotel and a few ramshackle wooden houses, barely discernible in the all-pervasive mist. Nevertheless, director John Moxey and
cameraman Desmond Dickinson work wonders with their limited

189

resources, and with the help of Patricia Jessel's magnificent witch produce a genuinely frightening atmosphere of all-pervasive evil.

Subotsky was by no means totally committed to horror, and Amicus's first official production was Richard Lester's *It's Trad Dad!*. But after the failure of its mistimed sequel, *Just for Fun*, in 1963, Subotsky wrote, as a sort of homage to Ealing's supernatural thriller *Dead of Night*, an omnibus film which Freddie Francis directed as *Dr Terror's House of Horror*. Peter Cushing, Christopher Lee, Michael Gough, Katy Wilde and Peter Madden were borrowed from Hammer, but Subotsky also provided an opportunity for Donald Sutherland, Max Adrian and Ursula Howells to make impressive horror debuts, and the film is well up to Hammer production standards. Commercially it was very successful, and Amicus followed up with three mediocre horror features – *The Skull*, *The Psychopath* and *The Deadly Bees*, all directed by Freddie Francis and based on stories by Robert Bloch – before Subotsky had the brighter idea of returning to the compendium format and using several of Bloch's stories at a time. *Torture Garden* (d. Freddie Francis, 1968) was followed by *The House That Dripped Blood* (d. Peter Duffell, 1970) and *Asylum* (d. Roy Baker, 1972), which Amicus interspersed with *Tales from the Crypt* (d. Freddie Francis, 1971) and *Vault of Horror* (d. Roy Baker, 1973) based on the 50s American EC comics. The final two entries in the cycle – *Tales That Witness Madness* (d. Freddie Francis, 1973), based on stories written by the actress Jennifer Jayne, and *From Beyond the Grave* (d. Kevin Connor, 1974), with a script by Robin Clarke and Raymond Christodoulou – were decidedly inferior.

By the late 60s a number of young directors were entering the horror field. David Greene made an impressive debut with *The Shuttered Room* in 1967, but he showed no desire to specialise in horror films; Stephen Weeks, a protégé of Christopher Lee, was brought in by Amicus to make a Freudian reinterpretation of the Jekyll and Hyde story, *I, Monster*. Peter Sasdy and the less promising Alan Gibson made their debuts at Hammer with *Taste the Blood of Dracula* and *Crescendo*. And Gordon Hessler, who had worked as a story editor on *Alfred Hitchcock Presents* in America and made a low-budget murder mystery, *Catacombs/The Woman Who Wouldn't Die*, at Shepperton, switched from producing to directing *The Oblong Box*.[39] By far the most promising newcomer, however, was Michael Reeves.

Determined to break into film-making, Reeves had sought out Don Siegel, the director he most admired, and persuaded him to take him on as his assistant. On the strength of that experience he was given some sequences of an Italian horror film – *The Castle of the Living Dead* – to direct, and at the age of twenty-two directed his first feature, the very low-budget *Revenge of the Blood Beast* (*La Sorella di Satana*). He then made two films in Britain for Tigon, a branch of the Laurie Marsh property empire which had Tony Tenser, the most imaginative of the exploitation producers, as its guiding force. Tigon's horror record is extremely patchy, and *The Sorcerers* (1967) is flawed by its cheap sets and the general aura of sleaze which was to envelop whole areas of the British film industry in the next decade. Set against this is an improbable but interesting story. A discredited old hypnotist (Boris Karloff) invents a machine which enables him not only to control the actions of someone he has programmed, but also to experience what his guinea-pig is feeling. He persuades a vaguely discontented young man (Ian Ogilvy) to submit to the experiment and, with the enthusiastic support of his wife (Catherine Lacey), he vicariously enjoys the thrill of discotheques, sports cars and the company of sexy young women. Such feelings prove too much for his wife's sanity, and in a mad urge for greater and greater sensation she has the young man murder his sexual partners. In desperation, Karloff wills the young man to crash his car and they share his fiery denouement as their flat goes up in flames. Like *Peeping Tom*, the film can be seen as an allegory about the cinema and the vicarious experience of the spectator. As Robin Wood argues:

> From the point in the film when we are alerted to such implications, our own response becomes uncomfortable and self-questioning: to what extent do *we*, like Catherine Lacey, want the young man to commit horrible murders while we sit back in our seats in second-hand security? And are we so sure that the 'security' isn't a delusion? Are we, like the old woman, contaminated? Does the release of our baser instincts threaten to overwhelm and obliterate all our finer feelings?[40]

Reeves's next film, *Witchfinder General*, is set in the past but there is no sense of a fantastic, fairytale world which encloses even the most frightening of the Gothic horror films. Superficially *Witchfinder General* would seem to relate more to John Gilling's *The Scarlet Blade* or Baker and Berman's *The Hellfire Club* than to the mainstream of horror, but even their darker cousins – *The Pirates of Blood River, Devil Ship Pirates* – don't treat power, violence, cruelty and revenge in the bleakly harrowing way that Reeves does. The England the film presents – most of the film was shot on location – is in many ways a traditional one – green fields, browsing sheep, cool shady woods, picturesque village churches – but the characters who inhabit it are not the usual stereotypes. The hero is a Roundhead, not a Cavalier, and there is none of the dreary sentimentality about King Charles and his cause which afflicts even Ken Hughes's *Cromwell*. There are no cheery, good-natured villagers (the reassuringly familiar faces of the Hammer character actors), who would be out of place in a world where evil is not a threat from the castle on the hill which can be combated with garlic and crucifixes, but a dull, cowardly acquiescence in spite and cruelty. In *Witchfinder General*, the goodness of ordinary people can be relied upon even less than the impartiality and fairness of those in authority.

The young couple at the centre of the film are in a similar position to Veronica Carlson and Simon Ward in *Frankenstein Must Be Destroyed* in that their happy, uncomplicated lives are caught up and ruined by a thoroughly evil man, but the forty-year age gap between Reeves and Fisher is manifested in the very different perspective they adopt. Reeves's lovers are essentially as superficial and uninteresting as Fisher's – Ian Ogilvy's handsome Richard Marshall and his sidekick played by Nicky Henson make unsophisticated young heroes, and Hilary Dwyer's Sarah is a sweet but essentially colourless heroine. But it is their ordinariness which makes them special, which makes their tragedy universal. Reeves knows these people (Ogilvy acts in all three of the films Reeves completed) and stirs our sympathy for them in a way that Fisher never does for Hammer's young couples. If such ordinary decent people can be engulfed in a tide of horror, can be degraded and destroyed by figures in authority with popular backing, then the world is a bleak place.

Robin Wood complains that although Vincent Price 'gives a very accomplished performance, he always remains Vincent Price in costume'.[41] Price's horror film persona was as fixed as that of Christopher Lee and Peter Cushing: in the Corman/Poe films (with the unsatisfactory exception of *The Masque of the Red Death*) his characters are sinister but fundamentally sympathetic. Reeves only gradually reveals to us in *Witchfinder General* that Matthew Hopkins is irredeemably evil; Price's sad, crumpled face continually gives rise to the hope that he will in the last resort show mercy, that he will sicken of the sadism and grossness that he sets in motion. Indeed, his attitude towards Sarah is that of a father towards a wayward daughter, and the final bloody denouement, which costs Richard his soul and Sarah her sanity, comes to seem like the retribution of a wronged son on a monstrous father.[42]

The Oblong Box, the last film Reeves worked on, was based on an Edgar Allan Poe story, scripted by veteran Welwyn director Lawrence Huntington and backed by AIP, the company responsible for Corman's Poe series.[43] Tragically Reeves died from an overdose of sleeping pills before shooting began and the producer, Gordon Hessler, had to take over as director. The story is potentially more interesting than that of *Witchfinder General*. A white man supposedly responsible for a black child's death is put under a witchdoctor's curse which makes him horribly misshapen. As his brother (Vincent Price) – who is the real guilty party – admits, a price has to be paid for colonial exploitation: 'Sin and retribution. We sinned out there in Africa all right. Plundering their land, and we're still stealing their wealth, though they're too innocent to know it. Yes, Edward's fate can only be our punishment, our kind of retribution.' And Alastair Williamson's Sir Edward, his deformed features concealed under a velvet hood, is initially at least a sympathetic monster. As he explains to the doctor (Christopher Lee) to whom he has been brought by body-snatchers after being buried alive: 'You're looking at someone who must be quite unique, even in your experience. A man turned inside out through sorcery and a handful of powders and obscure drugs. My mind's been unhinged, my face destroyed. I've been killed and then brought miraculously back to life. I am a very remarkable creature, doctor.'

Hessler has proved himself a competent but undistinguished director, and here he seems to have no very clear idea of what to do with these interesting elements. Sir Edward's relationship with Sally Geeson's sexy Victorian housemaid – a working-class beauty prepared to tolerate an aristocratic beast because he treats her with gratitude and respect – which might have provided an emotional centre for the film, is soon jettisoned, and sympathy for Sir Edward evaporates as he becomes a maddened killer wreaking vengeance on all and sundry. In contrast to their powerful performances in *Witchfinder General*, Vincent Price and Hilary Dwyer are left floundering around trying to find a focus for their roles and their relationship is insipid to the point of meaninglessness. Thus the ending on a freeze-frame (borrowed from *Witchfinder General*) of Dwyer staring fixedly at Price (who has been bitten by the mad Sir Edward) as he assumes the aspect and outlook of his disfigured brother seems to signify exasperated distaste rather than tragic revelation.

Tigon's follow-up to *Witchfinder General*, *Satan's Skin* (1970, d. Piers Haggard, later retitled *Blood on Satan's Claw*), is cruder but more effective. There is the same gloomy vision of the English peasantry as stupid and brutal, but the authorities, in the form of Patrick Wymark's earthily reassuring judge, can be relied upon for justice. Reeves's film is hardly concerned with the occult at all: nobody in *Witchfinder General* shows any indication that witchcraft is anything more than a convenient stigma with which to brand and destroy unwanted or unliked members of the community. *Satan's Skin* is less cynical. The village girls and boys stumble on dark practices which enable them to call up tangible devils and to create a millennial society that challenges and undermines the existing order. The film's picture of witchcraft as a cruel children's game is compelling; but, uncertain of where its sympathies lie, *Satan's Skin* peters out disappointingly, with the witches collapsing ignominiously before the bulky authority of Patrick Wymark.[44]

In collaboration with Chris Wicking, an articulate scriptwriter with a genuine interest in horror films who had written additional dialogue for *The Oblong Box*, Hessler made two more films before returning to America to find his niche as a director of television films. *Murders in the Rue Morgue* was apparently so changed by the distributors (AIP) as to make nonsense of Wicking and Hessler's intentions. *Scream and Scream Again*, made for Amicus and AIP, seems to have survived more or less intact, despite the hostility of Milton Subotsky to its explicit approach to sex and violence. The story, involving an alien who assumes the guise of a Ceausescu-like monster, murdering his way to political control of the world with the help of convincingly human androids, is ingenious. Unfortunately the film's most interesting characters – a very down-to-earth police inspector played by Alfred Marks and a misprogrammed android played by Michael Gothard (the existentially tortured hero of *Herostratus*), who preys on disco dolly birds and is possessed of superhuman strength beneath his frilly purple shirt – are sacrificed in order that Vincent Price, Peter Cushing and Christopher Lee, who really only play cameo roles, can earn their star billing, and the film fails to realise its potential.

British horror seemed to survive and flourish in the early 70s, but it was an Indian Summer rather than a new dawn. With the withdrawal of American finance, British film-makers were confined to smaller budgets and horror films could be made cheaply enough to make most of their money back on the home market. There were a handful of interesting experiments – Brian Clemens's *Captain Kronos – Vampire Hunter*, the Wicking-scripted *Blood from the Mummy's Tomb* and *Demons of the Mind*, and Robin Hardy and Anthony Shaffer's *The Wicker Man* (characteristically cut about and mishandled by the distributors) – but they petered out in the mid-70s. And while American cineastes inventively reworked old conventions in films like *The Texas Chainsaw Massacre*, *The Howling* and *An American Werewolf in London*, the British film industry could manage only bleak, grubby films like *The House of Whipcord* and its successors.

The Uncanny, the Marvellous and the Fantastic
Tzvetan Todorov makes a useful distinction between three types of supernatural literature: the uncanny, the marvellous and the fantastic. In the uncanny, 'events are related which may be readily accounted for by the laws of reason, but which are, in one way or another, incredible, extraordinary, shocking, singular, disturbing or unexpected. ... It is uniquely linked to the sentiments of the characters and not to a material event defying reason.'[45] In the marvellous, events which we would think of as impossible (a man being made from dismembered corpses, a creature that sucks human blood and can only die by having a wooden stake driven into its heart) are accepted as part of the normal order of things. Thus Fisher's films, where zombies, vampires and werewolves exist and only unenlightened fools question that brains and

even souls can be transferred from body to body, can be classed as marvellous, and the Sangster-scripted thrillers like *Taste of Fear* and *Nightmare* as uncanny.

Todorov's third category, the fantastic, poised uneasily between the marvellous and the uncanny, precisely describes Jacques Tourneur's 1940s films *Cat People* and *I Walked With a Zombie*. Here it is impossible to determine whether the bizarre events which occur are figments of a fevered imagination or manifestations of the supernatural. In Tourneur's British horror film, *Night of the Demon* (1957), the appearance of the Fire Demon (which several critics objected to) presents us with irrefutable evidence of the reality of satanic forces and shifts the film from the fantastic to the marvellous, making it intellectually, though not necessarily emotionally, less satisfying. Ambiguous excursions into the supernatural are rare in British cinema, though a sort of heritage can be derived from Gainsborough's *A Place of One's Own*, Thorold Dickinson's *Queen of Spades* and Ealing's supernatural compendiums *Halfway House* and *Dead of Night*. So the success of Jack Clayton's *The Innocents* is all the more surprising.

Todorov regarded Henry James's *The Turn of the Screw*, on which the film is based, as a classic example of the fantastic, and Clayton works hard to retain the ambiguity of James's narrative.[46] The visual style he evolves with his cameraman Freddie Francis is impressively restrained and consistent, their use of multiple dissolves, for example, sucking us gently into a subjective world which may signify the drift of Miss Giddens (Deborah Kerr) into madness but may equally indicate the presence of supernatural forces. Surreal images which occasionally intrude are similarly ambiguous: a ghost which seems to leave a tear, a huge beetle crawling out of the mouth of a stone cupid. We see the ghosts but we see them in moments of dead time when the world seems to stop, which could mean that we are witnessing a hallucination of the governess's aroused imagination – no one else can see what she sees – or we are sharing her psychic privilege of being able to see evil forces at work. Sometimes, as when she sallies forth with her candle in her flowing white nightgown, Miss Giddens seems to be an intrepid psychic investigator. Sometimes – along with Mrs Gosse (Megs Jenkins), the solid, sensible housekeeper – we are alienated by her hysterical behaviour. Undoubtedly the children are precocious, odd, manipulative, but if they are involved in some bizarre game of supernatural fantasy there is no reason to believe they are in the 'terrible danger' their governess thinks they are in. Deborah Kerr's performance is sophisticated and convincing, though, and at the end we are unsure whether she has won a major victory over the forces of evil or whether her own sexual repression has allowed her to destroy the lives of the children she is entrusted with.

Nothing resembling Clayton's sad Victorian ghosts was to appear again in the 60s. *The Tomb of Ligeia*, where hypnotism, dreams and morbid imagination never quite account for the supernatural presence of Verden Fell's dead wife, Sydney Hayers's *Night of the Eagle* (1961) and Dearden and Relph's last film, *The Man Who Haunted Himself* (1970), where Roger Moore is disturbed and eventually driven to suicide by his murderous double, enter fully into the realm of the fantastic; but more common were excursions into the supernatural which teeter on the brink, suggesting that ghosts and demons do exist but leaving an escape hatch that perhaps all we have seen is illusory.[47] As Niall MacGinnis's touchy, learned, insecure satanist enquires in *Night of the Demon*, 'Where does imagination end and reality begin? What is this twilight, this half world of the mind? ... How can we differentiate between the powers of darkness and the powers of the mind?'

Despite the fact that witchcraft attracted greater interest in the 60s than it had for a long time, the eleven films made during this period which dealt with contemporary witchcraft are a disappointing bunch, and none of them manages the impact (not to mention the commercial success) of Polanski's *Rosemary's Baby*. Lance Comfort's *Devils of Darkness*, made for Planet in 1964, is undeniably shoddy, its mixture of Celtic vampirism and smart-set witchcraft unconvincing. But the film's hero is played by the ever-reliable William Sylvester, and there is some satisfaction to be derived from the way in which the most boring characters are killed off by an avenging bat. Tigon's *The Curse of the Crimson Altar* (d. Vernon Sewell, 1968), despite the presence of Barbara Steele and Boris Karloff and a script based on H. P. Lovecraft's *Dreams in the Witch's House*, is disappointing. Barbara Steele – the star of Mario Bava's *La Maschera del Demonio* and Roger Corman's *The Pit and the Pendulum* – has little to do except appear in green paint and an exotic headdress, and the early part of the film, where chubby, inane young men and vacant-looking dolly birds hold an orgy while Michael Gough scuttles round as a mad butler and Christopher Lee sits upstairs by his log fire perusing his learned books, promises the worst. Fortunately, some redeeming qualities later materialise – a complex inter-meshing of dream and reality, a non-obvious plot, a real location (W. S. Gilbert's reputedly haunted house), and the photography of John Coquillon (which had added visual distinction to *Witchfinder General* and *The Oblong Box*) – but as a whole the film is a wasted opportunity.

Of the two American-backed films, *The Haunting* (1963), directed by Robert Wise (who had made *Curse of the Cat People* and *The Body Snatcher* for Val Lewton in the 40s and was to go on to make *The Sound of Music*), is close to *The Innocents* in its clever creation of atmosphere and unresolved ambiguities. But its haunted house theme is one that British cinema has rarely touched on, and despite the presence of Claire Bloom and Richard Johnson it is best regarded as a Hollywood film made in England. Lee Thompson's *Eye of the Devil* (1968) sets up the fascinating premise of the continuing existence of fertility cults in France which need to sacrifice rich landowners to ensure good crops. But the cast – David Niven, Deborah Kerr, Sharon Tate, David Hemmings, Donald Pleasence – look uncomfortable in their roles, and a meanderingly dull script robs the film of much of its interest. Don Sharp's *Witchcraft* (1964, for Robert Lippert) and Cyril Frankel's *The Witches* (1966, for Hammer) are more predictable but more satisfying. Sharp's film displays his usual competence and stylishness and, like *The Witches* (scripted by Nigel Kneale and photographed by Arthur Grant), creates a convincing picture of insular, incestuous everyday life in the English countryside. The two most interesting films, though, are *Night of the Eagle* and *The Devil Rides Out*.

Night of the Eagle, like *Circus of Horrors* directed by Sidney Hayers for Independent Artists, is based on a story by the science fiction writer Fritz Leiber, and like *Night of the Demon* it has a complacent rationalist forced to abandon his conviction that the supernatural does not exist. As one would expect, Hayers directs with less ingenuity than Tourneur, and the story does not have the gripping simplicity of M. R. James's *The Casting of Runes* on which *Night of the Demon* is based. But Margaret Johnston's pasty-faced academic monster is as interesting an adversary as Niall MacGinnis's satanic magician in Tourneur's film, and the relationship between Peter Wyngarde and his wife (Janet Blair) is more complex than the predictable romance between Dana Andrews and Peggy Cummins. Wyngarde plays Norman Taylor, a lecturer at a College of Medicine whose keenness and intelligence seem likely to elevate him over the heads of duller but older colleagues, but witchcraft unexpectedly intrudes into this realistic scenario of academic life.

When Norman finds occult paraphernalia in his kitchen, he refuses to take seriously his wife's warning that this is all that protects him from the College witches, and he burns them. His life now begins to drift into a nightmare confusion of reality and illusion, but his descent is as much into a female labyrinth as it is into the supernatural. His burning of his wife's charms and talismans is a violation, almost a rape, which leaves her naked and vulnerable and him confused. As he confesses in exasperation: 'I'm not convinced about anything. If we were to investigate all the strange rituals performed by women based on so-called intuition, half the female population would be in asylums. I don't know what to think!' Just as his wife loses the props which help her cope with her malevolent surroundings, Norman has the supports of his rational universe kicked away. There might be reasonable explanations for a van appearing from nowhere and nearly running him over, for one of his students trying to shoot him, for mysterious phone calls and threatening presences at the door, but Norman's life, which

Night of the Eagle: burning the charms (Janet Blair, Peter Wyngarde)

had been one of smooth and comfortable success, is now under siege. In a climactic scene in a derelict seaside church, he desperately improvises a ceremony to protect his wife; and though he sweeps away the little shrine he has built, his plea to something outside himself is rewarded by her appearance, wet, bedraggled and zombie-like, from the sea which would have claimed her.

As in *Night of the Demon*, a real monster makes an appearance – the stone eagle which comes to life and flaps menacingly (its tow rope clearly visible) through the college corridors – but its existence is more questionable than that of the Fire Demon, and *Night of the Eagle* remains a psychological horror story, its hesitation over the existence of the supernatural fulfilling Todorov's definition of the fantastic.

The satanists of *Night of the Demon* and *Night of the Eagle* are both destroyed by the demons they have conjured up. The same sort of nemesis awaits Charles Gray's coldly avuncular Mocata in *The Devil Rides Out* (1967), but a different sort of morality informs Fisher's film. In *Night of the Demon* and *Night of the Eagle*, the hero is blind to the evil forces being used against him but his basic goodness enables him to win through against a malevolent but slightly pathetic rival. In *The Devil Rides Out*, Christopher Lee's Duc de Richleau is as awake to the supernatural as Cushing's Van Helsing, and there is the familiar struggle between good and evil which is evident in Fisher's Frankenstein and Dracula films.[48] Pirie sees the film as the fullest expression of Fisher's world view, but there are serious problems. Richleau is a humourless bore, Leon Green's Rex Van Ryn a buffoon, and Patrick Mower's Simon Aron a nonentity. The women are better: Sarah Lawson's upper-middle class resilience is used effectively to convey a civilised rejection of the disorder threatened by the supernatural, and Nike Arrighi's Tanith is a genuinely exotic heroine. But Lawson is only given two good scenes – her chilling encounter with Mocata, and her assumption of Tanith's personality during the final ceremony – and the relationship between Tanith and the stolid Van Ryn is very poorly developed. For an effective climax to this little cycle of occult movies, one has to wait until 1973 and *The Wicker Man*.

The other important group of horror films made in the 60s are contemporary thrillers which involve madness or the illusion of madness – what Todorov calls 'an experience of limits' – rather than supernatural forces.[49] One could include Otto Preminger's *Bunny Lake is Missing*, David Greene's *The Shuttered Room* (like *The Curse of the Crimson Altar*, based on an H. P. Lovecraft story) and *I Start Counting*, but again this was an area which Hammer – and in particular Jimmy Sangster – specialised in. *Maniac* (1963), directed by Michael Carreras; *Paranoiac* (1963), *Hysteria* (1964), *Nightmare* (1964), all directed by Freddie Francis; and *Crescendo* (1969), directed by Alan Gibson, as well as Richard Matheson's similarly contrived *Fanatic* (1965), directed by Silvio Narizzano, all have moments of interest but only *Nightmare* is more than a routine production. *Taste of Fear* (1960) and *The Nanny* (1965), which were also scripted by Sangster for Hammer, stand out largely because they are directed by Seth Holt.

Holt is one of the great might-have-beens of British cinema, directing only six modest films – *Nowhere to Go*, *Station Six Sahara*, *Taste of Fear*, *The Nanny*, *Danger Route*, and *Blood from the Mummy's Tomb* (which had to be completed by Michael Carreras) – before he died in 1971.[50] *Taste of Fear* is a suspense film worthy of Hitchcock, where plot implausibilities only surface long after the film has ended. Douglas Slocombe's glistening black and white photography and Bernard Robinson's simple but convincing sets give an almost formal perfection to the film. But in contrast to *Psycho* or *Vertigo*, where the characters carry an unbearably sad weight of experience on their shoulders, Susan Strasberg, Ronald Lewis, Ann Todd and Christopher Lee, good though their performances are, exist only as part of the mechanics of a complex plot.[51]

The Nanny is more significant than *Taste of Fear*, sharing with *The Innocents*, *A High Wind in Jamaica* and *Our Mother's House* a fascination with the destructive potential of children, and combining it with *The Servant* and *Night Must Fall*'s fear of the indispensable but dangerous servant. In contrast to the rootless characters of *Taste of Fear* and the oddly indeterminate casts of *The Servant* and *Night Must Fall*, James Villiers, Jill Bennett and Wendy Craig's Belgravia monsters are searingly convincing – sufficient reasons in themselves for the anti-social behaviour of ten-year-old Joey. And Holt draws from Bette Davis a magnificently restrained performance as the mad but over-whelmingly sympathetic Nanny – her brain disintegrating under the strain of pandering to the inanities of the upper-middle classes – which almost lifts the film on to a tragic plane.[52]

According to Robin Wood, 'the true subject of the horror genre is the struggle for recognition of all that our civilisation represses or oppresses: its re-emergence dramatised, as in our nightmares, as an object of horror, a matter for terror, the "happy ending" (when it exists) typically signifying the restoration of repression.'[53] But Wood is writing about the American horror films of the 70s, which relate closely to the society which produced them. Hammer's Gothic romances are dominated by conventions and represent an unreliable guide to the changing fantasy life of the 60s. One might suggest that the vampire films – the dominant myth of the international horror scene in the 60s – with their aura of voluptuous, insistent sexuality, had something to do with dreams of sexual plenitude aroused by greater permissiveness in dress and behaviour; but as with the realist films, it is less a question of reducing them to sociological phenomena than of considering the role they play in the history of popular culture.[54]

9
EXPLORING THE UNDERWORLD

In an atmosphere controlled by real and imaginary fears, murder no longer seems the great unpardonable act, only the mechanism of last resort. The best melodrama finds subtlety on the far side of shock by creating complex patterns of identification for the reader (and in Hitchcock's case the audience), forcing him to reconcile the experiences of criminal and victim and to perceive elements of both in himself. He is reminded that the destructive act, in its rejection of conventional limits, has a strong primitive appeal. (Gavin Lambert, *The Dangerous Edge*, 1975)[1]

Our Policemen are Wonderful

In 1946 George Orwell wrote an article on 'The Decline of the English Murder', lamenting the fact that the traditional English murder – furtive, domestic, carefully planned, involving long-repressed hatreds and passions – was being pushed out by American-style casual killings which reeked of 'dance halls, movie palaces, cheap perfume, false names and stolen cars'.[2] He was writing in the wake of wartime crimes like the Cleft Chin murder and in the midst of a cycle of spiv films. In the 50s there was a remarkable reversal. Peace returned to the underworld and the crime rate dropped, and in Anglo-Amalgamated's *Scotland Yard* series the nosy neighbours, suspicious landladies, men with guilty secrets, women with secret passions, amnesia, dreams, and mysterious happenings in suburbia which Orwell thought had passed away, enjoyed a long Indian summer. *Scotland Yard's* 'stories of human weakness, of greed and envy, of cunning and stupidity', dredged from the annals of crime by the lugubrious Edgar Lustgarten, had to share the bottom end of the market with low-budget spiv films (*Street of Shadows*, *Soho Incident*, *The Blue Parrot*) and films exploring the violent world of teenage hoodlums (*Cosh Boy*, *The Young and the Guilty*), lorry drivers (*The Long Haul*, *Hell Drivers*), and prostitutes

(*The Flesh is Weak, Passport to Shame*). But most 50s first features, like Charles Frend's *The Long Arm* and John Ford's *Gideon's Day*, celebrated the integrity and heroism of the police.

By the end of the decade less reverential attitudes to the police began to surface. In television, the cosy world of *Dixon of Dock Green* was disrupted by the noisy sirens of *Z-Cars*; and in the cinema, hymns to the Scotland Yard detectives were superseded by a group of remarkable films – *Beyond This Place, Blind Date, Hell is a City, The Criminal* and *Never Let Go* – which presented a less comfortable view of the underworld and a less flattering one of the police.

Beyond This Place (1959), based on an A. J. Cronin novel, directed by Jack Cardiff for the small distribution company Renown (which also backed Siodmak's *The Rough and the Smooth*), and starring Van Johnson and Vera Miles, looks like an American *film noir* with its low-key lighting and doom-laden plot; but its use of Liverpool locations and the presence of Bernard Lee – one of the best and most flexible of British character actors before he was swallowed up by his role as 'M' in the Bond films – root it solidly in English society. Johnson, evacuated to America after his father is convicted of murder during the war, returns to discover a web of apathy and corruption obscuring his father's innocence. The Liverpool police, in contrast to the friendly, honest men of Scotland Yard, are sour, unhelpful and susceptible to

A gloomy, oppressive world where power and authority are in the hands of cynics and psychopaths: Van Johnson and Emlyn Williams, *Beyond This Place*

202

pressure from local dignitaries. With the help of a shy, sexually damaged librarian and a crusading newspaper editor, the depressed hero succeeds in seeing justice done, but prison has turned the jovial, lovable man he remembers into a bitter, brutalised thug, and it is a precarious, uncertain victory that is won against the forces of darkness.

Beyond This Place bears comparison with Joseph Losey's first important British film, *Time Without Pity* (1957), though there it is the inadequate father who has to prove his son's innocence. Leo McKern, the villain of *Time Without Pity*, is the newspaper editor in *Beyond This Place*; Emlyn Williams, who wrote *Time Without Pity*, is its villain; and along with their overlapping personnel both films share a sense of little people adrift in a gloomy, oppressive world where power and authority are in the hands of cynics and psychopaths. *Time Without Pity*, despite Michael Redgrave's performance, stays within 'B' movie conventions, its characters subordinated to its plot, its action mechanical. But Losey's next two films, *Blind Date* (1959) and *The Criminal* (1960), broke new ground.

Blind Date was made for Independent Artists, a small production company run by Julian Wintle and Leslie Parkyn, who had worked as Rank contract producers in the early 50s. Their biggest success came early in 1959 with *Tiger Bay*, Lee Thompson's film about an inquisitive child and a Polish seaman who has shot his adulterous girlfriend and is on the run from a grim, humourless policeman. *Blind Date*, released five months later, is superficially similar. Again a young foreigner is accused of murdering a woman, again a hard-bitten police detective is determined to nail him for the crime; but there the similarity ends. Thompson employs proto-Kitchen Sink backgrounds and explores weighty themes of freedom and responsibility, youth and age, guilt and innocence. *Blind Date* is a conventional British murder mystery, which Losey transforms into a critique of a repressive, class-ridden society. In *The Servant*, *King and Country*, *Accident* and *The Go-Between*, Losey's treatment of the English class system is always that of an outsider, fascinated and slightly appalled. *Blind Date*, despite its French *femme fatale* and its Dutch hero, is bolder and more polemical, the only one of Losey's British films to validate his left-wing credentials.

Stanley Baker's Inspector Morgan is the son of a chauffeur on uneasy terms with his middle-class colleagues and superiors, unwilling to temper his policeman's professionalism to accommodate their self-protective corruption, but acutely conscious of the threat to his career that his uncompromising attitude represents ('Going to the top calls for something a little more than the constable mentality, it calls for an understanding of the deeper meanings of public service,' he is warned). His adversary, Jan Van Rooyen (Hardy Kruger), the irreverent young artist he suspects of murder, is also working-class (the son of

203

a coal-miner), but he has fallen in love with a cold *haute couture* beauty, Jacqueline Cousteau (Micheline Presle). Morgan believes the boy to be guilty but suspects some collusion with the murdered woman's rich and influential lover. His attempt to confront them with one another unexpectedly reunites Jan with his treacherous mistress, and the film's ending speaks volumes about the ravages exacted by a society polluted by materialism and repression.

The plot's resolution turns on Jacqueline, the real murderer, who has carefully framed Jan for her crime, acknowledging that she is – as Morgan refuses to believe – his lover. Jan taunts her, 'Be careful, don't reveal anything. No feeling of any kind. You shouldn't have to worry, you've had a lifetime of experience in pretending and hiding your feelings.' But her sophisticated amorality, a mask for the indulgent stupidity of the over-privileged, is dissolved by his innocence and vitality, and her sad, doll-like façade cracks when he demands why she went on with her mad plot rather than trusting in his love for her: 'What was it? You were too old for me? Were you afraid of that? But you were young to me, all the things that should have happened to you when you were a girl I was bringing to you.' She leaves him cursing, but she is a tragic rather than a pathetic figure, damned by the conflict between the false social values she has lived her life by and the reality of truth and beauty with which Jan has tempted her.

Blind Date is a textbook example of how a director at the height of his powers can make a great film despite an unremarkable story and limited financial resources. *The Criminal*, which Losey made the following year for Anglo-Amalgamated, had more difficulty overcoming these obstacles.[3] What was no doubt a neat, if superficial, story by Jimmy Sangster, sprouts metaphysical wings in Alun Owen's screenplay and is further complicated by Losey's increasing tendency to leave his narratives loose and open-ended. The result is a fascinating hodge-podge. The depiction of life in prison is stark and authentic compared to anything that had come before, though Losey's use of Brechtian devices like the calypso-singing black prisoner who comments on the action seems out of place. Patrick Magee's chief screw, a peculiar mixture of religiosity and cynicism, and Noel Willman's *New States-man*-reading Governor might look like caricatures, but prison autobiographies like Jim Phelan's *Jail Journey* and Wilfred Macartney's *Walls Have Mouths* suggest that monsters such as these were by no means rare in the prison system.

Bannion (Stanley Baker), the central character, was ostensibly based on the Soho racketeer Albert Dimes, and though Dimes was involved in protection rather than armed robbery and served little time in prison, *The Criminal* is distinguished by its well-informed view of the underworld. The operation of a convict hierarchy in prison, the conflict between individual initiative and the need to work as part of a

'... all the things that should have happened to you when you were a girl I was bringing to you': Hardy Kruger, Micheline Presle in *Blind Date*

well-financed team, even the division between policemen who empathise with criminals and those who think of them as scum, give the film a sharp-edged authenticity conspicuously absent from earlier British crime films.[4] This is marred by Bannion's messy love-life. Jill Bennett looks as if she has drifted in from a Continental art-house movie, and Margit Saad's transformation from promiscuous sex kitten to devoted fiancée would look rushed even in a sexploitation film, but Losey's boldness in using popular generic forms to explore issues above love, death and the problems of being an individualistic hero in a corporate society is impressive.[5]

Stanley Baker is the key figure in 60s crime films, just as Jack Hawkins had been in the 50s. Hawkins's Superintendent Halliday (in *The Long Arm*) and Inspector Gideon (in *Gideon's Day*) are hardworking, happily married and unimpeachably honest. Baker's characters are usually vulnerable, unhappy, ambivalent, and from 1960 onwards he tended to play sympathetic criminals rather than policemen. His last police role is in *Hell is a City* (1960), directed by Val Guest for Hammer.

The city in question is not some metaphysical Alphaville or even rough, tough Sheffield or Glasgow, but Manchester – the home of the *Guardian*, *Coronation Street* and the Hallé orchestra. Baker plays Inspector Martineau, a cynical detective locked into an unhappy,

Prince of the city: Martineau (Stanley Baker) establishes his credentials with a
Manchester street-girl in *Hell is a City*

childless marriage (with Maxine Audley). He is a close cousin to *Blind
Date*'s Inspector Morgan and to the Liverpool policeman Baker plays
in Dearden and Relph's 1957 film *Violent Playground*. But *Violent
Playground* is a social problem film and *Blind Date* a murder mystery.
In *Hell is a City*, the escape of a robber who has a grudge against
Martineau leads to a vivid exploration of the Manchester underworld.
Guest makes full use of Arthur Grant's atmospheric Hammerscope
photography to capture a north of England which is as gritty and real
as that of the Kitchen Sink films. Dimly lit billiard halls, glittering
crowded pubs, a gathering outside a moorland village for an illegal
game of pitch and toss, the dark wet streets, make their Manchester
seem as exciting and dangerous as New York.

Martineau is a satisfyingly complex character, as hard-working a
policeman as Gideon of the Yard, but one whose home life is in tatters
and whose methods are rather rougher. He reassures one character,
'I've walloped you when you've been a rough boy, but I've never laid a
hand on you to make you admit anything', and threatens another,
'There were four men on that job and I want four men. If I don't get
the fourth I'll get your kid brother.' The film ends with him walking
into the rainy night, rejecting the advances of the friendly barmaid
who could make him happy but reluctant to return to his cold, loveless
home. Efforts have to be made to suspend disbelief that Baker (whose
own northern accent is sporadic) and John Crawford (the American
brought in to play the chief villain) are local Manchester boys who

went to school together, but the world they inhabit is brought alive by Grant's photography and the gallery of well-rounded supporting characters one comes to expect in a Guest film. George A. Cooper's jolly rogue of a publican, Vanda Godsell's glowingly sensual barmaid, Donald Pleasence's latter-day Sam Grundie besotted with bored, unvirtuous Billie Whitelaw, and the small-time crooks scared of Crawford and scared of the murder he has implicated them in, give the film a richness of texture which more than makes up for the routine story.

John Guillermin's *Never Let Go* (like *Blind Date* made for Independent Artists) is more violent than *Hell is a City* and *The Criminal*, and was consequently more critically disparaged. But Alun Falconer's script is refreshingly original and this tight, clever revenge thriller offers insights into British society as it entered the 'age of affluence'. Richard Todd plays an infuriatingly petty-minded cosmetics salesman, John Cummings, who thinks he's never had it so good until a gang of teenage delinquents (led by Adam Faith) steal his new Ford Anglia. He has not insured it against theft and without his car he stands to lose his job. Determined to recover it at all costs, he doggedly follows a trail which leads him to a prosperous car salesman, Lionel Meadows (Peter Sellers), who beneath his smooth exterior is a dangerously volatile criminal.

Todd's John Cummings is a similar character to Attenborough's Tom Curtis in *The Angry Silence* (released only a couple of months

Turbulent youth: Adam Faith and his gang, *Never Let Go*

207

earlier). Both are little, ordinary men forced by circumstances and their conscience to take on a violent, malevolent world. But *Never Let Go* is more honest and consistent. In contrast to the greasy caricatures of *The Angry Silence*, Adam Faith's leather boys seem genuinely threatening – dropping Cummings's soap samples into his tea and mobbing him with their bikes – but they collapse into humdrum, vulnerable, powerless young people once the fun is over, less equipped to deal with the world than Cummings himself. And whereas the ending of *The Angry Silence* is irritatingly contrived (Tom Curtis's blinding by the leather boys shocks the workers back to their senses), *Never Let Go* allows Cummings's determination to retrieve his Ford Anglia, which overrides concern for his family's safety and the smooth working of a police operation, to become an obsession inextricably tied up with his own masculinity.[6]

The most marked difference between the two films, though, is that in place of a dumb shop steward and a shadowy agitator, *Never Let Go* has one of the great villains of screen history. Sellers, at the peak of his creative powers, gives a marvellous performance, less nuanced than the comic caricatures of *I'm All Right Jack* and *Heavens Above*, but consequently more intense and powerful. Lionel Meadows is frightening in the Tod Slaughter tradition of melodrama villains – slamming a radiogram lid down on the fingers of the luckless Faith, tipping over a fish tank and crushing underfoot Mervyn Johns's beloved terrapins, and finally exploding into self-destructive fury as the interfering activities of the 'little lipstick pedlar' threaten to bring down his criminal empire.

After *Hell is a City*, Guest went on to make *Jigsaw*, set in Brighton, again with Arthur Grant as his photographer, and with Jack Warner in the main police role. By this time Warner was inseparably identified with Dixon of Dock Green and to some extent *Jigsaw* is a reversion to the 'copperolatry' of the 50s. There is the familiar fascination with police procedure, the insistence that policemen are good sorts who patiently endure the arrogance, stupidity and apathy of the public; but Guest breathes new life into the old myths. Warner is obviously comfortable in his part and is able to imbue his police inspector with convincing idiosyncrasies: his tetchiness at having to give up smoking and choose between tea without sugar and a fat paunch, his inability to delegate and his awareness of his own weakness in delivering Dixonian homilies. Placed among Guest's stock company of eccentrics – Peter Ashmore's fussy little teacher, Norman Chappell's colour-blind delivery boy, Michael Goodliffe's slimy vacuum-cleaner salesman, Yolande Donlan's improbable virgin – he seems to be making a one-man stand against the onrush of the affluent society. As he declares, on discovering that Goodliffe's salesman is not after all the murderer, despite being a compulsive womaniser and an embodiment of everything that's wrong with the affluent society: 'I'm not a prude, but a man like that makes me want to take a bath.' It is this conflict of values, superimposed on to a neatly plotted murder mystery, which makes the film so fascinating.

Sidney Hayers's *Payroll* (1962) continued the tradition of setting a tough crime thriller in a clearly defined English provincial town, but it is less imaginative than the Guest/Grant films. Its ingredients are excellent – a good team of villains (Michael Craig, Tom Bell, Kenneth Griffith), a vengeful security guard's widow (Billie Whitelaw), and fresh and exciting locations in and around Newcastle – but they don't quite jell. Too much time is spent on uninteresting characters, particularly the cowardly wages clerk who helps the gang in order to raise money for his faithless French wife, and the villains are disappointingly developed. Kenneth Griffith doesn't get beyond the stereotype of the weak but decent crook who abhors violence, Michael Craig's cruel good looks remain unexploited, and Tom Bell, brilliant in his intimations of psychopathic inarticulacy, is snuffed out before he can play a major role.

The Rank Organisation had a policy of offering 'family entertainment', but it acted on the assumption that a leavening of crime films was essential to a healthy diet. Its distribution arm handled – and substantially financed – *Tiger Bay*, *Blind Date* and *Never Let Go*, as well as the social problem thrillers *Sapphire* and *Victim*, and a handful of low-budget crime films made by Wolf Rilla, Leigh Vance and John Lemont – *Witness in the Dark*, *The Shakedown*, *And Women Shall Weep* and *Piccadilly Third Stop* (though Lemont and Vance's last, and best, film, *The Frightened City*, went to Anglo-Amalgamated). Thus it was not altogether surprising that Rank should be directly responsible for *The Informers* (d. Ken Annakin, 1963), the most interesting successor to *Never Let Go*. The script was by Alun Falconer, but it was closely based on a novel by Douglas Warner (with the much better title of *Death of a Snout*), which in turn relied heavily on the memoirs of Chief Superintendent John Gosling, a founder member of the 'Ghost Squad' (an undercover unit formed to combat serious crime in the late 1940s). The film deals with the serious and still relevant question of to what extent the police should interact with the underworld, and strongly endorses Gosling's view that 'however one may dislike the informer, no police force can function efficiently without him.'[7]

Inspector Johnnoe (Nigel Patrick) is not impressed when his superior (Harry Andrews) tells him that with modern methods of police surveillance there is no longer any need to rely on informers. One of his best 'snouts' is murdered shortly after phoning in a tip-off, and Johnnoe descends into the underworld to bring the culprit to book. He soon realises that a flashy, sadistic character called Bertie Hoyle (Derren Nesbitt) is in some way involved, but after raiding Bertie's luxur-

The Informers: Colin Blakely and some friends from the demolition business

ious home (without a search warrant) he is framed by the crooks and suspended from his job for alleged corruption. He unofficially continues his investigations, but it is the dead snout's brother (Colin Blakely) who – with some friends from the demolition business – wreaks vengeance on Bertie and enables Johnnoe to unmask and arrest the shifty villain who is behind the set-up. Nigel Patrick played the unimpeachably upright detective in charge of the murder investigation in *Sapphire*, but he had appeared in more disreputable roles in the past (most memorably the smooth-talking spiv, Bar Gorman, in *Noose*) and he has the right degree of roguish unconventionality to make Johnnoe believable. With its convincing underworld characters and quarrelsome, imperfect policemen, *The Informers* represents something of a high point in the development of British crime films. The characters might be stereotypes – the tough but honest detective and his loyal, long-suffering wife, the seedy criminal mastermind and his dangerously flashy front-man, the hard-bitten but vulnerable whore, the irredeemably shifty snout – but they come across as quirkily individual and there is little of the cosy moralising that afflicts so many British crime thrillers. A handful of critics did notice its potential at the time, but it is depressingly symptomatic of attitudes to British cinema that the film has subsequently vanished into critical oblivion.[8]

210

B Films

By 1965 the British crime film as a genre was beginning to look thin and sickly. Denis Gifford's *British Film Catalogue* lists forty-six crime films for 1962; by 1965 there were only twenty-two, and half of these were spy films like *Thunderball* and *The Liquidator*, which had little in common with the traditional British crime film. Part of the change was to do with the decline of the 'B' film: after 1965 second-feature production was virtually abandoned in favour of low-budget productions for sex and horror double bills. British 'B' films – of which crime was the staple diet – had a poor reputation and no one lamented their passing. An irate Frederick Woods had written in *Films and Filming* in 1959:

> These films – it's still safe to generalise – are inept, stupid, badly written and acted, ludicrous and worthless. The only entertainment one gets is from the unintentional laughs. For the rest – boredom, impatience and a ruining of one's appreciation of the main feature. They are a cheat. We, the public, do not pay only to see the main feature; we pay for the whole programme, and if half the programme stinks, then we should get up and throw the seats at the screen.[9]

The films Woods describes, where clichéd characters are crowded together in cardboard sets and given unreal dialogue to speak, certainly existed, but often there is at least one actor (Anthony Dawson in Baker and Berman's *Hour of Decision*, Susan Stephen in the Danzigers' *Return of a Stranger*, for example) who manages to bring the film to life, and the nightclubs, warehouses and country hideaways where the action takes place have acquired a period charm.

This disreputable type of 'B' film in its late 50s and early 60s form is perhaps best represented by the work of Guido Coen and Charles Saunders, two *maudit* protégés of Filippo del Giudice (who had brought films like *In Which We Serve*, *Henry V* and *Hamlet* to the screen in the 40s). *Naked Fury*, for example, which they made for Butchers in 1959, has just about all the stock ingredients which Frederick Woods complains about: an improbable American hero (Reed de Rouen), a squabbling gang with bitchy wives and girlfriends, an innocent and helpless heroine, and even a fiery finale in a deserted dockside warehouse. In fact, it is an exciting little film with clearly developed characters and a convoluted but satisfying plot – the gang disintegrates under the moral dilemma of what to do with the innocent (and attractive) girl who has witnessed them (accidentally) murder her father. *Jungle Street*, which Coen and Saunders made in 1961, is virtually a teenage social problem film, and attempts to raise the issue of capital punishment. It was predictably condemned by the *Monthly Film Bulletin* as a 'dreary second feature, with a number of amateurish strip-tease acts dispiritingly presented to eke out a feeble, formulary plot', which 'as an exercise in crime and punishment has neither point nor moral force'.[10] Without wishing to deny the film's flaws, its exploration of a grimy world of shortened horizons and stunted development which affluence has touched in only the most superficial way is fascinating. And its young protagonists, David McCallum, Kenneth Cope, Jill Ireland – fragile, brutal, vulnerable, rebellious – are disturbingly true to life.

From the late 50s attempts were made to produce higher quality 'B' films. Julian Wintle and Leslie Parkyn, who took over the small Beaconsfield studios when they set up Independent Artists in 1958, resolved that their one-hour featurettes would be of the same standard as their feature films. Independent Artists employed talented directors like Pat Jackson, Don Sharp, Vernon Sewell and Sidney Hayers. The films (Jackson's *Seven Keys*, Sharp's *The Professionals*, Sewell's *The Man in the Back Seat*, Hayers's *Violent Moment*, for example) are better made than most 'B' films, but they are marred by a conservative smugness – the police are always right, honesty is the best policy, crime is for mugs – which makes them disappointingly tame.[11] A similar criticism can be made of the Boulting Brothers' *Suspect* (1960), another worthy attempt to prove to the industry that cheap films did not have to be bad films, which despite a likeable cast – Peter Cushing, Thorley Walters, Virginia Maskell, Tony Britton, Donald Pleasence – and a script by Nigel Balchin, founders on an over-respectful attitude to authority. Shoddy though it is, the twilight world of *Naked Fury*, *The Gentle Trap*, *Danger By My Side*, *Jungle Street*, and their numerous brethren, where exotic characters talk in pseudo-American accents and spend their time in strip-clubs and gambling dens when they are not cracking safes or hijacking lorries, seems infinitely more attractive.[12]

In the early 60s the policy of bringing over American actors to star in British 'B' films was abandoned. A new breed of British actor – Alan Dobie, Alfred Burke, Kenneth Cope, Michael Coles, Lee Montague, Nigel Green, Derren Nesbitt, Dudley Foster, even Sean Connery before he was snapped up for the James Bond role – had emerged who were quite tough enough to take on underworld rivals and the police. None of them, however, quite had the weight of the Californian William Sylvester, who stayed on to give excellent performances in a trio of films – *Offbeat*, *Information Received* and *Blind Corner* – which typify the virtues and vices of early 60s low-budget crime films. *Offbeat* (directed by Cliff Owen for British Lion in 1960) has Sylvester as an MI5 man chosen for an undercover police operation 'because he doesn't look like a policeman' (he looks even less like an MI5 agent). He successfully infiltrates a gang of thieves and finds that in contrast to the lonely, suspicious existence he has pursued up to now, he is among people who are loyal, decent and trustworthy. He falls in love with the

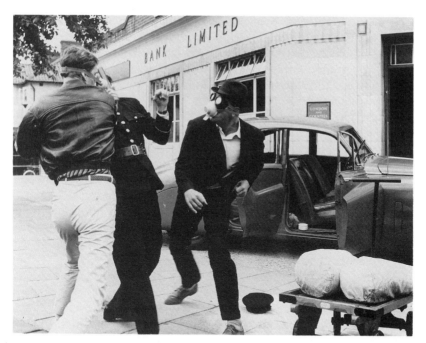

Americanised B movies: *Danger By My Side*

young widow (Mai Zetterling) of the 'peterman' he has been recruited to replace, and there is a real sense of sour disillusion when the untrusting, treacherous police catch up with the gang.[13]

Information Received (1961), directed by Robert Lynn and photographed by Nicolas Roeg, deals with a similar situation, but here loyalties are less complex as the woman Sylvester might have fallen in love with (Sabina Sesselman) turns out to be a murderous *femme fatale*, interested only in framing him for the murder of her unwanted husband. *Blind Corner* (1963), directed by Lance Comfort for Mancunian, looks like a reversion to the worst type of 50s (or 30s) jealous husband drawing-room thriller. But it is fascinating as a perfectly preserved fossil of a long dead form, and Sylvester's character – a blind composer continually distracted from his serious music by the need to write pop songs in order to pay for his wife's extravagant lifestyle – is firmly anchored in the 60s. The transfer of his affections from Barbara Shelley, his selfish, malevolent wife, to Elizabeth Shepherd, his stoically loving secretary, charts a satisfying path from indulgence and obsession to creativity and respect.[14]

By the late 50s Anglo-Amalgamated's *Scotland Yard* films were beginning to look old-fashioned, and the marvellously sonorous title sequence (police cars tear through night-time London to Scotland Yard as a stentorian voice intones, 'Scotland Yard! Nerve centre of London's Metropolitan Police, headquarters of its department of

213

Criminal Investigation. Scotland Yard! A name that appears on almost every page of the annals of crime detection. Scotland Yard! Where night and day a determined body of men carries on a relentless, unceasing crusade against crime') was truncated.[15] The stories, too, seemed to lose their way and there was nothing after 1959 to match the energetic inventiveness of Ken Hughes in early episodes like *The Dark Stairway*, *The Drayton Case* and *The Missing Man*, and Paul Gherzo in *The Mysterious Bullet*, *The Stateless Man* and *Fatal Journey*. In 1962 the series was replaced by *The Scales of Justice* which, with its tinny theme music by the Tornadoes (Billy Fury's backing group) and its tales of sex-obsessed salesmen and drunken drivers, faithfully evoked the new spirit of affluence. In filmic terms, however, it turned out to be much thinner soil. Edgar Lustgarten looked shifty and uncomfortable in the modern glass and concrete surroundings, like a vampire caught in the sunlight, and only twelve episodes were produced, compared to the forty episodes of *Scotland Yard*.

Anglo-Amalgamated was much more successful with the hour-long Edgar Wallace films it made between 1960 and 1964.[16] Earlier Wallace adaptations had tended to dwell on the macabre, but Anglo's films, relying heavily on location shooting to supplement the limited resources of Merton Park studios, were made with brusque realism. This had the effect of making typical Wallace locked-door mysteries like *The Malpas Mystery* and *The Clue of the Twisted Candle* look irritatingly contrived, but where the action could be brought up to date without too much violence to the plot – generally those stories involving crooked businessmen cheating and blackmailing their way to wealth (*The Share Out*, *Partners in Crime*), treacherous sexual relationships (*Ricochet*, *Man Detained*, *Never Mention Murder*), or small-time criminals adrift in a hostile world (*Man at the Carlton Towers*, *Marriage of Convenience*, *Five to One*, *Face of a Stranger*) – gripping, powerful films emerged. Distinguishing between directors is not easy. Allan Davis, Peter Duffell, Quentin Lawrence, Geoffrey Nethercott, David Eady, even Sidney Hayers, seem to bring nothing of note to their episodes, though the stolid professionalism of Montgomery Tully, a veteran of *Scotland Yard*, is evident in *The Man Who Was Nobody*, which is also notable for its upper middle-class beatniks. Robert Tronson, Gerard Glaister and Gordon Flemyng turn out more than their fair share of the good episodes, but two of the best – *Incident at Midnight* (d. Norman Harrison) and *Never Mention Murder* (d. John Nelson Burton) – are made by directors with no traceable track record. Clive Donner's *Marriage of Convenience* and *The Sinister Man* are very stylish, and clearly marked him out for higher things. But the most satisfying films are those directed by John Moxey, particularly *Face of a Stranger*, an improbable story about an ex-convict who visits his cellmate's blind wife and inadvertently takes his place, which Moxey transforms into a *Blind Date*-like tragedy of love, greed and betrayal with stunningly effective performances by Rosemary Leach as the blind *femme fatale* and Jeremy Kemp as the muddle-minded ex-convict.

Last Days of the British Crime Film

Until the mid-60s the crime genre had remained resistant to the general trend to switch from black and white to colour. But from 1966 onwards even low-budget crime films like Anglo's *Scales of Justice* series were being made in colour, and Charles Crichton's *He Who Rides a Tiger* and Otto Preminger's *Bunny Lake is Missing* are the last significant black and white crime films made in Britain.

Bunny Lake is Missing (1965), is a good example of conservative Hollywood professionalism, one of the few distinguished films made by the Hollywood old guard in the 60s. *He Who Rides a Tiger* (1965) is solidly in the tradition of the modestly budgeted indigenous British film (though ironically it was produced by a fly-by-night producer who ran out of money halfway through production). It was directed by Charles Crichton (his last feature film before *A Fish Called Wanda*), a director most closely identified with Ealing.[17] Both films seem to stand at a crossroads, aware that society has changed radically, but holding back from participating in those changes. Preminger hints that London is not what it was in Gideon of the Yard's day – a student demonstration, a pop group (the Zombies) on the pub television – but the England he concentrates on is one of old-fashioned eccentrics who fit neatly into the hoary old story of a mother whose child disappears so thoroughly that the police are sceptical whether she ever existed. Martita Hunt plays a dotty old lady tucked away in the attic of the school from which Bunny has disappeared, Finlay Currie the Dickensian shopkeeper who mends Bunny's doll and thus proves her existence, Noël Coward a television personality with a penchant for whips, and Laurence Olivier a Scotland Yard detective whose drab exterior conceals a sharp intelligence. Olivier's policeman is as harassed as Jack Warner's in *Jigsaw*, but he is less certain that the decency and sobriety he represents will win through. Confronted by a psychotic villain and helped by assistants who talk about 'bloody perverts' and threaten child molesters with bloody reprisals, his downbeat quirkiness incorporates a sad acknowledgment that traditional values have crumbled and a more open and more dangerous society now exists.

Crichton's Ealing origins are faintly discernible in *He Who Rides a Tiger*. Metaphors like cars whizzing down leafy lanes stand in for actual love-making and the Dr Barnardo's orphanage presided over by Ray McAnally is a bit too good to be true. But in its attitudes the film is surprisingly modern. This is partly a matter of casting. The burglar, Peter Rayston, is played with an almost Bogart-like resonance by Tom

215

He Who Rides a Tiger: Peter Rayston (Tom Bell), safebreaker

Bell, an actor who made impressive appearances in a number of early 60s films (*The Criminal*, *A Prize of Arms*, *Payroll* and *The L-Shaped Room*) but whose film career was stymied after he allegedly insulted the Duke of Edinburgh at a film industry dinner in 1962.[18] He brings to the role just the right degree of arrogance, vulnerability and violence, warmth and recklessness required of a dyed-in-the-wool villain. Bell makes a totally sympathetic character out of what one suspects was meant to be an ambivalent mixture of good and evil, and the film endorses his crook's view of the world in a way that Crichton would never have done at Ealing. Crichton's most famous Ealing film, *The Lavender Hill Mob*, celebrates a perfect crime, but its villains are honest little men tempted into crime by a sense of adventure that leaves them uncorrupted. In *He Who Rides a Tiger*, Peter's robberies and the life they lead to are shown to be wrong and futile, but his bravery and generosity is unquestioned and the Scotland Yard inspector (Paul Rogers), whom one might have expected to represent Crichton's point of view, is cold and unsympathetic. In attempting to persuade Peter's honest, middle-class girlfriend (Judi Dench) to betray him, he tells her: 'He might have a soft heart and a good physique ... but he's a dangerous, vicious, ruthless, useless man.' But this moral

216

stance is undermined by the irony that she is first attracted to Peter when they unite to rescue an injured fox, another 'dangerous, vicious, ruthless, useless' creature which is disposed of as vermin by the vet they take it to for treatment.

From the mid-60s onwards a vacuous internationalism seemed to seep into the British crime film. Peter Yates's *Robbery* (1967), a fictionalisation of the Great Train Robbery of 1963, bravely tried to update the genre with daring heists and exciting car chases, but this left little room for psychological depth. It is a very competent film (much better than the 1988 reworking of the same material, *Buster*) which makes excellent use of locations, and Stanley Baker gives a good performance as a Bannion-like criminal grown cleverer and more cynical. But legal and perhaps moral difficulties made it impossible to get too close to Bruce Reynolds, Buster Edwards, Ronnie Biggs and the rest, and in comparison with their real-life counterparts, Yates's train robbers are disappointingly colourless.[19]

Yates's flair for well-organised action sequences led to Hollywood and *Bullitt*. Back in Britain, the crime genre seemed to lose itself among a host of tepid caper movies – most of them starring Michael Caine – and the secret agent films that followed in the wake of James Bond. The usual pattern followed by the British crime film involved the detection of a crime and the apprehension of the guilty party, though the theme is often complicated by a digression into police procedure (*Gideon's Day*), low-life background colour (*Hell is a City*) or romance (*Blind Date*). Sometimes the task of detection and apprehension is shared between the police and an independent partner – in *The Informers*, for example, where the murdered snout's brother pursues his own investigations; or in *Bunny Lake is Missing*, where it is Bunny's mother rather than Inspector Newhouse who unmasks and confronts her psychotic brother. In bleaker films this partnership becomes unbalanced. In *Time Without Pity*, *Beyond This Place* and *Never Let Go*, the police are at best ineffectual, at worst obstructive, and the hero's task is fulfilled in an atmosphere of anomie and despair.

In caper films the pattern is different, the main emphasis being on the carrying out of an elaborate fraud or robbery, with detection and pursuit playing a less important part than the exploration of tensions within the gang. A film like *Robbery* (or Sidney Hayers's *Payroll*) mixes the two types, with the preparation and execution of the 'caper' followed by the rapid disintegration of the gang responsible and a shift towards their pursuit and apprehension (by Billie Whitelaw's vengeful widow in *Payroll*, by James Booth's Scotland Yard inspector in *Robbery*). The caper films of the late 60s hardly concern themselves with detection, and compensate for their amorality by treating their subject humorously. The linear antecedents of the late 60s caper films are not *The Criminal* or Cliff Owen's taut *A Prize of Arms* (1962), but *Two Way*

Stretch or even *The Lavender Hill Mob*. In these earlier films, however, comic interaction between the characters makes up for skimpy action sequences, whereas in *The Italian Job* (1969) and its ilk exciting action sequences enliven the dull interplay between poorly developed characters. *The Italian Job*, directed by Peter Collinson, has a vulgar package-holiday vitality and flashy stunt sequences; *Deadfall* (1968), Bryan Forbes's contribution to the genre, is graced by the last significant performance of Eric Portman, which almost makes its weak plot forgivable; and Dearden and Relph's *Only When I Larf* (1968) explores interesting sexual and class tensions. But most of the characters in these films – along with those in Cyril Frankel's *The Trygon Factor*, Gerry O'Hara's *Maroc 7*, Pete Walker's *The Big Switch*, Ronald Neame's *Gambit*, Peter Hall's *Perfect Friday* – seem to belong to a Ruritanian jet set weighed down by an ennui which no amount of jauntiness can disguise.[20] Compared to these embarrassingly unfunny films, the secret agent cycle seems almost refreshing.

The Dangerous Edge
Until the 60s, spies and secret agents seemed to weave in and out of thrillers, melodramas, war films, even comedies, without having a defined genre of their own. The Cold War gave rise to gloomy, paranoid fantasies like John and Roy Boulting's *Seven Days to Noon* and *High Treason*, but by the late 50s the spy and the secret agent, on film if not in books, seemed to be a spent force. In 1960, for example, only four films dealing with espionage were released in Britain, two of them (John Moxey's *Foxhole in Cairo* and Jack Lee's *Circle of Deception*) set in the Second World War, one of them (Carol Reed's *Our Man in Havana*) a superior comedy, and the other, the Boultings' *Suspect*, a tired, low-budget reworking of their worries about gullible liberal scientists and pacifist organisations being used as fronts by foreign agents. It is not surprising, then, that Cubby Broccoli and Harry Saltzman had difficulty finding financial backers for their projected series of James Bond films.

Ian Fleming's Bond was in some ways an aberration, a throwback to the intensely patriotic heroes of Sapper, Dornford Yates and John Buchan, where one Englishman was more than a match for twenty foreigners and Britain was still the greatest world power. But Fleming disguises his old-fashioned hero in smart new clothes. Whereas Bulldog Drummond and Richard Hannay fought for King and Empire and were burdened with the duties of a ruling elite, Bond, though undeniably patriotic, is driven more by the need to defend his right to enjoy Tiptree strawberry jam and speckled brown eggs and have his cigarettes made for him specially by Morlands of Grosvenor Street. And while the old heroes had taken only a polite interest in women, Bond had a healthy and frequently indulged sexual appetite.[21]

Penelope Houston points out that the best things about the novels – Fleming's ability to convey the sensation of fast driving, to get across his gourmet's knowledge of food, to make comprehensible the technicalities of gambling – were not qualities which would transfer easily to the cinema.[22] But the Bond films – exotic, colourful, tongue-in-cheek – had their own distinctive assets. In the 50s, Broccoli and his then partner Irving Allen had successfully instilled a Hollywood-like lavishness into their Warwick film productions (*The Red Beret, Cockleshell Heroes, The Killers of Kilimanjaro, The Trials of Oscar Wilde*, for example), and Broccoli was able to draw on the services of Warwick stalwarts like scriptwriter Richard Maibaum, cameraman Ted Moore, director Terence Young and, most important, art director Ken Adam. The Bond films combined the spectacle evident in Warwick's films (and in war epics like *The Bridge on the River Kwai* and *The Guns of Navarone*, for which there was a diminishing market as the Second World War retreated into history) with the traditional elements of the old 'thick-ear melodramas' built round Bulldog Drummond and Dick Barton: a bizarre and thoroughly evil villain, beautiful but dangerous women, impossibly difficult assignments which only a hero of almost godlike inviolability could carry out successfully. Broccoli and Saltzman retained Fleming's obsession with the material by-products of a glamorous and affluent lifestyle, but with Scot Sean Connery as Bond that lifestyle came to seem classless, international, almost *nouveau riche.*

Dr No was a big enough commercial success to enable Saltzman and Broccoli to continue with their projected series of Bond films. But critical reaction, at least among the 'quality' critics, was at best superciliously approving (as Penelope Houston put it in *Sight and Sound*, 'the film makes almost no appeal that is not to everyone's worst instincts'), and Connery was less successful in convincing the critics than the public with his performance. John Coleman in the *New Statesman* thought Connery 'an invincibly stupid-looking secret service agent' and the *Monthly Film Bulletin* found him 'a disappointingly wooden and boorish Bond', though to anti-Bond man Derek Hill in *Tribune* he combined 'exactly the right mixture of strong-arm fascist and telly commercial salesman'.[23] Critical resistance crumbled with *From Russia With Love*; as Arkadin, the *Sight and Sound* gossip columnist, put it: 'Clearly everyone knew at the outset that it must be a big popular success, and no one was going to be caught napping by giving it just a short, casual notice.'[24] But the industry proved slow to respond to Bond's success. Between *Doctor No* and *From Russia With Love* the only other spy films were three low-budget Cold War thrillers and Dearden and Relph's *The Mind Benders* (interesting more for Dirk Bogarde's transformation from happy family man to jealous sadist after being brainwashed into believing his wife, Mary Ure, has been

219

unfaithful to him, than for its sketchy espionage framework).[25] Between *From Russia With Love* and *Goldfinger* there was only *Carry on Spying*, the first and best attempt to parody the new spy film; *Hot Enough for June*, a limp-wristed Betty Box and Ralph Thomas Bond spoof with Bogarde as an amateur spy; and Robert Tronson's *Ring of Spies*.

Tronson's film, based on the Portland Down affair of 1961, is a splendid apotheosis of the Cold War melodrama. It centres on Henry Houghton, a cipher clerk at the Portland Down Underwater Weapons Research Establishment, who for materialistic rather than ideological reasons supplied the Russian spy Gordon Lonsdale with secret documents. Houghton himself had no access to confidential information but he seduced a middle-aged, and hitherto impeccably loyal, senior secretary, Ethel Elizabeth Gee, to help him. Houghton's drinking bouts and Miss Gee's increasingly expensive lifestyle attracted suspicion, and they were followed to the house in Ruislip which was the centre of Lonsdale's operations. After an unpromising start, the film settles down into sleazily convincing realism. William Sylvester's Lonsdale is not allowed much depth, but Bernard Lee's boozy, shambling Henry Houghton and Margaret Tyzack's Miss Gee – her prim exterior cracking open to reveal a seething mass of desires and ambitions – become fascinating, almost tragic figures. The story of how they rationalise away their scruples, overcome their fear, exult in getting the better of their patronising superiors and then drift into greed

The amoral attitudes of the classless, materialist, affluent society: Bernard Lee, William Sylvester, Margaret Tyzack in *Ring of Spies*

220

and discontent and carelessness, comes to seem like a warning less of the corrupting power of Communism than of the dangers awaiting those who shed the bonds of conventional morality and assume the amoral attitudes of the classless, materialistic, affluent society.

Ring of Spies foreshadows John Le Carré's sad, lonely world where espionage is the preserve of 'little men, drunkards, queers, hen-pecked husbands, civil servants playing cowboys and Indians to brighten their rotten lives', as Leamas explains in *The Spy Who Came in from the Cold*. It is significant that the secret agent film only began to emerge as a coherent genre with the filming of novels by Le Carré and Len Deighton, both of whom belong to the seedy, unglamorous world explored by Graham Greene and Eric Ambler in the 30s and 40s rather than to the flamboyant jet-setting of Fleming's Bond.

Harry Saltzman acquired the rights to Len Deighton's popular novels in case Bond should lose his grip on the public imagination (most of the novels had been written in the 50s, and Fleming died in 1964). Deighton's contribution to the spy thriller is to invent an English equivalent of the colloquial American developed by Raymond Chandler and Dashiell Hammett for the thriller, and to use it to revitalise the spy story in a way that retains the democratic ethos of the Greene/Ambler novels but updates it to the slicker, faster, smarter society of the 60s. Deighton's hero, unnamed in the books, christened Harry Palmer in the films, is a deliberate contrast to Bond. Where Bond is urbane, handsome, upper middle-class, an officer and a gentleman (even in the films, Connery is suave and well-heeled), Palmer is a grammar school boy from Burnley, vaguely leftwing (he buys the *New Statesman*, the *Morning Star* and *History Today* in *The Ipcress File*) and continually trying to fiddle his expenses to make ends meet. Bruce Merry, in his study of the contemporary spy thriller, sees Palmer rather than Bond as the typical secret agent:

> Professionalism cuts absolutely across class barriers. The spy no longer comes from the pre-war British ruling class. So the thriller places a particular emphasis on the non-privileged boy's desire to make good in an expensive environment. We are back to the old state school vs. public school dichotomy which has loomed so large in post-war British writing. More often than not, the agent is a grammar school man, while his boss in London comes from the upper crust.[26]

Saltzman takes Palmer even further down the social scale, making him a working-class Cockney, 'insubordinate, insolent, a trickster, perhaps with criminal tendencies'. It was a role ideally suited for the as yet untapped talents of Michael Caine, whose only big part until then had been as a foppish officer in *Zulu*. Here, with his glasses, Cockney accent and insolent charm, he was much more at home, and Harry Palmer was to set the parameters of Caine's screen persona for the next twenty years.

The Bond films were big and glossy, with exciting action sequences, exotic locations and extravagant sets taking precedence over character and relationships. The more modestly budgeted Deighton films – *The Ipcress File* (1965), *Funeral in Berlin* (1966) and *Billion Dollar Brain* (1967) – were idiosyncratic, quirky and deliberately downbeat. *The Ipcress File* dispenses with the Beirut and South Pacific locations of the book and sets its action in a seedy London of warehouses, railway stations, supermarkets, parking meters, rainy streets, dimly lit libraries, and the rabbit warren of offices which house the dubious Military Intelligence unit Palmer works for. This is hardly Swinging London, and Sidney Furie's mannered, effect-seeking direction signals restless unease rather than morning-of-the-world optimism.

It was difficult for *Funeral in Berlin* and *Billion Dollar Brain* to live up to the promise of *The Ipcress File*, which depended for its success less on its plot than on the novelty of Caine's Harry Palmer and an espionage world characterised by grimy offices and cracked cups rather than luxury apartments and expensive nightclubs. But both films have interestingly complex plots and a strong sense of place. *Funeral in Berlin*, directed by Guy Hamilton straight from his success with *Goldfinger*, moved the relationship between Bond and Palmer closer. Hamilton's direction is neutral and unobtrusive compared to Furie's, but in the melodramatic setting of West Berlin (in the novel much more of the action takes place in London) this is quite appropriate; and the feeling for melancholy city streets which Hamilton had shown in *The Party's Over* combines with Otto Heller's photography to give an evocative picture of Berlin scarred by its massive ugly wall.

Coming in from the Cold

By the early 60s relations between Russia and the West had warmed sufficiently (despite the Cuba crisis) to allow a more relaxed and playful treatment of international intrigue and the dangers of world war. In the transition of James Bond from novel to film, the Russian Intelligence service SMERSH is pushed into the background by the international crime cartel SPECTRE in deference to the lessening of Cold War tensions. Bulgarians in *Dr No*, North Koreans and Red Chinese in *Goldfinger*, play subsidiary roles, but the only Russians who figure as major villains are mavericks like Rosa Klebb in *From Russia With Love*, who has already defected to SPECTRE. The Cold War was still fought in low-budget spy thrillers like *The Limbo Line* (1968) and *The Executioner* (1970), but it rarely intruded into major productions.[27] Still, Colonel Stok (Oscar Homolka) in *Funeral in Berlin* is something else, a more lovable Russian than any seen since the pro-Soviet euphoria of the middle years of the war, an echo of Eric Ambler's Zaleshoff in his (pre-war) *Cause for Alarm*. The fact that he lies about wanting to retire and grow roses in an English garden, and that his protestations that there is no place in modern Russia for an old Bolshevik who helped storm the Winter Palace are false, is irrelevant. We enjoy the joke as much as he does when he gets the better of Kreutzman, the Berlin escape expert, and his Nazi-like followers.

The same anti-Cold War bias informs Ken Russell's *Billion Dollar Brain*, the last of the Deighton trilogy. Palmer, having resigned from the secret service, runs a seedy private eye business, and, rejecting his old boss's attempt to re-recruit him, flies to Helsinki where he meets Leo Newbegin, a figure from his shady past who is involved in the scheme of a mad American general to foment rebellion against Communist rule in Latvia. Once again Colonel Stok (and Françoise Dorléac's Anya, his glamorous, murderous agent) is favourably contrasted with the scheming, maniacal Americans. Russell's style is more like Furie's than Hamilton's in striving after effects, but Furie tends to rely on peculiar angles, on allowing his characters to block or distort the screen, on devices like voice-overs and disorienting locations. Russell is bolder but cruder with his shock cuts and contrived compositions, and he readily borrows from other film-makers. General Midwinter's torchlit meeting is modelled on a similar sequence in Fritz Lang's *Fury*, and his invasion of Latvia on Eisenstein's Battle on the Ice sequence in *Alexander Nevsky*. It would be tempting to suggest that the predominantly hostile critical reaction to the film was politically motivated, but apart from the welcome extended to the film in the *Morning Star* and by unpredictable Eric Rhode in the *Listener*, the attitude of the British critics was more a seen-it-all-before indifference and an irritation with the eccentricities of Russell's style than any sort of political objection. And no one seems to have noticed Russell's point that General Midwinter's intervention in Latvia was a parody of Lyndon Johnson's in Vietnam.

Deighton's novels are clever, quirky, lightweight, essentially detective stories transferred to the secret agent idiom. Le Carré is much more solemn and pessimistic. Like Fleming, he writes about the world of espionage as an insider, but whereas Fleming deliberately transposes what he knows to a fantasy world, Le Carré remains doggedly earthbound, wrestling with the murky moral dilemmas that spying throws up. He inherits the moral uneasiness of Graham Greene, complaining that 'Bond on his magic carpet takes us away from moral doubt, banishes perplexity with action, morality with duty. Above all, he has the one piece of equipment without which not even his formula would work: an entirely evil enemy.' For Le Carré, 'There is no victory in the Cold War, only a condition of human illness and a political misery.'[28] Surprisingly, in view of their uncompromisingly

British subject matter, all three Le Carré films made in the 60s were directed by Americans for Hollywood companies. Obviously this had a great deal to do with the mechanics of the international film industry, but it is significant that (despite Senator McCarthy) America had a group of left-liberal film-makers – Martin Ritt, John Frankenheimer, Fred Zinnemann, Sidney Lumet, Elia Kazan – which had no real equivalent in Britain, except perhaps for Karel Reisz and John Schlesinger, both of whom were distracted unprofitably into a big-budget costume film in the mid-60s.[29]

Martin Ritt's *The Spy Who Came in from the Cold* (1965) squats like a toad on the zany optimism of the Swinging 60s. Oswald Morris's black and white photography has a bleak elegiac quality, and there are no heroics, no real adventures. Cyril Cusack's Control argues at the beginning of the film that 'You can't be less wicked than your enemy simply because your government's policies are benevolent, can you?'[30] In contrast to the Len Deighton films, where Harry Palmer on the one side and Colonel Stok on the other win through and the madmen and evil-doers get their just deserts, here the good characters – Richard Burton's Leamas, Claire Bloom's Nan, Oskar Werner's Fiedler – who are human and fallible, are sacrificed to a mad system. That the film is moving rather than depressing is a tribute to the performances Ritt evokes from his cast. Burton's depths of Celtic gloom give a magnificent weightiness to Leamas, the bitter alcoholic sufficiently disillusioned with his masters to defect; and the performance is all the more sophisticated for being a role Leamas is playing to fool the enemy but which, as the Byzantine convolutions of the plot unravel, becomes impossible to disentangle from his real identity. The other characters – Claire Bloom's naive, honest Nan, a touchstone of sanity and integrity without which Leamas cannot go on; Cyril Cusack's Control; Bernard Lee's unctuously aggressive grocer; Michael Hordern's gay contact man; Beatrix Lehmann's frigidly kindly interrogator; Oskar Werner's judicious Fiedler, politely concealing his contempt for Leamas's untidy treachery; and Peter Van Eyck's cold, brutal Mundt – seem to have lives and personalities of their own too, and between them they create a microcosm of a world caught up in fruitless, endless conflict.

According to scriptwriter Paul Dehn, Martin Ritt had been adamant that no sensationalism, no concessions to glamour, be introduced into *The Spy Who Came in from the Cold*:

> Thereafter, not only was my dialogue keyed-down from melodrama to drama and from drama to flat realism – witty exit lines, long speeches, pregnant pauses and continuity devices of remarkable brilliance went flying out my office window to splinter on the asphalt jungle of the Paramount lot below – but the *performance* of what I had written (once shooting had started) was purposefully

224

The Deadly Affair: Mendel (Harry Andrews) snoozing among his birds and rabbits

pared, pruned, damped, clipped and shorn of even the minor histrionic affectations with which our actors thought to mirror nature. Ritt held that the merest hint of theatrical vocalisation or gesture . . . distorted nature.[31]

Dehn also scripted Sidney Lumet's *The Deadly Affair* (1966), based on Le Carré's first novel *Call for the Dead*, which, though hardly less grim than *The Spy Who Came in from the Cold*, has an almost Hitchcockian plot which allowed for semi-comic cameos (from Lynn and Corin Redgrave, Roy Kinnear, Max Adrian) and provided a climax in a theatre auditorium against the backcloth of Marlowe's gruesome *Edward II*. In *The Spy Who Came in from the Cold* the relationship between Leamas and Nan is central (though this is more apparent in the film than in the book). Leamas's faith in the world as fruitful and benevolent has long burnt out, and once Nan is dead he refuses to save his own life. In *The Deadly Affair* the relationship between Dobbs (James Mason) and Anne (Harriet Andersson), his 'nymphomaniac' wife, is more negative. Dobbs's spiritual rebirth, his escape from the limbo of soured ambition and failed marriage which traps so many of Le Carré's characters, derives from his friendship with Mendel (Harry Andrews), an old detective who comes out of retirement to help him resolve a mystery which his superiors want to sweep under the carpet.

225

Commercial considerations put paid to Lumet's wish to make the film in black and white, but Freddie Young's muted colour helped create a vision of England as a sleepy backwater wherein lurks treachery and brutality rather than tranquillity. Anne and her lover Dieter (Maximilian Schell), Dobbs's wartime protégé, are duplicitous but almost transparently so, and more interest accumulates around Mendel and Simone Signoret's Elsa Fennan. Mendel, living out his retirement in sleepy contentment among his pet rabbits and birds, provides Dobbs with a refuge and proves to be violent and efficient when called back to the active world. Elsa, a concentration camp survivor, seems to provide the film with its moral centre, warning Dobbs, whom she blames for her husband's suicide: 'You dropped a bomb from the sky, don't come down here to look at the blood and hear the screaming.' In fact it is she more than Dobbs who is the guilty party, but Signoret's passionate lies are so convincing that the plot almost founders on our willingness to believe her.

The Looking Glass War (1969) proved difficult to adapt for the screen. The Woolfs had originally acquired the novel for Jack Clayton to direct, but script problems proved insuperable and the project was shelved until 1969 when it was taken up by the American screenwriter Frank R. Pierson (who was to go on to write *The Anderson Tapes* and *Dog Day Afternoon* for Lumet) for his directorial debut. The women in the film – Anna Massey, Maxine Audley, Vivien Pickles, Pia Degermark and Susan George – all give memorable performances, but the main relationships are between men, and Pierson radically altered the focus of the novel by casting Christopher Jones, a young American who had achieved minor stardom as a television Jesse James and as the pop idol President of *Wild in the Streets*, in the central role as Leiser. Le Carré's Leiser is a middle-aged car salesman tempted into undertaking a misconceived espionage mission by nostalgia for the comradeship and shared dangers of the war. Pierson's Leiser is a young Polish seaman who has jumped ship and agrees to undertake the mission in exchange for permission to stay in Britain with his pregnant girlfriend. Le Carré's novel is an indictment of the tragic folly brought about by old men playing war games: 'the tragic ghosts, the unfallen dead of the last war', whose source of energy 'lies not in the war of ideas but in their own desolate mentalities'.[32] In the film, we first see the athletic Leiser through the eyes of the elderly secret service chiefs Leclerc (Ralph Richardson) and Haldane (Paul Rogers) as they watch him playing squash, and there is a constant sense of the old being parasitic on the young, of old men using the power they have accumulated over the years to live vicariously through the energetic but powerless young.

Pierson adds a further contrast, between the footloose, almost hippy-like Leiser and Anthony Hopkins's Avery, the young, straight, secret service patriot responsible for his training. Leiser and Avery

226

function as Cain and Abel-like brothers. Leiser is irreverent, disrespectful: a young man who feels indifference, even contempt for his elders. After a violent training fight with Avery, Leiser suddenly, motivelessly, kisses the cold, grey Haldane full on the lips. Avery is dutiful, orthodox, resentful not of authority but of his wife's unwillingness to accept his old-fashioned, deferential patriotism. There is, however, a degree of solidarity between them. The sequence in the pub where, the night before the mission, Avery and Leiser get drunk together – Avery sulky about his relationship with his wife, Leiser bitter that the pregnant girl who was the justification for his involvement in espionage has had an abortion – perceptively explores that shared male excitement in dangerous adventure which overrides nationality, class and lifestyle. Leiser's life is sacrificed to the fantasies of these old fools, but he is never under any illusion about the madness of the enterprise; and it is Avery whose ideals are shattered, shouting bitterly at his superiors as they pack up and prepare to abandon Leiser to his fate, 'I always thought fathers were supposed to love their sons, now I know they don't, they hate them!'

The novel, and the film, fall into two parts, dealing first with Leiser's recruitment and training, and then with his mission, which goes disastrously wrong. Leiser's mission is dealt with more extensively in the film, though Le Carré's emphasis on moral dilemmas rather than exciting action is retained. Leiser's involvement with a fey, enigmatic girl (Pia Degermark) and a child who asks difficult questions ('What do birds dream about?') seems to be taking the film into the terrain of European art cinema. But the conflict between recklessly self-destructive young East Europeans and the rigidly repressive state apparatus created by their elders mirrors that between Leiser (and in the end, Avery) and their elderly, dangerously out of touch spymasters.

A Successful Formula?

The tendency to dismiss the plethora of spy films made in the 60s as weakly derivative is understandable. The Betty Box/Ralph Thomas film *Hot Enough for June* (1963), Val Guest's *Where the Spies Are* (1965) and *Assignment K* (1967), John Gilling's *Where the Bullets Fly* (1966) and Anthony Mann's *A Dandy in Aspic* (1968) are all disappointing, and they are merely the tip of an iceberg of spy films – *Licensed to Kill, Crossplot, Some May Live, Hammerhead, The Limbo Line, Subterfuge, Circus of Fear, Sumuru, The Executioner, The Man Outside* – which are probably best left submerged. But even bad spy films have a certain resonance. As Bruce Merry points out:

The fit between the standard pattern of the folk tale and the modern spy thriller is a strikingly precise one. . . . The gods no longer help the hero, and wizards no longer hand him a book of spells which explain the terms of his challenge and the crucial points of his adventure. But the fictional spy must cope with the same language and culture problems of every mythic traveller. Like all protagonists who cannot depend on the same degree of skill and panache in their support team, the secret agent lives in a tension between paranoia and self-fulfilment – the staple diet of the popular imagination.[33]

This mythic quality might explain why Michael Anderson's *The Quiller Memorandum*, Sidney Furie's *The Naked Runner*, and Seth Holt's *Danger Route*, all deeply flawed films, are nevertheless so compelling.

The Quiller Memorandum (1966) is the only 60s film to come out of the sub-genre of the spy thriller which deals with the enduring legacy of the Nazis. These thrillers tend to divide into stories centring on a hunt for Nazi gold hidden during the war (featured in the subplot of *Funeral in Berlin*) and stories about the unearthing of a powerful Nazi organisation (as in Frederick Forsyth's *The Odessa File*). *The Quiller Memorandum*, written by Elleston Trevor under the pseudonym Adam Hall, is interesting in that the uncovering job is an entirely British operation. Its hero, Quiller, worked as an undercover agent during the war, helping prisoners to escape the death camps, and his bitter memories of Nazi atrocities give the book a pungent anti-German tone.

The casting of George Segal as Quiller necessitated changes in the plot which caused problems with motivation and plausibility. Segal is too young to have rescued Jews from the concentration camps, and an unconvincing conflict between casual but professional American Quiller and his supercilious, amateurish British spymasters (George Sanders, Robert Flemying, Alec Guinness) is substituted for his long-running duel with the Nazis. To set against this, Harold Pinter's screenplay deserves credit for jettisoning the novel's alarmingly melo-dramatic plot in which the Nazis come close to precipitating a world war in collusion with Franco, Nasser and the Mafia. Anderson and his cinematographer Erwin Hillier present Berlin in a new and interesting way, as an ugly mixture of ill-lit streets, high-rise hotels and urban motorways with not even a glimpse of the Wall. And in place of the sexually fetishised *Führerbunkerkind* who threatens to (though never does) throw Quiller's coldly mechanical brain into confusion, there is a gentle, reticent junior schoolteacher (Senta Berger) whose deadly ambiguity gives the film a promise of originality and complexity which it almost fulfils.[34]

Seth Holt's *Danger Route* and Sidney Furie's *The Naked Runner* (both 1967) are thematically similar to each other, but their treatment could not be more different. Furie's increasingly extravagant style – out of focus chairs block half the screen, disembodied voices intervene unexpectedly, giant close-ups of coffee cups loom threateningly – makes it a very disconcerting film and it is easy to lose patience with it. But once one ceases to worry about realism and begins to see the film as the nightmare of its central character, it begins to make satisfying sense. Like Le Carré's Leiser, Sam Laker (Frank Sinatra) is a wartime operative who is re-recruited for a mission into East Germany. As all he is required to do is to deliver a watchstrap to a jeweller in Leipzig, there is no need for the elaborate training of *The Looking Glass War*. But the mission appears to be equally ill-fated. Within hours of delivering his message, Laker is arrested and threatened with death. It is soon apparent that this is part of a Machiavellian plot: the East German security officer (Derren Nesbitt) is in fact a British agent and Laker's real mission, which he will be tricked into performing, is to shoot an escaping spy. By the end of the film this has come to seem wildly improbable, but as in John Guillermin's *Never Let Go* and Trevor Preston and Jim Goddard's 1984 Eurothriller *Parker*, the disruption of a middle-aged man's life after years of soft living (the hero of *Never Let Go* is a cosmetics salesman, Laker designs office furniture) by the need to enter a world of violence is very disturbing. The ending, where Laker, after shooting his victim, throws away his gun and rushes through a dark tunnel to confront the man he thought he had killed (the hated East German security officer) and the man who had sent him on the disastrous mission, is ludicrous on a plot level but it makes a satisfying end to Laker's nightmare.

Danger Route is more modest and conventional, marred by a stingy budget and Amicus's insistence on keeping its length down to ninety-two minutes (most spy thrillers last around 110 minutes). Thus its satisfactions are more those of a tight, economical 'B' film than the emotional excesses offered by spy films as different as *The Spy Who Came in from the Cold* and *Goldfinger*. Seth Holt brings together a talented cast – Richard Johnson, Gordon Jackson, Harry Andrews, Maurice Denham, Sam Wanamaker, Carol Lynley, Diana Dors, Sylvia Sims – and slots them into convincing characters in a complex plot full of class tensions and cruel surprises. The film's weakness lies in the shallowness of the relationships between the characters, which, except for that between Johnson and Diana Dors, are irritatingly underdeveloped. How far this was Holt's fault is questionable. The big Frenchman who emerges from nowhere as the villain's henchman and the odd little interlude between Johnson's class-conscious hatchet man and the upper-class wife (Sylvia Sims) of his control look like fragments from lost subplots, and one suspects that producer Milton Subotsky might have been responsible for some injudicious pruning.[35]

It is difficult to draw a firm line between spoofs and straight spy films. *The Spy Who Came in from the Cold* and *Carry On Spying* are obviously worlds apart, but the Bond films from *Goldfinger* onwards

Jonas (Richard Johnson) and Mrs Gooderich (Diana Dors), convincing characters in a complex plot: *Danger Route*

became increasingly humorous, while a film like *Where the Spies Are* starts as a comedy and grows increasingly black as the death toll mounts. Films which openly declare their intentions to be funny rather than frightening – *Carry On Spying, The Intelligence Men, Our Man in Marrakesh* – tend to work better than more ambitious films like *Hot Enough for June, Where the Spies Are, Modesty Blaise* and *Casino Royale*. MGM's *The Liquidator* (d. Jack Cardiff, 1965) succeeds where it apes its more lowly budgeted brothers and relies on comic perform-ances from Eric Sykes, John Le Mesurier, Akim Tamiroff and a ridi-culous but likeable plot (a government assassin who is too squeamish to assassinate anybody is persuaded by enemy agents to 'practise' on the Duke of Edinburgh). In contrast, *Casino Royale* is a ragbag of poorly executed sketches with appalling 'guest performances' from Peter Sellers and Orson Welles and a horde of glamorous starlets. Even with the lapse of time, when one might have expected to find carelessly scattered pearls among the debris, there is little to take home apart from the phantasmagoric torture sequence directed by Nicolas Roeg, and Woody Allen's dream of a world populated by beautiful women where no man but himself is allowed to grow over four feet six inches high. Joseph Losey's *Modesty Blaise*, based on a newspaper comic strip, is much more technically accomplished, but it is undermined by a weak script and smirky, indulgent performances by Monica Vitti, Dirk Bogarde and Terence Stamp. The film has undeniably impressive moments – Joe Melia's clown meeting a gruesome death between the legs of Rossella Falk, the nicely handled explosion with which the film opens, Monica Vitti's Op Art dungeon (indeed, Richard MacDonald's production design almost makes the film worthwhile) – but Losey seems to have little understanding of the genre he attempts to subvert and his smart-alecky tricks backfire more often than not.[36]

The feminist inversion of male chauvinist myths which one might have expected to find in *Modesty Blaise* appears rather unexpectedly in two films made by Betty Box and Ralph Thomas which revived the pre-war secret agent Bulldog Drummond. It would be difficult to refute the claim that *Deadlier Than the Male* and *Some Girls Do* are bad films – jokes are mistimed, actors poorly directed, the sets are tacky and the scripts clichéd – but they have interesting thematic strands and a redeeming vulgarity. Richard Johnson's Drummond is tougher but more fallible than Bond, and he doesn't always get the girl. In *Some Girls Do* his zany, Goldie Hawn-like sidekick undergoes metamorphosis after metamorphosis, eventually ending up as a Russian spy who steals the Magic Box and leaves Drummond stranded with only a grubby, shop-soiled robot for consolation. Though in both films he gets the better of his arch-rival, Carl Petersen, most of the violent action is carried out by a murderous female duo (Sylva Koscina and Elke Sommer in *Deadlier Than the Male*, Daliah Lavi and Beba Loncar in *Some Girls Do*) who tear through the film wreaking vengeance on men with sadistic glee.

The only British spy film which succeeds both as a comedy and a thriller is Dick Clement and Ian La Frenais's *Otley* (1968). Like Harry Palmer, Gerald Arthur Otley (Tom Courtenay) is a working-class grammar school boy, but he has made no effort to get to the top and his involvement in espionage is fortuitous and traumatic. Clement and La Frenais had made their reputation in television with their working-class situation comedy *The Likely Lads*, and *Otley* has the advantage of an intelligent, witty script full of convincingly idiosyncratic characters, such as Leonard Rossiter's chatty, practical contract killer, Romy Schneider's au pair turned intelligence officer and Ronald Lacey's snivellingly sadistic heavy. What lifts the film out of the ordinary run of spy spoofs is its solid rooting in mundane reality. The long tracking shot down Portobello Road which carries the titles introduces us to a London which has stopped swinging and settled down to become a shambling, easy-going, bohemian backwater. When Otley is dragged from this comfortable world into a nightmare of murder, treachery and double-dealing, he protests loudly ('Have a go at my psyche but leave me body alone,' he tells his persecutors), and his attempts to hang on to the landmarks of his everyday existence – culminating in a driving test which turns into a crazy car chase – creates a comic tension which Courtenay exploits to the full.

231

Degenerate Britain

David Greene's flashily directed *Sebastian* (1968), produced by Michael Powell and based on a story by Leo Marks (who had worked as a code-breaker during the war), can only tentatively be classified as a spy film. *Sebastian* divides its time between the dreaming spires of Oxford and a high-tech code-breaking centre in the Barbican, and focuses on the relationship between Dirk Bogarde's Sebastian, an Oxford don whose computer-like brain makes him indispenable to MI6, and Susannah York's Jenny, the bright young woman he recruits to join his staff of pretty assistants. Greene not only manages to get both Susannah York and Dirk Bogarde to act like interesting human beings but overcomes the impediments of Swinging London film-making – meaningless plot, bad rock music, affairs between sexy dolly birds and successful but unhappy middle-aged men – to create a vision of Britain in the 60s which looks more acute and perceptive now than it did at the time in its mixture of cruelty and tenderness, carelessness and ambition, modernity and tradition, radicalism and conformity.

Despite its glittering surface, *Sebastian* shares thematic concerns with the films of the Le Carré school. Lilli Palmer's Elsa Shahn is somewhere between Margaret Tyzack's Miss Gee in *Ring of Spies* – a foolish woman who is tricked into handing over secret information – and Simone Signoret's Elsa Fennan in *The Deadly Affair* – an embittered radical to whom loyalties to the British government are irrelevant. Sebastian himself is patriotic but weary and disillusioned, like Leamas and Dobbs and Avery acutely conscious of the emotional damage caused by a lifetime's devotion to espionage. As he complains bitterly: 'I fill my mind with patterns of mistrust. I make them and I break them, I allow them to infest my mind. And all I get out of them are secrets I don't want to know. I'm a kind of septic tank for all the world's ugly secrets.'

There is also a strand of sexual disturbance, of a deeper unease with the world, which might be attributed to the writer Leo Marks and the co-producer Michael Powell were it not a characteristic of all four of the films David Greene made in Britain in the 60s.[37] Amid the light-headed romping around there is a peculiarly brutal scene where a fading pop singer (Janet Munro, in her last role before an untimely death four years later) is coerced by her agent (the normally benevolent Ronald Fraser) into luring Bogarde into taking LSD and flying out of the window. This gives the film a chilling dimension which carries over into Greene's next film, *The Strange Affair* (1968), the first of a new generation of crime films which use the permissiveness of the Swinging Sixties to display a more explicit treatment of sex and violence.

By 1968 drug arrests and the police handling of demonstrations had disillusioned many middle-class people about the impartiality and fairness of the British police, but the process had begun five years earlier

Old-fashioned policeman ill-adjusted to a brash new world: Pierce (Jeremy Kemp) and Charley Small (Barry Fantoni) in *The Strange Affair*

when the Challenor Affair hit the headlines. Challenor was a Detective-Sergeant in central London who, after slipping up with the wrongful arrest of a journalist, was discovered to be in the habit of planting false evidence on his victims. Though a psychiatrist found Challenor 'very mad indeed' and there were claims that he was the one bad apple in an otherwise uncorrupt police force, a survey carried out in 1963 revealed that '42.4 per cent of the population thought that the police took bribes; 34.7 per cent thought that they used unfair methods of getting information; and 32 per cent thought that they might distort evidence in court.'[38] With *The Strange Affair*, these attitudes found belated expression in a feature film.

The Strange Affair breaks with all the conventions of the British police thriller. Its policemen are at best fools and madmen, at worst irredeemably corrupt. The London it is set in is not one of Big Ben, Tower Bridge and quaint, narrow streets, but of concrete office blocks, multi-storey car parks, garish modern pubs and a heliport crowded with the white-clad supporters of an Indian guru. And though the jazzy score and the flashy colour associate it with other Swinging London films, the story is unusually gloomy. A keen, well educated young man, Peter Strange (Michael York), joins the police to do something useful for society and finds he is dealing with a thoroughly unpleasant bunch of people. He becomes embroiled with a rich and promiscuous flower-child (Susan George), whose kinky relatives film them in bed; a sadistic gangster (Jack Watson) and his sons, who drill holes in his cheeks; and a peculiarly obsessive policeman, Detective-Sergeant Pierce (Jeremy Kemp). Pierce, like Nigel Patrick's Inspector Johnnoe in *The Informers*, defies his superiors and mingles with the flotsam and jetsam of the underworld. But he is a much more ambiguous figure than Johnnoe. He inherits Challenor's psychotic tendencies and he uses blackmail to force Strange into planting false evidence on the villain when he is unable to catch him by orthodox methods. Strange is a sympathetic character (if one can stomach Michael York's milk-and-water charm) and is in a way the representative of the public. He is shocked by the conduct of his fellow constables, who lie to cover their mistakes, and perplexed and disturbed by Pierce. Mary Grigg, in her book on the Challenor affair, makes the point that:

> The public expects the police force to combat crime; and it also expects the police to do this successfully without the slightest impropriety. Police officers had discovered in practice, however, that they could either catch criminals or behave properly, but that it was difficult to do both. They were therefore dithering constantly between satisfying the public in one respect and not offending it in the other.[39]

Pierce is a good policeman in the Johnnoe/Gosling mould, treating his informers fairly and being rewarded with good tip-offs. But he is thwarted by his superiors, one of whom is a bigoted disciplinarian who sneers at Pierce's reliance on 'information received', the other a slimy hypocrite in the pay of the gangsters. The film ends on an extraordinarily bleak note, with Strange in prison, Pierce mad, and the gangsters and corrupt police carrying on as usual.

There are no policemen in *Performance*, but like *The Strange Affair* it explores the darker side of the Swinging 60s. It was completed in 1968, but its financial backers, Warner-Seven Arts, regarded it as an evil, decadent film and refused to release it. Only when the company was taken over in 1970 did more enlightened policies prevail, and even then the release was poorly handled and provoked mixed and confused reactions. Nicolas Roeg was unusual among cameramen who become directors (Jack Cardiff, Guy Green, Freddie Francis) in being able to combine his rich visual sense with a sophistication in unravelling narrative and an ability to inspire extraordinary performances from actors. Here James Fox, hitherto typecast as an upper-class wimp, is stunningly effective as a working-class hoodlum, and it is a mark of the film's sophistication that Fox's intense acting combines so well with the casual naturalism of Mick Jagger, Anita Pallenberg and Michele Breton. *Performance* is such an idiosyncratic film that it is difficult to squeeze it into the crime genre, but its first half deals more explicitly, more openly, more violently with the modern underworld than any previous British film. *The Strange Affair* showed violence, torture, corruption, but it still operated within a recognisable and familiar set of values, even if they were approached with irony and cynicism. In *Performance*, all that goes out of the window and is replaced by the drug culture's amoral exploration of inner worlds.

Donald Cammell, the film's writer and co-director, seemed able to cross over from the hippy underground into the criminal underworld with surprising facility. His first effort, *Duffy* (1968, d. Robert Parrish), a hippy high-life caper movie with James Mason, James Coburn, Susannah York and James Fox, had suffered from a weak score and unsympathetic direction. But as in *Performance*, the central relationship is between an underworld hustler (Coburn) and a decadent hippy (ironically, in view of his role in *Performance*, James Fox). *Performance* is more daring, moving from the sadistic masculine world where Chas (Fox) operates to Turner's (Jagger) womblike netherworld without recourse to a routine plot. Pherber (Pallenberg) and Turner's exploration of Chas's sexuality, and the savage parody of his macho ethos in Jagger's 'Memo from Turner', sum up the questing, challenging spirit of the 60s. It was a sign of the times that the first two major crime films of the 1970s, Mike Hodges's *Get Carter* and Michael Tuchner's *Villain*, with their sad, throwaway, sexually subdued and abused women, should celebrate that ethos.[40]

10

FRYING TONIGHT

> I never read the proclamations of generals before battle, the
> speeches of fuehrers and prime ministers, the solidarity
> songs of public schools and left-wing political parties,
> national anthems, Temperance tracts, papal encyclicals and
> sermons against gambling and contraception, without seem-
> ing to hear in the background a chorus of raspberries from
> all the millions of common men to whom these high senti-
> ments make no appeal. (George Orwell, *Horizon*, 1942)[1]

Comic Traditions

Writing the history of British comedy in the 60s is like reviewing a play
in which the actors have walked out halfway through the performance,
leaving a cast of cleaners, stagehands and volunteers from the audience
to stagger through the remains of the play. Historically, comedy had
been the one consistently successful area of British film production.
Stan Laurel and Charlie Chaplin made their careers in Hollywood, but
Britain's silent cinema produced at least one prolific and popular comedian, Fred Evans, whose 'Pimple' character featured in over a
hundred films between 1912 and 1922; and in the 1920s, when film
production in Britain was at its lowest ebb, the comedienne Betty
Balfour provided one of the few bright spots.[2] After the coming of
sound, film producers scoured variety halls, seaside concert parties,
West End revues, for comedians whose appeal would transfer to film.
The vehicles they provided for George Formby, Max Miller, Gracie
Fields, Jack Hulbert and Cicely Courtneidge, Tom Walls and Ralph
Lynn, Sandy Powell, Leslie Fuller and the rest, tended to be crudely
improvised, but the comedians themselves proved remarkably dur-
able. By the mid-1930s Formby was rivalling Gary Cooper and Clark
Gable in popularity, and Gracie Fields had more fans (in Britain) than
Greta Garbo and Marlene Dietrich.

Cultural barriers remained intact. Formby and Fields just about managed to cross the class divide, but their rougher northern cousins like Duggie Wakefield and Frank Randle remained confined to working-class audiences, while the silly ass antics of the Aldwych farceurs was aimed primarily at the 'better-class halls'. Wartime populism produced less class-specific forms of comedy. Films starring popular radio entertainers like Arthur Askey and Tommy Handley, whose zany modern humour appealed to a wide cross-section of people, and war films built round ordinary (i.e. respectable working-class or lower middle-class) people – *Millions Like Us*, *Waterloo Road*, *The Foreman Went to France*, *The Bells Go Down* – pointed the way to comedies of everyday life such as *Holiday Camp* and *Passport to Pimlico*. It was this sort of comedy of incident and character that emerged as the dominant form in the 50s, though feeding into it was the tradition of sentimental upper middle-class comedy enshrined in Terence Rattigan's *French Without Tears*, Esther McCracken's *Quiet Wedding*, Dodie Smith's *Dear Octopus* and William Douglas Home's *The Chiltern Hundreds*, which showed that the higher orders were just as endearing and ordinary as the workers.

In the 50s, variety, which had sustained the music-hall tradition through the inter-war years, slowly collapsed into a senescence of girly shows and smutty jokes. In contrast, brisk, bright, middle-class comedy was the staple diet of the British film industry, and films like *Genevieve* (1953, d. Henry Cornelius) and *Doctor in the House* (1954, d. Ralph Thomas) spearheaded a solid phalanx of medium-budget comedies which commanded a loyal and substantial audience. The young doctors and engineers played by Dirk Bogarde and Kenneth More embodied the frothy optimism of the New Elizabethan age, combining a playful rebelliousness against lovable authority figures (generally played by James Robertson Justice) with a respect for steam trains and vintage cars and an adolescent enthusiasm for girls which didn't descend to the reality of sex.

Genevieve and *Doctor in the House*, the top box-office films of 1953 and 1954, accept and enjoy the real world to the extent that Raymond Durgnat is able to class them as comedies of affluence.[3] Most of the comedies made by Ealing and by John Grierson's Group 3 in the 50s – *The Titfield Thunderbolt*, *Meet Mr Lucifer*, *The Love Lottery*, *Brandy for the Parson*, *Laxdale Hall* – combine whimsical nostalgia with a primly censorious attitude towards bus companies, television personalities and the *nouveau riche* who are held responsible for eroding the old ways of life. More robust attitudes survived in the groundswell of barrack-room and below-decks comedies which began with Jack Raymond's adaptation of R. F. Delderfield's *Worm's Eye View* in 1951 and continued until the early 60s, when the phasing out of National Service allowed the army, the navy and the airforce to return to decent and unfunny obscurity.

In 1959, British film comedy seemed to be in good shape. In his end of year round-up, Josh Billings of the *Kinematograph Weekly* reckoned *Carry On Nurse* and *I'm All Right Jack* to be the top two box-office films of the year, and several other British comedies – *The Square Peg*, *Carry On Teacher*, *Operation Bullshine*, *The Sheriff of Fractured Jaw* (a spoof Western starring Kenneth More and Jayne Mansfield, directed by Raoul Walsh), *I Only Arsked* and *The Bridal Path* – were among the dozen or so runners-up. But time was running out for the small-scale black and white comedy which had been the mainstay of the British film industry since the early 30s. In 1962, thirty-six British comedies were released. In 1964 there were only eleven, and in the second half of the 60s stage farces, service comedies, rural whimsy and old crock films seemed in danger of extinction.[4]

The Last of the Good Old Days
Ealing, the studio most closely associated with comedy, was passed over to the BBC in 1955, but there were occasional attempts made to keep alive the Ealing tradition. Charles Frend's *Barnacle Bill* (1957), Cyril Frankel's *Alive and Kicking* (1958), Dearden and Relph's *The Smallest Show on Earth* (1957), *Rockets Galore* (1958), *Desert Mice* (1959) and *The Man in the Moon* (1960), Jack Arnold's *The Mouse that Roared* (1959) and Lewis Gilbert's *Light Up the Sky* (1960), are all rather half-hearted, but Charles Crichton's *The Battle of the Sexes* (1959), Dearden and Relph's *The League of Gentlemen* (1960), Michael Truman's *Go to Blazes* (1962) and Robert Hamer's *School for Scoundrels* (1960) update the old formulas more inventively.

Crichton, the most undemonstrative of the Ealing directors, had displayed an unexpected awareness that something other than antiquated steam trains and mischievous bank clerks existed beyond Ealing's village green by making a highly charged melodrama, *Floods of Fear* (with Howard Keel, Cyril Cusack and Anne Heywood) in 1958. When he returned to the fold to make *The Battle of the Sexes* for Balcon's Bryanston consortium, he was able to do so with a certain amount of irony. It is a typical Ealing subject, with its evocation of an old-fashioned world of small businesses and long-serving employees. But in contrast to an early Ealing comedy like *Cheer Boys Cheer* (1939), this world is now a nostalgically evoked caricature. Peter Sellers and a collection of Scottish eccentrics preserve their time-honoured methods against the reforming zeal of a female American efficiency expert (Constance Cummings), but they outwit her only by the unmanly trick of having her declared insane.

The League of Gentlemen was much happier to embrace the modern world. For Alexander Walker the film, 'with its target of quick capital gains, was the ideal comedy for a boom-time economy'.[5] Jack Hawkins, disgruntled at being put out to grass, takes revenge on society by recruiting a team of ex-officers with extremely undistinguished records to carry out a commando-style bank raid. Bryan Forbes's witty script combines well with Dearden's clear and uncluttered direction. The ending – with the smooth-as-clockwork operation foiled by a car numberplate-spotting schoolboy – is predictably conformist, but it is cleverly masked by the farcical intrusion of a Colonel Blimp-like buffer (Robert Coote) who generates such tension and confusion that the arrival of the police seems almost an irrelevance.

Michael Truman had been unlucky at Ealing. Hardly had he made his first feature, *Touch and Go*, than the studio closed down, and his career as a director never really took off. *Go to Blazes* (made for ABPC in CinemaScope and Technicolor) is the last film to succeed in taking the Ealing ethos into the 60s. Truman's direction is adequate rather than inspiring, but the film combines a fresh, plausible plot (bank robbers train as firemen to effect an undercover entry into a bank) with meticulous observation – from kiddies hula-hooping and teenagers dancing to Cliff Richard records to 'Ban the Bomb' painted on the garage door and Golden Shred marmalade on the breakfast table – and the best comedy cast since *The Ladykillers*. Norman Rossington, Daniel Massey and Dave King make an unlikely trio of robbers, but their mismatched personalities and acting styles give the film an uncosy edge and set off the comic caricatures of Robert Morley, Miles Malleson, Dennis Price, Wilfrid Lawson, Maggie Smith and the rest. Everybody is glowingly good-natured (except for Arthur Lowe's prison warder and Wilfrid Lawson's scrap metal dealer), but the reality of decor and detail – King and Rossington arriving early in the getaway fire engine because the police have held up the traffic for them, and getting sidetracked into dealing with Derek Nimmo's flooded flat – ensures that the film doesn't fall into the whimsy of most late Ealing films.

Robert Hamer had left Ealing much earlier than Crichton, Dearden and Truman and was always something of a maverick. *School for Scoundrels*, his last completed film before his death in 1963, is, ironically, about taking short cuts to social success.[6] Based round Stephen Potter's concept of one-upmanship, the film follows the fortunes of an ineffectual young man (Ian Carmichael) as he struggles for supremacy with waiters, women, and Terry-Thomas. The first half – in particular a sequence where used-car salesmen Peter Jones and Dennis Price ('Dudley and Dunstan Dorchester: the Winsome Welshmen') perpetrate a trick even Richard Nixon would be proud of – has its moments of cruel humour and seems to offer insight into the rewards society offers to avarice and malice. As Raymond Durgnat suggests:

It indicates the heavy crudity of middle-class ploys, while establishing that exacerbated dread of hostile judgement, that terrorized and often unjustified certainty of every betrayal of non-stock emotion being silently noted, possibly to be non-committally held against one, which renders the Englishman so constrained, and gives the stiff upper lip its roots, not only in stoicism, but in fear.[7]

But when, with the benefit of a course in 'lifemanship', Carmichael is reborn as a winner, the film becomes increasingly predictable, and Janette Scott's squeaky-clean heroine works her way back into the plot to provide a cloyingly sentimental ending.

School for Scoundrels is more British Lion than Ealing, sharing the same world as the Boulting Brothers' satires. They had begun promisingly in 1956 with *Private's Progress* which, in offering middle-class mickey-taking – as opposed to working-class griping – about the army, seemed to offer something new. But its successors – *Brothers in Law* (1957), *Lucky Jim* (1957) and *Carlton-Browne of the FO* (1959) – are too jolly to qualify as satire, and it was only with *I'm All Right Jack* (1959) that the Boultings took a proper bite at the cherry. Launder and Gilliat, their stablemates at British Lion, continued the saga of the monstrous schoolgirls of St Trinian's and were responsible for a disappointingly slack political satire, *Left, Right and Centre* (1959) and a thin piece of Celtic whimsy, *The Bridal Path* (1959). Then unexpectedly they hit home with Peter Sellers in *Only Two Can Play* (1962), a downbeat comedy of provincial life which is much more successful than the Boultings' *Lucky Jim* in capturing the mixture of anger, bloody-mindedness and cruel humour of Kingsley Amis's early novels.

The charladies' revenge: Peggy Mount, *Ladies Who Do*

By the early 60s even Bryanston was attempting to engage satirically with the pretensions of the affluent society. *Ladies Who Do* (1963, d. C. Pennington-Richards) is much less ambitious than *Only Two Can Play* and was one of the films Rank and ABC considered too undistinguished to be shown on their circuits. But the idea of a gang of charladies raiding the waste-paper bins of their stockbroker employers to play the market and outwit unscrupulous property developer Harry H. Corbett is irresistible, and the film was a box-office success when it was eventually allowed into the cinemas.[8] Freddie Francis's first film, *Two and Two Make Six*, and Roy Baker's *Two Left Feet*, which make similarly brave attempts to come to terms with contemporary life, were also casualties of the 1963 log-jam, but Jay Lewis's *Live Now – Pay Later*, the Boultings' *Heavens Above!* (1963) and Clive Donner's *Nothing But the Best* were too brash to ignore and fared better with the cinema chains.

Modest inputs of new energy came from Joan Littlewood's adaptation of her stage success *Sparrows Can't Sing* (1963) and Ken Russell's feature debut *French Dressing* (1963). Despite their directors' very different approach, the two films are surprisingly similar. Both use James Booth and Roy Kinnear, both are made in black and white largely on location, and both aim at unpretentious populist humour.[9] Russell's visual flair manifests itself in sequences like the mayor and council arriving on roller-skates, a cinema riot with people escaping through a gigantic close-up of Marisa Mell's mouth, and the Walter Raleigh joke which Lester recycles in *A Hard Day's Night* (gallant hero spreads cloak over puddle to prevent lady getting her feet wet, lady steps on cloak and disappears down hole). But it doesn't make up for an inferior cast and a silly story. *Sparrows Can't Sing* hardly has a plot, but its characters – virtually created by the actors who play them – are solidly rooted in East End life. Kinnear and Booth are excellent, but the film also has the huge advantage of Barbara Windsor, a bubbly, sexy, lovable blonde with an infallible sense of right and wrong which is continually betrayed by her sensual instincts. Murray Melvin and Barbara Ferris have so little to do that they seem almost wasted, but they are infinitely more attractive than the displaced starlets Russell is landed with in *French Dressing*.

Tony Hancock, with Peter Sellers the greatest comedian of the postwar period, made a successful transition from radio to television, but his two feature films were disappointing. *The Rebel* (1961), written by Hancock's long-standing scriptwriters Ray Galton and Alan Simpson and directed by Robert Day, is long-winded and heavy-handed at times, and Galton and Simpson don't cope well with the romantic interest, a problem which afflicts all films centred on physically unappealing middle-aged comedians. But the central idea of Hancock becoming a Gauguin-like painter who casts aside respectability to pur-

241

Barbara Windsor, heroine of the high-rise East End: *Sparrows Can't Sing*

sue his art among the beatniks of Paris works well.[10] The film was popular in Britain, but (retitled *Call Me Genius*) attracted hostile reviews in America and flopped badly.

Seeking greater artistic control on his next film, Hancock dispensed with the services of Galton and Simpson and collaborated with the film critic Philip Oakes on the story of a seaside entertainer holding out against the impatient and insensitive commercialism pushed by grasping town councillors and his own socially ambitious wife. *The Punch and Judy Man* (1962) has a good plot, and Sylvia Syms brings exactly the right note of brittle resentment to the part of the wife. But in his desire for artistic control Hancock chose a young and inexperienced director, Jeremy Summers, who proved to have little sense of comic timing, and the film is allowed to sprawl indulgently along and then rushed hurriedly to a conclusion.[11] No doubt if Hancock had gone to Herne Bay and participated in *French Dressing*, or Russell had gone to Bognor Regis and directed *The Punch and Judy Man*, there would have been monumental personality clashes. But if Russell's film lacks a weighty centre, Hancock's lacks zest and inventiveness, and it seems a pity that no one thought of combining the talents of these two lower middle-class egotists.

Peter Yates's *One Way Pendulum* (1964) was in retrospect the most daring of these early 60s attempts to expand the horizons of British film comedy. Beckett, Ionesco, Adamov, Genet and Pinter had created a 'theatre of the absurd' of international significance by the late 1950s, and if N. F. Simpson was not quite in the same league there was the advantage that his plays relied on visual fantasies which might better adapt to film than the more outlandish but mainly verbal absurdism of *Waiting for Godot* or *The Bald Prima Donna*. Unfortunately, Yates dithers between going for the madness of everyday life (explored in 'Armchair Theatre' productions like Pinter's *A Night Out* or David Perry's apocalyptic *The Trouble With Our Ivy*) and the outright lunacy of the Goons. Simpson's bizarre ideas – the speak-your-weight machines trying to sing the 'Hallelujah Chorus', the do-it-yourself Old Bailey kit – creak only fitfully into life and, ironically, *One Way Pendulum* now seems less anarchic and disturbing than the Brian Rix farce *The Night We Got the Bird* (1960, d. Darcy Conyers). Here, there is no attempt at visual or any other sort of sophistication, but the rooting of bizarre events in the mundaneness of everyday lower middle-class life is more secure. Rix's continually frustrated bridegroom, Dora Bryan's

A world which is familiar but totally absurd. Brian Rix, *The Night We Got the Bird*

243

flirty but prim bride and Ronald Shiner's dead husband reincarnated as a voyeuristic parrot interact in such a way as to create a world which is familiar but totally absurd.

Woodfall, the company responsible for *One Way Pendulum*, had more success with Richard Lester's *The Knack*, which finds a visual style – negative images, disjunctive cuts, intrusive vox pop interpolations – to express a view of the world as absurd but full of exciting possibilities. It was an attitude and a style that crept into Swinging London films like *Morgan*, *Help!*, *Smashing Time* and *The Bliss of Mrs Blossom*. But the onset of permissiveness seems to have thrown traditional British comedy forms into confusion, and even those strands which do cross the mid-decade divide – Norman Wisdom and Peter Sellers films and the *Carry On* series – show serious signs of strain.

Peter Sellers

Sellers's parents were variety performers and by the time he was three he was joining them on stage in miniature top hat and tails to sing 'My Old Dutch'. Even before he became a household name as one of the Goons, his impersonations of Churchill, Humphrey Bogart, Jimmy Durante and Groucho Marx were getting him bookings at prestigious venues like the London Palladium.[12] Sellers and his collaborators on the 'Goon Show' (1950–57) – Harry Secombe, Spike Milligan and Michael Bentine – were impatient of traditional music-hall humour and built on the surreal inventiveness of wartime radio shows like *Band Waggon*, *Happidrome* and *ITMA* to create a new sort of irreverent, subversive, absurd comedy. This was transferred to television in Sellers and Milligan's *A Show Called Fred* (directed by Richard Lester) and Michael Bentine's *It's a Square World*, and provided styles and ideas for youth films like *The Knack* and *Catch Us If You Can*. But Sellers's own film career was built round the creation of bizarre but believable eccentrics who are at their best when rooted in British culture.

Two low-budget Goon films were made in the 50s – *Down Among the Z Men* (1952) and *The Case of the Mukkinese Battlehorn* (1956) – and Sellers played the junior member of Alec Guinness's gang in *The Ladykillers*, but the first of his fully matured comic monsters is Sonny Macgregor, the hypnotically hypocritical television quizmaster in Mario Zampi's *The Naked Truth* in 1957. *The Naked Truth* was followed by roles in four films – *Up the Creek*, *Tom Thumb*, *Carlton-Browne of the FO*, and *The Mouse That Roared* – which don't extend beyond comic caricature. But Fred Kite, the Stalinist shop steward in *I'm All Right Jack*; Mr Martin, Constance Cummings's Crippen-like adversary in *The Battle of the Sexes*; Dodger Lane, the cagey, pampered gang boss who uses Wormwood Scrubs as a convenient base from which to launch a jewel robbery in *Two Way Stretch*; and the

Comic monsters: Peter Sellers in *Battle of the Sexes*

explosively malevolent Lionel Meadows in *Never Let Go*, are all characters of depth and originality. In his next four films – *The Millionairess*, *Mr Topaze* (which Sellers directed), *Only Two Can Play* and *The Dock Brief* – he played more complex, more 'realistic' characters, all of them essentially 'little men'. But as Doug McVay points out, Sellers

> lacks the dynamic impudence of a Chaplin, so that his Little Men are a trifle too small for comfort. By endeavouring to be subtle and discreet, he frequently tends to efface himself beyond the bounds of desirability, and his attempts at wit and sentiment coalesce into a rather tentative and negative atmosphere of sketchiness.[13]

McVay perceptively notes that Sellers seemed comfortable with these nondescript specimens of humanity only 'with scenes of either drily cold aplomb or else fantastic idiosyncrasy', and concluded that he was 'intrinsically a simple and stylised performer, not a complicated and realistic one; that he is most suited to single-toned parts, and suave, snide or savage parts into the bargain.'[14] But Sellers was not content to find success as a comic type like Terry-Thomas, Leslie Phillips or Lionel Jeffries, who adopted a persona which remained fundamentally unchanged throughout their film careers.[15]

Sellers's talent for mimicry (which had led him to take absurd risks impersonating high-ranking officers during the war) developed into a form of possession:

245

He came to see himself as a form of medium – as if the film characters had entered his body, transfusing his personality so powerfully with their own that they took him over. From that it was to be just a short jump in credulity to the point where he convinced himself that these were not simply fictitious characters, the offspring of some screenwriter's imagination – they were 'lives' that he himself, whoever *he* might be, had lived at other times, in other places, under other names. Acting, in short, was a process of past-life recall.[16]

This might have been a convenient way for Sellers to explain his deep involvement in the roles he played, but it is evident that his most convincing characters express unacknowledged aspects of his own personality. Sonny Macgregor's contempt for his television audience in *The Naked Truth* is different from Sellers's hatred of variety hall audiences 'with two-thousandths of an inch foreheads' only in that it is hypocritically concealed. Alexander Walker relates how after Spike Milligan had been driven to almost suicidal despair by a hostile audience at the Coventry Hippodrome, Sellers went on the next night, scrapped his prepared act and contemptuously proceeded to baffle his audience by playing them gramophone records.[17] Lionel Meadows's dyspeptic violence which breaks out into uncontrollable rages in *Never Let Go* spilled over into Sellers's home life. 'It was an appreciable time before his menacing glare and crude manner, which disconcerted any dinner guests, had faded, leaving a drained, apologetic and apprehensive husband almost scared by himself.'[18] An underlying threat of violence is evident in all Sellers's best parts, except where it is transmuted into the equally daunting sincerity of Fred Kite's bloody-minded utopianism in *I'm All Right Jack*, the Reverend Smallweed's Christian goodwill in *Heavens Above!*, and Inspector Clouseau's self-immolating zeal in *The Pink Panther* and its successors.

After *Heavens Above!*, Peter Sellers was virtually lost to the domestic British comedy. His performances in *Lolita* and *Dr Strangelove* led to Hollywood and *The Pink Panther*, and in any other period he would have stayed there, but in the 60s he was able to return to Britain and still play major roles in big-budget international films. Unfortunately, except for *A Shot in the Dark* (1964) – the best of the Clouseau films – and *What's New Pussycat?* (1965), the films he appeared in – *The Wrong Box* (1966), *After the Fox* (1966), *Casino Royale* (1967), *The Bobo* (1967), *The Magic Christian* (1969), *Hoffman* (1970) and *There's a Girl in My Soup* (1970) – are films which ought to be shipped to a desert island and screened continuously to those responsible for them. Whether one blames the British film industry, the Americans, Anglo-American culture, or Sellers himself, what is undeniable is the terrible waste of Britain's finest film comedian.[19]

Norman Wisdom

Norman Wisdom was something of a throwback to good-hearted music-hall clowns like George Formby or even Stan Laurel. As Richard Dacre explains, he was part of the

> last generation of comics to have the tremendous advantage of at least the remnants of a live variety circuit to use as a training ground, learning timing and perfecting presentation through experience on the boards. The process of working up from the 'wines and spirits' to top-billing, perfecting single routines through repetition, was irreplaceable in developing knockabout physical comedy and verbal timing.[20]

But it was television which brought Wisdom to prominence. Unlike Sellers, who created a whole gallery of comic monsters, Wisdom confined his ingenuity, like Chaplin, Formby and most of the early film comedians, to variations on a single character: the bullied, good-hearted, disaster-prone little man he called 'the Gump'. Film critics never had much time for low-brow British film comedy, and Wisdom, sentimental without being vulgar, was particularly vulnerable to critical contempt. This in turn made it difficult for him to find more satisfactory vehicles for his talents than the increasingly banal projects offered by the Rank Organisation.

John Paddy Carstairs, the director assigned to the first seven Wisdom films, was a colourful, multi-talented character, and *Trouble in Store* (1953), *Up in the World* (1956) and *The Square Peg* (1958) are well organised and effective comedies. At the end of the decade he was succeeded by Robert Asher (brother of cameraman Jack Asher), who was more susceptible than the worldly, hard-boiled Carstairs to Wisdom's insistence on the importance of pathos. This was not in itself a disadvantage. As early as 1955 David Robinson, the one national critic to have any time for Wisdom, pointed out that the Gump

> always *tries* to be right, but never succeeds – except of course by a happy last-minute fluke. His motive is a mania . . . to be friendly. This is not in itself new, of course; the perennial problem of clowns and children is the impossibility in this world of loving and being loved all the time. The resulting rebuffs are the mainspring for the pathos which is an essential of Wisdom's work.[21]

In *Follow a Star* (1959), the fact that his girlfriend is crippled works very well, tying in usefully with Wisdom's castrating dependence both on her and on the Machiavellian crooner (Jerry Desmonde) who 'steals' his voice. And in *The Bulldog Breed* (1960), the pathos surrounding Wisdom's little man, such a washout with women that he

247

Situating Norman in the real world: Susannah York, Reginald Beckwith, Norman Wisdom in *There Was a Crooked Man*

joins the navy as the only alternative to suicide, at least avoids the strains on credulity of a standard film comedy romance. Both films were commercially successful, but Wisdom was eager to expand his repertoire and in 1960 he broke free of Rank to make two films for United Artists, *There Was a Crooked Man* (1960) and *The Girl on the Boat* (1961).

There Was a Crooked Man is ably directed by theatre director Stuart Burge. It retains the traditional Wisdom format of innocent Norman falling among thieves and scoundrels but eventually escaping unscathed to win the girl and bring happiness to those who deserve it, but Burge takes it all rather more seriously than Carstairs and Asher, and what the film loses in inspired slapstick it gains in better characterisation and plausibility of plot. Wisdom's role as a good-natured ex-commando with a peculiar facility for explosives takes him, predictably, into the underworld and prison, but also to a grim northern mill-town which – having ensured that the mill owner/speculator rather than the townspeople will pay the bill – he proceeds to blow up to make way for a smart, clean new town. There are the usual absurd complications, but the attempt to situate Norman in the real world works very well.[22]

The Girl on the Boat, directed by Henry Kaplan, is based on a novel by P. G. Wodehouse and has Wisdom strangely cast as an upper-class

248

dilettante. He struggles gamely with the part, but fails to rid himself entirely of his cloth-cap image and his problems are compounded by the miscasting of Millicent Martin as the dizzy flapper Norman pursues. Together they are hopelessly unconvincing as Wodehouse characters and though the film has its moments, it only briefly takes off into that frenzy of manic confusion which both Wisdom and Wodehouse achieve at their best. The presence of Richard Briers and Sheila Hancock, who are much more appropriately cast and in no way subordinate to Wisdom, only serves to throw the film further out of kilter.

Changes to the Wisdom persona did not go down well at the box-office, and the two United Artists films were much less successful than their predecessors. Wisdom returned to Rank for a further two films – On the Beat (1962) and A Stitch in Time (1963) – but, his popularity restored, he again grew restive and turned down the script for Turn Again, Wisdom, Rank's projected 1964 Wisdom film, complaining that 'They don't seem to realise that I have grown up and can get laughs without falling downstairs.'[23] But he found it difficult to break out from the confines of the British film industry and the expectations of his audience. His 1965 film, The Early Bird, has a dialogue-less ten-minute sequence with Norman continually falling down stairs as he stumbles about half asleep attempting to get ready for his early morning milk round, but the rest of the film holds few surprises. Press for Time (1966), his final film for Rank, was expected to open new avenues, but when shooting began Robert Asher told the Evening News:

> This is to be a formula Wizzy film, he wants to get away from the formula but they don't want him to. You can see their point actually. They shove a Wizzy picture out at Christmas and the money pours in. The Little Man is just like the Pied Piper. The kids follow him wherever he goes. Showing a Wizzy film is like owning a bank.[24]

Perhaps because of all the last-minute dithering it is a poorly scripted and directed film, redeemed only by one brilliant sequence where Norman, fearing his bicycle will be stolen by the rapacious local children, insists on bringing it into the luxurious home of the town's Mayoress and, in trying to park it, ends up with the bicycle and himself suspended from the ceiling. Despite playing a major role in William Friedkin's The Night They Raided Minsky's (1968), Wisdom failed to establish himself in Hollywood and returned to Britain to make What's Good for the Goose (1969, d. Menahem Golan) for Tigon. Its setting among the dregs of the Swinging Sixties – Wisdom is a timid bank clerk who falls for a promiscuous young swinger (Sally Geeson) – gives it a gruesome sort of appeal, but it did his career little good and turned out to be his last feature film.

Attempts were made to launch other comedians who had become popular through television. Associated British, having missed out on Norman Wisdom, signed up Charlie Drake and Tony Hancock, but neither venture prospered. Four quite ingenious vehicles were provided for Drake – *Sands of the Desert* (1960, d. John Paddy Carstairs), *Petticoat Pirates* (1961, d. David Macdonald), *The Cracksman* (1963, d. Peter Graham Scott) and *Mister Ten Percent* (1967, d. Peter Graham Scott) – but they failed to create anything like the commercial impact of the Wisdom films.[25] Rank tried to duplicate their success with Wisdom by recruiting Eric Morecambe and Ernie Wise, brilliant pier-end entertainers who had proved even more effective on television. Unfortunately, their comic genius proved less adaptable to the narrative demands of feature films. *The Intelligence Men* (1965), *That Riviera Touch* (1966) and *The Magnificent Two* (1967) have wonderfully funny sequences but they don't hold together as films. *The Intelligence Men* has a good script but is sloppily directed by Robert Asher. Cliff Owen provided much tighter direction on the other two films, but this was a mixed blessing since it allowed little space for Eric and Ernie's genial, relaxed humour to build up momentum.

'Infamy! Infamy! They've all got it in for me!'

The *Carry On* series began unremarkably with an ordinary barrack-room comedy, *Carry On Sergeant* (1958), based on R. F. Delderfield's play *The Bull Boys*. It is almost a spoof of Carol Reed's famous war film *The Way Ahead*, with William Hartnell again playing a tight-lipped Sergeant-Major trying to whip his gang of assorted misfits into an effective fighting unit. In contrast to Richard Lester's *How I Won the War* (1967), which treats the same subject with savage derision, *Carry On Sergeant* is sunnily good-natured. The Sergeant-Major has a heart of gold, the blustering camp commander (Eric Barker) softens to allow a newly wedded recruit leave to consummate his marriage, and in a surprising echo of wartime populism, Kenneth Williams's awkward, snooty intellectual shows himself patient and sympathetic enough to bring the camp's failure (Norman Rossington) – whom everyone else has given up on – up to scratch. With National Service still very much part of everyday experience the film proved an unexpected box-office success, and producer Peter Rogers had the bright idea of keeping together his comic team (Kenneth Connor, Hattie Jacques, Charles Hawtrey, Kenneth Williams and Eric Barker) and taking them on to explore other institutions.[26] Hospitals seemed to figure almost as prominently as the army in the national psyche, and *Carry On Nurse* (1959), for which Leslie Phillips and Joan Sims were recruited, proved so popular that it launched the *Carry On* films as an unstoppable series. *Carry On Teacher* (1959) stars Ted Ray as the headmaster of a run-down secondary modern school and is in some ways more successful than its more serious rivals (*Spare the Rod*, *Term of Trial* and *To Sir, With Love*) in treating rebellious children and harassed teachers with realistic sympathy.

With *Carry On Constable* (1960), *Carry On Regardless* (1961), *Carry On Cruising* (1962), and *Carry On Cabby* (1963) the series drifted into the doldrums, but new blood in the form of Bernard Cribbins, Jim Dale and Juliet Mills (in *Carry On Jack*, 1963) and Barbara Windsor (in *Carry On Spying*, 1964) and scriptwriter Talbot Rothwell gave the series a new lease of life. *Carry On Cleo* (1964) has an energy and inventiveness which subsequent films were never quite to recapture. Higher than usual production values (thanks to the left-behind sets of Fox's attempt to film *Cleopatra* in England) help, but it is as an ensemble comedy that the film succeeds. Kenneth Connor's nine-stone-weakling character reaches its apotheosis in Hengist Pod, an Ancient Briton who gains an undeserved reputation for ferocity. Sid James looks like a gone-to-seed Richard Burton as Mark Anthony, Amanda Barrie's thin, pert, unpretentiously sexy Cleopatra compares well with Elizabeth Taylor, and the other *Carry On* regulars play parts in which they are so effortlessly at home – Kenneth Williams as a vain and cowardly Caesar, Joan Sims a dowdy Calpurnia, and Charles Hawtrey the old and lecherous sage, Seneca – that one hardly notices the lack of a storyline.

The idea of parodying other film genres produced mixed results. *Carry On Screaming* (1966) is only very patchily funny, despite the horrid glee Kenneth Williams brings to his task of transforming nubile young women into wax dummies, but *Carry On Cowboy* (1966), *Follow That Camel* (1967) and *Don't Lose Your Head* (1967) benefit from solider than usual stories and the gauche charm of Jim Dale and Angela Douglas. After *Carry On Screaming*, Peter Rogers left Anglo-Amalgamated for Rank, and it was Anglo's insistence that they retain copyright over the *Carry On* title which prevented the first two Rank films from using it. However, the films had always been made at Pinewood and distributed by Rank Film Distributors, and the series' subsequent decline would appear to have more to do with flagging ingenuity and an inability creatively to come to terms with the new permissive climate.[27]

The early *Carry On* films relied on innuendo and double meaning in a similar way to the seaside postcards of Donald McGill. Ian Johnson juxtaposes George Orwell's essay on McGill with an example from *Carry On Nurse*:

'In one postcard, captioned "They didn't believe her", a young woman is demonstrating, with her hands held apart, something about two feet long to a couple of open-mouthed acquaintances. Behind her, on the wall, is a stuffed fish in a glass case, and beside that is a photograph of a nearly naked athlete. Obviously it is not the fish that she is referring to, but this could never be proved.' Likewise when in *Carry On Nurse* a nurse remarks upon a patient's embarrassment at pulling down his trousers: 'All that fuss over such a little thing . . .' you can't prove anything either.[28]

As sexual taboos dissolved, such evasions seemed childish and unnecessary (though the embarrassments they expose remained as powerful as they had ever been). In the old repressive society, humour came from the juxtaposition of sexual fantasies and grim reality – the ugly misshapen middle-aged man dreaming of sex with an attractive pliable young girl and being pulled up short by his stout, argumentative wife. The permissive 60s seemed to offer a different scenario where middle-aged men could at least share the favours of sexually liberated young women, and the remaining *Carry On* films – *Carry On Doctor* (1968), *Carry On Up the Khyber* (1968), *Carry On Camping* (1969), *Carry On Again Doctor* (1969), *Carry On Loving* (1970), *Carry On Up the Jungle* (1970) – and their increasingly tattered 1970s successors like Norman Wisdom's *What's Good for the Goose* and Peter Sellers's *There's a Girl in My Soup*, are dominated by this magnetic but unsavoury myth.

Late 60s Comedies
Except for the *Carry On* films, which had a peculiar momentum of their own, early and late 60s comedies seem to occupy different worlds. *The Great St Trinian's Train Robbery* (1966), for example, drops all the old regulars except for George Cole, Richard Wattis and a sadly diminished Eric Barker, and substitutes smutty sexual innuendo for the endearing eccentricity of Alastair Sim and Joyce Grenfell. Like 1960s town planning, which pulled down friendly terraces and replaced them with shopping precincts and high-rise flats, it now seems a dreadful mistake. But no doubt at the time it seemed that film comedy had to change or die. Television had already captured the high ground with *Hancock's Half Hour*, the Benny Hill and Morecambe and Wise shows, and series like *The Rag Trade*, *Steptoe and Son*, *Till Death Us Do Part* and *Dad's Army*, *That Was the Week That Was* and its successors, Peter Cook and Dudley Moore's *Not Only . . . But Also*, and *Monty Python's Flying Circus*.

Attempts were made to reach an international audience with Ken Annakin's lavish relaunch of the old crock cycle in *Those Magnificent Men in Their Flying Machines* (1965) and *Monte Carlo or Bust!* (1969), and comic caper films expanded from the parochial level of Mario Zampi's *Too Many Crooks* and Michael Truman's *Go to Blazes* to the international heists of *Gambit* and *The Italian Job*. But more elaborate machines and more exotic locations were a poor substitute for likeable

252

characters and neatly tied up plots, and big budgets and illustrious casts did not necessarily make for better films.

The realisation that, with the unceasing efforts of the Clean-Up TV campaigners and the liberalisation of cinema censorship, film comedy could attract audiences with greater sexual explicitness had a baleful effect on the *Carry On* series. As Andy Medhurst writes, 'By their increasing sexual directness ... they put an end to the very traditions of innuendo that sustained them for so long. After Barbara Windsor's brassiere had at last burst (in *Carry On Camping*, 1969) where was the humour in teasing about the possibility of such an occurrence?'[29] The middle-class comedies of Ralph Thomas and Betty Box which had dominated the 50s took some advantage of the new permissive climate, with blandly asexual Dr Sparrow (Dirk Bogarde) being succeeded by unctuously lecherous Dr Burke (Leslie Phillips). But if *Doctor in Clover* (1966) and *Doctor in Trouble* (1970) are more gutsy than *Doctor in Distress* (1963) they are still half-hearted, their morality still tied to the safer, cosier world of the pre-permissive society. Sex comedies as such don't really get under way until the end of 1970, with the release of a low-budget brothel farce (*Games That Lovers Play*, d. Malcolm Leigh) and two films about penises (*The Statue*, d. Rod Amateau, and Box/Thomas's *Percy*). Apart from the international films, the largest groups of comedies were those which spun off from or closely resembled television comedy, and adaptations of stage successes.

The television spin-offs divide into two groups. The least contentious are the solidly realist social comedies like British Lion's *Till Death Us Do Part* (1968, d. Norman Cohen), which might be classed alongside the two Bill Naughton adaptations, *The Family Way* (1966, d. Roy Boulting) and *Spring and Port Wine* (1970, d. Peter Hammond). They are unadventurously orthodox in terms of style but have some merit in their genuine exploration of social themes and their warm, unpatronising affection for the lives of their very ordinary protagonists. The other group, *30 is a Dangerous Age, Cynthia* (1967, d. Joe McGrath), *Bedazzled* (1967, d. Stanley Donen), *The Rise and Rise of Michael Rimmer* (1970, d. Kevin Billington), *Every Home Should Have One* (1970, d. Jim Clark), belated children of the satire boom, employ a battery of cinematic tricks – fast motion, rapid montage, animated insertions – to disguise what unfortunately tend to be over-extended ragbags of old television sketches. *The Rise and Rise of Michael Rimmer*, for example, starts promisingly as a *Nothing But the Best* for the late 60s, with Peter Cook as a mysterious public relations expert who moves into a traditionally (and badly) run advertising agency and proceeds with stoat-like implacability to traumatise everyone from the Managing Director downwards and make them completely dependent on him. This neat twenty-minute parable on the power of the 'image-makers' is then extended for a further eighty minutes as with ponder-

A horrid fascination: *The Bliss of Mrs Blossom*

ous predictability Cook goes on to bring down the Labour government, take over the Tory party, become Prime Minister, and dispense with democracy entirely.

These late 60s satires share characteristics with theatrical adaptations such as *Work is a Four Letter Word* (from Henry Livings's play *Eh?*), *The Bliss of Mrs Blossom* (Alec Coppel), *Entertaining Mr Sloane* and *Loot* (Joe Orton) and *A Severed Head* (Iris Murdoch and J. B. Priestley). For the uninitiated some of these films must seem unwatchably awful, but as examples of 60s tastelessness Joe McGrath's *The Bliss of Mrs Blossom* (1968), Silvio Narizzano's *Loot* (1970) and Jim Clark's *Every Home Should Have One* exercise a horrid fascination. The haphazard, fragmentary structure allows moments of redeeming hilarity to escape – Bob Monkhouse's Ronnie Laing-like psychotherapist delving into the unconscious of bra manufacturer Mr Blossom ('the Orpheus of the undie world'), the Snow White toothpaste car full of dwarves which whizzes through *Every Home Should Have One*, the police bulldozer laying waste to garden gnomes in *Loot*. But like headless chickens they seem to run round in ever-decreasing circles. The absurdism, the view of the world as a ridiculously irrational and unpredictable place, which they strive for, fails to convince because unlike Roman Polanski's bleak, casual, cruelly funny *Cul de Sac*, they present only a shallow pastiche of the real world which has no immediate or symbolic importance.

254

Richard Lester's *How I Won the War* (1967) and *The Bed Sitting Room* (1969) have a boldness and integrity which deserves more sympathy, but unlike *The Knack* and *Help!* they are esoteric works and failed to reach a mass audience. By the early 70s, the British film industry was restricting its ambitions in the field to sex comedies and adaptations of television sit-coms like *On the Buses*.

11

HOLLYWOOD'S ENGLAND

Then everything along the bus route into the city upset me. The houses seemed so small, and the flower-bordered front paths, down which men in three-piece suits came hurrying off to work, seemed too bright and neat and prepared. Men were carrying umbrellas, whistling errand boys on bicycles were weaving in and out of the traffic, bright orange tile roofs curved gaily over pebble-dash fronts. Bay windows, broad clean pavements, narrow, tarmacked road ways, lurking buses, everything was just as it was in the Ealing comedy movies. It was all nice and wholesome and harmless. (Martin Green, *A Mirror for Anglo-Saxons*, 1961)[1]

The Shadow of Hollywood

In trying to reverse the neglect into which the study of British cinema has fallen, there is a tendency to ignore the fact that from the middle of the First World War onwards the British film industry has been dominated by Hollywood; that since 1916 anything from 50 to 97 per cent of the films shown in Britain have been American. In the 1920s the production of British films seemed to be going into terminal decline and was only saved by the Cinematograph Films Act of 1927 which made it compulsory for cinemas to show a quota of British films, initially only 5 per cent but rising to 20 per cent by 1935. To ensure that there was a supply of films for the exhibitors to show, distributors were required to carry a similar quota of British films on their books. At 20 per cent this meant that MGM, for example, had to offer twelve British films in 1935 to set against its sixty American films. The Americans responded by making their British films as cheaply as possible, provoking considerable hostility about 'quota quickies'.

After the war British film production was sufficiently well-established for the distributors' quota to be abandoned, but Hollywood's own problems changed American attitudes towards production in

Britain. The rapid spread of television ownership had a devastating effect on cinema admissions, and the 1949 'divorcement' decrees which forced the majors to divest themselves of their cinema chains spelt the end of the old studio system. 'Runaway' production, films made by Americans outside Hollywood, became increasingly important and Britain – where the majors could utilise blocked exhibition earnings, take advantage of lower labour costs, and qualify for the Eady Levy subsidy provided they used crews and casts that were predominantly British – became an attractive alternative to Hollywood. By 1956 one third of the films made in Britain had some form of American involvement.[2] In contrast to the quota quickie days of the 30s, the predominant trend was to make big-budget pictures which would appeal to American as well as British audiences. Many of these films – Warner Brothers' *Moby Dick*, MGM's *Mogambo*, Disney's *Rob Roy* – had little to identify them as British beyond the presence of character actors like James Robertson Justice, Bernard Miles or Finlay Currie. Even where the films were set in contemporary Britain (Ford's *Gideon's Day*, for example) pains were taken to make it look as much like the Britain familiar to cinemagoers from Hollywood productions like *Manhunt*, *Cluny Brown* and *Ministry of Fear*, where cuddly Cockneys and friendly bobbies on bicycles lived fog-shrouded lives under the shadow of Big Ben and the Houses of Parliament. War films – Warwick's *Cockleshell Heroes* (1955, d. José Ferrer), Sam Spiegel's *The Bridge on the River Kwai* (1957, d. David Lean) – were more realistic, but they were first and foremost colourful spectacles and their British subject matter was incidental.[3]

American involvement in the British 'New Wave' was minimal. Warner Brothers had backed *Look Back in Anger* only because of the box-office potential of Richard Burton, and the Woolfs – who had made many of their films as Anglo-American productions – had to put up their own money for *Room at the Top*. Columbia did back later Romulus productions like *The L-Shaped Room* and *The Pumpkin Eater* and 20th Century-Fox made *Sons and Lovers* (1960, d. Jack Cardiff), an impressively bleak film despite its American leading man. But more typical of American production in Britain was Disney's *In Search of the Castaways* (1961, d. Robert Stevenson) and MGM's Agatha Christie series – *Murder She Said* (1961), *Murder at the Gallop* (1963), *Murder Ahoy* (1964) and *Murder Most Foul* (1964) – with Margaret Rutherford heading a cast of dotty British eccentrics. United Artists' success with *Doctor No*, *Tom Jones* and *A Hard Day's Night* heralded a new era.[4]

The energy and panache of the Beatles and Bond films, the success of British pop music, and the development of the myth of Swinging London made British society suddenly exciting, charismatic and fashionable. After decades in which Britain had followed American trends, it seemed that the process had been reversed. London was seen as the centre of a youth-oriented cultural revolution which young Americans found fascinating and appealing. By the mid-60s all the majors and two mini-majors – Filmways and Avco-Embassy – had set up British production subsidiaries. According to the NFFC, by 1966 75 per cent of production finance came from American sources. A year later it was 90 per cent.[5] American and Continental directors were brought over (Preminger for *Bunny Lake is Missing*, Truffaut for *Fahrenheit 451*, Antonioni for *Blow Up*), but it was generally British talent which was sought after. As David Robinson recalled at the end of the decade: 'Perhaps at no time in the remembered history of the cinema had the money-men been so receptive to new people and new ideas. It was a brief Utopia.'[6]

United Artists

Since the 30s, when it had backed Alexander Korda's *The Private Life of Henry VIII*, United Artists had been the most active of the American companies in Britain. In the late 50s and early 60s it had been responsible for a mixed but not unlikeable group of films. Two intelligent films about the IRA, *Shake Hands With the Devil* (1959, d. Michael Anderson) and *A Terrible Beauty* (1960, d. Tay Garnett), two refreshingly unusual Norman Wisdom comedies, *There Was a Crooked Man* and *The Girl on the Boat*, were made alongside Sidney Furie's horror films *Doctor Blood's Coffin* (1961) and *The Snake Woman* (1961) and Ronald Neame's stodgy but commercially successful *Tunes of Glory* (1961) and *I Could Go On Singing* (1963). The infusion of new blood in 1962/3 – Broccoli/Saltzman, Woodfall, Richard Lester – encouraged United Artists to invest more heavily in British production.

George Ornstein, who had been responsible for commissioning *Tom Jones* and the Beatles and Bond films, left the company in 1964 to work with Broccoli and Saltzman on *Thunderball* and *You Only Live Twice* before taking over as Paramount's British production head. But United Artists' production programme remained remarkably stable throughout the decade. This did not automatically spell box-office success. After *Tom Jones*, Tony Richardson seemed to lose his popular touch. His two experiments with Jeanne Moreau, *Mademoiselle* (1966) and *The Sailor from Gibraltar* (1967), perhaps deserve more serious treatment than they have received, but their appeal could hardly be expected to extend beyond a small circle of art cinema aficionados and even there they were unsympathetically received. Richardson's final three 60s films, *The Charge of the Light Brigade* (1968), *Laughter in the Dark* (1969) and *Ned Kelly* (1970), are less abstruse but have a petulant quality which makes it difficult to like them.

Richard Lester was only slightly more successful in avoiding the late 60s doldrums. The inventiveness of *A Hard Day's Night*, *The Knack* and *Help!* was shackled in Melvin Frank's conventional screenplay for

The Bed-Sitting Room: Mrs Ethel Shroake (Dandy Nichols)

A Funny Thing Happened on the Way to the Forum (1967) and seemed to lose its way in the muddled tragi-comedy of *How I Won the War* (1968). With admirable loyalty, though with a breathtaking disregard for commercial considerations, United Artists stuck by Lester and allowed him to go ahead with *The Bed-Sitting Room* (1969). It is his most outlandish film, a macabre post-holocaust comedy peopled by characters who metamorphose into rooms and wardrobes and spend their lives in railway carriages and dustbins, the sort of film which, daft though it is, is so unique that one is glad it was made. But commercially it was a non-starter and it seriously jeopardised Lester's career.

There were post-Ornstein attempts at United Artists to introduce new blood. Clive Donner made *Here We Go Round the Mulberry Bush* for the company in 1967, and Ken Russell was signed up by Harry

259

Saltzman to make *Billion Dollar Brain*. He stayed with United Artists to make his first two really successful films, *Women in Love* (1969) and *The Music Lovers* (1970). But these slightly risky films were carefully balanced by big-budget productions aimed at an international audience, such as Basil Dearden and Michael Relph's trilogy, *Woman of Straw* (1964, with Gina Lollobrigida, Sean Connery and Ralph Richardson), *Masquerade* (1965, with Cliff Robertson and Jack Hawkins) and *Khartoum* (1966, with Charlton Heston and Laurence Olivier).

Saltzman and Broccoli were together responsible for the Bond films but both men also embarked on independent ventures. Saltzman was successful with his Len Deighton adaptations, but after *Billion Dollar Brain* he gave up on Harry Palmer and cast Michael Caine in a grubby war film, *Play Dirty* (1969, d. André de Toth), and in the enormously expensive *Battle of Britain* (1969, d. Guy Hamilton), where Caine's unmistakable Cockney accent makes him one of the few expensive stars who is not reduced to anonymity by their flying gear. Broccoli devoted his spare time to an even duller project, *Chitty Chitty Bang Bang* (1968, d. Ken Hughes), an extravagant children's musical which despite Ken Adam's sets and good cameo appearances from Lionel Jeffries and Robert Helpmann obstinately refuses to take off.

United Artists' most prolific suppliers, Woodfall and the American independent producers the Mirisch Brothers (ten films each between 1963 and 1970), came from opposite ends of the film-making spectrum. The Mirisch Brothers were responsible for the Inspector Clouseau films – *The Pink Panther* (1963, d. Blake Edwards), *A Shot in the Dark* (1964, d. Blake Edwards) and *Inspector Clouseau* (1968, d. Bud Yorkin, with Alan Arkin struggling unsuccessfully to emulate Sellers) – and a bevy of solidly predictable war films (*633 Squadron*, *Attack on the Iron Coast*, *Submarine X–1*, *Hell Boats*, *Mosquito Squadron*) which display those conventional heroics that Lester and Richardson mock in *How I Won the War* and *The Charge of the Light Brigade*. Woodfall relied mainly on the eclectic, increasingly erratic Tony Richardson, but also supplied pleasingly offbeat films like Peter Yates's *One Way Pendulum* (1964), Desmond Davis's *The Girl With Green Eyes* (1964), Richard Lester's *The Knack* (1965) and Ken Loach's *Kes* (1969).

Between 1968 and 1970 United Artists backed thirty-one British films, depressingly few of which were either commercially successful or artistically worthwhile.[7] But among them were two boldly controversial interpretations of well-known literary subjects, Billy Wilder's *The Private Life of Sherlock Holmes* (1970) and Ken Russell's *Women in Love* (1969). Wilder's film, co-produced by the Mirisch Brothers and Polanski's collaborator Gene Gutowski, is admittedly a bit of a hodgepodge. It was conceived as a compendium of at least four Holmes stories, but nobody bothered to work out how long the resulting film would be and in the two-hour version of the film that was finally released only two of them survive. Though there are no overt connections, the two stories combine to make the film a harmonious whole.[8] The first, a brief account of how Holmes, invited to marry a Russian ballerina, excuses himself by hinting that he is homosexually attached to Watson, introduces themes which are explored more fully in the second story. Here, in what constitutes the main body of the film, the arrival of a half-drowned amnesiac at 221B Baker Street precipitates Holmes and Watson into a deadly fairy-tale world where they have to deal with a beautiful but dangerous woman, the Loch Ness Monster, Queen Victoria, and a primitive submarine. Robert Stephens's Holmes emerges as a tragic figure, a brilliant man kept at arm's length by an Establishment wary of his unconventionality, for whom the unravelling of mysteries and the dangerous pleasures of cocaine are incomplete remedies for the boredom and futility of a dilettante's life. The film seems afflicted with Holmes's own *fin de siècle* languor and there is little of the excitement of Gene Gutowski's earlier, cruder excursion into Sherlock Holmes territory, *A Study in Terror*, but it is still a moving, intelligent, original approach to the Holmes legend.

D. H. Lawrence was a potent cultural influence in the 60s. The decade opened with the *Lady Chatterley's Lover* trial and Jack Cardiff's film of *Sons and Lovers* and ended with three films based on Lawrence's novels: Raymond Stross's Canadian adaptation of *The Fox* (1967, d. Mark Rydell) and Christopher Miles's *The Virgin and the Gypsy* (1970), which are worthy but dull; and Ken Russell's *Women in Love*, which is much more adventurous.[9] Whereas *The Fox* and *The Virgin and the Gypsy* are very short novels, *Women in Love* is long and complex and the process of condensation provoked the hostility of literary critics. F. R. Leavis, Lawrence's champion since the 30s, considered it 'an obscene undertaking' and asserted that no one 'who had any inkling of the kind of *thing* the novel is, or how the "significance" of a great work of literature is conveyed, or what kind of thing significance is, could lend himself to such an outrage.'[10] But it is Russell's outrageous lack of respect which enabled him to make *Women in Love* a film in its own right rather than a weak reflection of a literary masterpiece. His imagery – Gudrun performing an Isadora Duncan-like dance to intimidate a herd of shaggy, horned cows, the drowned lovers entwined in death, the firelit wrestling match – is vigorous and accessible and not yet, as it was to become in his later films, indulgently personal.

Paramount
Paramount backed only seven films in Britain between 1959 and 1964: two Tarzan adventures and Hammer's *The Man Who Could Cheat Death*, Guy Hamilton's light comedy *A Touch of Larceny* (1959), Richard Quine's *The World of Suzie Wong* (1960), Cy Endfield's *Zulu*

(1963) and Peter Glenville's *Becket* (1963). In the second half of the decade the company was much more prolific, and at least until 1969, when things began to fall apart, managed to put together a varied and interesting production programme. No doubt this was partly the influence of George Ornstein, the hero of Alexander Walker's *Hollywood England*, who was appointed head of Paramount's production in Britain in November 1966.[11] But *Alfie*, the company's biggest success, predated his arrival and Paramount, like most British and American distribution companies, had informal links with a number of producers and directors and tended to stick with them. Of key importance was the actor Stanley Baker who, after appearing in *Zulu* and *Sands of the Kalahari* (1965) – both directed by Cy Endfield – set up his own production company, Oakhurst, with Michael Deeley and Barry Spikings to make *Robbery* (1967). It was followed by *Where's Jack?* (1968), with Baker as thief-taker Jonathan Wild and Tommy Steele (who had starred in the expensive Paramount musical *Half a Sixpence* the previous year) as his nemesis Jack Sheppard, and *The Italian Job*, directed by Peter Collinson (who had already made *The Penthouse*, *Up the Junction* and *The Long Day's Dying* for Paramount).

Films that might have gone to United Artists, Woodfall's *Inadmissible Evidence*, Desmond Davis's *Smashing Time*, Lindsay Anderson's *If....*, Harry Saltzman's *Funeral in Berlin*, went to Paramount. Ornstein's influence was crucial in Paramount deciding to back Zeffirelli's *Romeo and Juliet* (1968) and Anderson's *If....*, both of which were commercially successful, and though he found no equivalent to the hugely profitable Bond films, he did back David Greene and Peter Collinson, two young directors who looked as promising in the late 60s as Richardson and Lester had done five years earlier. Collinson declined into a pedestrian director and Greene returned to directing American TV movies, but the films they made for Paramount are interesting.[12] Greene, who had made his first feature for Warners (*The Shuttered Room*), made *Sebastian* and *The Strange Affair*, two of the freshest, most exciting films of the 60s, for Paramount. Collinson followed up *The Penthouse* and *Up the Junction* with *The Long Day's Dying* (1968). It was castigated by most of the critics for being an anti-war film which celebrates war, but Charles Wood's script (from a novel by Alan White) in its tight, modest way works better than his more ambitious efforts for *How I Won the War* and *The Charge of the Light Brigade*.[13]

David Hemmings's interior monologue, around which the film is structured, is precisely about the attractions of wartime adventure to someone who is ideologically opposed to the whole business. Hemmings's realisation that he actually likes the excitement and danger and isn't too worried about death comes across more effectively than the anti-war chest-beating of *How I Won the War*, *The Charge of the Light*

Brigade and *Oh! What a Lovely War*. Collinson fuses Brian Probyn's newsreel-impressionist camerawork with underplayed but rivetingly convincing performances from Hemmings, Tony Beckley, Alan Dobie and Tom Bell, and makes us feel the danger, the boredom, the challenge of their situation. The flaw is in the ending. Perhaps it is inevitable that everyone should die, but that they should die so confusingly, so anonymously, puts a dampener on the lively intelligence which animates the film.

Other Ornstein projects – Joe McGrath's *The Bliss of Mrs Blossom*, Peter Medak's *Negatives* (1969) and Ted Kotcheff's *Two Gentlemen Sharing* (1969) – worked out less well and he confessed to Alexander Walker that he 'sometimes felt that he was presiding over the frenzied disintegration of the very trends he had helped to initiate in the early 1960s.'[14] By the end of the decade Ornstein had gone and the company was relying on industry stalwarts Dearden and Relph, Ken Annakin and Richard Attenborough for films like *Only When I Larf*, *The Assassination Bureau*, *Monte Carlo or Bust!* and *Oh! What a Lovely War*. They proved to be disappointingly unpopular, and in 1970 Paramount released no British films at all.

Warner Brothers

Warners' part-ownership of ABPC meant that until the late 60s they rarely bothered to make British films of their own, and when they did they were often British-based films shot largely on location and with an international cast. Woodfall's *Look Back in Anger* was eligible because of Richard Burton, and Romulus's *Term of Trial* because of Laurence Olivier and Simone Signoret, but more typical Warner Brothers films were Fred Zinnemann's *The Sundowners* (1961), José Quintero's *The Roman Spring of Mrs Stone* (1962), and Delmer Daves's *The Battle of the Villa Fiorita* (1965), which showed little trace of their British origins.[15] Surprisingly, then, Warners was responsible for one of the first fully-fledged Swinging London films, *Kaleidoscope* (1966, d. Jack Smight), with Susannah York and Warren Beatty joining forces for a caper among boutiques, discotheques and casinos. It was successful enough to encourage further investment in British films, but Warners tended to rely on North American directors – Sidney Furie for *The Naked Runner* (1967), Franklin Schaffner for *The Double Man* (1967), Robert Parrish for *The Bobo* (1967).

The most interesting of Warners' 1967 films came from outside, from Anglo-Amalgamated, which although it acted autonomously was a subsidiary of ABPC and distributed its films through Warner-Pathé. *Far from the Madding Crowd* (d. John Schlesinger), Anglo's only venture into really big-budget film-making (it cost $4 million) was a box-office flop in America. Presumably – as an epic rather than a melodrama, with bitty, cinematically unconventional romantic re-

Swinging Londoners in Wessex: Terence Stamp, Julie Christie, *Far from the Madding Crowd*

lationships – it was difficult to sell to a mass audience unfamiliar with the book. Aesthetically, however, the film is a considerable achievement. Frederic Raphael's script is admirably faithful to Thomas Hardy's long, complex novel, and Nicolas Roeg's photography presents an achingly beautiful picture of the English countryside. In an enlightening review in *Sight and Sound*, James Price observes:

> It is an obtrusively painterly film with references from Hogarth (Temperence and Soberness Miller) to Corot and even (the sleeping reapers/the Land of Cockayne) Breughel: these allusions, together with the images of sowing, sheep-dipping and harvesting, emphasising as they do the Arcadian character of the story, create feelings both of timelessness and of a time from which an urban audience is totally cut off. It is here, it seems to me, that the specific appeal of the film lies. The actors may not all be convincing in their parts and the story may be pretty thin, but pastoral myth for the smokebound consumer is as potent as it was in the time of Beaumont and Fletcher.[16]

The problem is in the casting. It is not so much that Julie Christie, Alan Bates and Terence Stamp give poor performances (though their Dorset accents leave something to be desired) but that they are so closely associated with Swinging London that they seem too indelibly modern to fit into Hardy's Wessex, and it is difficult to shake off the feeling that at any moment they may discard their funny voices and fancy dress and rush off to Annabel's.[17] Peter Finch, in the smallest and least rewarding of the four principal parts, and nearly all the backing cast look and act impressively authentic, and if, as James Price suggests, we view the film as a pastoral, then one might expect and excuse the appearance of Swinging London royalty among the peasants. But it gives this very long film (169 minutes) an air of insubstantiality.

By 1968, Warners' London office seemed to be losing its way. While in Hollywood Richard Lester was making his best film, *Petulia*, and Peter Yates his greatest commercial success, *Bullitt*, for Warners, all that the British end could offer was a muddled, ponderous Western, Edward Dmytryk's *Shalako*, and two overblown costume films, Gordon Flemyng's *Great Catherine* and Terence Young's *Mayerling*. Despite their poor box-office performance, Warners continued to turn out unexciting films such as their ponderous adaptations of Chekhov's *The Sea Gull* (1968, d. Sidney Lumet), Giraudoux's *The Madwoman of Chaillot* (1969, d. Bryan Forbes) and Joe Orton's *Entertaining Mr Sloane* (1970, d. Douglas Hickox), and Kevin Billington's disappointingly silly *The Rise and Rise of Michael Rimmer*. The brief sojourn of George Ornstein at the company (August 1969–February 1970) seems to have had little effect and, ironically, the one film of which Warners could have been proud, Roeg and Cammell's *Performance*, they did their best to disown.[18]

MGM

MGM was the most conservative, and with its huge, well-equipped Borehamwood studios, the most influential of the American majors. While United Artists were exploring new trends and recruiting new talent, MGM preferred to rely on films which determinedly turned their back on the brave new world of the 60s. MGM's favoured director for its prestige British films was Anthony Asquith, who in his later years had joined forces with Anatole de Grunwald and Terence Rattigan to make increasingly banal celebrations of the rich and empty-headed – *The Doctor's Dilemma* (1958), *Libel* (1959), *The VIPS* (1963), *The Yellow Rolls Royce* (1964) – which perfectly suited MGM's taste for overblown escapism. The other mainstay of MGM's production programme was a series of adaptations of Agatha Christie novels starring Margaret Rutherford as Miss Marple, so cosy that they make even the most innocuous Ealing comedy look daring.

Interesting films from MGM tended to be made almost by default. MGM's policy of recycling past successes clashed creatively with Karel Reisz and Albert Finney's desire to escape the Kitchen Sink in *Night*

Must Fall (1964), by no means a wholly satisfactory film but one which at least tries to be bold and adventurous. *Young Cassidy* (1964) was finished by Jack Cardiff after John Ford fell ill during the first few days of shooting. As a result it lacks the harmonious and elegiac qualities Ford might have given it but – like Cardiff's other Anglo-American films, *Sons and Lovers* and *The Long Ships* – it has a visual exuberance which makes it enjoyable to watch. Jack Clayton's *Our Mother's House* (1967) was presumably commissioned because Clayton was a prestige director who had chosen not to make a film since *The Pumpkin Eater* in 1963 and who could be relied upon for quality and professionalism. *Our Mother's House* is indeed immaculately made, but it resolutely ignores Swinging London to explore (more subtly than Peter Brook's *Lord of the Flies* but less interestingly than Mackendrick's *A High Wind in Jamaica*) a dangerously irrational children's world, and it is an uncompromisingly uncommercial film.

Blow Up was another prestige project which on paper looked even more risky. Antonioni had never made a film in Britain and had shown no indication of any willingness to bow to commercial pressures and make his films open and accessible. Thus *Blow Up* is something of a surprise. Admittedly at times it is mysterious and abstruse, but its picture of Swinging London, with David Hemmings as a David Bailey-like photographer, ensured it widespread popularity. It now seems to add up to much less than was thought at the time, its un-explained events clumsy rather than haunting. Nonetheless, compared to other MGM late-60s films – Peter Glenville's *Hotel Paradiso* (1966), Lee Thompson's *Eye of the Devil* (1967), Jack Cardiff's *The Mercenaries* (1968), Brian G. Hutton's *Where Eagles Dare* (1969) – it is a beacon of intelligence and originality.

Richard Fleischer's *The Vikings* and Jack Cardiff's *The Long Ships* had proved the box-office potential of the savage Nordic epic, so the idea of casting David Hemmings as King Alfred and bringing in Clive Donner (who had given him his first proper part in *Some People*) to make a fashionable, youth-oriented account of Alfred's struggles against the Danes must have seemed a good one. Donner's attempt to understand Alfred's life as a struggle between spiritual and earthly desires is both historically and metaphysically valid, but Dark Age history was not the forte of most film reviewers and *Alfred the Great* (1969) seems to have hit a collective critical blind-spot. Apart from the scholarly Michael Billington (who complained that Alfred shouldn't have been shown reading Latin until he was forty) and the always unpredictable Eric Rhode (who wanted to know why the film hadn't shown Alfred burning the cakes), the British reviews did little more than snigger at 'historical inaccuracies' – that the Danes speak English for example. And America wasn't interested in an intellectually am-bitious film about an obscure English king.[19] The dialogue does oc-

266

Monk becomes king: Colin Blakely, David Hemmings, *Alfred the Great*

casionally lapse into bathos (in the not wholly convincing relationship between Guthrum and Aelswith for example), but in its attempt to find a vernacular idiom for complex ideas it is more satisfactory than Robert Bolt's *A Man for All Seasons* and James Goldman's *The Lion in Winter*. Alfred's tormented attitude to his own sexuality, his dogged insistence on the superiority of a religion where intellect rules passion, his guilt about blood-lust and carnal desire, are authentic ninth-century Saxon concerns and Donner is remarkably successful in making them relevant to a twentieth-century audience.

Commercially MGM had much to thank Stanley Kubrick for, but the profits made by *2001* were not enough to make up for losses on the ill-timed remake of *Goodbye Mr Chips* (1969, d. Herbert Ross), with its slushy vision of public school life looking pathetically unconvincing after Lindsay Anderson's *If. . . .*, and on the brave but poorly received *Alfred the Great*. In February 1970 MGM's new managing director, James T. Aubrey, announced that the company's British operations would cease and the Borehamwood studios be closed down.

20th Century-Fox
Until 1966 Fox was cautious and discerning in its choice of films, and many of the more interesting American-backed films of the early 60s – Michael Powell's *The Queen's Guards*, Jack Cardiff's *Sons and Lovers*, Jack Clayton's *The Innocents*, Guy Green's *The Mark*, Charles Crichton's *The Third Secret* – came from the company. These rather unusual

267

films were interspersed with cheap but popular horror films like Robert Lippert's *The Earth Dies Screaming*, *Witchcraft* and *The Curse of the Fly*, and international films like *Those Magnificent Men in Their Flying Machines*, *A High Wind in Jamaica* and *The Blue Max* (1966, d. John Guillermin) – which were more conveniently based in Britain than in Hollywood. Fox coped with Swinging London badly, backing a string of gimmicky, pretentious films – Joseph Losey's *Modesty Blaise* (1966), Stanley Donen's *Bedazzled* (1967), Michael Cacoyannis's *The Day the Fish Came Out* (1967), Bryan Forbes's *Deadfall* (1968), Guy Green's *The Magus* (1968), John Krish's *Decline and Fall* (1968) and Fielder Cook's *Prudence and the Pill* (1968).

Two for the Road (1966), also directed by Stanley Donen but with a script by Frederic Raphael, explores in convincing detail the history of a relationship between a 'classless' young couple (Audrey Hepburn and Albert Finney) but it misses the satirical bite of *Nothing But the Best* and the flair and ambition of *Darling*, and its protagonists never quite rise above being smug and dull and deserving of unhappiness. Mike Sarne's *Joanna*, commissioned by Richard Zanuck over the heads of the London office and very much a maverick film, captures more convincingly and excitingly than any other film made in the 60s the reckless hedonism of London at the height of its permissive phase. But it proved as unsuccessful at the box-office as Fox's other Swinging London films. By 1969 the company had returned to more conventional subjects, relying on dull but safe directors like Ronald Neame for *The Prime of Miss Jean Brodie* (1969) and Lee Thompson for *The Most Dangerous Man in the World* (1969), and taking risks only on modestly budgeted films like *All the Right Noises* (1969), where a workmanlike director (Gerry O'Hara) and an underused but charismatic star (Tom Bell) almost guaranteed success.

Columbia

Columbia, like Fox and MGM, relied on solid mainstream entertainment films in the 50s and early 60s but was briefly seduced by the attractions of Swinging London. Columbia tended to rely on American independent producers working in Britain. Sam Spiegel supplied them with *The Bridge on the River Kwai* (1957, d. David Lean), *Suddenly Last Summer* (1959, d. Joseph L. Mankiewicz), *Lawrence of Arabia* (1962, d. David Lean), and *The Night of the Generals* (1967, d. Anatole Litvak); Carl Foreman with *The Key* (1958, d. Carol Reed), *The Guns of Navarone* (1962, d. Lee Thompson), *The Victors* (1963, d. Carl Foreman), *Born Free* (1966, d. James Hill) and *Otley* (1969, d. Dick Clement); and Irving Allen (with his partner Albert R. Broccoli until 1961) with *The Bandit of Zhobe* (1959, d. John Gilling), *Killers of Kilimanjaro* (1959, d. Richard Thorpe), *The Trials of Oscar Wilde* (1961, d. Ken Hughes), *The Long Ships* (1964, d. Jack Cardiff), *Ham-*

merhead (1968, d. David Miller), *Run Wild, Run Free* (1969, d. Richard Sarafian) and *Cromwell* (1970, d. Ken Hughes). Visiting American directors contributed similarly prestigious films like Richard Brooks's *Lord Jim* (1965) and Fred Zinnemann's *A Man for All Seasons* (1966), though Otto Preminger's *Bunny Lake is Missing*, Sidney Lumet's *The Deadly Affair* and Frank L. Pierson's *The Looking Glass War* are more personal, intimate films and, despite being directed by Americans, more relevant to British culture than the epics directed by Lean and Lee Thompson. Columbia also had long-standing links with the Woolf brothers' Romulus and provided financial backing for *The L-Shaped Room*, *The Pumpkin Eater*, *Life at the Top* and *Oliver!* (1968, d. Carol Reed).

Columbia was responsible for *Georgy Girl* and *To Sir, With Love*, two of the most profitable Swinging London films, but in retrospect they can be seen as good old-fashioned stories with a few 60s trimmings and the same might be said for Kevin Billington's deliberately unzany *Interlude*. The company had its mistakes too, both small and forgivable ones like Joe McGrath's *30 is a Dangerous Age, Cynthia* (1967) and large and inexcusable ones like Bryan Forbes's *The Wrong Box* (1966) and producer Charles Feldman's *Casino Royale* (1967). But Columbia survived the Swinging London phenomenon better than the other American majors. *A Man for All Seasons* won the 1966 Best Picture Oscar and in commercial terms was by far the most successful of the 60s British historical films; *Oliver!* also won the 1968 Best

Trouble in Virginia Water: Ann Bell, Nicol Williamson in *The Reckoning*

269

Picture Oscar and was the only one of the big-budget British musicals to make healthy profits. At the end of the decade Columbia was still making refreshingly idiosyncratic films: Frank Pierson's *The Looking Glass War*, Richard Fleischer's *Ten Rillington Place*, Ken Hughes's *Cromwell* and Jack Gold's *The Reckoning*. Gold's film, scripted by John McGrath, is a stylish reworking of the *Room at the Top* theme, with Nicol Williamson's Michael Marler, drunken, violent, and unscrupulous in his deployment of backstreets methods in the boardroom, as much a symbol of working-class aspirations in the late 60s as Joe Lampton had been a decade earlier.

Universal

Since the late 1930s Universal's films had been distributed in Britain by Rank and the company had no history of involvement in film production in Britain. In the early 60s Universal backed occasional Disney-like projects such as Cornel Wilde's *Lancelot and Guinevere* (1962), Richard Thorpe's *The Truth About Spring* (1964) and Ross Hunter and Ronald Neame's *The Chalk Garden* (1964); and, through a deal with Hammer which allowed the British company the right to remake Universal's horror classics of the 30s, picked up three or four Hammer horror films a year. By 1965 Universal seemed to have given up entirely on production in Britain, but a policy change by its parent company MCA led to Jay Kanter being sent over to organise an ambitious, adventurous programme of films which would take advantage of the lower labour costs, the deep pools of talent and the trendy ambience that London was now thought to possess.

The dozen or so films released by Universal between 1966 and 1970 are a fascinating bundle of the experimental and daring and the dully conventional, but worthy though many of these films are the programme as a whole seems to manifest all the worst aspects of Hollywood's England. The most striking feature is how the cost of a film seems to have no relationship to its quality. Charlie Chaplin's *A Countess from Hong Kong* (1966), a slow and inept farce with continuity lapses which would shame the lowest budgeted exploitation film, cost three and a half million dollars, twice as much as Karel Reisz's *Isadora*, a film which for all its faults looks lavishly and painstakingly made. *Boom!* and *Secret Ceremony*, small-scale art films with tiny casts and virtually no dramatic action, cost more than twice as much as Truffaut's *Fahrenheit 451*, and four or five times as much as Peter Watkins's *Privilege*.

This did not necessarily mean that Losey and Chaplin were inefficient film-makers, and most of their budgets were taken up by the huge salaries commanded by their stars – Sophia Loren, Marlon Brando, Richard Burton and Elizabeth Taylor. The Chaplin film is simply a poorly directed farce which was presumably made because

270

sentimental nostalgia ousted more objective commercial considerations, but the Losey films are different. Within the framework of art
cinema they are as well made as, for example, Bergman's *Winter Light*
or *The Silence*, and offer the same sort of rewards, but Universal was
expecting something like Mike Nichols's *Who's Afraid of Virginia
Woolf?*, which had won Oscars and had been commercially very successful. As Losey himself ruefully put it: 'I was the first person ever to
make a picture with the Burtons that lost money, which is largely due
to the fact that while we, the Burtons and I, got along superbly well,
and continued to, the public that wanted to see my films didn't want to
see the Burtons and the public who wanted to see the Burtons didn't
want to see my kind of film.'[20] Both *Secret Ceremony* and *Boom!* have
an impenetrable obscurity which alienated audiences, but they also
have an integrity and a visual beauty which makes them memorable.
Taylor and Burton in *Boom!*, Taylor and Mia Farrow and Robert
Mitchum in *Secret Ceremony*, give impressive performances and both
films might be seen as honourable experiments which, because of the
peculiarities of the film industry, became commercial follies on an
absurdly grand scale.

Isadora (1969) looked an altogether more likely prospect. The
dancer Isadora Duncan, with her reckless defiance of convention and
her connections with revolutionary Russia, was a marvellously appropriate subject for the 60s, and after *Morgan* Karel Reisz must have
seemed the ideal director. But *Morgan* had been fired by David
Mercer's passionately 'committed' script. In *Isadora* it is Reisz's
curious detachment which is most apparent, and as James Price commented in *Sight and Sound*: 'Isadora was a cause: you were either
stupidly for her or stupidly against her. But *Isadora* is too intelligently
and in the last resort too coldly handled for any such alignment to take
place.'[21] Reisz's neutrality is emphasised by the structure of the film.
Writing about the unsuccessful Sydney Box epic *Christopher Columbus*
in 1949, Campbell Dixon of the *Daily Telegraph* made the point that
some lives – and Columbus was a classic case – just don't have a
dramatic shape. Isadora Duncan's life did, as Ken Russell in one of the
best of his dramatised television documentaries had shown. By starting
at the beginning (the beginning of her career as a dancer at least) and
ending with her death, Russell presents a moving tragedy of a talented,
inventive woman bursting into creative life like a Roman candle and
quickly burning out. Reisz's three scriptwriters – Margaret Drabble,
Melvyn Bragg and Clive Exton – collaborate to squeeze all excitement,
drama and dignity out of Isadora Duncan's life, starting from her last
stages of decline into poverty, lechery and absurdity and then flashing
back to show how a silly woman tricked a gullible public into believing
in her for a time and then drifted into a wilderness of aimless nostalgia.
The awful, central tragedy of her life – the drowning of her two

271

children – is passed off as another picturesque incident rather than the cause of her suicidal despair.

Reisz has too deep a well of resources to make a bad film and (helped by Larry Pizer's photography) parts of the film are imbued with poetic beauty. But whereas Ken Russell's Isadora, Vivien Pickles, has an energy and enthusiasm which makes her dancing mesmeric even at its most absurd, Reisz's Isadora, Vanessa Redgrave, fine actress though she is, never quite dispels the feeling that her enemies were right and she really is 'some kind of a governess from Milwaukee who's taken to prancing about the stage with her boots off'.

For Alexander Walker, *Privilege* provided 'no better example of what should have been a profitable union between pop culture and the avant garde'.[22] But like Kubrick's *2001*, Watkins's film suffers from a portentous pessimism which makes it in turns irritating and endearing. Kubrick's obelisk god controlling or guiding or monitoring the progress of man no longer seems a very profound inspiration for his journey into space and the film's main redeeming feature is the sad, mad, lonely computer HAL 9000 which still seems a powerful metaphor for the empty 'have a nice day' soul of America. Watkins's wheeler-dealer executives manipulating their zombie-like pop star might seem closer to reality (though in Britain pop star managers tended to be less equipped to deal with power and money than their protégés), but Watkins, having departed from the *vérité* realism of his television films, never seems to know whether to make his characters realistic types or caricatures.

Jay Kanter complained that his decision to back films which were adventurous, original and heavily reliant on British talent received scant support from the cinema circuits, and that 'the failure of several of our films to get any really significant showing in Britain (despite tie-up with Rank) has had repercussions back in Hollywood.'[23] Alexander Walker laments the failure in particular of Albert Finney's *Charlie Bubbles* (1967), endorsing Finney's fiercely held view that it was a casualty of the stupidity of British exhibitors. The story of a successful working-class writer going back up north to visit his roots (like Lindsay Anderson's *The White Bus*, it was written by Shelagh Delaney) is intelligently explored, and an unusually droll humour pervades the best sequences – in Charlie's house with all the rooms linked by closed circuit television, Charlie's midnight encounter with Yootha Joyce in a motorway service station, a seduction sequence ending on Liza Minnelli's hairpiece lying in the post-coital bed – but it is a film of fragments. Finney, perhaps in recompense for the fluffiness of his role in *Two for the Road*, staggers through the film in a state of zombie-like depression, and avoids the problem of a proper ending by waking up to find a balloon in the back garden on which he drifts away.

Walker also defends *Three into Two Won't Go* (1969), directed by Peter Hall, finding its failure inexplicable: 'Set in a new, bright, rootless housing estate for the executive class, it pinned down a generational conflict in English society with unusual truth and lack of compromise. It should have had an instant appeal to youth, if only for its honesty and apart from the fact that the teenager was a winner all the way on her own terms.'[24] In fact, the teenager (Judy Geeson) is cold, unscrupulous, alienated, and the generational conflict boils down to the sour exploration of a common 60s theme: the fascination for older men of a relationship with a sexually provocative teenage girl. The cast (Rod Steiger, Claire Bloom, Peggy Ashcroft, Judy Geeson) and cameraman (Walter Lassally) are formidable enough to withstand even the worst director; and Andrea Newman, upon whose novel the film is based, has a gift for creating unpleasant, obsessional characters whose purgatorial sufferings hold a horrid fascination (in the TV series *Bouquet of Barbed Wire*, for example), but here they are muffled and coddled and analysed and made to seem unjustifiably significant. Instead of full-blooded melodrama, Hall offers watered-down art.

The British exhibition system, with its two big circuits and its rigid patterns of blanket release, was particularly hard on interesting failures of the sort that Universal produced, but one can still argue that Kanter's programme was disastrously misconceived. The most interesting films – *Privilege, Charlie Bubbles, Fahrenheit 451, Isadora, Boom!* and *Secret Ceremony*, Jack Gold's *The Bofors Gun* – are almost perversely anti-commercial. Some of the others – Hall's *Work is a Four Letter Word* and *Three into Two Won't Go*, Anthony Newley's *Can Heironymus Merkin Ever Forget Mercy Humppe and Find True Happiness?*, even Michael Winner's *I'll Never Forget What's 'Is Name*, are messily indulgent, and the more commercial films made to balance out the programme – *A Countess from Hong Kong, The Night of the Following Day* – uninspiringly dull.

In February 1969 Kanter resigned and Universal reverted to its earlier policy of making films in Britain only when British locations seemed essential. Its next two major productions were *Anne of the Thousand Days*, produced by the veteran Hal Wallis, and Hitchcock's *Frenzy*.

Disney

Disney, the other Hollywood major, made only fourteen films in Britain between 1959 and 1970, and none of them is of much interest. *Swiss Family Robinson* (1961, d. Ken Annakin) and *In Search of the Castaways* (1962, d. Robert Stevenson) were big hits at the box-office but they now look very twee. *Greyfriars Bobby* (1961, d. Don Chaffey) has a sad romantic quality which holds in check the expected sentimentality, and its successor, *The Three Lives of Thomasina* (1964, d.

273

Don Chaffey), though much more schematic, evokes powerful fairy-tale echoes in the feud between the little girl and her father and the little boys' fascination with Susan Hampshire's white witch. *The Moonspinners* (1964, d. James Neilson), with Hayley Mills and Peter McEnery, seemed to indicate a turn towards adventure stories for and about teenagers, but during the later 60s the Disney operation in Britain was virtually dormant and there was no follow-up until Robert Butler's *Guns in the Heather* in 1969.

The Beginning of the End

It is extraordinary that the three waves of ambitious, prestigious film-making in Britain – 1933–37, 1944–49, 1963–69 – should all founder amidst a welter of expensive costume dramas. Ironically, it was not the bold, experimental radicals like Ken Loach and Lindsay Anderson whose films lost money and caused the Americans to pack their bags and scurry away, but big-budget prestige productions on subjects that seemed innocuously safe, like Paramount's *Half a Sixpence*, United Artists' *Battle of Britain* and MGM's *Goodbye Mr Chips*. But this time the situation was complicated by the fact that it was Hollywood's own problems which were the cause of the crisis. The 60s were years of muddle and confusion for the Hollywood majors, many of which were taken over by non-film conglomerates (United Artists by Transamerica, Paramount by Gulf and Western, Warner Brothers by Kinney National). Money was poured into blockbusters in a desperate attempt to win back audiences, and losses incurred on British films were more than equalled by home-grown disasters like Fox's *Hello Dolly* and *Star!*, Universal's *Sweet Charity* and Paramount's *Darling Lili*. In 1969 MGM declared a loss of $35 million, Fox of $36.8 million and Warners of $52 million. The other majors, with the exception of Disney, fared little better.[25]

In November 1969, the *Economist* warned Hollywood that it was time to wake up to reality:

> In face of the massive contraction in audiences, the structure of the industry has hardly changed. The process of merger or takeover and subsequent rationalisation to produce a few profitable companies capable of attracting finance like any other companies has not happened, and the entry of the conglomerates makes it all the more difficult to happen. So each company (except United Artists) has its own studios each producing fewer films and each has its own home and overseas distribution system processing fewer films.[26]

The process of building a new Hollywood was a painful one, and the next few years saw an increasing contraction in the direct production activities of the majors as studios were developed for real estate or

274

opened to tourists. But between 1967 and 1971 the success of a number of American films – *Bonnie and Clyde, The Graduate, Easy Rider, Midnight Cowboy, Butch Cassidy and the Sundance Kid, Woodstock, Mash, Five Easy Pieces, Carnal Knowledge* – seemed to indicate that Hollywood no longer needed to look at Britain for the sort of fresh, dynamic, youth-oriented films that might revive its fortunes. Once British films ceased to make big profits, there was little reason for the majors to maintain expensive London-based production operations. Americans continued to make films in Britain, but increasingly they were British only in the sense that they were made in British studios and British craftsmen had helped to make them (the *Star Wars* and *Indiana Jones* cycles for example). With admissions down from 601 millions in 1959 to 193 millions in 1970, the domestic market was now only able to support modestly budgeted horror films and sex comedies, and the British film industry gradually ceased to exist as an entity separate from television.[27]

CONCLUSION

> ... it is common experience that a previously unobserved coherence may become apparent in the course of time or through increased familiarity with a work. If we *come* to perceive the pattern, it was presumably always available for our perception. The argument spins away and leaves us continually looking over our shoulders at posterity with judgement in suspense. (Victor Perkins, *Film as Film*, 1972)[1]

Interviewing Alfred Hitchcock in 1962, François Truffaut puzzled over the difference between Hitchcock's British and American films and suggested that

> to put it bluntly, isn't there a certain incompatibility between the terms 'cinema' and 'Britain'? This may sound far-fetched, but I get the feeling that there are national characteristics – among them, the English countryside, the subdued way of life, the stolid routine – that are anti-dramatic in a sense ... it seems to me, these national characteristics are in conflict with plastic stylisation and even with the stylisation of the actors.[2]

In the 60s there was a real attempt to break with this cinema of – as Lindsay Anderson called it – 'the stiff upper class lip', to make films which might catch the quickening tempo of a changing Britain. What strikes one now about the Kitchen Sink films is not the supposedly drab settings (and with the passage of time their canals and steam trains and factories look evocatively poetic) but their confidence and vitality. *This Sporting Life*, for example, might be harrowingly gloomy but Richard Harris's Samson-like Machin, pulling down his world around him rather than acquiescing in compromise and conformity, proves that 'the subdued way of life, the stolid routine' of the English could be rebelled against and rendered cinematically exciting.

276

Film critics easily tired of realistic stories in urban industrial settings and the 'new wave' directors lessened their allegiance to 'the poetry of the everyday'. Richardson (with *Tom Jones*), Schlesinger (with *Darling*), Reisz (with *Morgan*) and Anderson (with *If. . . .*) joined with other new directors such as Richard Lester and Clive Donner to set the parameters of a cinema capable of exploring the affluent, youth-oriented society that emerged in the 60s. Their efforts attracted little support. Philip French, in one of the first attacks on the cinema of 'Swinging London', saw 1963 'as a turning point on the crooked road from the wheelwright's shop to the boutique' and complained:

> If the British films of the previous four years appeared to have been guided by the editors of the *New Left Review*, Richard Hoggart and the Opies, then those of the three years that followed looked increasingly as if they had been made under the personal supervision of the regius professor of Applied Camp at the Royal College of Art.[3]

The embarrassment of British film critics at films which are extravagant, stylish, experimental, has resulted in misconceptions about 60s British cinema which have been exploited by post-60s film-makers like Alan Parker and David Puttnam.

It is not that the 'Red London Bus' movies complained of by Parker and Puttnam don't exist – from the mid-60s onwards most films were shot in colour and on location, which generally meant London – but it is a term which encompasses such radically different films as to be meaningless. In Sidney Furie's *The Ipcress File*, Michael Caine escapes from what he thought was an Albanian dungeon to be nearly run over by a number 22 bus on its way to Bethnal Green; in Jack Clayton's *Our Mother's House*, Dirk Bogarde wins over his hostile brood of children by taking them on a number 68 to see the dinosaurs at Crystal Palace; in James Clavell's *To Sir, With Love*, the title sequence crosses Tower Bridge, picks up Sidney Poitier on a number 15 and follows him into the grimy reaches of Dockland; and in *Secret Ceremony*, contact between Leonora and Cenci is first made on the top deck of a number 27 passing through Kentish Town.

None of these films is a 'Swinging London' film, and the breed turns out to be much rarer than one might expect and by no means synonymous with what is worst about 60s British cinema. For the really bad films one has to look at adaptations of ill-suited stage material like Peter Hall's *Work is a Four Letter Word*, attempts to get 'with it' by stolidly conservative directors like Bryan Forbes's *The Wrong Box* and Ronald Neame's *Gambit*, or indulgently budgeted extravaganzas like *Casino Royale*. The American-financed boom foundered not on ill-conceived experiments like *Can Heironymus Merkin Ever Forget Mercy Humppe and Find True Happiness?* (which, whatever its faults, cost

277

only $500,000) but on expensively old-fashioned musicals like *Half a Sixpence* and *Goodbye Mr Chips*.

Puttnam claimed in 1986 that in the 60s 'we made maybe the longest consistent run of lousy movies that's been managed by any country in the last fifty years history of the cinema'.[4] Yet I have found it difficult to keep this book down to a reasonable length because of the large number of films deserving of attention. *Carry On* films, Hammer's horror films and Anglo-Amalgamated's Edgar Wallace series are constantly recycled on television and seem to have become a permanent part of media culture. No one, I think, would claim the *Carry On* films to be aesthetically distinguished but their stereotyped characters and situations obviously still have a relevance to large sectors of British society, and 60s horror films – *Plague of the Zombies*, *Witchfinder General*, *Night of the Eagle*, Fisher's and Francis's *Frankenstein* and *Dracula* films – have survived censorship, mutilation and the constant re-use of their motifs and images to remain significant films.

Admittedly, in their frantic attempt to come to terms with a rapidly changing society, film-makers failed as often as they succeeded and some 60s films are sloppily indulgent just as some 50s films are mind-numbingly conventional and some 40s films are simplistically patriotic. But if the picture of decadence and excess is a true one, how does one explain why Ken Russell and Lindsay Anderson, Clive Donner and Richard Lester, Karel Reisz and Tony Richardson, Jack Clayton and John Schlesinger, made their best films in the 60s? Or why young directors like David Greene and Jack Gold, Mike Hodges and Kevin Billington made such promising films as *The Strange Affair* and *Get Carter*, *Interlude* and *The Reckoning*, and subsequently drifted into anonymity? Puttnam's judgment is wildly off the mark. Taken as a whole, the 1960s saw a greater number of significant and exciting films made in Britain than at any time before or since.

APPENDIX

A GUIDE TO THE 1960s IN BRITAIN

1959

Parking meters introduced to London (January)

CND organises march from Aldermaston to Trafalgar Square with 50,000 supporters (Easter)

Obscene Publications Act (July)

General Election: Conservative majority of 100 (October)

First stretch of M1 motorway opened (November)

John Stephen opens his first shop in Carnaby Street

Publication of *The Establishment* (ed. Hugh Thomas), Colin MacInnes's *Absolute Beginners*. (J. K. Galbraith's *The Affluent Society*, Raymond Williams's *Culture and Society* and Kenneth Allsop's *The Angry Decade* first came out in 1958; Tom Maschler's anthology *Declaration* and Richard Hoggart's *The Uses of Literacy* in 1957.)[1]

Significant films

Room at the Top, Too Many Crooks, Passport to Shame, Carry on Nurse, Tiger Bay, No Trees in the Street, The Hound of the Baskervilles, Sapphire, Beyond This Place, Look Back in Anger, The Mummy, Carry On Teacher, I'm All Right Jack, Blind Date, The Rough and the Smooth, The Stranglers of Bombay, Follow a Star, Please Turn Over, Battle of the Sexes[2]

1960

Hugh Carleton Greene becomes Director General of the BBC (January)

Harold Macmillan makes his 'Winds of Change' speech (February)

Betting and Gaming Act (July)

Princess Margaret marries Anthony Armstrong Jones (July)

Traffic Wardens introduced to relieve police of burden of coping with parking offences (September)

Lady Chatterley's Lover trial (October)

End of National Service (November)

The contraceptive pill introduced in Britain.

Publication of R. D. Laing's *The Divided Self*.

Significant films

Our Man in Havana, Two Way Stretch, The Flesh and the Fiends, Hell is a City, The League of Gentlemen, Peeping Tom, The Running, Jumping and Standing Still Film, School for Scoundrels, Sons and Lovers, The Trials of Oscar Wilde, Never Let Go, The Brides of Dracula, The Entertainer, There Was a Crooked Man, The Criminal, Watch Your Stern, Beat Girl, Saturday Night and Sunday Morning, The Pure Hell of St Trinian's

1961

Beyond the Fringe opens in London (May)

Britain applies to join the Common Market (July)

Arnold Wesker launches Centre 42 as a trade union-funded organisation for the arts (July)

Mass arrests of CND supporters after sit-down in Trafalgar Square (September)

First issue of *Private Eye* (October)

Publication of Martin Green's *A Mirror for Anglo-Saxons*, Raymond Williams's *The Long Revolution*.

Significant films

The Singer not the Song, No Love for Johnnie, The Rebel, The Mark, The Hellfire Club, Taste of Fear, Very Important Person, The Curse of the Werewolf, Payroll, Flame in the Streets, Whistle Down the Wind, Victim, A Taste of Honey, Gorgo, The Queen's Guards, The Day the Earth Caught Fire, The Innocents, The Young Ones

1962

Sunday Times launches its Colour Supplement (February)

Eric Lubbock wins the Orpington by-election for the Liberal Party (March)

Commonwealth Immigration Act restricts flow of black immigrants (July)

Beatles release first record, 'Love Me Do' (October)

That Was the Week That Was begins on BBC television (November)

Publication of Pilkington Report on Television, Anthony Sampson's *Anatomy of Britain*, Ray Gosling's *Sum Total*

Significant films

Only Two Can Play, Go to Blazes, HMS Defiant, Postman's Knock, Night of the Eagle, A Kind of Loving, It's Trad Dad!, The Phantom of the Opera, A Prize of Arms, Tiara Tahiti, Life for Ruth, Some People, Jigsaw, The Damned, The Boys, Billy Budd, Live Now – Pay Later, The Loneliness of the Long Distance Runner, Dr No, The Wild and the Willing, The Punch and Judy Man, Lawrence of Arabia, The Mind Benders, The L-Shaped Room, Station Six Sahara, The Kiss of the Vampire

1963

General de Gaulle vetoes Britain's entry into the Common Market
  (January)

Harold Wilson becomes leader of the Labour Party (January)

War Minister John Profumo resigns after admitting he has lied to the
  House of Commons about his relations with Christine Keeler (June)

Rediffusion launches *Ready Steady Go* (August)

Fifteen masked men rob the Glasgow to London mail train of £2½
  million (August)

Harold Wilson makes his 'White Heat of Technology' speech
  (September)

Harold Macmillan resigns as Prime Minister and is replaced by Sir
  Alec Douglas Home (October)

Mary Whitehouse begins her Clean Up TV campaign (November)

Publication of *Honest to God* by John Robinson, Bishop of Woolwich,
Professor Colin Buchanan's *Traffic in Towns* (recommending the building
of urban motorways), Lord Denning's Report on the Profumo
Affair, Dr Beeching's Report on British Railways (recommending that
a third of the railway network be axed), Lord Robbins' Report (recommending
the creation of six new universities – East Anglia, York,
Canterbury, Warwick, Lancaster and Essex).

Significant films

This Sporting Life, Sparrows Can't Sing, The Small World of Sammy Lee, The Leather Boys, Jason and the Argonauts, Ricochet, Sammy Going South, Heavens Above!, 80,000 Suspects, Billy Liar!, The World Ten Times Over, Tom Jones, The Caretaker, Unearthly Stranger, The Informers, The Party's Over, From Russia With Love, The Servant, Nothing But the Best, The Comedy Man, Carry on Jack, Dr Strangelove, Ring of Spies.

1964

Pirate station Radio Caroline begins broadcasting (March)

Mods and Rockers clash at Clacton and Margate (Easter and Whitsun)

BBC2 begins broadcasting (April)

John Bloom's Rolls Razor washing machine company goes bankrupt (July)

Barbara Hulanicki opens first Biba shop in London (September)

BBC begins controversial drama series: the 'Wednesday Play' (October)

General Election: Labour majority of 4 (October)

Terence Conran opens first Habitat shop in South Kensington

Publication of Marshall McLuhan's *Understanding Media*, Herbert Marcuse's *One Dimensional Man*, Stuart Hall and Paddy Whannel's *The Popular Arts*.

Significant films

Night Must Fall, The Third Secret, The Evil of Frankenstein, The Beauty Jungle, The Earth Dies Screaming, Carry on Spying, A Hard Day's Night, The Pumpkin Eater, A Shot in the Dark, The Gorgon, One Way Pendulum, It Happened Here, Face of a Stranger, The Tomb of Ligeia, Carry On Cleo, Never Mention Murder

1965

Death of Winston Churchill (January)

George Brown sets up the Prices and Incomes Board (April)

Poets of the World/Poets of Our Time Convention at the Albert Hall: the first public manifestation of the Underground (June)

Edward Heath replaces Sir Alec Douglas Home as leader of the Conservative Party (August)

George Brown publishes his National Plan for Britain's economy (September)

Harold Wilson opens the Post Office Tower (October)

Capital punishment suspended for a five-year experimental period (October)

Rhodesia declares UDI (November)

Race Relations Act (November)

Publication of *David Bailey's Box of Pin-Ups*, Peter Laurie's *The Teenage Revolution*.

Significant films

Young Cassidy, Lord Jim, Repulsion, The Ipcress File, A High Wind in Jamaica, The Big Job, Catch Us If You Can, The Knack, Four in the Morning, The City Under the Sea, The Collector, Darling, Help!, The Nanny, Bunny Lake is Missing, Dracula – Prince of Darkness, A Study in Terror, He Who Rides a Tiger, Invasion, Life at the Top, The Spy Who Came in from the Cold, Thunderball, The Plague of the Zombies

1966

General Election: Labour majority of 97 (March)

Trial of Moors Murderers Ian Brady and Myra Hindley (April)

Time publishes its 'Swinging London' article (April)

Seamen's strike begins (May)

England beat West Germany and win the football World Cup (July)

Charles Richardson and his associates arrested (July)

Launch of *It* celebrated with a party at the Roundhouse with music by Pink Floyd (October)

Industrial Reorganisation Corporation established to 'drag firms kicking and screaming into the twentieth century' (December)

UFO, the first Underground club, opens (December)

Significant films

Morgan, Cul de Sac, Alfie, Khartoum, Modesty Blaise, They're a Weird Mob, The Blue Max, Georgy Girl, Kaleidoscope, Fahrenheit 451, The Quiller Memorandum, The Family Way, The Deadly Affair, To Sir, With Love, Drop Dead Darling, The Night of the Generals, Don't Lose Your Head, A Man for All Seasons

1967

First issue of *Oz* (January)

London School of Economics occupied by students (March)

Technicolor Dream festival at Alexandra Palace (April)

Mick Jagger, Keith Richards and art dealer Robert Fraser tried for possession of drugs (June)

Beatles release 'Sergeant Pepper' album (June)

Drury Lane Arts Lab opens (July)

Dialectics of Liberation symposium at the Roundhouse (July)

Full-page advertisement in *The Times* claiming that 'The law against marijuana is immoral in principle and unworkable in practice' (July)

BBC2 begins broadcasting in colour (July)

Sexual Offences Act legalises homosexual acts between consenting adults in England and Wales (July)

Marine Broadcasting Offences Act drives Radio London and other pirate radio stations off the air (August)

BBC launches Radio One, Two, Three, Four (September)

Abortion Act (October)

First London mass demonstration against American involvement in Vietnam (October)

Dock strike begins (October)

Pound devalued from $2.80 to $2.40 (November)

British troops withdraw from Aden/South Yemen (November)

Significant films

Accident, Blow Up, Frankenstein Created Woman, Privilege, Dance of the Vampires, How I Won the War, You Only Live Twice, The Naked Runner, I'll Never Forget What's 'Is Name, Herostratus, Pretty Polly, Charlie Bubbles, Our Mother's House, Follow That Camel, Robbery, Far from the Madding Crowd, Quatermass and the Pit, Up the Junction, Billion Dollar Brain, Danger Route, Poor Cow, Sebastian, Smashing Time, Interlude, Here We Go Round the Mulberry Bush, The White Bus

1968

'I'm Backing Britain' campaign launched (January)

Big demonstrations against American involvement in Vietnam (March and October)

Enoch Powell makes his anti-immigrant 'Rivers of Blood' speech (April)

Decimalisation of British currency begins (April)

Ronan Point tower block severely damaged by gas explosion (May)

Ron and Reggie Kray arrested (May)

First *Time Out* published (August)

Lord Chamberlain loses his powers of censorship over the theatre (September)

Publication of Jeff Nuttall's *Bomb Culture*

Significant films

The Strange Affair, 2001 – a Space Odyssey, Inadmissible Evidence, The Charge of the Light Brigade, The Devil Rides Out, Oliver!, Petulia, Witchfinder General, The Bliss of Mrs Blossom, Boom!, Dracula Has Risen from the Grave, Otley, Secret Ceremony, Twisted Nerve, The Long Day's Dying, Mrs Brown You've Got a Lovely Daughter, If. . . ., Joanna, Sympathy for the Devil

1969

Labour publishes its White Paper on trade union reform, *In Place of Strife* (January)

Hugh Carleton Greene resigns from the BBC (March)

Bernadette Devlin elected as Republican MP for Mid-Ulster (April)

Rolling Stones Hyde Park concert commemorates the death of Brian Jones (July)

Isle of Wight pop festival (August)

British Army moves into Belfast and Derry (August)

'London Arts Commune' squat in 144 Piccadilly (September)

Divorce Reform Act (October)

Drury Lane Arts Lab closes (October)

BBC1 and ITV begin broadcasting in colour (November)

Death Penalty abolished (December)

Publication of Christopher Booker's *The Neophiliacs*, Nik Cohn's *Pop from the Beginning*, Peter Evans and David Bailey's *Goodbye Baby and Amen: A Saraband for the Sixties*.

Significant films

The Prime of Miss Jean Brodie, Some Girls Do, Isadora, Three into Two Won't Go, What's Good for the Goose, Where's Jack?, Oh! What a Lovely War, The Bed-Sitting Room, Frankenstein Must Be Destroyed, Kes, Alfred the Great, Age of Consent, I Start Counting, Laughter in the Dark, The Looking Glass War, Twinky, Women in Love

1970

Women's Liberation Conference at Ruskin College, Oxford (March)

Schoolkids' edition of *Oz*, which leads to June 1971 obscenity trial (May)

General Election: Conservative majority of 30 (June)

Start of the Angry Brigade campaign (September)

Publication of Richard Neville's *Playpower*, Germaine Greer's *The Female Eunuch*, Bernard Levin's *The Pendulum Years*, Robert Skidelsky and Vernon Bogdanor's *The Age of Affluence*

Significant films

The Reckoning, Praise Marx and Pass the Ammunition, Entertaining Mr Sloane, Every Home Should Have One, Taste the Blood of Dracula, Anne of the Thousand Days, Leo the Last, Cromwell, Loot, The Virgin and the Gypsy, The Private Life of Sherlock Holmes, Performance, Scrooge, Bronco Bullfrog, Get Carter, The Raging Moon, Ryan's Daughter, Satan's Skin, The Music Lovers, The Go-Between

Notes

1. There will sometimes be a discrepancy between the publication date here (which is when the book was first published) and the publication date in the bibliography (which is generally that of the latest and most easily available edition).

2. I have included in these yearly lists a number of minor but fascinating films – *Unearthly Stranger*, *Invasion*, *Face of a Stranger*, for example – at the expense of films I consider overblown and over-praised – *Lolita*, *Tunes of Glory* – and these are value judgments I would defend. But I have also included films – *Passport to Shame*, *Gorgo*, *Beat Girl*, *The Party's Over* – which are interesting despite their obvious flaws, and others – *Herostratus*, *What's Good for the Goose*, *Every Home Should Have One* – which retain a historical importance despite being bad films.

NOTES

INTRODUCTION

1. Alan Parker, *Personal View: A Turnip-Head's Guide to British Cinema*, transmitted ITV, 12 March 1986.
2. Peter York, 'Recycling the Sixties', reprinted in *Style Wars*, London, Sidgwick & Jackson, 1980, p. 182.
3. Paul Willemen, 'Sex, Class and Realism', *Framework*, no. 34, 1987, p. 114.
4. Lindsay Anderson, *Personal View: Free Cinema*, transmitted ITV, 19 March 1986.
5. R. Barton Palmer, 'What Was New About the British New Wave?', *Journal of Popular Film and Television*, vol. 14, no. 3, p. 133.
6. John Hill, *Sex, Class and Realism*, London, BFI, 1986, p. 3.
7. Penelope Houston, 'Seventy', *Sight and Sound*, Winter 1970, p. 4.
8. Thomas Guback, 'American Interests in the British Film Industry', *Quarterly Review of Economics and Business*, no. 7, 1967, p. 21.
9. David Robinson, 'Case Histories of the Next Renascence', *Sight and Sound*, Winter 1968–9, p. 36.
10. Barry Curtis, *Morgan: A Suitable Case for Treatment*, unpublished Polytechnic of Central London M.A. thesis, 1983, p. 27.
11. Jeffrey Richards, 'The Revolt of the Young', *Best of British*, A. Aldgate and J. Richards (eds.), Oxford, Basil Blackwell, 1983, p. 159.
12. *Little Shoppe of Horrors*, no. 4, April 1978, pp. 25–110. Dave Pirie's dossier, *Hammer: A Cinema Case Study*, London, BFI Education, 1980, is also useful.
13. Vincent Porter, 'The Studio System: From Film Study to Film History', paper delivered at the Mostra Internazionale del Nuovo Cinema, Pesaro, December 1982.
14. Ben Brewster, 'Film History in Film Studies Teaching', *Film and Media Studies in Higher Education*, Christine Gledhill (ed.), London, BFI Education, 1981.
15. Steve Neale and Andrew Higson, 'Introduction: Components of the National Film Culture', *Screen*, vol. 26, no. 1, 1985, p. 6.
16. Lawrence Alloway, *Violent America*, New York, Museum of Modern Art, 1969, p. 19.
17. This means that Peter O'Toole – who stars in all these films, as he does in *What's New Pussycat?*, *Great Catherine*, *Goodbye Mr Chips* and *Country Dance*, to which I have also devoted little attention – has regrettably been ignored.

1. A SAVAGE STORY OF LUST AND AMBITION

1. Arthur Marwick, '*Room at the Top*, *Saturday Night and Sunday Morning*, and the "Cultural Revolution" in Britain', *Journal of Contemporary History*, vol. 19, no. 1, January 1984, p. 149.

2. Lindsay Anderson, 'Get Out and Push', in *Declaration*, Tom Maschler (ed.), London, MacGibbon & Kee, 1957, p. 157.

3. For 1950s directors see 'British Feature Directors', *Sight and Sound*, Autumn 1958, pp. 289–304. Cyril Frankel, Alfred Shaughnessy and Philip Leacock began with Group 3; Julian Aymes, George More O'Ferrall, Peter Graham Scott in television; Peter Glenville, Peter Brook, Wendy Toye came from the theatre; Muriel Box, Leslie Norman, Guy Hamilton, Seth Holt, Noel Langley, Michael Relph, Guy Green and Jack Clayton became directors after serving an apprenticeship in producing, writing, editing or cinematography; Don Chaffey, Wolf Rilla, Jack Lee Thompson, Ken Hughes, Gerald Thomas (and John Guillermin and Michael Anderson, who made their debuts in 1949) worked their way up from low-budget 'B' films.

4. This is not meant to imply that Richardson, Anderson and Reisz were starry-eyed idealists. Richardson began his career in television, Anderson directed episodes of *Robin Hood*, and both Anderson and Reisz made TV commercials when they had the chance.

5. Alan Lovell and Jim Hillier, *Studies in Documentary*, London, BFI/Secker & Warburg, 1972, p. 142. Lovell also lists the six National Film Theatre Free Cinema programmes.

6. In the 50s the Woolfs financed their indigenous British films (like *Cosh Boy*) from their own resources and co-financed their international films (like *Moulin Rouge*) with American companies, usually Columbia.

7. A measure of James Woolf's uniqueness is that apart from David Puttnam, then an advertising rather than a film executive, he is the only film producer to be included in that lexicon of Swinging Sixties celebrities, *David Bailey's Box of Pin-Ups*, London, Weidenfeld & Nicolson, 1965.

8. Des Hickey and Gus Smith, *The Prince*, London, Leslie Frewin, 1971, p. 120, for Braine's description of Harvey as 'an exotic butterfly'.

9. Ibid., p. 121.

10. According to Kenneth Allsop, it was a 'shredded and de-sexed' version of the book that was serialised. *The Angry Decade*, London, Peter Owen, 1964, p. 90.

11. Alexander Walker, *Hollywood, England*, London, Harrap, 1986, p. 45.

12. John Braine, *Room at the Top*, Harmondsworth, Penguin, 1957, p. 29. Presumably because it sounds more 'northern', the Warley of the book becomes Warnley in the films.

13. Beatrice Varley and Wilfrid Lawson, Joe's aunt and uncle, had played innumerable working-class characters in British films, Lawson as far back as 1938 when he gave an unforgettable performance as Doolittle in Anthony Asquith's version of *Pygmalion*.

14. One can get an idea of Signoret's importance to the film by comparing her performance with that of Vivien Leigh (the Woolfs' original choice for the part) as a rich widow in love with a handsome young adventurer (Warren Beatty) in *The Roman Spring of Mrs Stone* (1961).

15. *Reynold's News*, 25 January 1959. I was told about *Room at the Top*'s censorship problems, its initial reception and its worldwide box-office success by Sir John Woolf in an interview in September 1988. The British Board of Film Censors' interesting file on the film paints the same sort of picture. Continuing interest in *Room at the Top* is evident in the Arthur Marwick article cited above and in R. Barton Palmer's 'What Was New in the British New Wave? Reviewing *Room at the Top*', *Journal of Popular Film and Television*, vol. 14, no. 3, Fall 1986, pp. 125–35.

16. Josh Billings, 'The Best in 1959', *Kinematograph Weekly*, 17 December 1959, p. 6.

17. Quoted by Robert Hewison, *In Anger*, London, Weidenfeld & Nicolson, 1981, p. 72.
18. In fact, *Look Back in Anger* was a rather delayed bombshell. The first perform-ance of the play in May 1956 aroused a flurry of interest among the critics but it was not until its second run in October that a five-minute extract shown on BBC television attracted the new and enthusiastic audience the Royal Court had been hoping for. According to Devine's stage director Michael Halifax: 'None of us thought we were going to last through the summer. The houses were appalling. Then, after the TV extract, all these people started arriving. People you never see in theatres. Young people gazing around wondering where to go and what the rules were. A completely new audience.' Quoted by Irving Wardle, *The Theatres of George Devine*, London, Jonathan Cape, 1978, p. 185.
19. Ironically it was Herbert Wilcox, the epitome of commercial film-making, who gave Kenneth Haigh, the original Jimmy Porter, his first big film part in his 1956 production *My Teenage Daughter*, casting him as an upper middle-class 'beatnik' who introduces Sylvia Syms to the Chelsea Set and causes his rich old aunt to have a heart attack.
20. Colin Young, 'Tony Richardson: An Interview in Los Angeles', *Film Quar-terly*, Summer 1960, p. 12.
21. Stanley Kauffman, *A World on Film*, New York, Harper & Row, 1968, p. 81.
22. *Look Back in Anger* cost £250,000, *The Entertainer*, £210,000, *Saturday Night and Sunday Morning*, £117,000. 'Tony Richardson: An Interview in Los Angeles', p. 11. Richardson acted as producer on *Saturday Night and Sunday Morning* before going to Hollywood to direct *Sanctuary*.
23. See Alan Sillitoe, 'What Comes on Monday', *New Left Review*, no. 4, July–August 1960, pp. 58–9; Rod Prince, 'Saturday Night and Sunday Morning – the Novel and the Film', *New Left Review*, no. 6, November–December 1960, pp. 15–17.
24. Walter Lassally, *Itinerant Cameraman*, London, John Murray, 1987, p. 63. The only book-length study of Karel Reisz is by George Gaston (*Karel Reisz*, Boston, Twayne, 1980), part of a useful series which includes books on Jack Clayton, Lindsay Anderson and John Schlesinger.
25. Quoted in Alexander Walker, *Hollywood, England*, p. 85.
26. Alan Lovell, 'Film Chronicle', *New Left Review*, no. 7, January–February 1961, p. 52.
27. Most of this information on Sillitoe comes from Michael Barber's radio series *The Angry Decade*, episode two, last broadcast on Radio Four on 24 July 1988. Though Braine and Sillitoe have little in common as writers, Braine also suffered from tuberculosis and wrote the first draft of *Room at the Top* while he was in hospital in 1952–3; see Allsop, *The Angry Decade*, p. 91.
28. Alan Sillitoe, *Saturday Night and Sunday Morning*, London, Pan, 1960, p. 120. In the film this speech is transposed from a period Arthur spends in an army training camp, which is not used in the film, to that of his recuperation after he is beaten up.
29. Alan Sillitoe, 'What Comes on Monday', *New Left Review*, no. 4, p. 59. When Sillitoe wrote this he was expecting the film to end on a final soliloquy. Tony Aldgate in his essay 'The Seeds of Further Compromise' in *Best of British* (A. Aldgate and J. Richards, eds., Oxford, Basil Blackwell, 1983) argues that by removing this, Reisz ended the film in ambiguity and confusion. Sillitoe, quoted by Alexander Walker, *Hollywood, England*, p. 85, and in an interview in the *Daily Mirror*, 28 January 1961, sticks to his original optimism.
30. According to Harry Saltzman, a Columbia Pictures executive told him that 'the Finney character looked tubercular, the women were most unappetizing and the factory locations were "some of the ugliest that had ever gotten into

any feature film meant for entertainment".' Alexander Walker, *Hollywood, England*, p. 88.

31. Majdalany's review, *Daily Mail*, 25 October 1960; box-office results reported in *Evening News*, 1 March 1961. Both can be found in the BFI Library microfiche for *Saturday Night and Sunday Morning*.
32. 'Tony Richardson: An Interview in Los Angeles', p. 13.
33. Walter Lassally, *Itinerant Cameraman*, p. 23.
34. Ibid., p. 69.
35. Tony Richardson, 'The Man Behind the Angry Young Man', *Films and Filming*, February 1959, p. 9.
36. Peter John Dyer, *Monthly Film Bulletin*, September 1962, p. 148. Most reviewers praised Tom Courtenay's performance and criticised Richardson's direction. Only the *Daily Herald* and the *Daily Worker*, the two most left-wing national newspapers, welcomed the film wholeheartedly.
37. Peter Harcourt, 'I'd Rather Be Like I Am', *Sight and Sound*, Winter 1962–3, p. 18.
38. Ibid., p. 19. See also Vicki Eves, 'Britain's Social Cinema', *Screen*, vol. 10, no. 6, November–December 1969. Andrew Higson's abstruse but rewarding 'Space, Place, Spectacle', *Screen*, vol. 25, no. 4–5, July–October 1984, presents a more sophisticated critique of *Saturday Night and Sunday Morning* and *A Taste of Honey* as representative examples of the Kitchen Sink cycle.
39. See for example *The Times*, 26 September 1962, and Peter Graham, *The Abortive Renaissance*, Axle Publications, 1963, p. 6.
40. Frank Norman, *Bang to Rights*, London, Secker & Warburg, 1958; Mark Benney, *Low Company*, London, Peter Davies, 1936. Benney writes about the treatment of juveniles in the 1930s, but the ethos is the same. Norman writes about corrective detention for adults which is based on the same principles as Borstal training. *The Loneliness of the Long Distance Runner* is certainly more convincing than the other two films centring on Borstal life, the disappointingly tame *The Boys in Brown* (1949) and the sensationalised *Scum* (1979).
41. Avis Bunnage had played Jo's mother in the original stage production of *A Taste of Honey*. Several other Royal Court and Stratford East actors made delayed entries into the film industry, most notably Alan Bates, the original Cliff of *Look Back in Anger*.
42. Topsy Jane was cast for the part of Liz in *Billy Liar!*, but she fell ill during filming and was replaced by Julie Christie. Alexander Walker, *Hollywood, England*, p. 166.
43. Raymond Durgnat, 'Loved One', *Films and Filming*, March 1966, p. 39.
44. In view of his association with Schlesinger, the most significant of Janni's earlier films is *White Corridors* (1950), a hospital drama directed by ex-documentarist Pat Jackson, though in commercial terms his most successful productions were *The Glass Mountain* (1948), a soft-centred melodrama; *A Town Like Alice* (1956), from the Nevil Shute novel; and *The Captain's Table* (1958), a comedy.
45. Carol Reed, BFI Library microfiche on *The Running Man*, and quoted by Peter Armitage in 'British Cinema: Attitudes and Illusions', *Film*, no. 36, Summer 1963, p. 17. Ironically, in view of Reed's disparaging comments, Tony Richardson's most substantial piece of critical writing, 'The Metteur en Scène' (*Sight and Sound*, October–December 1954, pp. 62–6), argues a convincing case for Reed as an auteur, pointing out that 'his heroes all react the same way: they run away from a reality that is too much for them'. This is as true of Reed's later films, *Our Man in Havana* and *The Running Man*, as it is of *Odd Man Out* and *The Third Man*.
46. Peter Armitage, 'British Cinema: Attitudes and Illusions', *Film*, no. 36, p. 22.

See also Ian Cameron's long review in *Movie*, no. 10, June 1963, 'Against This Sporting Life'; though unfair, it is powerfully and persuasively written.

47. See, for example, Arthur Machin's clash with his parents:

> Then, just for a moment, he saw that through my eyes there was nothing there at all. He saw the neighbourhood without its affections and feelings, but just as a field of broken down ambition. He might have wanted to be a footballer in *his* youth. My mother looked at him as if she'd been turned to stone. He just sat there, the little man with no trousers, his head shaking from side to side in bewilderment, his face screwed up with inadequacy and self-reproach, half-blinded with tiredness and with life-fatigue.

David Storey, *This Sporting Life*, Harmondsworth, Penguin, 1963, p. 112.

48. Lindsay Anderson, 'Sport, Life and Art', *Films and Filming*, February 1963, p. 16. Storey was equally adamant that their film was free of the 'sociological' preoccupations of earlier kitchen sink films:

> the prodigious step forward made by *This Sporting Life*, and the cause of its incredible impact within the industry and outside it, is that it deals essentially with human experience on a large scale, that it gains its emotional momentum, its energy, not from social issues and polemical issues that die after their day but purely from inner sources. Rather than externalising the tragedy of a purely human predicament in its social effect, it shows people as people and not as the ciphers of sociological speculation.

Quoted by Raymond Durgnat in 'Old Wine in New Bottles', *Film*, no. 39, Spring 1964, p. 32.

49. See Anne Francis, *Julian Wintle: A Memoir*, London, Dukeswood, 1986, pp. 68–70, for the reception of *This Sporting Life*.

50. Sir John Davis, quoted by Bernard Husra, 'Patterns of Power', *Films and Filming*, April 1964, p. 31. The speech was made at the Rank Theatre Division's Annual Showmanship Luncheon at the Dorchester Hotel, 12 December 1963.

51. Another aspect of popular enthusiasm for 'kitchen sink' subjects is the long-running television series *Coronation Street*. When it first appeared in 1960, the *Daily Mirror* television correspondent commented: 'The programme is doomed from the outset, with its dreary signature tune and grim scene of a row of terraced houses.'

52. Osborne's disparaging comment about the monarchy comes from 'It's Only Cricket', his essay in *Declaration*, p. 76.

53. John Hill, *Sex, Class and Realism*, London, BFI, 1986, p. 25.

54. D. E. Cooper, 'Looking Back on Anger', *The Age of Affluence*, Robert Skidelsky and Vernon Bogdanor (eds.), London, Macmillan, 1970, p. 257.

55. Martin Green, *A Mirror for Anglo-Saxons*, London, Longman, 1961, p. 18.

56. John Hill, 'Working Class Realism and Sexual Reaction', in *British Cinema History*, Vincent Porter and James Curran (eds.), London, Weidenfeld & Nicolson, 1983, p. 308.

57. John Hill, *Sex, Class and Realism*, pp. 157–66.

58. Geoffrey Gorer, 'The Perils of Hypergamy', *New Statesman*, 4 May 1957, p. 568.

59. Alan Sillitoe, *Saturday Night and Sunday Morning*, p. 36.

60. John Hill, *Sex, Class and Realism*, p. 174. Hill is least convincing in his treatment of *A Taste of Honey* and *The L-Shaped Room* – Kitchen Sink films which do have a female protagonist. He argues that 'the tendency is less to endorse a female self-direction than to reaffirm the value of motherhood and re-insert their characters into a network of family relations' (p. 166). If one considers the other possible ends to *A Taste of Honey* – Jo's African Prince

returning from the sea, Geoffrey overcoming his sexual orientation and settling down with Jo, a miscarriage freeing her from the burden of pregnancy – Jo's stoical acceptance of her mother's return might be better seen as a recognition of the importance of inter-female relations (it is obvious that her mother needs Jo far more than Jo needs her) rather than a reactionary affirmation of the importance of the family unit.

2. 80,000 PROBLEMS

1. John Berger, 'Look at Britain', *Sight and Sound*, Summer 1957, pp. 12–13.
2. Raymond Williams, 'A Lecture on Realism', *Screen*, vol. 18, no. 1, Spring 1977, pp. 61–74.
3. Virginia Maskell committed suicide shortly before her performance in Kevin Billington's *Interlude* was universally praised by the critics. Janet Munro died struggling to make a comeback in 1972. Rachel Roberts committed suicide in 1980.
4. Ken Hughes, like John Guillermin, was an unabashed admirer of American action pictures and his 50s 'B' films are exuberantly inventive. Unfortunately, after *The Trials of Oscar Wilde* his 60s films are something of a disappointment, though *Drop Dead Darling* (1966) and *Cromwell* (1970) have their moments. See Allen Eyles, 'Ken Hughes – A Passion for Cinema', *Focus on Film*, no. 6, Spring 1971, pp. 42–51. For Ken Adam, see Roger Hudson, 'Three Designers', *Sight and Sound*, Winter 1964, pp. 26–31.
5. Victor Perkins, 'The British Cinema', *Movie*, no 1, June 1962, p. 5. For more sympathetic assessments of Dearden and Relph's films, see Raymond Durgnat, 'Two On a Tandem', *Films and Filming*, July 1966, pp. 26–33; Carrie Tarr, '*Sapphire*, *Darling* and the Boundaries of Permitted Pleasure', and John Hill, 'The British "Social Problem" Film – *Violent Playground* and *Sapphire*', in *Screen*, vol. 26, no. 1, January–February 1985; Richard Dyer, '*Victim* – Hermeneutic Project', *Film Form*, vol. 1, no. 2, 1977; and Andy Medhurst, '*Victim* – Text as Context', *Screen*, vol. 25, nos. 4–5, July–October, 1984. John Hill's *Sex, Class and Realism*, London, BFI, 1986, and Raymond Durgnat's invaluable *A Mirror for England*, London, Faber & Faber, 1970, deal with social problem films generally.
6. Colin MacInnes, *City of Spades*, London, MacGibbon & Kee, 1957.
7. Derek Monsey, *Sunday Express*, 10 May 1959.
8. Horace is played by Robert Adams, who had begun his career in British films back in 1935 alongside Hughie Green in Carol Reed's *Midshipman Easy*.
9. Raymond Durgnat, *A Mirror for England*, p. 196.
10. Andy Medhurst, '*Victim* – Text as Context', pp. 31–3. See James Robertson, *The Hidden Cinema*, London, Routledge, 1989, pp. 119–26, for *Victim*'s passage through the BBFC.
11. Of Dearden and Relph's subsequent films, *Woman of Straw* (1964), *Masquerade* (1965) and *Khartoum* (1966) are well-made international productions; *Only When I Larf* (1968), *The Assassination Bureau* (1969) and *The Man Who Haunted Himself* (1970) are afflicted by a jaded shoddiness shared by several other late 60s films.
12. Attenborough was closely associated with the Boultings in the 1940s, following up the success of *Brighton Rock* with the starring role in *The Guinea Pig*, made for Filippo del Giudice's Pilgrim Films, the company responsible for *Chance of a Lifetime*, a middle-of-the-road precursor of *The Angry Silence*. Pilgrim Films was taken over by the Woolfs and, renamed Remus, was the production company they used to make *Room at the Top*.
13. Letter to *Tribune*, 15 April 1960.

14. Guy Green is best compared with Jack Lee Thompson, a director I have neglected here. Lee Thompson's *Tiger Bay* (1959), *No Trees in the Street* (1959), *North West Frontier* (1959) and *The Guns of Navarone* (1961) fall into my period, but for most of the 60s he worked in America, returning for the unsatisfactory quartet, *Eye of the Devil* (1966), *Before Winter Comes* (1969), *The Most Dangerous Man in the World* (1969) and *Country Dance* (1970). Green too went to Hollywood, though not until after making *The Mark*, a social problem film which despite the best efforts of the National Film Archive I have been unable to trace.

15. Raymond Durgnat, *A Mirror for England*, p. 73; *Daily Herald*, 16 May 1960, for the attitude of the Ipswich factory workers.

16. According to Forbes, the Mills were extremely reluctant to entrust their story and their daughter to an untried director. See Bryan Forbes, *Notes for a Life*, London, Collins, 1974, pp. 296–7, 300–1. John Mills's own debut as a director, *Sky West and Crooked* (1965), was much less successful, artistically and commercially, than *Whistle Down the Wind*, despite an excellent performance from Hayley Mills.

17. Brian Baxter, 'Bryan Forbes', *Film Dope*, no. 17, April 1979, pp. 7–9.

18. Alexander Walker, *Hollywood, England*, London, Harrap, 1986, pp. 102–6, 246–8, has useful background information on the setting up and demise of Allied Film Makers.

19. Michael Balcon, *A Lifetime of Films*, London, Hutchinson, 1969, p. 195.

20. *Woman in a Dressing Gown* (1957) and *No Trees in the Street* (1959) were both directed by Lee Thompson, whose melodramatic style seems ill-matched to Willis's naturalistic scripts. He was more fruitfully deployed on *Yield to the Night* (1956), which stars Diana Dors as a thinly disguised Ruth Ellis.

21. A clue to Roy Baker's anonymity is given in an interview with *Films and Filming*, in which he confesses his lack of interest in fashioning a personal visual style:

> From the point-of-view of somebody who thinks he knows his technique, I feel that I can devote myself to working with the actors without worrying about technique. The actor is the mode of expression ... when you come up against a tensely emotional scene, say of a man and his wife having a squabble, in a situation where 'souls are bared', then it's solely upon the actor that you have to rely, because there's no montage construction that can help you out. You have got to see it in their eyes and they must mean it and live the part with utter sincerity.
> 'Discovering Where the Truth Lies', *Films and Filming*, May 1961, p. 17.

Like Karel Reisz, he approaches his melodramatic subjects with a clear-eyed detachment and the attention he pays his actors brings rich rewards: John Mills gives three of his best performances in Baker's *The October Man*, *The Singer Not the Song* and *Flame in the Streets*.

22. A copy of the 'Armchair Theatre' production of *Hot Summer Night* is preserved in the National Film Archive.

23. The emphasis on colour is also evident in a sequence where Kathy and her black boyfriend go swimming together and in the casting of Sylvia Syms, a pale English rose, in place of olive-skinned, dark-eyed Andrée Melly. Other points about the cast worth making are that Gomez, who is unseen in the TV version, is played by Earl Cameron, the respectable black doctor in *Sapphire*. And that Ruth Dunning, who plays Nell in *Hot Summer Night*, would have been familiar to television viewers from her role as the mother in the BBC's first soap opera, *The Grove Family*, which ran from 1953 to 1956.

24. John Hill discusses Willis's films in *Sex, Class and Realism*, pp. 97–104.

Raymond Durgnat suggests a fascinating alternative scenario for *Flame in the Streets* in *A Mirror for England*, pp. 62–4. Durgnat is also the only writer to attempt an analysis of Roy Baker's style, *A Mirror for England*, pp. 239–42.

25. See the BFI Library microfiche on *Flame in the Streets* for critical reaction. The *Monthly Film Bulletin* (John Gillett) and the *Financial Times* (David Robinson) were lukewarm and *Tribune* (Derek Hill) contemptuous, but the *Daily Telegraph* (Patrick Gibbs), *Evening Standard* (Alexander Walker), *Spectator* (Isabel Quigly), *Morning Star* (Nina Hibbin) and *Films and Filming* (Raymond Durgnat), while finding several faults with the film, thought it a worthwhile and likeable enterprise.

26. Comedies did occasionally stray into the political arena, most notably in John Paddy Carstairs's patchy but hilarious *The Chiltern Hundreds* (1949), and in Launder and Gilliat's *Left Right and Centre* (1959), which is theoretically more interesting but in practice rather insipid.

27. According to Christopher Booker, the *Sunday Times*'s first colour supplement included a photo-feature on Lincoln, 'paying particular attention to its jazz club, its art students, its coffee bars, its electronics factory, its go-ahead young repertory company and its dynamic young architect.' *The Neophiliacs*, London, Collins, 1970, p. 49. The issues of cultural conflict for a working-class boy at university are dealt with more passionately and more convincingly in Dennis Potter's play *Stand Up, Nigel Barton* (1965).

28. If one wanted to pursue the parallel, then Dearden and Relph appear to oscillate between the *Guardian* and the *Daily Telegraph*, Willis represents the gorblimey populism of the *Mirror*, and Box/Thomas, with their constant anxiety about etiquette and class relations, the *Daily Mail*.

29. Despite its topicality *80,000 Suspects* was a commercial disaster, doing worse in box-office terms than any other film released on the Odeon circuit in 1963. See Terence Kelly, Graham Norton and George Perry, *A Competitive Cinema*, London, Institute of Economic Affairs, 1966, p. 74. Preserved on the BFI Library microfiche for Val Guest is a useful filmography compiled by three London School of Film Technique students who regarded him as a great director, but the only writer to deal with Guest's films in any detail is Raymond Durgnat; see *A Mirror for England*, pp. 132–5, 221–2.

30. John Hill, *Sex, Class and Realism*, p. 125.

31. Lawrence Alloway, *Violent America*, New York, Museum of Modern Art, 1969, p. 34.

3. CRITICAL DEBATES

1. Lawrence Alloway, 'Critics in the Dark', *Encounter*, February 1964, p. 55.
2. William Whitebait (George Stonier) had given way to John Coleman at the *New Statesman*, Fred Majdalany to Quentin Crewe on the *Daily Mail*, Campbell Dixon to Patrick Gibbs on the *Daily Telegraph*, Caroline Lejeune to Penelope Gilliatt at the *Observer*, Josh Billings to Bill Altria on the *Kine Weekly*, Jympson Harman to Felix Barker on the *Evening News*, Reg Whiteley to Dick Richards on the *Daily Mirror*, Milton Shulman to Alexander Walker on the *Evening Standard*.
3. Dilys Powell, *Films Since 1939*, London, Longmans Green, 1947, p. 39.
4. See John Ellis, 'Art, Culture and Quality: Terms for a Cinema in the '40s and '70s', *Screen*, vol. 19, no. 3, Autumn 1978, and Robert Murphy, *Realism and Tinsel*, London, Routledge, 1989, Chapter 5, 'Great Expectations', for post-war cinema and the critics.
5. Michael Balcon at Ealing was committed to making socially responsible films of a sort, but John Davis and Earl St John at Pinewood, and Robert Clark and

his Warner Brothers partners at Elstree, valued 'family entertainment' above everything else.

6. Grierson's *Sight and Sound* column, 'A Review of Reviews', ran from April–June 1954 to January–March 1955. Clearly no love was lost between him and Anderson. The 'Sulky Fire' articles appeared in the January–March and July–September issues for 1952 and the January–March issue of 1953.

7. 'Stand Up! Stand Up!', *Sight and Sound*, Autumn 1956, pp. 63–9; Taylor's letter appeared in the same issue, p. 110.

8. Lindsay Anderson, 'Commitment in Film Criticism', *Universities and Left Review*, no. 1, Spring 1957, pp. 44–8.

9. Lindsay Anderson, 'French Critical Writing', *Sight and Sound*, October–December 1954, p. 105.

10. The crucial Bazin essays – 'The Ontology of the Photographic Image', 'The Myth of Total Cinema', 'The Evolution of the Language of Cinema', 'The Virtues and Limitations of Montage' – are reprinted in *What is Cinema?* vol. 1, translated by Hugh Gray, Berkeley, Los Angeles and London, University of California Press, 1967. See Charles Barr, 'CinemaScope: Before and After', *Film Quarterly*, vol. 16, no. 4, Summer 1963, pp. 4–24, for a useful articulation of Bazin's arguments.

11. See Richard Roud, 'The French Line', *Sight and Sound*, Autumn 1960, pp. 167–71.

12. Ian Cameron, Editorial, p. 36; Mark Shivas, 'The Commercial Cinema: A Few Basic Principles', p. 39; Victor Perkins, 'Fifty Famous Films 1915–45', p. 36; in *Oxford Opinion*, no. 38, April 1960.

13. Peter John Dyer, 'Counter Attack', *Film*, 26, November–December 1960, p. 8.

14. See 'The Current Picture', *Film*, no. 27, January–February 1961, p. 7, for announcement, and 'The Current Picture', *Film*, no. 28, March–April 1961, pp. 4–5, for a report of this critical debate, 'Pistols for Three, Coffee for One', held at the Kensington Central Library on 28 January 1961. *The Critical Debate*, compiled by Jim Cook for the BFI Education Department, provides a useful selection from the most important articles.

15. Penelope Houston, 'The Critical Question', *Sight and Sound*, Autumn 1960, p. 163.

16. Ibid., p. 165.

17. Paddy Whannel, 'Room at the Top', *Universities and Left Review*, no. 6, Spring 1959, pp. 21–2; Stuart Hall, 'Jimmy Porter and the Two-and-Nines', *Definition*, no. 1, February 1960, pp. 9–14; Boleslaw Sulik, 'Saturday Night and Sunday Morning', *Definition*, no. 3, Autumn 1961, pp. 16–18; Alan Lovell, 'What Comes on Monday', *New Left Review*, no. 4, July–August 1960, pp. 58–9.

18. Victor Perkins, 'The British Cinema', *Movie*, no. 1, June 1962, p. 3.

19. Victor Perkins, 'The British Cinema', *Movie*, no. 1, p. 7, for Seth Holt; Victor Perkins, 'Clive Donner and Some People', *Movie*, no. 3, September 1962, pp. 22–5; Ian Cameron, 'Sammy Going South', *Movie*, no. 9, May 1963, pp. 29–30; Robin Wood, 'Michael Reeves – In Memoriam', *Movie*, no. 17, Winter 1969–70. *Movie* also published a long article by Philip French on Richard Lester (no. 14, Autumn 1965, pp. 5–11), and followed it up with a twelve-page interview (no. 16, Winter 1968–9, pp. 16–28); Raymond Durgnat's article on Michael Powell was first published in *Movie* (with Durgnat disguised as O. O. Green) and the first (regrettably the only) proper study of a British studio, Charles Barr's *Ealing Studios*, London and Newton Abbot, Cameron & Tayleur and David & Charles, 1977, came out as a *Movie* book. Paul Mayersberg, the most flexible of the *Movie* editors, interviewed Alex-

ander Mackendrick about *High Wind in Jamaica* on the BBC Third Programme, 26 May 1965.

20. Gilles Jacob, 'Nouvelle Vague or Jeune Cinema', *Sight and Sound*, Winter 1964–5, p. 5, claims that 'over 170 directors made their first features between 1959 and 1963'.

21. Geoffrey Nowell-Smith, 'Movie and Myth', *Sight and Sound*, Spring 1963, p. 62. Thomas Elsaesser, 'Two Decades in Another Country', in *Superculture*, C. W. E. Bigsby (ed.), Ohio, Bowling Green University Press, 1975, pp. 199–216, covers the same ground but he is much more critical of this cultural miscegenation.

22. Richard Hoggart, 'A Sense of Occasion', *Speaking to Each Other*, vol. 1, Harmondsworth, Penguin, 1973, p. 39. First published in *Conviction*, N. Mackenzie (ed.), 1958.

23. For the development of film education see Jim Cook and Jim Hillier, *The Growth of Film and Television Studies 1960–1975*, unpublished BFI Education Department Paper, April 1976; Paddy Whannel, 'Film Education and Film Culture', *Screen*, vol. 10, no 3, May–June 1969, pp. 49–59, sets out how a course might be constructed around John Ford.

24. The key text is Peter Wollen's *Signs and Meanings in the Cinema*, London, Secker & Warburg/BFI, 1969. Robin Wood, the Cambridge auteurist who became *Movie*'s most articulate and coherent critic, returned from a three-year sojourn in Canada to find British film culture transformed: '. . . everything has subtly changed, to an extent that I have only gradually begun to measure. Everyone has read books I had never heard of, in disciplines I scarcely knew existed; everyone was talking about semiology, and about "bourgeois ideology" . . .' Robin Wood, 'In Defence of Art', *Personal Views*, London, Gordon Fraser, 1976, p. 33. Wood entered into a debate with Alan Lovell in the pages of *Screen*: Alan Lovell, 'Robin Wood – A Dissenting View', *Screen*, vol. 10, no. 2, March–April 1969; Robin Wood, 'Ghostly Paradigm and H. C. F. An Answer to Alan Lovell', *Screen*, vol. 10, no. 3, May–June 1969; Alan Lovell, 'The Common Pursuit of True Judgement', *Screen*, vol. 11, nos. 4/5, Autumn 1970.

25. Raymond Durgnat, 'The Impotence of Being Ernest', *Views*, no. 8, Summer 1965, p. 76. Hall and Whannel's attitude was considerably more moderate than that expressed by Arnold Wesker in his article 'Two Lost Generations'. He gloomily suggests that working-class youths are so irredeemably corrupted by the pap fed them by Hollywood that it would be a waste of time making films which tried to reach them and the only sensible thing to do was to write them off and make a fresh start on the children. *Definition*, no. 1, February 1960, pp. 40–1.

26. Raymond Durgnat, 'The Impotence of Being Ernest', p. 80. Durgnat's review is followed by a 'committed' riposte from Oliver Williams defending *The Popular Arts*. Despite the value of *The Popular Arts* in opening up new approaches to media education, time has revealed Durgnat's judgments on the popular culture of the early 60s as much more acute than Hall and Whannel's.

27. George Melly, *Revolt into Style*, Harmondsworth, Penguin, 1972, p. 14.

28. Richard Hamilton, 'For the Finest Art Try Pop', *Gazette*, no. 1, 1961, reprinted in *Collected Works 1953–82*, London, Thames & Hudson, 1982, p. 42.

29. Robert Hewison, *Too Much*, London, Methuen, 1986, p. 46. The NUT's conference papers were published as *Discrimination and Popular Culture*, Denys Thompson (ed.), Harmondsworth, Penguin, 1964. Hamilton's lecture, 'Popular Culture and Personal Responsibility', was eventually published in his *Collected Works*.

30. Lawrence Alloway, 'Monster Films', *Encounter*, January 1960, pp. 70–2; Derek Hill, 'The Face of Horror', *Sight and Sound*, Winter 1959, pp. 6–11; Lawrence Alloway, *Violent America*, New York, Museum of Modern Art, 1969.

31. Lawrence Alloway draws on the work of art critic Erwin Panofsky, particularly his 'Iconography and Iconology' (in *Meaning in the Visual Arts*, Garden City, 1955); Robin Wood, the most influential of the English auteurists, on the literary scholar F. R. Leavis (see Wood's essay 'In Defence of Art', in *Personal Views*, pp. 33–75).

32. Lawrence Alloway, 'The Long Front of Culture', *Cambridge Opinion*, no. 17, 1959, reprinted in *Pop Art Redefined*, Suzi Gablik and John Russell (eds.), London, Thames & Hudson, 1982. Walter Benjamin, 'The Work of Art in the Age of Mechanical Reproduction', reprinted in *Film Theory and Criticism*, Gerald Mast and Marshall Cohen (eds.), New York, London and Toronto, Oxford University Press, 1974, pp. 612–34.

33. Lawrence Alloway, *Violent America*, p. 34.

34. It is perhaps a mistake to lump the *Movie* editors together. See 'Differences', *Movie*, no. 8, April 1963, pp. 28–34, for a discussion between Mark Shivas, Ian Cameron, Paul Mayersberg and Victor Perkins. Mayersberg's position, which comes quite close to that of Alloway, is more clearly expressed in 'The Art That Never Was', a talk he gave on the BBC Third Programme in March 1963 (a transcript of which can be found in the BFI Library). Robin Wood's differences with Victor Perkins are explored in 'Big Game', in Wood's *Personal Views*, pp. 11–29.

35. Raymond Durgnat, 'The Mass Media – A Highbrow Illiteracy?', *Views*, no. 4, Spring 1964, p. 51.

36. George Melly, *Revolt into Style*, pp. 16–19; Ray Gosling, *Sum Total*, Faber & Faber, London, 1962, p. 75.

37. Raymond Durgnat, 'Puritans Anonymous', *Motion*, no. 6, Autumn 1963, p. 3.

38. Raymond Durgnat, 'Standing Up for Jesus', *Motion*, no. 6, Autumn 1963, p. 27. Their position as mavericks outside the mainstream of film criticism and their affection for the films of John Ford eventually reconciled Durgnat to Anderson. See Durgnat's review of Anderson's *About John Ford*, *Cineaste*, vol. 12, 1983, pp. 56–8.

39. Raymond Durgnat, 'Standing Up for Jesus', *Motion*, no. 6, p. 38.

40. Jim Hillier, *Cahiers du Cinéma*, vol. 2, London, Routledge/BFI, 1968, p. 15. *Positif* enthusiastically championed British horror films (and in particular Terence Fisher) at a time when British critics – with the exception of Alloway and Durgnat – regarded them as pernicious rubbish.

41. *A Mirror for England* is reviewed sympathetically by Dave Pirie in *Time Out*, 10–17 June 1973, p. 49; and by Charles Barr in *Monogram*, no. 3, 1972, pp. 43–4.

42. Alan Lovell, *British Cinema, the Unknown Cinema*, BFI Seminar Paper, March 1969, available in the BFI Library. The only books on British cinema to come out of the committed or auteurist schools are Jim Hillier and Alan Lovell's *Studies in Documentary*, London, Secker & Warburg/BFI, 1972, Charles Barr's *Ealing Studios*, and Dai Vaughan's *Portrait of an Invisible Man*, BFI, 1981.

4. ART and COMMERCE

1. J. G. Weightman, 'High, Low and Modern', *Encounter*, September 1960, p. 67.

2. Dilys Powell, *Films Since 1939*, London, Longmans Green, 1947, p. 22.

3. Ivan Butler, *To Encourage the Art of the Film*, London, Robert Hale, 1971, p. 178.

4. 'The Front Page', *Sight and Sound*, Autumn 1965, p. 159. See Geoffrey Nowell-Smith, 'Chasing the Gorgon', *Sight and Sound*, Spring 1965, p. 60, and Ian Cameron, 'Mark Shivas: Framed', *Sight and Sound*, Winter 1988–9, p. 21, for more positive responses to this cultural mix.

5. Peter Baker, 'The Foreign Papers', *Films and Filming*, February 1964, p. 41. See also 'The Front Page', *Sight and Sound*, Summer 1964, pp. 107–8, for comments on the distribution of *Vivre sa Vie*, *L'Année Dernière à Marienbad* and *Viridiana* in Britain.

6. Robert Vas, 'Arrival and Departure', *Sight and Sound*, Spring 1963, p. 56.

7. One could add to this list all sorts of theatrical adaptations, from Zeffirelli's *Romeo and Juliet* to Silvio Narizzano's *Loot*. The three film versions of John Le Carré's novels – *The Spy Who Came in from the Cold*, *The Deadly Affair* and (in particular) *The Looking Glass War* – are also ambitious and pretentious enough to qualify as art films. But it is part of my argument that the division between art films and entertainment films is only provisionally useful, and they will be dealt with in their proper place among the other spy/secret agent films.

8. Paul Mayersberg, 'The Art That Never Was', broadcast BBC Third Programme, March 1963 (transcript in BFI Library). Mayersberg and Mark Shivas were the only two significant critics of their generation to become involved in film production.

9. Penelope Houston, 'Keeping Up With the Antonionis', *Sight and Sound*, Autumn 1964, p. 165.

10. Richard Thorpe made several films in Britain. Around the time Reisz was remaking *Night Must Fall* he was busy on a John and Hayley Mills vehicle, *The Truth About Spring*.

11. The most useful and perceptive review of *Night Must Fall* is by Alan Lovell in *Peace News*, 5 June 1964, reproduced on the BFI Library microfiche for the film. See also George Gaston, *Karel Reisz*, Boston, Twayne, 1980, pp. 47–60. See Alexander Walker, *Hollywood, England*, London, Harrap, 1986, pp. 146–51, for a detailed account of the genesis, production and reception of *Night Must Fall*.

12. The moment when this fusion took place might be taken, symbolically at least, as the Dialectics of Liberation Conference held at the Roundhouse in London in July 1967, for which see Robert Hewison, *Too Much*, London, Methuen, 1986, pp. 134–9; Jeff Nuttall, *Bomb Culture*, London, Paladin, 1970, p. 58; and Nigel Fountain, *Underground*, London, Routledge, 1988, pp. 49–50. Mercer returned to Laing's ideas more explicitly in his television play *In Two Minds* (1967), directed by Ken Loach, who also directed a cinema version of the same play, *Family Life* (1971).

13. Barry Curtis, *Morgan, a Suitable Case for Treatment*, Polytechnic of Central London M. A. thesis, 1983, p. 2. Curtis's account is convoluted but stimulating and useful. *A Suitable Case for Treatment*, directed by Don Taylor, was transmitted on BBC television in November 1962 and, according to Curtis, the tape was wiped soon after and no copy survives. The most perceptive and sympathetic review of *Morgan* is by Michael Kustow in *Sight and Sound*, Summer 1966, p. 144. Raymond Durgnat, *Films and Filming*, June 1966, pp. 6–7, is surprisingly hostile.

14. John Russell Taylor, 'The Collector', *Sight and Sound*, Autumn 1965, p. 201.

15. *David Bailey's Box of Pin-Ups*, London, Weidenfeld & Nicolson, 1965, James Woolf. Of the reviews of *The Collector* preserved on the BFI Library microfiche, the most acute is that by Dilys Powell in the *Sunday Times*, 17 October

1965. There is a useful section on the film in Michael A. Anderegg's *William Wyler*, Boston, Twayne, 1979, pp. 205–14.

16. In the novel Fowles saddles Clegg with the unlikely name of Ferdinand in order to press the ironic parallel with the handsome prince who loves Miranda in *The Tempest*; naturally Miranda calls him Caliban. In the film he becomes Freddie.

17. See Geoffrey Gorer, 'The Perils of Hypergamy', *New Statesman*, 4 May 1957, reprinted in *Protest*, Gene Feldman and Max Gartenberg (eds.), London, Souvenir Press, 1959.

18. Critical reaction to *Repulsion* was mixed: Alexander Walker (*Evening Standard*), Patrick Gibbs (*Daily Telegraph*), Kenneth Tynan (*Observer*) and David Robinson (*Financial Times*) enthusiastically in favour of the film; Dilys Powell (*Sunday Times*) and Isabel Quigly (*Spectator*) critical but not unperceptive; Nina Hibbin (*Daily Worker*), Richard Roud (*Guardian*) and John Coleman (*New Statesman*) crassly dismissive. The best subsequent analyses of the film are Ivan Butler's in *Horror in the Cinema*, pp. 83–9; Virginia Wright Wexman's in her *Roman Polanski*, Boston, Twayne, 1985, pp. 43–57; and Gretchen Bisplinghoff's 'Codes of Feminine Madness' in *Film Reader* 5, 1982, pp. 37–40. For the critical reaction to *Peeping Tom*, see Ian Christie, 'The Scandal of *Peeping Tom*', in *Powell, Pressburger and Others*, Ian Christie (ed.), London, British Film Institute, 1973, pp. 53–9; Jean-Paul Török, 'Look at the Sea: *Peeping Tom*', *Powell, Pressburger and Others*, pp. 59–62; and Ian Johnson, 'A Pin to See the Peepshow', in *Motion*, no. 4, *Companion to Violence and Sadism in the Cinema*, February 1963, pp. 36–9.

19. The career of Harry Waxman, who photographed *Sapphire*, shadows that of Otto Heller, who photographed *Peeping Tom*. Both experimented with 'noirish' lighting in the 40s (Heller in *They Made Me a Fugitive*, *Temptation Harbour* and *The Queen of Spades*, Waxman in *Brighton Rock*) and garish Eastman Colour in the late 50s (Heller in *Peeping Tom*, Waxman in *Sapphire*).

20. *Peeping Tom* can usefully be compared with *Twisted Nerve* (1968), directed by Roy Boulting, photographed by Harry Waxman and scripted by Leo Marks, who also wrote *Peeping Tom*. Boulting's handling of the similar story of an attractive but psychotic young man's murderous relationships with women is less assured than Powell's, but it is an interesting film, undeserving of the contemptuous neglect with which it has been treated.

21. Penelope Houston, 'Keeping Up With the Antonionis', *Sight and Sound*, Autumn 1964, p. 167. See Elizabeth Wilson, *Only Half Way to Paradise*, London, Tavistock, 1980, pp. 154–61, for a discussion of *The Pumpkin Eater* and other women's novels of the 60s.

22. See Dilys Powell in the *Sunday Times*, Thomas Wiseman in the *Sunday Express*, Patrick Gibbs in the *Daily Telegraph* and the anonymous review in *The Times*, all included on the BFI Library microfiche for *The L-Shaped Room*, for sympathetic assessments of the film. Francis Wyndham in *Sight and Sound*, Winter 1962–3, pp. 40–1, is representative of the hostile reviews.

23. Julie Christie's Liz in *Billy Liar!*, which was released at the same time as *The World Ten Times Over*, is little more than a cameo role but her impact was considerable. Dinah in *Catch Us If You Can* (released April 1965) is almost a carbon copy of Ginnie, though Barbara Ferris – tough despite her fragility, pragmatic despite her zaniness – brings different qualities to the role.

24. See the BFI Library microfiche for *The World Ten Times Over* for Walker and Wiseman's reviews. Walker's favourable reviews of off-beat films are often absent or even repudiated in *Hollywood, England*. See also Raymond Durgnat, *A Mirror for England*, London, Faber & Faber, 1970, pp. 204–5, for a brief but perceptive comment on the film.

25. See Kevin Brownlow, *How It Happened Here*, London, Secker & Warburg/ BFI, 1968, for the cost of the film and a full account of how it was made. Margaret Hinxman in the *Sunday Telegraph*, 5 May 1968, and Penelope Houston in the *Spectator*, 10 May 1968, both cost *Herostratus* at £10,000; Sir John Woolf gave me figures of around £350,000 for *The L-Shaped Room* and *The Pumpkin Eater* in an interview in September 1988.

26. The most interesting reviews of *Herostratus* were written by John Weightman, 'A Pad in Paddington', *Encounter*, June 1968; and Jan Dawson, *Monthly Film Bulletin*, June 1968, p. 87. Levy's guide to how to view the film is reproduced on the BFI Library microfiche for *Herostratus*. See also Raymond Durgnat's letter defending the film in *Encounter*, September 1968, p. 91.

27. For the early development of the British avant-garde, see Jan Dawson and Claire Johnston, 'Declarations of Independence', *Sight and Sound*, Winter 1969–70, pp. 28–32, and 'More British Sounds', *Sight and Sound*, Summer 1970, pp. 144–7. For *Bronco Bullfrog*, see David Robinson, 'Around Angel Lane', *Sight and Sound*, Summer 1970, pp. 132–3; for *Praise Marx and Pass the Ammunition*, see Jan Dawson's review in *Sight and Sound*, Autumn 1969, p. 214, though the most revealing comparison is with Tariq Ali's *Street Fighting Years*, London, Fontana/Collins, 1988.

28. See 'Hammer: Yesterday, Today and Tomorrow', *Little Shoppe of Horrors* no. 4, April 1978, p. 110, for Losey and *X the Unknown*. Julian Wintle, the executive producer of *This Sporting Life*, wanted Losey to direct the film with Stanley Baker as Machin, but they failed to agree on how to treat the story and Wintle turned to Reisz and Anderson instead. Anne Francis, *Julian Wintle*, Dukeswood, 1968, p. 65. Of the innumerable books and articles on Losey, the best is Michel Ciment's *Conversations With Losey*, London and New York, Methuen, 1985. Ciment manages to keep his admiration well below the sycophantic level.

29. Michel Ciment, *Conversations With Losey*, p. 214.

30. John Russell Taylor makes an interesting comparison between *The Servant* and Clive Donner's adaptation of Pinter's *The Caretaker*, 'The Servant and The Caretaker', *Sight and Sound*, Winter 1963–4, pp. 38–9. Donner transfers the play to the screen very simply – the film was made on a very limited budget – but he succeeds in bringing it to life much better than William Friedkin does in his grindingly slow version of *The Birthday Party* (1968) and than David Jones's uninspiring *Betrayal* (1982). Polanski's *Cul de Sac* (1966) shares Pinter's savagely absurd world but realises it with much greater humour, pathos and conviction.

31. Penelope Gilliatt, *Sight and Sound*, Winter 1964–5, pp. 37–8; *Monthly Film Bulletin*, December 1964, pp. 171–2; Isabel Quigly, *Spectator*, 4 December 1964. Charles Barr's review in *Movie* is more perceptive and more critical but he still regards *King and Country* as 'completely remote from the standard Dearden–Relph item which could have been run up from the same source material.' *Movie*, no. 12, Spring 1965, p. 25.

32. Pauline Kael is much less indulgent to her fellow countryman than British critics like Tom Milne (*Sight and Sound*) and Richard Roud (*Monthly Film Bulletin*). She describes *Accident* as 'a fascinating, rather preposterous movie, uneven, unsatisfying, but with virtuoso passages of calculated meanness', and concludes, 'It has an archness which I associate with a kind of well-written but fundamentally empty novel. *Accident* is, despite what Losey and Pinter say in it, for and of "the upper classes".' 'The Comedy of Depravity', reprinted in *Kiss Kiss Bang Bang*, London, Calder & Boyars, 1970, pp. 105–9.

33. See Michel Ciment, *Conversations With Losey*, pp. 273–96, Philip Strick, 'Mice in the Milk', *Sight and Sound*, Spring 1969, pp. 77–8, and 'Interview

with Joseph Losey', *Cinema*, no. 3, June 1969, p. 21, for favourable comment on *Boom!* and *Secret Ceremony*. Alexander Walker, *Hollywood, England*, pp. 354–7, is guardedly critical.

34. Woolf insisted on Reed as director, overcoming the opposition of Columbia, the film's backers. Interview with author, September 1988. See Pauline Kael, 'The Concealed Art of Carol Reed', in *Going Steady*, London, Temple Smith, 1970, pp. 200–5, for a sympathetic analysis of *Oliver!*, and Robert Moss, *The Films of Carol Reed*, London, Macmillan, 1987, for a detailed assessment of Reed's career.
35. Alain Silver and James Ursini, *David Lean and His Films*, London, Leslie Frewin, 1974.
36. Philip Kemp, 'Mackendrickland', *Sight and Sound*, Winter 1988–9, p. 52.
37. In 1969 Mackendrick moved out of the commercial jungle to become Dean of the Film and Video Department at the California Institute of the Arts.
38. Other British films made in Africa in the 60s – *Born Free* (1965), *Africa Texas Style* (1967), *An Elephant Called Slowly* (1969) – tended to concentrate on the animals.
39. The BBC radio interview between Mackendrick and Paul Mayersberg, 26 May 1965, which is transcribed on the BFI library microfiche for *High Wind in Jamaica*, is full of useful information. The film is intelligently reviewed by Philip French, *Observer*, 23 May 1965, and Allen Eyles, *Films and Filming*, August 1965, pp. 29–30.
40. The most perceptive review of *Sammy Going South* is by Ian Cameron in *Movie*, no. 9, May 1963, pp. 29–30.
41. Simon Raven, 'Perish By the Sword', in *The Establishment*, Hugh Thomas (ed.), London, Anthony Blond, 1959. Andrew Sinclair, *The Breaking of Bumbo*, London, Faber & Faber, 1959. Sinclair went on to film his novel for Bryan Forbes at Elstree in the late 60s, but the company thought the resulting film too bad to release. It was screened by Channel 4 in 1987. See also Kevin Billington's fascinating documentary on the Household Brigade, *All the Queen's Men* (1966).
42. Quentin Crewe, *Daily Mail*, 12 October 1961, included along with the reviews of other newspaper critics on the BFI microfiche for *The Queen's Guards*.
43. *Monthly Film Bulletin*, November 1966, pp. 172–3; *Guardian*, 21 October 1966; *The Times*, 20 October 1966.
44. Sylvia Lawson, 'They're a Dull Mob', *Nation*, 17 August 1966.
45. Raymond Durgnat (as O. O. Green), 'Michael Powell', *Movie*, no. 14, Autumn 1965.
46. Penelope Houston, *Spectator*, 22 November 1969.
47. In its use of an island setting and the casting of James Mason as a roguish but essentially honourable philanderer, *Age of Consent* has a precursor in Ted Kotcheff's *Tiara Tahiti*. Kotcheff, another Canadian who made his name directing plays on television, was also responsible for *Life at the Top* (1965), the underrated sequel to *Room at the Top*. *Age of Consent* can also be compared to Polanski's *Cul de Sac*. In contrast to Mason's mellow, mature artist who finds tranquillity and love on his island, Donald Pleasence's cold, rainy island becomes increasingly nightmarish as his life disintegrates around him.
48. Alan Lovell, *British Cinema: The Unknown Cinema*, BFI Education Seminar paper, 1969, p. 7.

5. WHEN DINOSAURS RULED THE EARTH
1. Harry Hopkins, *The New Look*, London, Secker & Warburg, 1963, p. 332.
2. The best source for cinema statistics is Appendix 2 of the Monopolies Com-

mission's *Report on the Supply of Films for Exhibition in Cinemas*, London, HMSO, 1966, p. 92.

3. For the introduction of CinemaScope and the Fox/Rank quarrel see Political and Economic Planning, *The British Film Industry*, London, 1958, pp. 139–40; and Richard Hamilton, 'Glorious Technicolor, Breathtaking Cinemascope and Stereophonic Sound', in *Collected Works 1953–82*, London, Thames & Hudson, p. 117.
4. FIDO press statement, quoted in PEP, *The British Film Industry*, p. 143.
5. *Report on the Supply of Films for Exhibition in Cinemas*, p. 26.
6. John Davis, *Kinematograph Weekly*, 16 October 1958, p. 6. Davis set out the case for rationalisation in 'Intermission – The British Film Industry', *National Provincial Bank Review*, 1958, pp. 1–12.
7. John Spraos, *The Decline of the Cinema*, London, Allen & Unwin, 1962, p. 84.
8. See *Kinematograph Weekly*, 16 October 1958, pp. 6–7, 23 October 1958, p. 6.
9. Figures from Report of Cinematograph Films Council Sub-Committee on Trading Practices, reproduced in ACTT, *Survival or Extinction: A Policy for British Films*, London, ACTT, 1964, pp. 27–45. See also Penelope Houston, 'The Power of the Circuits', *Sight and Sound*, Autumn 1963, p. 174.
10. Allen Eyles and Marcus Eavis's survey, 'Focus on Exhibition', *Motion*, no. 2, Winter 1961–2, pp. 13–16, 38, deals interestingly with alternatives to the Rank/ABC duopoly, in particular the Classic circuit which succeeded 'in adroitly balancing really old titles with recent continental successes'. See Geoffrey Nowell-Smith, 'Chasing the Gorgon', *Sight and Sound*, Spring 1965, p. 60, for how a discerning film enthusiast could profit from the proliferation of film programmes.
11. Ian Cameron, 'Saving the Cinema', *Spectator*, 7 February 1964, p. 178.
12. Keith Robertson, interview with author, 8 January 1986.
13. *Kinematograph Weekly*, 14 December 1961, p. 4.
14. *Kinematograph Weekly*, 16 October 1958, p. 6.
15. Terence Kelly, *A Competitive Cinema*, London, Institute of Economic Affairs, 1966, p. 69.
16. Obscurity surrounds the identity of these martyred films. The best guide is Terence Kelly, *A Competitive Cinema*, p. 35, though Kelly lists only thirteen films while Jolyon Wimhurst, 'Movies at a Halt', *Statist*, 30 December 1963, p. 863, writes of 'a queue of perhaps eighteen first feature and thirteen second feature films'. See also Penelope Houston, 'Whose Crisis?', *Sight and Sound*, Winter 1963–4, pp. 26–9. Robert Clark, defending ABPC's record in the booking of films from independent producers on to their circuit, pointed out that in the four years 1960–63, 107 British films were shown, 66 of them from sources with which ABPC had no connection. Of the remaining 41 – which were handled by Warner-Pathé, the distribution company ABPC co-owned with Warner Brothers – 36 were made by independent producers with financial backing from ABPC, and only five came from the company's own production unit. Quoted from Clark's letter to *The Times*, 20 December 1963, by Bernard Husra, 'Patterns of Power', *Films and Filming*, April 1964, p. 51.
17. For comment on the Monopolies Commission Report see: 'Movies and Monopolies': Part 1, *Film and Television Technician*, January 1967, pp. 5–7, 24–5, Part 2, February 1967, pp. 44–7; Penelope Houston, 'Monopoly', *Sight and Sound*, Winter 1966–7, pp. 15–16; Terence Kelly, 'Chicken-hearted Champion of Competition', *Films and Filming*, January 1967, pp. 34–5.
18. Figures from Monopolies and Mergers Commission, *Films: A Report on the Supply of Films for Exhibition in Cinemas*, HMSO, 1983, pp. 5, 9. While no doubt more enterprising management could have done more to arrest the decline of the cinema it would be wrong to assume that Rank and ABC were

cynical or incompetent in running their cinemas. Terence Kelly noted in 1966: 'Rank has completely rebuilt ten cinemas and has been modernising others recently at a cost of some £3 million a year. It has also opened eight new cinemas. Since the war ABC has completely modernised twenty-three cinemas and in the last ten years it has spent over £12 million on maintenance and repairs. It has opened eight new cinemas and plans more.' But he concludes sadly that 'According to Rank, the return on investment in renovating cinemas is low – a mere 3.7 per cent.' Kelly, *A Competitive Cinema*, p. 46. From a purely business point of view one can hardly blame Rank for putting its money into photocopiers.

19. ABPC churned out films from their Elstree and Welwyn studios in the 30s, but they were merely programme-fillers and the profitability of the ABC cinemas rested on the prestige Hollywood films shown in them. Gaumont British/ Gainsborough deserves more serious consideration, and for the period between 1931 and 1945 the films made at Islington and Shepherd's Bush constitute an identifiable and interesting studio product.

20. Frederic Raphael, *Two for the Road*, London, Jonathan Cape, 1967, p. 10.

21. Terence Kelly, *A Competitive Cinema*, p. 50. The NFFC deal, undertaken at the time of the Monopolies and Mergers investigation, involved Rank and the NFFC jointly financing five films – *They're a Weird Mob*, *Romeo and Juliet*, *I Was Happy Here*, *The Sandwich Man* and *Maroc 7*. The experiment was not repeated. Kelly reports that ABPC had a similarly limited involvement in production. 'In 1960–3, though its own production unit made only five films the group provided finance – usually 70 per cent or more of the budget – for another thirty-six films by outside producers.' *A Competitive Cinema*, p. 51.

22. The Danziger Brothers, based at New Elstree studios (a converted warehouse), were extremely prolific in the late 50s, but they had abandoned production by 1962 and their story belongs to the previous decade.

23. Anglo-Amalgamated had been absorbed by Warner-Pathé in 1962, but it continued to exist as an autonomous production unit until EMI took over ABPC in 1969. By the early 70s Nat Cohen, Anglo's managing director, had become the driving force of the new company and the most influential producer in the industry. His unprejudiced commercialism is best seen in his justification for backing Ken Loach's radical films *Poor Cow* and *Family Life*: 'I can't see any harm in Socialist films. If the public want Socialist films, and there are directors who want to make them, no harm in that.' 'Carry on Cohen', Charles Nicholl, *Daily Telegraph*, 7 December 1973.

24. Michael Balcon, *A Lifetime of Films*, London, Hutchinson, 1969, p. 195.

25. NFFC Annual Report for the year ended 31 March 1959, p. 4. See also Penelope Houston, 'The Front Page', *Sight and Sound*, Autumn 1959, p. 109.

26. NFFC, 1959, p. 8.

27. For the British Lion story see Bernard Husra, 'Patterns of Power', *Films and Filming*, April 1964, pp. 49–56; Mark Shivas, 'British Lion', *Movie*, no. 14, Autumn 1965, pp. 1–4; and Michael Balcon, *A Lifetime of Films*, pp. 202–9.

28. See Michael Balcon, *A Lifetime of Films*, p. 201, and Alexander Walker, *Hollywood, England*, London, Harrap, 1986, p. 151, for the end of Bryanston. Rediffusion was interested in Bryanston's backlog of films, not in continuing production.

29. Connery's replacement at the end of the decade, George Lazenby, proved how wrong Broccoli and Saltzman were in thinking that a mere physical presence was sufficient for Bond.

30. See Kingsley Amis, *The James Bond Dossier*, London, Jonathan Cape, 1965; Philip Larkin, 'The Batman from Blades', *Required Writing*, London, Faber & Faber, 1983, pp. 266–70.

31. For Lester see Neil Sinyard, *The Films of Richard Lester*, London, Croom Helm, 1985; Philip French, 'Richard Lester', *Movie*, no. 14, Winter 1965, pp. 5–11; and Mark Shivas and Ian Cameron, 'Interview With Richard Lester', *Movie*, no. 16, Winter 1968–9, pp. 16–29. For the Beatles see (in particular) George Melly, *Revolt into Style*, Harmondsworth, Penguin, 1972, pp. 62–82, and Tony Bicat, 'Fifties Children: Sixties People' in *The Age of Affluence 1951–64*, Robert Skidelsky and Vernon Bogdanor (eds.), London, Macmillan, 1970, pp. 329–34.

6. BRAVE NEW WORLD

1. Ray Gosling, 'I Like You Full Stop', *Queen*, 15 September 1961, p. 120. Jeff Nuttall quotes almost the entire article in *Bomb Culture*, London, Paladin, 1970, pp. 114–15.
2. Robert Hewison, *Too Much*, London, Methuen, 1986, p. 6.
3. Christopher Booker, *The Neophiliacs*, London, Collins, 1969, p. 132.
4. Andrew Shonfield, *British Economic Policy Since the War*, Harmondsworth, Penguin, 1958.
5. The economic boom was celebrated in an issue of *Queen*. According to Booker, Macmillan handed copies round to his Cabinet at one of their last pre-election meetings. *The Neophiliacs*, p. 141.
6. See John Barnes, 'The Record', in *The Decade of Disillusion*, Chris Cook and David McKie (eds.), London, Macmillan/St Martin's Press, 1972, p. 17, for Macmillan's reshuffle; and Booker, *The Neophiliacs*, p. 176, for Henry Brook.
7. Christopher Booker, *The Neophiliacs*, p. 192.
8. Post-war criticism of 'mass culture' in Britain began with J. B. Priestley, who formulated his concept of 'admass' during his travels in America in the mid-50s. 'Admass' was his name 'for the whole system of an increasing productivity, plus inflation, plus a rising standard of material living, plus high-pressure advertising and salesmanship, plus mass communications, plus cultural democracy and the creation of the mass mind, the mass man.' J. B. Priestley and Jacquetta Hawkes, *Journey Down a Rainbow*, London, Heinemann-Cresset, 1957. Richard Hoggart used the term 'shiny barbarism' to describe squeaky-clean American teen culture, which in film terms was soon to manifest itself in beach-party movies starring the likes of Frankie Avalon and Annette Funicello. Richard Hoggart, *The Uses of Literacy*, Harmondsworth, Penguin, 1958, p. 193. For conflicting views of Wesker's achievement with Centre 42, see Robert Hewison, *Too Much*, pp. 17–24, and Jeff Nuttall, *Bomb Culture*, pp. 55–8.
9. Irving Kristol, 'High, Low, and Modern', *Encounter*, August 1960, p. 34. More constructive attitudes to mass/popular culture can be found in John Weightman's reply to Kristol, *Encounter*, September 1960, pp. 66–9; and in Lawrence Alloway's 'The Long Front of Culture', *Cambridge Opinion* 17, 1959, reprinted in Suzy Gablik and John Russell (eds.), *Pop Art Redefined*, London, Thames & Hudson, 1969, pp. 41–3.
10. See Robert Hewison, *Too Much*, pp. 12–14, for the Pilkington Report. BBC2 began broadcasting in April 1964.
11. In addition to *Live Now – Pay Later* and *Nothing But the Best*, a number of comedies concerned themselves with 'the affluent society', most notably Tony Hancock's *The Punch and Judy Man* (1962, d. Jeremy Summers), Bryanston's *Ladies Who Do* (1963, d. C. M. Pennington-Richards), and Joan Littlewood's *Sparrows Can't Sing* (1963).
12. Peter Glenville, an actor turned director whose most memorable screen role was as the snivelling spiv Jimmy Rosso in *Good Time Girl*, was the Woolfs' alternative choice for the director of *Room at the Top* (it was his idea to bring in Simone

Signoret). When Clayton turned down *Term of Trial*, Glenville was thus a natural choice. He went on to make *Becket* (1964) for Paramount and *Hotel Paradiso* (1966) for MGM but his loyalties were to the theatre rather than to film.

13. Raymond Durgnat, *A Mirror for England*, London, Faber & Faber, 1970, p. 44.

14. Jack Trevor Story, *Live Now Pay Later*, Harmondsworth, Penguin, 1963, p. 121.

15. BFI Special Collection, *Live Now – Pay Later*: letter from John Trevelyan to Jack Hanbury, 27 March 1962.

16. Raymond Durgnat, *A Mirror for England*, p. 46. There is a sort of follow-up to *Live Now – Pay Later*, *This is My Street* (1963, d. Sidney Hayers), with Ian Hendry and June Ritchie once again in the leading roles. See John Hill, *Sex, Class and Realism*, London, British Film Institute, 1986, pp. 167–8.

17. See Kenneth More, *More or Less*, London, Hodder & Stoughton, 1978, pp. 180–203. More's chance of a career in Hollywood was lost when – for reasons which had nothing to do with the quality of his performance – he was cut out of William Wyler's *The Collector*.

18. Expectations that the romantic reunion between Chick and Judy is going to lapse into *Look Back in Anger* whimsy ('Once upon a time there were three bears') are rudely disappointed ('And now the bastards are everywhere').

19. The television play, *The Best of Everything*, based on a short story by Stanley Ellin, was also scripted by Raphael and had Terence Alexander, Gary Raymond (Cliff in the film version of *Look Back in Anger*) and Diane Clare (the heroine of *Plague of the Zombies*) in the roles played by Denholm Elliot, Alan Bates and Millicent Martin in *Nothing But the Best*.

20. See Charles T. Gregory, 'There'll Always be Room at the Top for Nothing but the Best', *Journal of Popular Film*, vol. 2, no. 1, Winter 1973, pp. 59–73, for a detailed, if peculiarly biased, comparison of the two films. *Nothing But the Best* might be as fruitfully compared to *The Servant* in its treatment of a sly chancer battening on to an upper-class degenerate and destroying him; or to Ian McEwan and Richard Eyre's *The Ploughman's Lunch* (1983), a cynical reworking of the theme of a young man of humble origins trying to climb the greasy pole.

21. Julie Christie, 'Everybody's Darling', in *Very Heaven: Looking Back on the Sixties*, Sara Maitland (ed.), London, Virago, 1988, p. 171. In real life Christie's rejection of the conventional trappings of stardom – shared by other 60s icons like Sandie Shaw and Cathy McGowan and the post-Beatles pop groups – make her, rather than Diana, the model for modern women. Mark Boxer's *London Life* magazine, which for its brief existence was the most authentic voice of Swinging London, took for its girl of 1966 Lucy Bartlett, a twenty-four year-old Christie lookalike, commenting that in spite of her upper middle-class upbringing, 'an almost peasant-like concealment of wealth governs her existence, a sort of conspicuous non-consumption which rates dungarees higher than Dior.' Jack Wilton, 'Girls Like Lucy', *London Life*, 8–14 January 1966, p. 26.

22. See Carrie Tarr's perceptive article, '*Sapphire*, *Darling* and the Boundaries of Permitted Pleasure', *Screen*, vol. 26, no. 1, January–February 1985, pp. 50–65.

23. *Daily Mail*, 14 September 1965. Schlesinger later expressed dissatisfaction with the film in his interview with David Spiers, *Screen*, vol. 11, no. 3, Summer 1970, pp. 8–10, as did Raphael in his introduction to the published script of *Two for the Road*, London, Jonathan Cape, 1967, pp. 28–9.

24. See Mark Abrams, *The Teenage Consumer*, London, Press Exchange, 1959, and Peter Laurie, *The Teenage Revolution*, London, Anthony Blond, 1965.

25. Robert Hewison, *Too Much*, p. 59, for higher education figures; Geoffrey Pearson, *Hooligan: A History of Respectable Fears*, London, Macmillan, 1983, for the activities of pre-50s teenage gangs.

25. For women's fashion see Barbara Bernard, *Fashion in the Sixties*, London, Academy Editions, 1978, and Barbara Hulanicki, *From A to Biba*, London, W. H. Allen, 1984; for men's fashion see Nik Cohn, *Today There Are No Gentlemen*, London, Weidenfeld & Nicolson, 1971.
27. Even mods had their antecedents. Nineteen-year-old Roy Kerridge's 'A Teenage Who's Who', *New Statesman*, 24 September 1960, pp. 423–6, deals in detail with the now forgotten proto-mods whom he calls (technically, not pejoratively) Yobs. See also Richard Barnes, *Mods!*, London, Eel Pie Publishing, 1979; Stanley Cohen, *Folk Devils and Moral Panics*, London, MacGibbon & Kee, 1972; Dick Hebdidge, *Subcultures*, London, Methuen, 1979; Stuart Hall and Tony Jefferson (eds.), *Resistance Through Rituals*, London, Hutchinson, 1976; Colin MacInnes's articles, 'Pop Songs and Teenagers' and 'Sharp Schmutter', reprinted in *England, Half English*, London, Hogarth Press, 1986, 'Old Youth and Young', *Encounter*, September 1967, pp. 29–35, and his novel *Absolute Beginners*, London, MacGibbon & Kee, 1959.
28. Young people became an increasingly important part of the cinema's audience. Peter Laurie claims that: 'Since the spread of television in the middle fifties, this has become almost entirely a teenage medium. ... In fact as the young are driven out of their homes by television and the split with the older generations, the cinema has become one of the few second homes available to them.' *The Teenage Revolution*, p. 68. I am indebted to Jonathan Simmons's unpublished MA thesis, *British Youth Problem Feature Films*, Polytechnic of Central London, 1983, particularly for his detailed analysis of *The Boys* and *Some People*.
29. Sidney Furie's mixed bag of early features includes two horror films (*Dr Blood's Coffin* and *The Snake Woman*), an odd social problem melodrama (*During One Night*), and the film which launched him on the international market, *The Ipcress File*.
30. *Films and Filming*, June 1962, p. 40.
31. Peter Laurie, *The Teenage Revolution*, pp. 25–6; Jeff Nuttall, *Bomb Culture*, p. 34. See also Gillian Freeman, 'On Location at the Ace', *New Statesman*, 21 February 1964 (reproduced on the BFI Library microfiche for *The Leather Boys*).
32. Thomas Wiseman, *Sunday Express*, 26 January 1964.
33. See Gordon Gow's interview with Raymond Stross, 'Love Yourself Sufficiently', *Films and Filming*, March 1971, pp. 18–22.
34. Also of crucial importance were the cameramen Larry Pizer, who went on to photograph *Four in the Morning*, *The World Ten Times Over*, and (with Gerry Turpin) *Morgan*; and the art director Peggy Gick, who also worked on *The World Ten Times Over*.
35. Peter Laurie gives the following example: 'As late as 1960, Neil Carter, a part-time youth leader with six years' experience in Huddersfield, was sacked because he let his teenage members rock and roll, play billiards, table tennis and darts. The County Youth Service is reported to have said: "The teenagers should be encouraged to take part in handicrafts, classical music and could enter the drama festivals we organise." ' *The Teenage Revolution*, p. 43. Ray Gosling's autobiographical *Sum Total*, London, Faber & Faber, 1962, was written after the failure of his attempt (at the age of twenty-one) to organise a very different sort of youth club.
36. See Victor Perkins, 'Clive Donner and Some People', *Movie*, no. 3, September 1962, pp. 22–5, for a perceptive account of the film.
37. Tommy Steele is essentially a 1950s phenomenon, though he starred in Paramount's unsuccessful adaptation of his stage show *Half a Sixpence* (1967) and *Where's Jack?* (1968), in which his sunny charm is well matched against Stanley Baker's dark malevolence. See Colin MacInnes, 'The Pied Piper from Bermondsey', *Encounter*, December 1957, reproduced in *England, Half English*,

306

for a sympathetic assessment of Steele as a pop singer. For the significance of late 50s/early 60s English pop stars, see Ray Gosling's 'Dream Boy', *New Left Review*, no. 3, May–June 1960, pp. 30–4, reprinted in *Screen Education*, no. 12, January–February 1962, pp. 6–12.
38. Cliff Richard made two more feature films, *Finders Keepers* (1966, d. Sidney Hayers) and *Take Me High* (1974, d. David Askey), which were much more modestly successful.
39. Nik Cohn, *Pop from the Beginning*, London, Weidenfeld & Nicolson, 1969.
40. Robert Hewison's figures concisely sum up this explosion of British pop music: 'Between 1960 and 1963 only ten records by British artists were bestsellers in the U.S.; between 1964 and 1967 there were 173, 25 of them by the Beatles.' *Too Much*, p. 66.
41. Peter Laurie, *The Teenage Revolution*, p. 104.
42. Nik Cohn dismisses Tommy Steele: 'He was that all-time showbiz cliché, the lovable cockney, always merry and bright. He had turned into a pop Max Bygraves.' It is instructive to compare *A Hard Day's Night* with *It's All Happening* (1963) which – despite a script from Wolf Rilla's old collaborator Leigh Vance and direction by Don Sharp – has Tommy in a Max Bygraves-like role as an ex-Barnados Home boy putting on a show with Russ Conway, the George Mitchell Minstrels and long forgotten balladeers Johnnie de Little and Dick Kallman to raise money for similarly deprived children.
43. Ray Brooks in *Some People* (and, in 1966, *Cathy Come Home*), Michael Crawford in Philip Leacock's *The War Lover* (1962).
44. *Help!*, made in colour in 1965, is full of visually impressive jokes but the character actors – Leo McKern, Eleanor Bron, Victor Spinetti, Roy Kinnear – look uncomfortable in a plot that is too camped up to have any substance, and the Beatles themselves retreat almost into anonymity. *Magical Mystery Tour* (1967), which Lester had nothing to do with, has four good songs ('The Fool on the Hill', 'I Am the Walrus', 'Blue Jay Way' and 'Your Mother Should Know') but it is technically on the level of an expensive home movie.
45. The best attempt to treat Boorman as an auteur is Michel Ciment's *John Boorman*, London, Faber & Faber, 1986, but even Ciment has to work hard to extrapolate significance from Boorman's films.

7. SWINGING LONDON
1. Piri Halasz, 'You Can Walk Across it on the Grass', *Time*, 15 April 1966, p. 32.
2. Jeff Nuttall, *Bomb Culture*, London, Paladin, p. 40.
3. See Steve Humphries and John Taylor, *The Making of Modern London 1945–1985*, London, Sidgwick & Jackson, 1986, for the changing face of London; Alan Sked and Chris Cook, *Post-War Britain: A Political History*, Harmondsworth, Penguin, 1979, p. 119, for government housing targets
4. The Moors Murders troubled the libertarian left as well as the traditionalist right. See Jeff Nuttall, *Bomb Culture*, pp. 127–30.
5. Sidney Poitier considered that he had been allocated an 'offensively meagre "take it or leave it" budget'. See *This Life*, London, Hodder & Stoughton, 1980, pp. 283–6.
6. *To Sir, With Love* grossed $19.1 million in the US market compared to, for example, *Help!*'s $5.33 million, *Alfie*'s $8.5 million, *From Russia With Love*'s $9.8 million and *Tom Jones*'s $16.95 million.
7. Peter Laurie, *The Teenage Revolution*, London, Anthony Blond, 1965, p. 54.
8. Arthur Marwick, *British Society Since 1945*, Harmondsworth, Penguin, 1982, pp. 117, 173, 175.
9. Elizabeth Wilson, *Only Halfway to Paradise*, London, Tavistock, 1980, p. 110.

10. The phrase is Philip French's, from 'The Alphaville of Admass', *Sight and Sound*, Summer 1966, p. 108, which is useful for *Alfie*'s history before it was filmed. Two other Bill Naughton plays were filmed in the 60s – *Honeymoon Deferred* (as *The Family Way*, 1966, d. Roy Boulting) and *Spring and Port Wine* (1970, d. Peter Hammond) – and they show him to be in the wry, moral northern tradition of Harold Brighouse and J. B. Priestley. But in one of his short stories, 'The Little Welsh Girl' in *Late Night on Watling Street*, London, MacGibbon & Kee, 1959, he had explored the relationship of two Elephant and Castle spivs with a naive country girl who is the prototype for Annie (Jane Asher) in *Alfie*.

11. Isabel Quigly, *Spectator*, 1 April 1966.

12. *Time*, 2 September 1966.

13. Alexander Walker, *Hollywood, England*, London, Harrap, 1986, p. 262.

14. Reviews of *Smashing Time* tended to be short and condescending. The best exceptions are Margaret Hinxman in the *Sunday Telegraph* (3 December 1967) and Michael Billington in *The Times* (28 December 1967), which express guarded approval. See *Evening Standard*, 29 December 1967, for Alexander Walker's review. Bruce Lacey, who also plays the trendy pie-shop owner, was a founder member of the Alberts, famous for their 'Evening of British Rubbish', as well as the inventor of the ingeniously destructive automata who run amok in *Smashing Time*.

15. *What's New Pussycat?* (1965) was American-financed and shot in Paris but its probing at the boundaries of the sexually permissible makes it comparable to the Swinging London films. See Mark Shivas and Ian Cameron's interview with Donner, 'What's New Pussycat?', *Movie*, no. 14, Autumn 1965, pp. 12–16. In Gordon Gow's interview with Clive Donner, he claimed that 'the notion of Swinging London' was 'anathema to me'. 'The Urge of Some People', *Films and Filming*, July 1969, p. 7.

16. 'The Urge of Some People', pp. 7–8. Geoffrey Gorer, 'The Perils of Hypergamy', *New Society*, 4 May 1957, p. 568.

17. Robin Wood and Ian Cameron, *Antonioni*, London, Studio Vista, 1968, p. 138.

18. Penelope Gilliatt, 'The Spectre of the Shrinking Brainpan', *New Yorker*, 27 April 1968.

19. See Bill Harding, *The Films of Michael Winner*, London, Frederick Muller, 1978, pp. 42–8, for an enthusiastic assessment of *I'll Never Forget What's 'Is Name*. Wendy Craig's performance in the film, coupled with that of Sarah Miles in *Lady Caroline Lamb*, suggests that *The Servant* might have worked better if their roles had been reversed. But in the light of *Performance* and *Death in Venice*, one might say the same about James Fox and Dirk Bogarde.

20. According to *Kinematograph Weekly*, 14 December 1968, p. 6, there were four British films in the top ten general releases of the year: *Up the Junction*, *Poor Cow*, *Here We Go Round the Mulberry Bush* and *Carry on Doctor*. The *Kine Weekly* is an unreliable source for box-office returns after the retirement of Josh Billings in 1963, but there is little doubt that the four films mentioned here were commercially very successful.

21. *Up the Junction* was photographed by Arthur Lavis, who had brought a documentary realism to Terence Fisher's *The Earth Dies Screaming*. His garish colour on *Up the Junction* contrasts with Brian Probyn's irrepressibly romantic photography on *Poor Cow*, where even the most sordid slums look picturesque. (Loach would have preferred to make the film in black and white.) Probyn's photography in Collinson's next film, *The Long Day's Dying* – impressionistic, blurry, hand-held – is absolutely appropriate.

22. Pauline Kael, *Going Steady*, London, Temple Smith, 1970, p. 25.

23. *Variety*, 20 November 1968; *Hollywood Reporter*, 12 November 1968. After it

had been greeted with jeers by the audience at Cannes, few critics were prepared to defend *Joanna*, the honourable exceptions being Gordon Gow in *Films and Filming*, Hollis Alpert in the *Saturday Review*, and more surprisingly both Margaret Hinxman and Eric Shorter in the *Daily Telegraph*.

24. Victor Davis, *Daily Express*, 13 May 1968, claimed that *Joanna* exposed 'the King's Road crowd as beautiful, hollow lifewasters' and quoted Sarne: 'I am showing the aimlessness and pointlessness – and also the cures – so that we can live life *today*. ' In *Films and Filming*, December 1968, p. 53, Sarne, a writer, actor and pop singer (best known for his pop hit 'Come Outside') was quoted perhaps more accurately as wishing to show 'an environment I know well, the world of artists and criminals and the idle, aimless society which makes up the metropolitan scene.'

25. R. Gilbert, 'London's Other Underground', *Town*, March 1967. Surprisingly film-makers paid little attention to the Underground. Peter Whitehead, like Don Levy and Raymond Durgnat one of Thorold Dickinson's protégés from the Slade School of Art, made two evocative documentaries: *Wholly Communion* (1966), a *cinéma vérité* account of the Poetry Conference at the Albert Hall of June 1965; and *Tonite Lets All Make Love in London* (1967), in which, by interviewing Julie Christie, Mick Jagger, David Hockney, Michael Caine, Edna O'Brien and Andrew Oldham, Whitehead attempted to find out what it was that made London so appealing. There was the Beatles' psychedelic fairy-tale *Yellow Submarine* (1969) and *Magical Mystery Tour* (1967), but narrative films about late 60s youth culture – drugs, squatting, alternative life-styles – hardly got beyond low-budget efforts like John Pearse's *Moviemakers* (1971) and Barney Platts-Mills's *Private Road* (1971). There are glimpses of hippy high-life in London and Tangiers in Donald Cammell's *Duffy* (1968, d. Robert Parrish), but its hero (James Coburn) is more of a sharp 50s hipster than a flower-power hippy, and only in *Performance* was there an attempt to explore the inner world of the alternative culture.

26. Walter Lassally sees the film 'despite its many faults as a better mirror of the "Swinging Sixties" than such films as *Smashing Time* or *Here We Go Round the Mulberry Bush*'; and points out that 'Mike was closer to the core of that society than the directors of those films were, and this more than made up for his lack of directorial experience.' *Itinerant Cameraman*, London, John Murray, 1987, p. 111.

27. A number of other films which deal with women and romance might be included here except that they have little relevance to Swinging London. Guy Green's *Pretty Polly* (1967) looks old-fashioned (it is based on a Noël Coward story and set mainly in Singapore), but there is a refreshing honesty about the relationship between Hayley Mills and Shashi Kapoor. Jack Cardiff's *Girl on a Motorcycle* (1968) is visually his most ambitious colour film since *Black Narcissus*, but such is the arty pretentiousness of Ronald Duncan's script that he seems uncertain whether he is supposed to be making pretty picturebook pornography like *Emmanuelle* and *Bilitis* or a deep study of perverse sexuality like *Bad Timing*. *Take a Girl Like Me* (1970) – directed by Jonathan Miller, with a script by George Melly from a novel by Kingsley Amis, and starring Hayley Mills and Oliver Reed – has fascinating ingredients, but they mix into a disappointing film.

28. Barbara Ferris had been Sarah Miles's flighty schoolmate in *Term of Trial* and played a similar though more sympathetically viewed character in *Sparrows Can't Sing* before becoming a sort of poor man's 'Darling' as the pin-up heroine of *Catch Us If You Can*. Oskar Werner was already a well-established Viennese stage actor before reaching an international audience as one of Jeanne Moreau's lovers in *Jules et Jim*.

29. Critical reception of *A Touch of Love* was generally favourable, that of *A Nice Girl Like Me* contemptuously dismissive.
30. Desmond Davis made five films in the 60s – *The Girl With Green Eyes*, *The Uncle*, *I Was Happy Here*, *Smashing Time* and *A Nice Girl Like Me* – which are sufficiently consistent and original to qualify him as at least a minor auteur.
31. Jeff Nuttall, *Bomb Culture*, p. 7.
32. Watkins himself expressed dissatisfaction with the ending: 'There is absolutely no doubt that inadvertently – and I think that it is alone of my films in falling into this trap, at least I hope it's alone of my films – it does have a certain dismissal of the public which I very much regret now. I think if I were ever to make that film again, the only thing I would change would be the last few minutes.' Quoted by Joseph A. Gomez, *Peter Watkins*, Boston, Twayne, 1979, p. 84.
33. Nina Hibbin, *Morning Star*, 29 April 1967.
34. See Alexander Walker, *Hollywood, England*, pp. 350–1, for Rank's attitude to *Privilege*.
35. Quoted by David Robinson, 'Shooting If', *Sight and Sound*, Summer 1968, p. 131.
36. David Robinson, 'Shooting If', p. 111; the most perceptive reviews of *If. . . .* are by Gavin Millar in *Sight and Sound*, Winter 1968–9, pp. 42–3, and Paul Mayersberg in *New Society*, 19 December 1968, p. 923. For more detailed accounts and assessments see Jeffrey Richards, 'The Revolt of the Young', *Best of British*, Jeffrey Richards and Tony Aldgate (eds.), Oxford, Basil Blackwell, 1983, and Elizabeth Sussex, *Lindsay Anderson*, London, Studio Vista, 1969.
37. Eric Rhode, 'The British Cinema in the Seventies', *Listener*, 14 August 1969, p. 203. Rhode's article – along with Philip French's witty 'The Alphaville of Admass', *Sight and Sound*, Summer 1966, John Russell Taylor's 'Larking Back', *Sight and Sound*, Spring 1968, and David Robinson's introduction to his 'Case Histories of the Next Renascence', *Sight and Sound*, Winter 1968–9 – seem to be wrapped up in the fantasy world of the Swinging London films they attack. Thomas Elsaesser's 'Between Style and Ideology', *Monogram*, no. 3, 1972, is more substantial, but like Victor Perkins's polemic in the first issue of *Movie*, it is so negative in its approach to British cinema that it makes unrewarding reading. See Barry Curtis, *Morgan, A Suitable Case for Treatment*, unpublished Polytechnic of Central London M.A. thesis, 1983, pp. 18–28, for an intelligent defence of 60s film style.

8. OTHER WORLDS

1. Jean-Paul Török, 'H-Pictures (II)', *Positif*, July 1961, p. 49.
2. David Pirie, *A Heritage of Horror*, London, Gordon Fraser, 1973, p. 9.
3. Lawrence Alloway, 'Monster Films', *Encounter*, January 1960, p. 70.
4. Derek Hill, 'The Face of Horror', *Sight and Sound*, Winter 1959–60, p. 9.
5. The other vital factor in Hammer's success is Peter Cushing, a flexible, subtle actor who brings something new to each of his prolific film performances.
6. There is now a certain irony in the fact that directors with a flashy, obtrusive style like Tony Richardson, John Guillermin, Lee Thompson and Basil Dearden became associated with social realism while Fisher, with his precise, subtle style, should become Britain's best director of horror films. Basil Dearden had in fact worked on *Halfway House* and *Dead of Night*, and his last film, *The Man Who Haunted Himself*, is a sort of return (a very disappointing one) to those roots. Lee Thompson made the not very successful *Eye of the Devil*, and another director from the same school, Sidney Furie, directed *Dr Blood's Coffin* and *The Snake Woman* before turning, for a time, to social realism. Other horror

directors – Freddie Francis, Don Sharp, John Gilling – are less restrained than Fisher, but it was not until the early 70s that the rootless, restless, gimmicky style, by then associated with Michael Winner, Silvio Narizzano and Peter Collinson, made serious inroads into the horror film.

7. Pirie, *A Heritage of Horror*, p. 51. The whole of the first issue of *Midi-Minuit Fantastique*, May–June 1967, was devoted to Terence Fisher, but most English-speaking writers remained hostile. Carlos Clarens writes about 'Terence Fisher's pedestrian direction', *Horror Movies – An Illustrated Survey*, p. 174; John Brosnan thinks 'his directing style has always been static (he rarely moves the camera)', *The Horror People*, London, Macdonald and Jane's, 1976, p. 110; Ivan Butler complains of his 'excesses of sensationalism' and manages to dismiss his oeuvre in a couple of pages, *Horror in the Cinema*, New Jersey, A. S. Barnes and Co., 1979, p. 55; and as late as 1986 Leslie Halliwell describes Fisher as a 'competent journeyman', *The Dead That Walk*, London, Grafton, 1986, p. 58. More enlightened opinions can be found in 'Horror is My Business', an interview with Fisher by John Cutts and Raymond Durgnat in *Films and Filming*, July 1964, pp. 7–8; 'The Fruitation of Terence Fisher', an interview by G. R. Parfitt in *Little Shoppe of Horrors*, no. 3, February 1974, pp. 49–62; two articles by Harry Ringel, 'The Horrible Hammer Films of Terence Fisher' in *Take One*, May 1973, pp. 8–12, and 'Terence Fisher: The Human Side' in *Cine-Fantastique*, vol. 4, no. 3, Fall 1975, pp. 7–28; and Pirie, *A Heritage of Horror*, pp. 50–65.

8. Raymond Durgnat and John Cutts, 'Horror is My Business', *Films and Filming*, July 1964, p. 8.

9. The unusually muted colour of *The Curse of Frankenstein*, shot in Technicolor, can be compared with the much more garish Eastman Colour of *The Gypsy and the Gentleman*, *The Hellfire Club*, and Anglo-Amalgamated's trilogy – *Horrors of the Black Museum*, *Peeping Tom* and *Circus of Horrors*.

10. Derek Hill, 'The Face of Horror', p. 7. Hill's film criticism is frequently unperceptive but he played an invaluable role in British film culture through his New Cinema Club, which rescued films like Makavejev's *The Switchboard Operator* and Oshima's *Diary of a Shinjuku Thief* from the oblivion to which the BBFC wanted to consign them.

11. Ibid., p. 9.

12. Coleridge, quoted in D. P. Varma, *The Gothic Flame*, London, Arthur Barker, 1957, p. 131.

13. Varma, quoted in Pirie, *A Heritage of Horror*, p. 42.

14. Lawrence Alloway, 'Monster Films', p. 71.

15. See Colin Heard, 'Hammering the Box Office', *Films and Filming*, June 1969, pp. 17–18, and Vincent Porter, 'The Context of Creativity: Ealing Studios and Hammer Films', in *British Cinema History*, James Curran and Vincent Porter (eds.), London, Weidenfeld and Nicolson, 1983, for Hammer's commercial ethos.

16. Roy Ashton, the make-up man, and Christopher Lee both comment on the disappointing appearance of the Gorgon in 'Hammer: Yesterday, Today and Tomorrow', *Little Shoppe of Horrors*, no. 4, April 1978, pp. 63, 97.

17. The 'John Sansom' credited with the script is Jimmy Sangster. According to his own account, he 'supplied only the original concept as *Disciple of Dracula* many years before and Anthony Hinds revised it into the shooting script used for *Prince of Darkness*'. 'Hammer: Yesterday, Today and Tomorrow', p. 82.

18. Pirie, *A Heritage of Horror*, p. 55.

19. See Denis Gifford, *A Pictorial History of Horror Movies*, Exeter Books, New York, 1984, pp. 192–204, for early British horror films. Sidney Furie's *The Snake Woman* (1960), deals with a similar subject to that of *The Reptile*, but

according to *The Aurum Encyclopedia of Horror*, Phil Hardy, Tom Milne and Paul Willemen (eds.), London, Aurum Press, 1985, it is much inferior.

20. Pirie, *A Heritage of Horror*, p. 124.
21. Mario Praz, *The Romantic Agony*, London, Oxford University Press, 1970, p. 26.
22. Paul Willemen, *The Aurum Encyclopedia of Horror*, p. 180. Pirie also gives a fascinating analysis of *Frankenstein Created Woman*, comparing Christina to Keats's Lamia, 'the illusory incarnation of female beauty who has only recently been transformed from her true hideous shape'. *A Heritage of Horror*, p. 77.
23. Francis's distinguished career as a cameraman – in which capacity he still occasionally works – included *Time Without Pity*, *Room at the Top*, *Saturday Night and Sunday Morning*, *Sons and Lovers*, *The Innocents* and *Night Must Fall*. His collaboration with Jack Cardiff, another great cameraman turned director, on *Sons and Lovers* won him an Oscar. For its overall visual impact, however, *The Innocents* is his most impressive film. His story sense was somewhat at variance with that of the Hammer formula: 'I was more interested in the love affair between the boy and the girl than with Dracula, he was just a fly in the ointment. Unfortunately much of that was cut out by Hammer and I never had a chance to put it back again.' Brosnan, *The Horror People*, p. 229.
24. *Monthly Film Bulletin*, December 1968, p. 200. The same ill-judged comment is repeated in the generally more discerning *Aurum Encyclopedia of Horror*. See Gary Dorst, 'Dracula in Retrospect', *Little Shoppe of Horrors*, no. 4, April 1978, p. 115, for the commercial reception of *Dracula Has Risen from the Grave*.
25. Stephen R. Pickard, 'The Works of Jack Curtis', a useful history of production at Bray which lists the studios and locations where all Hammer's films were made. Jack Curtis was Hammer's supervisory electrician. *Little Shoppe of Horrors*, no. 3, February 1974, pp. 8–11.
26. See 'A Tribute to Bernard Robinson, 1912–1970', *Little Shoppe of Horrors*, no. 2, March 1973, pp. 8–11; and 'Hammer: Yesterday, Today and Tomorrow', *Little Shoppe of Horrors*, no. 4, April 1978, pp. 69–75.
27. Harry Ringel, 'The Horrible Hammer Films of Terence Fisher', *Take One*, May 1973, p. 16.
28. Pirie, *A Heritage of Horror*, pp. 20–1.
29. Edward Judd was something of a favourite in British science fiction films, beginning his career with a small part in *X The Unknown* (1956), progressing through Val Guest's *The Day the Earth Caught Fire* (1961) and the best of the Jules Verne/H. G. Wells adaptations, *First Men in the Moon* (1964), to *Invasion* (1966) and *Island of Terror* (1966). As well as his television work, Alan Bridges was responsible for *Act of Murder* (1964), an hour-long featurette for Anglo-Amalgamated which was slipped into the Edgar Wallace series when genuine Wallace material was running out. It is a pleasingly complex little film and might be preferred to some of Bridges's later films like *The Hireling* (1973) and *Return of the Soldier* (1982).
30. Pirie, *A Heritage of Horror*, p. 140. The predecessor of Hammer's exotic cycle is Don Chaffey's excellent imitation Italian epic, *Jason and the Argonauts* (1963), which like *One Million Years BC* relied on Ray Harryhausen for its special effects.
31. Phil Hardy (ed.), *The Aurum Encyclopedia of Science Fiction*, London, Aurum Press, 1984, is an invaluable guide to the genre. David Sylvester's interesting article, 'The Anglicisation of Outer Space', *Encounter*, January 1956, pp. 69–72, was unfortunately written too early to deal with anything later than *The Quatermass Xperiment*. *Quatermass and the Pit* was originally intended for production in 'December 1963 with Freddie Francis directing: Brian O'Brien, 'Backing the System', *Films and Filming*, September 1963, p. 51. See Alexander

Walker, *Stanley Kubrick Directs*, London, Abacus, 1972, pp. 224–67, and François Truffaut, 'Journal of *Fahrenheit 451*', *Cahiers du Cinéma in English*, no. 5, pp. 11–22, for more sympathetic accounts of *2001* and *Fahrenheit 451*.

32. Losey apparently intended Freya to be shot from one of the helicopters, making her death an impersonal state murder. I agree with Hammer that it is more poignant and makes more sense for Bernard to have to shoot her himself. Michel Ciment, *Conversations With Losey*, London, Methuen, 1985, pp. 196–206. See Raymond Durgnat, *A Mirror for England*, pp. 258–9, and Paul Mayersberg, 'Contamination', *Movie*, no. 9, May 1963, pp. 32–4, for perceptive interpretations of *The Damned*.

33. Continental critics, particularly Jean-Paul Török, were fascinated by these films, though the versions released in France were much less anaemic: 'The film by Robert Baker and Monty Berman (*Jack the Ripper*, 1958) seems to have the sole aim of getting its audience simply to react with disgust. A frantic accumulation of sordid details, the deliberate choice of the cast in particular, quite appalling to watch – none of this is designed for visual pleasure, and one might ask with some misgivings just what kind of audience the film had in mind. With this exhibition of functional horror, which at bottom aims to provoke nausea and repugnance, a zero degree of horror is arrived at.' *Positif*, July 1961, p. 45.

34. Pirie, *A Heritage of Horror*, p. 57; *The Aurum Encyclopedia of Horror*, p. 174. James Hill, the director, came out of documentaries and his first significant feature was a tenaciously literal adaptation of Arnold Wesker's *The Kitchen* (1961), backed by the ACTT. The play is a strange mixture of steamy melodrama and utopian whimsicality and needs a Borzage to bring it to life. Hill's handling of *A Study in Terror* is much better, but he moved on from horror to direct animal/adventure films like *Born Free* (1966), *Captain Nemo and the Underwater City* (1969) and *An Elephant Called Slowly* (1970).

35. Paul Willemen, *The Aurum Encyclopedia of Horror*, p. 188. The puzzled attitude of the mainstream critics at Polanski's willingness to work within genre conventions is best expressed in Tom Milne's comment that the film is 'an engaging oddity', 'long stretches . . . might have been lifted intact from any Hammer horror': *Monthly Film Bulletin*, January 1969, pp. 4–5. For Martin Ransohoff see David McClintick, *Indecent Exposure*, New York, William Morrow, 1982. Virginia Wright Wexman gives a fascinating analysis of *Dance of the Vampire*'s sexual tensions in *Roman Polanski*, Boston, Twayne, 1985, pp. 57–63. See also Ivan Butler, *The Cinema of Roman Polanski*, London/New York, Zwemmer/Barnes, 1970, pp. 117–142.

36. Roger Corman, quoted in *The Movie World of Roger Corman*, Philip di Franco (ed.), New York/London, Chelsea House, 1979, p. 34.

37. *Monthly Film Bulletin*, December 1964, p. 173. *The Tomb of Ligeia* is best analysed by David Pirie in *Roger Corman – the Millennic Vision*, David Will and Paul Willemen (eds.), Edinburgh Film Festival in association with *Cinema* magazine, 1970, pp. 62–6.

38. Correspondence between Michael Carreras and Max Rosenberg discussing Subotsky's script is reproduced in 'Hammer: Yesterday, Today and Tomorrow', *Little Shoppe of Horrors*, no. 4, April, 1978, p. 87. See 'Amicus: Two's a Company', *Little Shoppe of Horrors*, no. 2, March 1973, p. 21, for Subotsky's comments on *City of the Dead*.

39. See David Pirie, 'New Blood', *Sight and Sound*, Spring 1971, pp. 73–5. *The Shuttered Room* is something of a curate's egg but the good parts – Greene's ability to create suspense with Ken Hodges's constantly moving camera and Carol Lynley's china doll fragility – more than make up for a clumsy subplot about the distinctly unsupernatural threat posed by Oliver Reed and his gang of backwoods hooligans. Greene was also responsible for the suspense thriller *I*

Start Counting (1969), which I have been unable to track down. *I Monster* has an interesting and unusual score by Carl Davis and a sensitive, restrained performance by Christopher Lee, but the film had a troubled production history and it is marred by cardboard sets and a meandering storyline.

40. Robin Wood, 'In Memoriam: Michael Reeves', *Movie*, no. 17, p. 5.
41. Ibid., p. 6.
42. Two critics not noted for their sympathy towards British cinema were nevertheless sufficiently acute to pick up on Reeves's talent. John Russell Taylor – the writer of the letter which provoked Lindsay Anderson's article 'Stand Up! Stand Up! and the 'commitment' debate – gave sympathetic treatment to *The Sorcerers* and wrote a long intelligent review of *Witchfinder General*, provocatively but legitimately comparing its passion and intensity to that of *This Sporting Life*: *The Times*, 15 June 1967, 11 May 1968. Robin Wood wrote an exemplary piece of auteur criticism, 'Michael Reeves: In Memoriam' in *Movie*, no. 17, Winter 1969–70, pp. 2–6. There is also a useful section in Pirie, *A Heritage of Horror*, pp. 145–55.
43. Huntington had directed *This Man is Dangerous* and *Tower of Terror* at Welwyn, though his best film is James Mason's *The Upturned Glass* (1947).
44. From their subsequent careers, the creative force on *Satan's Skin* would seem to have been the writer, Robert Wynne-Simmons, rather than the director, Piers Haggard. Haggard's next venture into horror was *Venom* (1981), an unscary melodrama about a black mamba bringing nemesis to an inefficient kidnap gang, though in the intervening years he had shown considerable ingenuity in directing Dennis Potter's *Pennies from Heaven* and the 1979 television revival of *Quatermass*. Wynne-Simmons went on to produce, write and direct a Channel 4 film, *Outcasts* (1984), which, with more sympathy than *Satan's Skin*, deals with magic as an integral part of peasant culture.
45. Tzvetan Todorov, *The Fantastic*, Ithaca and New York, Cornell University Press, 1975, pp. 46–7.
46. There is a useful discussion of *The Innocents* in Gordon Gow's interview with Jack Clayton, 'The Way Things Are', *Films and Filming*, April 1974, pp. 11–14. Freddie Francis contradicts the usual view that the film's strange happenings are the products of Miss Giddens's fevered imaginings in his interview with John Brosnan: 'We had Deborah Kerr, a brilliant actress but always absolutely charming and no one could ever think she was slightly bonkers, so in the film all the suspicion fell on the children – whereas having read *The Turn of the Screw* one doesn't know whether it is the governess who is a bit strange or the children.' Brosnan, *The Horror People*, pp. 227–8.
47. By a sad coincidence, Basil Dearden himself was killed in a car crash in 1971, shortly after *The Man Who Haunted Himself* was released.
48. Fisher's world view is clearly mapped out in an interview with Harry Ringel: 'I have endeavoured, in the actors' performances and in the interpretation of the material scene by scene, to underline, wherever possible, that conflict, to bring to the audience's attention this conflict between the power of good and the power of evil. . . . We shall find in the end that evil is merely a mistaken concept for the absence of good. You see, there aren't two powers. There's only one. The power of evil is what we give to it. Of course, it is self-destructive in the end, because it is only given power by its victims, or its opponents. It doesn't have any power of its own. So its power will cease eventually. You know this is the ultimate millennium. But it is important to realise it will come to pass.' 'Terence Fisher: Underlining', *Cine-Fantastique*, vol. 4, no. 3, Fall 1975, pp. 20–2.
49. Tzvetan Todorov, *The Fantastic*, p. 48.
50. Paul Mayersberg, Victor Perkins and Mark Shivas interviewed Seth Holt in 1963, though the transcript was not published until after his death in *Film Dope*,

no. 25, November 1982, pp. 1–5. A fuller interview conducted by Kevin Gough-Yates was published in *Screen*, vol. 10, no. 6, November–December, 1969, pp. 4–23.

51. In its central theme of a girl being manipulated into madness *Taste of Fear* shares themes with Freddie Francis's *Nightmare*, and it is interesting to compare the two films. Holt's heroine (Susan Strasberg), despite being crippled, is never sexually vulnerable, and though helpless is always resourceful, a fragile but capable heroine. Jennie Linden in *Nightmare* – blonde, frightened, dishevelled – is altogether less in control of the situation and it is only the intervention of outsiders that brings the malefactors to justice. The relationship between Ronald Lewis and Susan Strasberg in *Taste of Fear* is one of misplaced trust, that between Jennie Linden and David Knight in *Nightmare* one of pathetic dependence. Nevertheless, *Taste of Fear* is basically a clever con-trick: it cheats by reworking the plot to provide only temporarily plausible explanations for what has happened. *Nightmare* dips more realistically into madness and the long coda dealing with the disintegrating relationship between the two murderers gives the film a structural and thematic complexity.

52. *Taste of Fear* and *The Servant* were photographed by Douglas Slocombe, *The Nanny* by Harry Waxman and *Night Must Fall* by Freddie Francis, but they share a similar visual style.

53. Robin Wood, *American Nightmare*, Toronto, 1979, p. 10.

54. In contrast to the huge numbers of Mexican and Italian vampires who rivalled Dracula, Hammer had a virtual monopoly over Frankenstein who, apart from any copyright problems, was very much the creation of Peter Cushing. Hammer's own attempt to replace Cushing with Ralph Bates in *The Horror of Frankenstein* failed dismally.

9. EXPLORING THE UNDERWORLD

1. Gavin Lambert, *The Dangerous Edge*, London, Barrie & Jenkins, 1975, p. 269.

2. George Orwell, 'The Decline of the English Murder', *Collected Essays, Journalism and Letters*, vol. 4, Harmondsworth, Penguin, 1980, pp. 124–8.

3. Anglo-Amalgamated's *Scotland Yard*, *Scales of Justice* and Edgar Wallace films dominated the 'B' film market, but surprisingly *The Criminal* seems to be their only feature-length crime film. After the EMI takeover at the end of the decade, Anglo-Amalgamated managing director Nat Cohen was responsible for commissioning films like *Get Carter* and *Villain*, as well as Joseph Losey's *The Go-Between*.

4. See Michel Ciment's *Conversations with Losey*, London, Methuen, 1985, pp. 184–9, and Robert Parker, *Rough Justice*, London, Fontana, 1981, p. 188, for the Dimes connection.

5. Robin Wood, 'The Criminal', in *Motion*, no. 6, Autumn 1963, p. 9.

6. Trevor Preston and Jim Goddard's *Parker* (1984) deals with the same sort of themes as *Never Let Go* almost as effectively in a 1980s EEC setting.

7. John Gosling, *The Ghost Squad*, London, W. H. Allen, 1959, p. 11.

8. Fortunately there is a viewing copy of *The Informers* in the National Film Archive.

9. Frederick Woods, 'Take *That* You Swine', *Films and Filming*, August 1959, p. 6.

10. *Monthly Film Bulletin*, December 1961, p. 170.

11. Nevertheless, Independent Artists' record as a production company is an impressive one. Its featurettes (Julian Wintle refused to call them 'B' films) also include Vernon Sewell's *House of Mystery* and John Krish's *The Unearthly Stranger*, and a production programme where *Blind Date*, *This Sporting Life*,

Never Let Go, and *Bitter Harvest* (an attempt to reset Patrick Hamilton's *Twenty Thousand Streets Under the Sky* in the 60s) rub shoulders with *Night of the Eagle* and *Circus of Horrors* deserves more credit than it has so far received. Wintle went on from Independent Artists to co-produce the first four series of *The Avengers*. See Anne Francis, *Julian Wintle: A Memoir*, London, Dukeswood, 1986.

12. The low status of 'B' films means that their survival is erratic. A surprising number have been shown on Channel 4 over the past few years, though of the films from the old-established production/distribution company Butcher's I have only managed to see Terry Bishop's *Life in Danger*, Charles Saunders's *Danger By My Side*, and Peter Maxwell's *Serena*, all of which are interesting, if hardly outstanding. Other Butcher's films, like Lance Comfort's *Breaking Point* (1960) and *Rag Doll* (1960), Francis Searle's *Freedom to Die* (1961) and *Gaolbreak* (1962), Peter Maxwell's *Impact* (1963) and Jim O'Connolly's *The Hijackers* (1963) look worth a glance.

13. Cliff Owen, who began his career directing episodes of *The Third Man* for television, was also responsible for *A Prize of Arms* (1961), a taut, lean film about three men – Stanley Baker, Tom Bell and Helmut Schmid – stealing an army payroll, which is almost too grim to be called a caper film. His subsequent career has been disappointing.

14. Elizabeth Shepherd played Ligeia and Lady Rowena in Corman's *The Tomb of Ligeia* and was to have replaced Honor Blackman (whom she closely resembles) in *The Avengers*. Comparisons can be drawn between *Blind Corner*, *Blind Date* and *Playback*, an Edgar Wallace adaptation directed by Quentin Lawrence for Anglo-Amalgamated in 1962. All three films involve a rich, sophisticated woman sexually ensnaring a young man in order to implicate him in murder. The characters, even the appearance, of Barbara Shelley (in *Blind Corner*), Micheline Presle (in *Blind Date*) and Margit Saad (in *Playback*) are remarkably similar, though it is a measure of the superiority of Losey's film that only in *Blind Date* does the woman become a complex and sympathetic character. William Sylvester found a sort of fame as Doctor Floyd in Kubrick's *2001*, though the part is less interesting than most of his 'B' film roles.

15. The Goons made a wonderful little parody of *Scotland Yard*, *The Case of the Mukkinese Battlehorn*, in 1956 (d. Joseph Stirling).

16. About thirty Wallace films were concurrently made in Germany, and though the Germans came over to make *Traitor's Gate* in 1964 (d. Freddie Francis), there seems to have been no co-operation between the two teams. Jack Nolan lists all the films based on Wallace stories in *Films in Review*, February 1967, pp. 71–85. A letter from Denis Gifford in the following issue adds a further twenty-five films and disqualifies some of the later Merton Park films which use the same format and the same production team but are not based on Wallace stories. Gifford's *The British Film Catalogue* reinstates *Never Mention Murder* and *We Shall See* as Wallace films. But see *Classic Images*, no. 109, July 1984, pp. 24–5; no. 126, December 1985, pp. c27–8; no. 127, January 1986, pp. c17–20; no. 128, February 1986, pp. 47–50, 61, c5, for up-to-date listings of Wallace films, which appear to have a substantial cult following.

17. Charles Crichton's post-Ealing career is due for reassessment. *Floods of Fear* (1958), *The Battle of the Sexes* (1959), *The Boy Who Stole a Million* (1960) and *The Third Secret* (1964) are all interesting films.

18. The story of Tom Bell's fall from grace is part of media mythology. The incident certainly happened: according to Sir John Woolf, Bell, justifiably disappointed at not winning a British Academy Award for his performance in *The L-Shaped Room*, drank too much and interrupted the Duke's speech. Though one might be sceptical about the Duke of Edinburgh's influence on the American-domi-

nated film industry, between *The L-Shaped Room* and *He Who Rides a Tiger*, Bell acted only in the Anglo-American *Ballad in Blue* and the Israeli *Sands of Beersheba* – and he wasn't offered a part in *The Liquidator*, the plot of which features an assassination attempt on the Duke.

19. Uncharismatic though they are, Yates's villains come uncannily close to the 'scrap metal dealers, used car salesmen, greengrocers, antique dealers and property consultants' associated with Bertie Smalls, the successful bank robber turned supergrass of the early 70s. See John Ball, Lewis Chester and Roy Perrott, *Cops and Robbers*, London, 1978, p. 24.

20. *The Trygon Factor* (1966) is interesting as a transition film. According to Richard Gordon in *Classic Images*, no. 128, February 1986, p. c5, it is based on an Edgar Wallace story. Produced by Rialto Film, the German company responsible for over thirty Wallace films in the 60s, the film is virtually a star vehicle for Stewart Granger, woefully miscast as Superintendent Cooper-Smith of Scotland Yard, but the main interest lies in the elaborate criminal operation organised by a group of ruthless nuns.

21. The role of women in the Bond novels is dealt with in some depth by Tony Bennett: 'In responding to the challenge posed by the girl, putting her back into place beneath him (both literally and metaphorically), Bond functions as an agent of sexist ideology, refurbishing its impaired structure by quelling the disturbance within it.' 'James Bond as Popular Hero', *Politics, Ideology and Popular Culture*, Milton Keynes, Open University Press, 1982. See also Tony Bennett and Janet Woollacott, *Bond and Beyond*, London, Macmillan, 1987. Alternative analyses of the Bond phenomenon can be found in Kingsley Amis, *The James Bond Dossier*, London, Jonathan Cape, 1965, and David Cannadine, 'James Bond and the Decline of England', *Encounter*, September 1979, pp. 46–55.

22. Penelope Houston, '007', *Sight and Sound*, Winter 1964–5, pp. 14–16.

23. Penelope Houston, *Sight and Sound*, Autumn 1962, p. 197; Peter John Dyer, *Monthly Film Bulletin*, 1962, p. 132; John Coleman, *New Statesman*, 9 October 1962; Derek Hill, *Scene*, 5 October 1962. Dilys Powell, *Sunday Times*, 7 October 1962, and Alexander Walker, *Evening Standard*, 4 October 1962, were much more positive.

24. 'Arkadin', *Sight and Sound*, Winter 1963–4, p. 31. The honeymoon continued with *Goldfinger* but *Thunderball* and *You Only Live Twice* were much less favourably received and George Lazenby's performance in *On Her Majesty's Secret Service* gave the critics the opportunity to be openly derisive. I prefer *Thunderball* and *You Only Live Twice*, untidy though they are, to *From Russia With Love* and *Goldfinger* and consider *Dr No* by far the best. *On Her Majesty's Secret Service* still seems to me a very dull film despite its ascension to cult status.

25. Television was much more on the ball. *Danger Man* (1959–62), *The Rat-Catchers* (1961–3) and *The Avengers* (1961–8) actually predate Bond, and the American series *The Man From UNCLE* was quick to follow in his footsteps. The three Cold War thrillers are *Hide and Seek* (d. Cy Endfield), *Master Spy* (d. Montgomery Tully), and *The Girl Hunters* (a Mickey Spillane film directed by Roy Rowland).

26. Bruce Merry, *Anatomy of the Spy Thriller*, Dublin, Gill & Macmillan, 1977, p. 60. Though as Bennett and Woollacott point out, there was a distinct shift in the nature of Bond in the transition from novels to films: '. . . he was now made to point in the opposite direction – towards the future rather than the past. Functioning as a figure of modernisation, he became the very model of the tough abrasive professionalism that was allegedly destined to lead Britain into the modern, no illusions, no holds-barred post-imperialist age, a hero of rupture rather than one of tradition.' *Bond and Beyond*, pp. 238–9.

317

27. An exception is Val Guest's *Where the Spies Are* (1965), which ties up its loose plot strands by having a Russian 'peace plane' tour the world dispensing torture and assassination. But it was not a great success and the *Monthly Film Bulletin* complained of a 'sour political note' being introduced into the proceedings.

28. John Le Carré (David Cornwell), 'To Russia, with Greetings', *Encounter*, May 1966, p. 6.

29. Reisz went on to *Isadora*, which makes its radical heroine look ridiculous, Schlesinger to *Far from the Madding Crowd*, though one of his best subsequent productions was a BBC television film, *An Englishman Abroad* (1983), which deals with the Le Carré-ish subject of a meeting between Guy Burgess and the actress Coral Browne in Moscow. There were a number of other left-wing film-makers in Britain, Lindsay Anderson and Ken Loach for example. But most of them would probably have agreed with the *Morning Star* that Le Carré was merely a sophisticated apologist for the Cold War

30. Le Carré himself expresses the opposite position in his reply to the Russian critic Voinov: 'For how long can we defend ourselves – you and we – by methods of this kind and still remain the kind of society that is worth defending?' *Encounter*, May 1966, p. 5.

31. Paul Dehn, 'The Spy Who Came in from the Cold', *Journal of the Society of Film and Television Arts*, no. 24 (*Spies on the Screen*), Summer 1966, p. 13.

32. John Le Carré, *Encounter*, May 1966, p. 6.

33. Bruce Merry, *Anatomy of the Spy Thriller*, p. 235.

34. The novel was originally called *The Berlin Memorandum*. Plot changes also make nonsense of the final sequence where Quiller wanders the deserted streets of Berlin followed by clusters of Oktober's men. In the book he is released in the hope that he will phone home and – as the Berlin telephone exchange has been infiltrated by the Nazis – give away the whereabouts of the British headquarters. In the film Quiller plays a cat and mouse game with Oktober's agents in his search for an unoccupied, unvandalised telephone but as he is obviously not going to reveal anything useful there seems little reason why they don't simply kill him.

35. Franklin Schaffner's *The Double Man* (1967) suffers from the same sort of mechanical quality, though there is little evidence of budget restraint here and the set-pieces – a murderous game of hide and seek in a deserted cable car station, a torchlit ski-run – have a slick Hollywood professionalism rarely matched in British films. As in *The Naked Runner*, a man is manipulated into a nightmare world by the supposed death of his teenage son. But here the son really is dead and the father, Dan Slater (Yul Brynner), a CIA agent, is so cold and ruthless that the brainwashed Russian double who is to take his place is exposed by his inability to emulate Slater's inhumanity. Intriguing though this is, it leaves few opportunities for emotional development.

36. *Modesty Blaise* did have sôme supporters. See David Wilson, *Monthly Film Bulletin*, June 1966, pp. 89–90, and Raymond Durgnat, 'Symbols and Modesty Blaise', *Cinema*, no. 1, December 1968, pp. 2–7.

37. David Greene began his career as an actor, but while touring North America was tempted into television and acquired a reputation as an efficient and ingenious director. In the late 60s he made four films in Britain – *The Shuttered Room*, *Sebastian*, *The Strange Affair* and *I Start Counting* – all of them stylish and original. He then returned to America and television, making only occasional excursions – *Godspell*, *Gray Lady Down* – into theatrical features. See David Robinson, 'Case Histories of the Next Renascence', *Sight and Sound*, Winter 1968–9, p. 39, for Greene's revealing comments on *Sebastian* and *The Strange Affair*.

38. *Observer*, 19 March 1971.

39. Mary Grigg, *The Challenor Affair*, Penguin, Harmondsworth, 1965, p. 126.
40. The most interesting analyses of *Performance* can be found in Jan Dawson's review in *Monthly Film Bulletin*, February 1970, pp. 27–8, and Philip French's article in *Sight and Sound*, Spring 1971, pp. 67–9. Paul Tickle's 'The Irresistible Rise of the Celluloid Villain', *Time Out*, 16 June 1981, pp. 12–13, takes *Performance* as the first real British gangster film, before which he can discern only gruff but kindly bobbies like George Dixon, and juvenile delinquents.

10. FRYING TONIGHT
1. George Orwell, 'The Art of Donald McGill', *Collected Essays, Journalism and Letters*, vol. 2, 1940–1943, Sonia Orwell and Ian Angus (eds.), Harmondsworth, Penguin, 1971, p. 193.
2. See Andy Medhurst, 'Music Hall and British Cinema' in *All Our Yesterdays*, Charles Barr (ed.), London, British Film Institute, 1986, p. 172, and Catherine Lamb, *Pimple: Britain's Greatest Comedian, and his Rivals*, unpublished Sunderland Polytechnic M.A. thesis, 1987.
3. Raymond Durgnat, *A Mirror for England*, London, Faber & Faber, 1970, p. 44.
4. My figures are from Denis Gifford's *The British Film Catalogue 1895–1985*, Newton Abbot, David & Charles, 1986. Gifford includes *A Home of Your Own*, the first and best of a series of almost silent slapstick shorts, Desmond Davis's *The Uncle*, which did not get a cinema release and is only marginally a comedy, and *The Rattle of a Simple Man*, which despite the presence of Harry H. Corbett is a melodrama/social problem film with a few comic touches.
5. Alexander Walker, *Hollywood, England*, London, Harrap, 1986, p. 104.
6. Robert Hamer, like his brother-in-law Seth Holt, seems to have been driven to an early death by the frustrations and disappointments involved in working in the British film industry. Hamer died in 1963 while working on the Boultings' *Rotten to the Core*, aged fifty-two; Holt died in 1971 while working on Hammer's *Blood from the Mummy's Tomb*, aged forty-nine.
7. Raymond Durgnat, *A Mirror for England*, p. 163.
8. Bill Altria lists *Ladies Who Do* among the forty or so top money-makers of 1964 in his 'Survey of Success', *Kinematograph Weekly*, 17 December 1964, p. 9, though this is by no means an infallible guide.
9. Roy Kinnear, though part of the *That Was the Week That Was* team, emerged through Joan Littlewood's Theatre Workshop and had roots in Wigan not Cambridge.
10. See Roger Wilmut, *Tony Hancock: 'Artiste'*, London, Bibliophile Books, 1986, pp. 115–16, 130–4.
11. See Philip Oakes, *Tony Hancock*, London, Woburn/Futura, 1975, pp. 70–86.
12. See Michael Sellers, *P.S. I Love You*, London, Collins, 1981, pp. 26–34, and Alexander Walker, *Peter Sellers*, London, Weidenfeld & Nicolson, 1981, pp. 11–67, for Sellers's early history.
13. Doug McVay, 'One Man Band', *Films and Filming*, May 1963, p. 45.
14. Ibid., p. 47.
15. This predictability could itself become a source of humour when used by sophisticated comics like Leslie Phillips and Terry-Thomas, as for example in *Carry On Constable* when new recruit P.C. Potter (Phillips) is exposed by a passing debutante as 'Potty Poodles', last seen at Fruity Fothergill's pyjama party, or in *Our Man in Marrakesh* when the fearsome Sheik El Caid (Thomas), whose veiled warriors have plucked Senta Berger and Tony Randall out of the desert to face what they expect to be a fate worse than death, drawls in his impeccable Eton and Oxford accent, 'I say, jolly nice of you to drop in, you're just in time for tea.'

16. Alexander Walker, *Peter Sellers*, p. 90.
17. Ibid., p. 70.
18. Ibid., p. 99. Sellers's son Michael further testifies to his father's violent unpredictability when working on *Never Let Go*, and adds the significant rider that 'Unfortunately these rows continued long after Dad had finished playing Lionel Meadows.' Michael Sellers, *P.S. I Love You*, pp. 63–4.
19. Sellers's career was also affected by his health. He had a serious heart attack in 1964 while working on Billy Wilder's *Kiss Me Stupid*, and he died, before he was fifty-five, in 1980.
20. Richard Dacre, *Trouble in Store: Norman Wisdom, a Career in Comedy*, Dumfries, T. C. Farries, 1991, p. 5.
21. David Robinson, 'A New Clown', *Sight and Sound*, April–June 1954, p. 213.
22. *There Was a Crooked Man* was also notable for Susannah York's debut as a surprisingly demure, dark-haired heroine. After the film's disappointing performance at the box-office, Burge returned to the theatre, though he did film his own production of *Uncle Vanya* (1962) and John Dexter's production of *Othello* (1965).
23. Wisdom to the *Evening News*, quoted by Richard Dacre, *Trouble in Store*, p. 42.
24. Quoted by Richard Dacre, *Trouble in Store*, p. 46. According to Keith Robertson, a long-serving executive with Rank Film Distributors, 'We never had a failure with Norman Wisdom's comedies. We put each one out on Boxing Day and it had got its cost back before we started making the next one in the summer.' Interview with author, 8 January 1986.
25. Charlie Drake's films have been dealt with so perfunctorily because I have not been able to see any of them. There are no viewing copies in the National Film Archive and in the five years I have been working on this book none of them has turned up on television. Regrettably even Raymond Durgnat gives Drake only a couple of mentions (*A Mirror for England*, London, Faber & Faber, pp. 173, 176) though his review of *The Cracksman* (*Films and Filming*, September 1963) is perceptive and sympathetic. John Hill draws an interesting comparison between *Operation Bullshine* (1959, d. Gilbert Gunn), where the comedy 'derives from the incompetence of women to adapt to military circumstances', and *Petticoat Pirates*, where it 'results from their successful confounding of male expectations by proving their worth in taking over a warship.' *Sex, Class and Realism*, London, British Film Institute, 1986, p. 170. But in fairness to *Operation Bullshine* one should note that its female leads – Carol Lesley and Barbara Murray – are a considerable advance on the shiny lipsticked dummies of its predecessor, *Girls at Sea* (1958, d. Gilbert Gunn).
26. Bob Monkhouse, who had played the romantic lead in *Carry on Sergeant*, did not appear in any further *Carry On* films, perhaps because of Rogers and Thomas's insistence on no particular actor getting star billing. Producer Bertram Ostrer launched a rival series which starred Monkhouse and relied on *Carry On* stalwarts like Kenneth Connor, Eric Barker and Charles Hawtrey for support, but it only ran to two films – *Dentist in the Chair* (1960, d. Don Chaffey) and *Dentist on the Job* (1961, d. Pennington Richards).
27. Peter Rogers and Gerald Thomas were amazingly prolific during their peak period between 1959 and 1965, turning out *Please Turn Over* (1959), *Watch Your Stern* (1960), *Twice Round the Daffodils* and *The Iron Maiden* (1962), *Nurse on Wheels* (1963) and *The Big Job* (1965) as well as ten *Carry On* films.
28. Ian Johnson, 'Have the British a Sense of Humour?', *Films and Filming*, March 1963, p. 52.
29. Andy Medhurst, 'Music Hall and British Cinema', p. 183.

11. HOLLYWOOD'S ENGLAND

1. Martin Green, *A Mirror for Anglo-Saxons*, London, Longman, 1961, p. 90.
2. *Kinematograph Weekly*, 13 December 1956, p. 79.
3. More parochially British films like *Reach for the Sky* and *The Dam Busters* were much less popular in America than they were in Britain.
4. Herbert J. Gans, in an otherwise useful article, is wrong in claiming that Kitchen Sink films like *Room at the Top* and *Saturday Night and Sunday Morning* 'were financed in varying degrees by American capital, since English investors have been reluctant to do so.' 'Hollywood Films on British Screens', *Social Problems*, vol. 9, no. 4, Spring 1962, p. 327.
5. NFFC Annual Report for year ending 31 March 1970, p. 5.
6. David Robinson, 'Case Histories of the Next Renascence', *Sight and Sound*, Winter 1968–9, p. 36.
7. Such generalisations should always be suspected and even in 1968, the worst year, it might be possible to mount a defence for Gerry and Sylvia Anderson's *Thunderbird 6*, Tony Richardson's *The Charge of the Light Brigade* and, for the really idiosyncratic film buff, Bud Yorkin's *Inspector Clouseau* and Ken Hughes's *Chitty Chitty Bang Bang*; but the other five United Artists films released that year (none of which was made by a British director) – *Attack on the Iron Coast* (d. Paul Wendkos), *Salt and Pepper* (d. Richard Donner), *Play Dirty* (d. André de Toth), *The File of the Golden Goose* (d. Sam Wanamaker) and *Hostile Witness* (d. Ray Milland) – have very few redeeming features.
8. See Bernard F. Dick, *Billy Wilder*, Boston, Twayne, 1980, pp. 139–47, for a detailed and useful analysis of *The Private Life of Sherlock Holmes*.
9. Michael Powell expressed admiration for *The Virgin and the Gypsy*, though it seems to me a predictable BBC-like literary adaptation. See also Neil Sinyard, *Filming Literature*, London, Croom Helm, 1986, pp. 50–3. Sinyard hasn't much time for any of the Lawrence adaptations.
10. Quoted by Ian Christie in his review of *Women in Love*, *Sight and Sound*, Winter 1969–70, p. 50. See also John Weightman, 'Trifling With the Dead', *Encounter*, January 1970, pp. 50–3, for a more protracted attack on Russell's treatment of Lawrence.
11. George Ornstein died in September 1978. There are obituaries on the BFI Library microfiche for him, but the best source for his role in the British film industry is Alexander Walker, *Hollywood, England*, London, Harrap, 1986.
12. Collinson's decline might have been due to the unpropitious climate for creative film-making in the 70s. He died of cancer in December 1980, aged forty-four. Greene's American television films, such as *Friendly Fire* and *Rehearsal for Murder*, have been consistently interesting.
13. *The Long Day's Dying* did win first prize at the San Sebastian Film Festival, but of the British critics only Alexander Walker (*Evening Standard*) and Eric Rhode (*Listener*) were prepared to express even grudging admiration and Rhode's endorsement was qualified by the fact that he thought 'the interior monologues and strange imagistic exchanges of Charles Wood's script' would be better off in a radio play.
14. Alexander Walker, *Hollywood, England*, p. 397.
15. Warner-Pathé, the distribution company jointly owned by Warner Brothers and ABPC, also handled Anglo-Amalgamated's films and, from 1965 onwards, most of Hammer's.
16. James Price, 'Far from the Madding Crowd', *Sight and Sound*, Winter 1967–8, p. 39.
17. Schlesinger protested that Bathsheba Everdene, in her refusal to conform to the conventions of nineteenth-century female behaviour, was herself a 'modern girl'. But behaviour and appearance are not synonymous and Julie Christie is far

321

too city-bred to convince us that she could run a sheep farm. See David Spiers, 'Interview with John Schlesinger', *Screen*, vol. 11, no. 3, Summer 1970, p. 10.

18. For the story of *Performance*'s genesis and troubled history see Alexander Walker, *Hollywood, England*, pp. 411–25.
19. Michael Billington, *The Times*, 17 July 1969; Eric Rhode, *Listener*, 24 July 1969. See Jocelyn Rickards (who designed the odd but effective costumes and married the director), *The Painted Banquet*, London, Weidenfeld & Nicolson, 1987, pp. 114–20; and Gordon Gow, 'The Urge of Some People', *Films and Filming*, July 1969, pp. 4–5, for the background to the making of *Alfred the Great*, and Derek Elley, *The Epic Film*, London, Routledge, 1984, pp. 154–5, for a refreshingly positive view of the film.
20. Michael Ciment, *Conversations With Losey*, London, Methuen, 1985, p. 276.
21. James Price, *Sight and Sound*, Spring 1969. *Isadora* was the sort of film that brought out the best in the critics, though the four most perceptive reviews – by James Price (*Sight and Sound* and *Financial Times*), Alexander Walker (*Evening Standard*), Eric Rhode (*Listener*) and Penelope Houston (*Spectator*) – came down, somewhat reluctantly, against the film.
22. Alexander Walker, *Hollywood, England*, p. 349.
23. John Russell Taylor, 'Backing Britain', *Sight and Sound*, Spring 1969, p. 114.
24. Alexander Walker, *Hollywood, England*, p. 347.
25. Figures are from Alexander Walker, *Hollywood, England*, p. 442.
26. 'Hollywood and Bust', *Economist*, November 1969, p. 69 (reprinted in *Film and Television Technician*, December 1969, pp. 8–9).
27. Figures from John Watson, 'The Changing Economics of the Cinema', *Three Banks Review*, June 1974, p. 35. For early manifestations of the emergence of New Hollywood see Axel Madsen, 'Fission, Fashion, Fusion', *Sight and Sound*, Summer 1968, pp. 125–6; and 'The Changing of the Guard', *Sight and Sound*, Spring 1970, pp. 63–5, 111

CONCLUSION

1. Victor Perkins, *Film as Film*, Harmondsworth, Penguin, p. 191.
2. François Truffaut, *Hitchcock*, London, Paladin, 1978, p. 140.
3. Philip French, 'The Alphaville of Admass', *Sight and Sound*, Summer 1966, p. 107.

BIBLIOGRAPHY

Aldgate, Tony and Richards, Jeffrey, *Best of British*, Oxford, Basil Blackwell, 1983.

Alloway, Lawrence, 'Monster Films', *Encounter*, January 1960, p. 70–2.

—— 'The Iconography of the Movies', *Movie*, no. 7, February–March 1963, pp. 4–6.

—— 'Critics in the Dark', *Encounter*, February, 1964, pp. 50–5.

—— *Violent America*, New York, Museum of Modern Art, 1969.

Allsop, Kenneth, *The Angry Decade*, London, Peter Owen, 1964.

Amis, Kingsley, *The James Bond Dossier*, London, Jonathan Cape, 1965.

Anderegg, Michael A., *William Wyler*, Boston, Twayne, 1979.

Anderson, Lindsay, 'French Critical Writing', *Sight and Sound*, October–December 1954, p. 105.

—— 'Stand Up! Stand Up!', *Sight and Sound*, Autumn 1956, pp. 63–9.

—— 'Sport, Life and Art', *Films and Filming*, February, 1963, pp. 15–18.

Andrews, Nigel and Kennedy, Harlan, 'Peerless Powell', *Film Comment*, May–June 1979, pp. 50–5.

Armes, Roy, *A Critical History of the British Cinema*, London, Secker & Warburg, 1978.

Armitage, Peter, 'The War of the Cults', *Motion*, no. 1, Summer 1961, pp. 4–6.

—— 'British Cinema: Attitudes and Illusions', *Film*, no 36, Summer 1963, pp. 16–24.

Association of Cinematograph, Television and Allied Technicians, *Survival or Extinction? A Policy for British Films*, London, ACTT, 1964.

—— *Nationalising the Film Industry*, London, ACTT, 1973.

Baker, Peter, 'The Foreign Papers', *Films and Filming*, February 1964, pp. 41–60.

Baker, Roy, 'Discovering Where the Truth Lies', *Films and Filming*, May 1961, pp. 17, 38.

Balcon, Michael, *Michael Balcon Presents . . . A Lifetime of Films*, London, Hutchinson, 1969.

Barlow, James, *Term of Trial*, Harmondsworth, Penguin, 1961.

Barnes, Richard, *Mods!*, London, Eel Pie Publishing, 1979.

Barr, Charles, *Ealing Studios*, London and Newton Abbott, Cameron & Tayleur/David & Charles, 1977.

Barr, Charles (ed.), *All Our Yesterdays*, London, British Film Institute, 1986.

Baxter, John, *An Appalling Talent: Ken Russell*, London, Michael Joseph, 1973.

Bean, Robin, 'Frames and Feelings: An Interview with Terence Stamp', *Films and Filming*, December 1968, pp. 4–10.

Bennett, Tony, 'James Bond as Popular Hero', *Politics, Ideology and Popular Culture*, Milton Keynes, Open University Press, 1982.

Bennett, Tony and Woollacott, Janet, *Bond and Beyond*, London, Macmillan 1987.

Berger, John, 'Look at Britain', *Sight and Sound*, Summer 1957, pp. 12–14.

Bernard, Barbara, *Fashion in the Sixties*, London, Academy Editions, 1978.
Betts, Ernest, *The Film Business*, London, Allen & Unwin, 1973.
Bigsby, C. W. E. (ed.), *Superculture*, Ohio, Bowling Green University Press, 1975.
Bisplinghoff, Gretchen, 'Codes of Feminine Madness', *Film Reader 5*, 1982, pp. 37–40.
Bogarde, Dirk, *Snakes and Ladders*, London, Chatto & Windus, 1978.
Booker, Christopher, *The Neophiliacs*, London, Collins, 1970.
Booth, M. R., *English Melodrama*, London, Herbert Jenkins, 1965.
Braine, John, *Room at the Top*, Harmondsworth, Penguin, 1959.
Braun, Eric, 'The Decade of Change', *Films and Filming*, December 1973, pp. 28–40.
Brooker, Nancy, *John Schlesinger: A Guide to References and Resources*, London/Boston, George Prior/G. K. Hall, 1978.
Brosnan, John, *The Horror People*, London, Macdonald & Jane's, 1976.
Brownlow, Kevin, *How It Happened Here*, London, Secker & Warburg/British Film Institute, 1968.
Butler, Ivan, *The Cinema of Roman Polanski*, London/New York, Zwemmer/Barnes, 1970.
—— *The Making of Feature Films – A Guide*, Harmondsworth, Penguin, 1971.
—— *To Encourage the Art of the Film*, London, Robert Hale, 1971.
—— *Horror in the Cinema*, New Jersey, A. S. Barnes & Co., 1979.
Callan, Michael Feeney, *Julie Christie*, London, W. H. Allen, 1984.
Cannadine, David, 'James Bond and the Decline of England', *Encounter*, September 1979, pp. 46–55.
Castelli, Louis and Cleeland, Caryn Lynn, *David Lean: A Guide to References and Resources*, London/Boston, George Prior/G. K. Hall, 1980.
Christie, Ian, *Arrows of Desire*, London, Waterstone, 1985.
Christie, Ian (ed.), *Powell, Pressburger and Others*, London, British Film Institute, 1973.
Christie, Ian and Collins, Richard, 'Interview With Michael Powell', *Monogram*, no. 3, 1972, pp. 32–8.
Ciment, Michel, *Conversations With Losey*, London, Methuen, 1985.
—— *John Boorman*, London, Faber and Faber, 1986.
Clarens, Carlos, *Horror Movies – An Illustrated Survey*, Secker & Warburg, 1968.
Cohen, Stanley, *Folk Devils and Moral Panics*, London, MacGibbon & Kee, 1972.
Cohn, Nik, *Pop from the Beginning*, London, Weidenfeld & Nicolson, 1969.
—— *Today There Are No Gentlemen*, London, Weidenfeld & Nicolson, 1971.
Cook, Chris and McKie, David, *The Decade of Disillusion: British Politics in the Sixties*, London, Macmillan, 1972.
Cook, Chris and Sked, Alan, *Post-War Britain: A Political History*, Harmondsworth, Penguin, 1980.
Cowie, Peter, 'Clayton's Progress', *Motion*, no. 3, Spring 1962 , pp. 34–40.
—— 'The Face of 63', *Films and Filming*, February 1963, pp. 19–27.
Cross, Robin, *The Big Book of British Films*, London, Charles Herridge/Sidgwick & Jackson, 1984.
Curran, James and Porter, Vincent (eds.), *British Cinema History*, London, Weidenfeld & Nicolson, 1983.
Curtis, Barry, *Morgan, a Suitable Case for Treatment*, unpublished Polytechnic of Central London M. A. Thesis, 1983.
Cushing, Peter, *Past Forgetting*, London, Weidenfeld & Nicolson, 1988.
Dacre, Richard, *Trouble in Store: Norman Wisdom, a Career in Comedy*, Dumfries, T. C. Farries, 1991.
Davenport, Nicholas, 'The State Muddle in Films', *Spectator*, 28 October 1966, pp. 562–3.

—— 'The Film Crisis', *Spectator*, 18 September 1971, p. 424.

Davis, John, 'Intermission – The British Film Industry', *National Provincial Bank Review*, 1958, pp. 1–12.

Dawson, Jan and Johnston, Claire, 'Declarations of Independence', *Sight and Sound*, Winter 1969–70, pp. 28–32.

Dehn, Paul, 'The Spy Who Came in From the Cold', *Journal of the Society of Film and Television Arts*, no, 24, Summer 1966, pp. 12–13.

Di Franco, Philip (ed.), *The Movie World of Roger Corman*, New York/London, Chelsea House, 1979.

Dick, Bernard F., *Billy Wilder*, Boston, Twayne, 1980.

Dorst, Gary, 'Dracula in Retrospect', *Little Shoppe of Horrors*, no. 4, April 1978, pp. 111–18.

Drake, Charlie, *Drake's Progress*, London, Robson Books, 1986.

Dundy, Elaine, *Finch, Bloody Finch*, London, Michael Joseph, 1980.

Durgnat, Raymond, *A Mirror for England*, London, Faber & Faber, 1970.

—— *Sexual Alienation in the Cinema*, London, Studio Vista, 1972.

—— 'Puritans Anonymous', *Motion*, no. 6, Autumn 1963, p. 3.

—— 'Standing Up for Jesus', *Motion*, no. 6, Autumn 1963, pp. 25–42.

—— 'Old Wine in New Bottles', *Film*, no. 39, Spring 1964, pp. 32–3.

—— 'The Mass Media – A Highbrow Illiteracy?', *Views*, no. 4, Spring 1964, pp. 49–59.

—— 'The Impotence of Being Ernest', *Views*, no. 8, Summer 1965, pp. 76–80.

—— (as O. O. Green), 'Michael Powell', *Movie*, no. 14, Autumn 1965, pp. 17–20.

—— 'Loved One', *Films and Filming*, February 1966, pp. 19–23, March 1966, pp. 37–40.

—— 'Losey: Modesty and Eve', *Films and Filming*, April 1966, pp. 26–33.

—— 'Losey: Puritan Maids', *Films and Filming*, May 1966, pp. 28–33.

—— 'Two on a Tandem', *Films and Filming*, July 1966, pp. 26–33.

—— 'Brain Drains: Drifters, Avant-Gardes and Kitchen Sinks', *Cinema*, no. 3, June 1969, pp. 12–15.

—— 'Britannia Waives the Rules', *Film Comment*, July–August 1976, pp. 50–9.

—— 'The Great British Phantasmagoria', *Film Comment*, May–June 1977, pp. 48–53.

Durgnat, Raymond and Armitage, Peter, 'Ten Years That Shook an Art', *Film*, no. 40, September 1964, pp. 22–33.

Durgnat, Raymond and Cutts, John, 'Horror is My Business', *Films and Filming*, July 1964, pp. 7–8.

Dyer, Richard, '*Victim* – Hermeneutic Project', *Film Form*, vol. 1, no. 2, 1977, pp. 3–22.

Eastaugh, Kenneth, *The Carry On Book*, Newton Abbot, David & Charles, 1978.

Elsaesser, Thomas, 'Between Style and Ideology', *Monogram*, no. 3, 1972, pp. 2–10.

Evans, Peter, *Peter Sellers: The Mask Behind the Mask*, New Jersey, Prentice-Hall, 1968.

—— *Goodbye Baby and Amen: A Saraband for the Sixties* (photographs by David Bailey), London, Condé Nast/Collins, 1969.

Everett, Peter, *You'll Never be 16 Again*, London, BBC Publications, 1986.

Eves, Vicki, 'Britain's Social Cinema', *Screen*, vol. 10, no. 6, November–December 1969, pp. 51–66.

—— 'The Structure of the British Film Industry', *Screen*, vol. 11, no. 1, January–February 1970, pp. 41–54.

Eyles, Allen, 'A Passion for Cinema: Ken Hughes', *Focus on Film*, no. 6, Spring 1971, pp. 42–51.

Eyles, Allen, with Robert Adkinson and Nicholas Fry (eds.), *The House of Horror*, London, Lorimer, 1981.

Eyles, Allen and Eavis, Marcus, 'Focus on Exhibition', *Motion*, no. 2, Winter 1961–2, pp. 13–16, 38.

Fairlie, Henry, 'Still Alive After All This Satire', *Queen*, December 1961, pp. 97–9.

Faulkner, Trader, *Peter Finch*, London, Angus & Robertson, 1979.

Feldman, Gene and Gartenberg, Max (eds.), *Protest*, London, Souvenir Press, 1959.

Fienburgh, Wilfred, *No Love for Johnnie*, London, Book Club, 1959.

Forbes, Bryan, *Notes for a Life*, London, Collins, 1974.

—— 'Talking About My Generation', *Town*, July 1966, pp. 30–1.

Fountain, Nigel, *Underground: The London Alternative Press 1966–74*, London, Routledge, 1988.

Fowles, John, *The Collector*, London, Pan, 1986.

Francis, Anne, *Julian Wintle: A Memoir*, London, Dukeswood, 1986.

French, Philip, 'Richard Lester', *Movie*, no. 14, Autumn 1965, pp. 5–11.

—— 'The Alphaville of Admass', *Sight and Sound*, Summer 1966, pp. 106–11.

Gablik, Suzi and Russell, John (eds.), *Pop Art Redefined*, London, Thames & Hudson, 1969.

Gans, Herbert J., 'Hollywood Films on British Screens', *Social Problems*, vol. 9, no. 4, Spring 1962, pp. 324–8.

Gaston, Georg, *Karel Reisz*, Boston, Twayne, 1980.

—— *Jack Clayton*, Boston, Twayne, 1981.

Gelmis, Joseph, *The Film Director as Superstar*, Harmondsworth, Penguin, 1974.

Gifford, Denis, *The British Film Catalogue 1895–1985*, Newton Abbot and London, David & Charles, 1986.

—— *A Pictorial History of Horror Movies*, Exeter Books, New York, 1984.

Gilbert, R., 'London's Underground', *Town*, March 1967.

Gillett, John, 'The State of the Studios', *Sight and Sound*, Spring 1964, pp. 55–61.

Gomez, Joseph A., *Ken Russell: The Adaptor as Creator*, London, Frederick Muller, 1976.

—— *Peter Watkins*, Boston, Twayne, 1979.

Gorer, Geoffrey, 'The Perils of Hypergamy', *New Statesman*, 4 May 1957.

Gosling, Ray, *Sum Total*, London, Faber & Faber, 1962.

—— 'I Like You Full Stop', *Queen*, 15 September 1961, pp. 120–1.

—— 'Dream Boy', *Screen Education*, no. 12, January–February 1962, pp. 6–12.

Gough-Yates, Kevin, 'Interview with Seth Holt', *Screen*, vol. 10, no. 6, November–December 1969, pp. 4–23.

Gow, Gordon, 'The Urge of Some People: An Interview with Clive Donner', *Films and Filming*, July 1969, pp. 4–8.

—— 'Love Yourself Sufficiently: An Interview with Raymond Stross', *Films and Filming*, March 1971, pp. 18–22.

—— 'The Way Things Are: An Interview with Jack Clayton', *Films and Filming*, April 1974, pp. 11–14.

—— 'Within the Cocoon – An interview with Tony Richardson', *Films and Filming*, June 1977, pp. 11–16.

—— 'A Bigger Canvas: An Interview with John Schlesinger', *Films and Filming*, September 1979, pp. 13–16.

Graham, Peter, *The Abortive Renaissance*, Axle Publications, 1963.

Green, Martin, *A Mirror for Anglo-Saxons*, London, Longman, 1961.

Gregory, Charles T., 'There'll Always Be Room at the Top for Nothing but the Best', *Journal of Popular Film*, vol. 2, no. 1, Winter 1973, pp. 59–73.

Guback, Thomas, *The International Film Industry*, Bloomington, Indiana University Press, 1969.

—— 'American Interests in the British Film Industry', *Quarterly Review of Economics and Business*, no. 7, 1967.

Halasz, Piri, 'You Can Walk Across It On the Grass', *Time*, 15 April 1966, pp. 32–42.

Hall, Stuart, 'Jimmy Porter and the Two-and-Nines', *Definition*, no. 1, February 1960, pp. 9–14.

Hall, Stuart and Whannel, Paddy, *The Popular Arts*, London, Hutchinson, 1964.

Halliwell, Leslie, *The Dead That Walk*, London, Grafton, 1986.

—— *Halliwell's Film Guide*, London, Granada, 1988.

Hamilton, Richard, *Collected Works 1953–82*, London, Thames & Hudson, 1982.

Harcourt, Peter, *Movies and Mythologies: Towards a National Cinema*, Toronto, Canadian Broadcasting Corporation, 1977.

—— 'I'd Rather Be Like I Am', *Sight and Sound*, Winter 1962–3, pp. 16–19.

Harding, Bill, *The Films of Michael Winner*, London, Frederick Muller, 1978.

Hardy, Phil, *The Aurum Film Encyclopedia vol. 2: Science Fiction*, London, Aurum Press, 1984.

Hardy, Phil, with Tom Milne and Paul Willemen (eds.), *The Aurum Film Encyclopedia vol. 3: Horror*, London, Aurum Press, 1985.

Harris, Jennifer, Hyde, Sarah and Smith, Greg, *1966 and All That: Design and the Consumer in Britain 1960–69*, London, Trefoil, 1986.

Heard, Colin, 'Hammering the Box Office', *Films and Filming*, June 1969, pp. 17–18.

Hewison, Robert, *In Anger: Culture in the Cold War 1945–60*, London, Weidenfeld & Nicolson, 1981.

—— *Too Much: Art and Society in the Sixties 1960–1975*, London, Methuen, 1986.

Hibbin, Sally and Nina, *What a Carry On*, London, Hamlyn, 1988.

Higson, Andrew, 'Space, Place, Spectacle', *Screen*, vol. 25, nos. 4–5, July–October 1984, pp. 2–21.

Hill, Derek, 'Defence Through FIDO', *Sight and Sound*, Summer–Autumn 1959, pp. 183–4.

—— 'The Face of Horror', *Sight and Sound*, Winter 1959–60, pp. 6–11.

—— 'A Writer's Wave?', *Sight and Sound*, Spring 1960, pp. 56–60.

—— 'The Habit of Censorship', *Encounter*, July 1960, pp. 52–62.

—— 'Where the Holy Spirit Leads', *Definition*, no. 3, Spring 1961, pp. 43–4.

Hill, John, 'Ideology, Economy and the British Cinema', *Ideology and Cultural Production*, M. Barret, P. Corrigan, A. Kuhn and J. Wolff (eds.), London, Croom Helm, 1979.

Hill, John, *Sex, Class and Realism*, London, British Film Institute, 1986.

—— 'The British "Social Problem" Film – *Violent Playground* and *Sapphire*', *Screen*, vol. 26, no. 1, January–February 1985.

Hillier, Jim, *Cahiers du Cinéma* vols. 1 and 2, London, Routledge, 1985, 1986.

Hillier, Jim and Lovell, Alan, *Studies in Documentary*, London, Secker & Warburg/British Film Institute, 1972.

Hoggart, Richard, *The Uses of Literacy*, Harmondsworth, Penguin, 1958.

—— *Speaking to Each Other, vol. 1: About Society*, Harmondsworth, Penguin, 1973.

—— 'We Are the Lambeth Boys', *Sight and Sound*, Summer–Autumn 1959, pp. 164–5.

Holston, Kim, *Starlet*, Jefferson and London, McFarland, 1988.

Houston, Penelope, 'Room at the Top?', *Sight and Sound*, Spring 1959, pp. 56–9.

—— 'The Critical Question', *Sight and Sound*, Autumn 1960, pp. 160–5.

—— 'The Power of the Circuits', *Sight and Sound*, Autumn 1963, p. 174.

—— 'Whose Crisis?', *Sight and Sound*, Winter 1963–4, pp. 26–8, 50.

—— 'Keeping Up With the Antonionis', *Sight and Sound*, Autumn 1964, pp. 163–8.

—— '007', *Sight and Sound*, Winter 1964–5, pp. 14–16.

—— 'Occupied Industry', *Sight and Sound*, Spring 1965, p. 59.

—— 'England Their England', *Sight and Sound*, Spring 1966, pp. 54–6.

—— (ed.), 'The Crisis We Deserve' (questionnaire answered by Kevin Billington, John Boorman, Kevin Brownlow, Jim Clark, Peter Hall and Dick Clement), *Sight and Sound*, Autumn 1970, pp. 172–8.

—— 'Seventy', *Sight and Sound*, Winter 1970–1, pp. 3–5.

Houston, Penelope and Gillett, John, 'Conversations with Nicholas Ray and Joseph Losey', *Sight and Sound*, Autumn 1961, pp. 182–7.

Hudson, Roger, 'Three Designers: interviews with Ken Adam, Edward Marshall and Richard Macdonald', *Sight and Sound*, Winter 1964–5, pp. 26–31.

—— 'The Secret Profession: interviews with two Lighting Cameramen, Douglas Slocombe and Walter Lassally', *Sight and Sound*, Summer 1965, pp. 113–17.

—— 'Putting the Magic in it: two editors, James Clark and Anthony Harvey, discuss their work', *Sight and Sound*, Spring 1966, pp. 78–83.

Hughes, Ken, 'Those Nutty Intellectuals', *Films and Filming*, January 1963, pp. 9–10.

Hulanicki, Barbara, *From A to Biba*, London, W. H. Allen, 1983.

Humphries, Steve and Taylor, John, *The Making of Modern London 1945–1985*, London, Sidgwick & Jackson, 1986.

Husra, Bernard, 'Patterns of Power', *Films and Filming*, April 1964, pp. 49–56.

Jacob, Gilles, 'Nouvelle Vague or Jeune Cinema', *Sight and Sound*, Winter 1964–5, pp. 4–8.

—— 'Joseph Losey or the Camera Calls', *Sight and Sound*, Spring 1966, pp. 62–7.

Jarvie, I. C., 'Media and Manners', *Film Quarterly*, 22, 1969, pp. 11–17.

—— 'Towards an Objective Film Criticism', *Film Quarterly*, 14, 1961, pp. 19–23.

—— *Towards a Sociology of the Cinema*, London, Routledge & Kegan Paul, 1970.

Johnson, Ian, 'The Reluctant Stars', *Films and Filming*, May 1962, pp. 24, 44.

—— 'We're All Right Jack', *Films and Filming*, September 1962, pp. 44–8.

—— 'A Pin to See the Peepshow', *Motion, no. 4: Companion to Violence and Sadism in the Cinema*, February 1963, pp. 36–9.

—— 'Have the British a Sense of Humour?', *Films and Filming*, March 1963, pp. 48–53.

Joyce, Paul, 'Nothing But the Best', *Film*, no. 45, Spring 1966, pp. 16–21.

Kael, Pauline, *I Lost it at the Movies*, Boston and Toronto, Little, Brown & Co., 1965.

—— *Kiss Kiss Bang Bang*, London, Calder & Boyars, 1970.

—— *Going Steady*, London, Temple Smith, 1970.

Katz, Ephraim, *The International Film Encyclopedia*, London, Macmillan, 1982.

Kelly, Terence, with George Perry and Graham Norton, *A Competitive Cinema*, London, Institute of Economic Affairs, 1966.

Kelly, Terence, 'Chicken-Hearted Champions of Competition', *Films and Filming*, January 1967, pp. 34–5.

Kemp, Philip, 'Mackendrickland', *Sight and Sound*, Winter 1988–9, pp. 48–52.

Kerridge, Roy, 'A Teenager's Who's Who', *New Statesman*, 24 September 1960, pp. 423–6.

Klemensen, Richard (ed.), 'Amicus: Two's a Company', *Little Shoppe of Horrors*, no. 2, March 1973, pp. 12–40.

—— (ed.), 'Hammer: Yesterday, Today and Tomorrow', *Little Shoppe of*

Horrors, no. 4, April 1978, pp. 23–110.

Knight, Chris, 'The Amicus Empire' (Interview with Milton Subotsky), *Cine-Fantastique*, vol. 2, no. 4, Summer 1973, pp. 5–18.

Korda, Michael, *Charmed Lives*, London, Allen Lane, 1980.

Kulik, Karol, *Alexander Korda:The Man Who Could Work Miracles*, London, W. H. Allen, 1975.

Kustow, Michael, 'Within and Without', *Sight and Sound*, Summer 1967, pp. 113–17.

Lambert, Gavin, *The Dangerous Edge*, London, Barrie & Jenkins, 1975.

Larkin, Philip, 'The Batman from Blades', *Required Writing*, London, Faber & Faber, 1983, pp. 266–70.

Lassally, Walter, *Itinerant Cameraman*, London, John Murray, 1987.

—— 'The Dead Hand', *Sight and Sound*, Summer 1960, pp. 113–15.

—— 'Communication and the Creative Process', *Film*, no. 37, Autumn 1963, pp. 18–24.

Laurie, Peter, *The Teenage Revolution*, London, Anthony Blond, 1965.

Le Carré, John, *The Looking Glass War*, London, Pan, 1966.

—— 'To Russia, with Greetings', *Encounter*, May 1966, pp. 3–6.

Leahy, James, *The Cinema of Joseph Losey*, London/New York, Zwemmer/Barnes, 1967.

Lee, Christopher, *Tall, Dark and Gruesome*, London, W. H. Allen, 1977.

Lee Thompson, J., 'The Still Small Voice of Truth', *Films and Filming*, April 1963, pp. 5–6.

Lellis, George, 'Recent Richardson – Cashing the Blank Cheque', *Sight and Sound*, Summer 1969, pp. 130–3.

Levin, Bernard, *The Pendulum Years*, London, Jonathan Cape, 1970.

Lovell, Alan, *British Cinema: The Unknown Cinema*, BFI Education Seminar Paper, March 1969.

—— 'The Best We've Got', *Definition*, no. 2, Summer 1960, pp. 3–4.

—— 'Notes on British Film Culture', *Screen*, vol. 13, no. 2, Summer 1972, pp. 5–15.

MacArthur, Colin, 'Polanski', *Sight and Sound*, Winter 1968–9, pp. 14–17.

McDougall, Gordon, 'To Deprave and Corrupt? An Examination of the Methods and Aims of Film Censorship in Britain', *Motion*, no. 2, Winter 1961–2, pp. 5–8.

MacInnes, Colin, *Absolute MacInnes*, London, MacGibbon & Kee, 1959.

—— *Out of the Way*, London, Brian & O'Keefe, 1979.

—— *England Half English*, London, Hogarth Press, 1986.

—— 'Old Youth and Young', *Encounter*, September 1967, pp. 29–35.

McVay, Douglas, 'One Man Band' (Peter Sellers), *Films and Filming*, May 1963, pp. 44–7.

—— 'The House That Jack Built' (Jack Clayton), *Films and Filming*, October 1967, pp. 4–11.

Madden, Paul (ed.), *British Television Drama 1959–1973*, London, British Film Institute, 1976.

Madsen, Axel, 'Fission/Fashion/Fusion', *Sight and Sound*, Summer 1968, pp. 125–6.

—— 'The Changing of the Guard', *Sight and Sound*, Spring 1970, pp. 63–5, 111.

Manvell, Roger, *New Cinema in Britain*, London, Studio Vista, 1969.

Marwick, Arthur, *British Society Since 1945*, Harmondsworth, Penguin, 1982.

—— '*Room at the Top*, *Saturday Night and Sunday Morning*, and the "Cultural Revolution" in Britain', *Journal of Contemporary History*, vol. 19, no. 1, January 1984, pp. 127–51.

Maschler, Tom (ed.), *Declaration*, London, MacGibbon & Kee, 1957.

Mason, James, *Before I Forget*, London, Hamish Hamilton, 1981.

Masters, Brian, *The Swinging Sixties*, London, Constable, 1985.

Mayersberg, Paul, 'The Art That Never Was', broadcast BBC Third Programme, March 1963 (transcript in BFI Library).

—— 'A National Cinema', *New Society*, 31 August 1967, pp. 296–7.

—— 'Tele-cinema', *New Society*, 1 February 1968, p. 165.

Medhurst, Andy, '*Victim* – Text as Context', *Screen*, vol. 25, nos. 4–5, July–October 1984, pp. 22–35.

Melly, George, *Revolt into Style*, Harmondsworth, Penguin, 1972.

Merry, Bruce, *Anatomy of the Spy Thriller*, Dublin, Gill & Macmillan, 1977.

Miller, Karl, 'A Sunday Dilemma: Getaway People and Ghetto People', *Sunday Times Magazine*, 14 December 1969, pp. 27–32.

Mills, John, *Up in the Clouds, Gentlemen, Please*, London, Weidenfeld & Nicolson, 1980.

Milne, Tom, *Losey on Losey*, London, Secker & Warburg/BFI, 1967.

Monopoly Commission *Report on the Supply of Films for Exhibition in Cinemas*, London, HMSO, 1966.

Moorhouse, Geoffrey, *Britain in the Sixties: The Other England*, Harmondsworth, Penguin, 1964.

More, Kenneth, *More or Less*, London, Hodder & Stoughton, 1978.

Mortimer, Penelope, *The Pumpkin Eater*, Harmondsworth, Penguin, 1964.

Moss, Robert F., *The Films of Carol Reed*, London, Macmillan, 1987.

Mottershead, Chris, 'Carry on Sinking', *Monogram*, no. 3, 1972, pp. 15–16.

Mowat, David, 'The Cinema's New Language', *Encounter*, April 1970, pp. 62–7.

Nairn, Tom, 'Roman Polanski', *Cinema*, no. 3, June 1969, pp. 22–6.

Neville, Richard, *Playpower*, London, Paladin, 1971.

Newman, Kim, *Nightmare Movies*, London, Bloomsbury, 1988.

Nolan, Jack, 'Edgar Wallace', *Films in Review*, February 1967, pp. 71–85.

Nowell-Smith, Geoffrey, 'Movie and Myth', *Sight and Sound*, Spring 1963, pp. 60–4.

—— 'Chasing the Gorgon', *Sight and Sound*, Spring 1965, p. 60.

Nuttall, Jeff, *Bomb Culture*, London, Paladin, 1970.

Oakes, Philip, *Tony Hancock*, London, Futura, 1975.

Oakley, C. A., *Where We Came In*, London, Allen & Unwin, 1964.

Orwell, George, 'The Art of Donald McGill, *Collected Essays, Journalism and Letters*, vol. 2, Harmondsworth, Penguin, 1980, pp. 183–95.

—— 'The Decline of the English Murder', *Collected Essays, Journalism and Letters*, vol. 4, Harmondsworth, Penguin, 1980, pp. 124–8.

Palmer, R. Barton, 'What Was New in the British New Wave? Re-viewing *Room at the Top*', *Journal of Popular Film and Television*, vol. 14, no. 3, Fall 1986, pp. 125–35.

Palmer, Scott, *A Who's Who of British Film Actors*, Metuchen, New Jersey, Scarecrow Press, 1981.

Parfitt, G. R., 'The Fruitation of Terence Fisher, *Little Shoppe of Horrors*, no. 3, February 1974, pp. 49–62.

Perkins, Victor, 'The British Cinema', *Movie*, no. 1, June 1962, pp. 3–7.

—— 'Clive Donner and Some People', *Movie*, no. 3, September 1962, pp. 22–5.

—— 'Censorship' (including interviews with John Trevelyan and Joseph Losey), *Movie*, no. 6, December 1962, pp. 16–22.

—— 'Forced to be free: Or Doing Business in a Great Art', *Movie*, no. 15, Spring 1968, pp. 17–18.

—— 'Supporting the British Cinema', *Movie*, no. 16, Winter 1968–9, pp. 13–16.

Perry, George, *The Great British Picture Show*, London, Pavilion Books, 1985.

—— *Movies from the Mansion: A History of Pinewood Studios*, London, Elm Tree

Books/Hamish Hamilton, 1976.

Phelps, Guy, *Film Censorship*, London, Victor Gollancz, 1975.

—— 'Art House', *Sight and Sound*, Winter 1983–4, pp. 12–14.

Philips, Gene, *The Movie Makers*, Chicago, Nelson-Hall, 1973.

—— *John Schlesinger*, Boston, Twayne, 1981.

—— 'John Schlesinger: Social Realist', *Film Comment*, Winter 1969, pp. 58–63.

Pickard, Stephen R., 'A Tribute to Bernard Robinson', *Little Shoppe of Horrors*, no. 2, March 1973, pp. 8–11.

—— 'The Works of Jack Curtis', *Little Shoppe of Horrors*, no. 3, February 1974, pp. 78–80.

Pirie, David, *A Heritage of Horror*, London, Gordon Fraser, 1973.

—— *Hammer: A Cinema Case Study*, London, BFI Education, 1980.

—— 'New Blood', *Sight and Sound*, Spring 1971, pp. 73–5.

Pitts, Michael R., 'The Cinema of Edgar Wallace', *Classic Images*, no. 126, December 1985, pp. 227–8; no. 127, January 1986, pp. c17–20; no. 128, February 1986, pp. 47–50.

Political and Economic Planning, *The British Film Industry 1958*, London, PEP, 1958.

Potter, Dennis, *The Glittering Coffin*, London, Victor Gollancz, 1960.

Pratley, Gerald, *The Cinema of David Lean*, London/New York, Tantivy/Barnes, 1974.

Praz, Mario, *The Romantic Agony*, London, Oxford University Press, 1970.

Raphael, Frederic, *Two for the Road*, London, Jonathan Cape, 1967.

Rayns, Tony and Eason, Patrick, 'Interview with Joseph Losey', *Cinema*, no. 3, June 1969, pp. 17–21.

Reid Banks, Lynne, *The L-Shaped Room*, Harmondsworth, Penguin, 1963.

Rhode, Eric, 'British Film-Makers', *Listener*, 26 September 1968, pp. 385–7.

—— 'The British Cinema in the Seventies', *Listener*, 14 August 1969, pp. 201–3.

Richards, Jeffrey, 'Maniac in the Cellar', *Monthly Film Bulletin*, September 1985, pp. 291–3.

Richardson, Tony, 'The Man Behind the Angry Young Man', *Films and Filming*, February 1959, pp. 9, 32.

Rickards, Jocelyn, *The Painted Banquet*, London, Weidenfeld & Nicolson, 1987.

Ringel, Harry, 'The Horrible Hammer Films of Terence Fisher', *Take One*, May 1973, pp. 8–12.

—— 'Terence Fisher: The Human Side', *Cine-Fantastique*, vol. 4, no. 3, Fall 1975, pp. 7–16.

—— 'Underlining: An Interview with Terence Fisher', *Cine-Fantastique*, vol. 4, no. 3, Fall 1975, pp. 19–28.

Roberts, John, 'British Mod Films of the 60s', *Classic Images*, no. 126, December 1985, pp. c26, 63.

Roberts, Rachel, *No Bells on Sunday*, London, Pavilion/Michael Joseph, 1984.

Robertson, James, *The Hidden Cinema*, London, Routledge, 1989.

Robinson, David, 'A New Clown', *Sight and Sound*, April–June 1954, p. 213.

—— 'Case Histories of the Next Renascence', *Sight and Sound*, Winter 1968–9, pp. 36–40.

—— 'Trevelyan's Social History', *Sight and Sound*, Spring 1971, pp. 70–2.

Rosenfeldt, Diane, *Richard Lester: A Guide to References and Resources*, London/Boston, George Prior/G. K. Hall, 1978.

—— *Ken Russell: A Guide to References and Resources*, London/Boston, George Prior/G. K. Hall, 1978.

Roszak, Theodore, *The Making of a Counterculture*, London, Faber & Faber, 1969.

Roud, Richard, 'The French Line', *Sight and Sound*, Autumn 1960, pp. 167–71.

Sampson, Anthony, *Anatomy of Britain*, London, Hodder & Stoughton, 1962.

331

Schlesinger, John, 'Blessed Isle or Fool's Paradise', *Films and Filming*, May 1963, pp. 3–10.

Sellers, Michael, *P.S. I Love You*, London, Collins, 1981.

Shivas, Mark, 'The Commercial Cinema: A Few Basic Principles', *Oxford Opinion*, no. 38, April 1960, pp. 38–40.

—— 'British Lion', *Movie*, no. 14, Autumn 1965, pp. 1–4.

Shivas, Mark and Cameron, Ian, 'Interview with Richard Lester', *Movie*, no. 16, Winter 1968–9, pp. 16–28.

Sillitoe, Alan, *Saturday Night and Sunday Morning*, London, Pan, 1960.

—— 'What Comes on Monday', *New Left Review*, no. 4, July–August 1960, pp. 58–9.

Silver, Alain and Ursini, James, *David Lean and his Films*, London, Leslie Frewin, 1974.

Sinyard, Neil, *The Films of Richard Lester*, London, Croom Helm, 1985.

—— *Filming Literature*, London, Croom Helm, 1986.

Skidelsky, Robert and Bogdanor, Vernon (eds.), *The Age of Affluence*, London, Macmillan, 1970.

Spiers, David, 'Interview with Jack Gold', *Screen*, vol. 10, no. 4–5, July–August 1969, pp. 3–18.

—— 'Interview with John Schlesinger', *Screen*, vol. 11, no. 3, Summer 1970, pp. 3–18.

Spraos, John, *The Decline of the Cinema*, London, Allen & Unwin, 1962.

Stamp, Terence, *Double Feature*, London, Bloomsbury, 1989.

Stanbrook, Alan, 'The Changing Face of Film Finance', *Investors Chronicle*, 5 August 1971, pp. 568–70.

Storey, David, *This Sporting Life*, Harmondsworth, Penguin, 1963.

Story, Jack Trevor, *Live Now, Pay Later*, Harmondsworth, Penguin, 1963.

Street, Sarah and Dickinson, Margaret, *Cinema and State*, London, British Film Institute, 1985.

Strick, Philip, 'Mice in the Milk', *Sight and Sound*, Spring 1969, pp. 77–8.

Sussex, Elizabeth, *Lindsay Anderson*, London, Studio Vista, 1969.

Swann, Paul, *The Hollywood Feature Film in Postwar Britain*, London, Croom Helm, 1987.

Swingewood, Alan, *The Myth of Mass Culture*, London, Macmillan, 1977.

Sylvester, David, 'The Anglicisation of Outer Space', *Encounter*, January 1956, pp. 69–72.

Tarr, Carrie, '*Sapphire, Darling* and the Boundaries of Permitted Pleasures', *Screen*, vol. 26, no. 1, January–February 1985, pp. 50–65.

Taylor, Derek, *It Was Twenty Years Ago Today*, London, Bantam Press, 1987.

Taylor, John Russell, *Anger and After: A Guide to the New British Drama*, London, Methuen, 1962.

—— *Directors and Directions*, London, Eyre Methuen, 1975.

—— 'Larking Back', *Sight and Sound*, Spring 1968, pp. 68–70.

—— 'Backing Britain', *Sight and Sound*, Spring 1969, pp. 112–15.

Terry, Sir John, 'Finance for Production', *Screen*, vol. 11, no. 4–5, 1970, pp. 123–8.

Thomas, Hugh (ed.), *The Establishment*, London, Anthony Blond, 1959.

Thompson, Denys, *Discrimination and Popular Culture*, Harmondsworth, Penguin, 1964.

Tickle, Paul, 'The Irresistible Rise of the Celluloid Villain', *Time Out*, 16 June 1981, pp. 12–13.

Todorov, Tzvetan, *The Fantastic*, Ithaca and New York, Cornell University Press, 1975.

Török, Jean-Paul, 'H-Pictures', *Positif*, May 1961, pp. 54–8; July 1961, pp. 41–9.

—— 'The Hazards of Insularity', *Monogram*, no. 3, 1972, pp. 11–14.

Trevelyan, John, *What the Censor Saw*, London, Michael Joseph, 1973.

—— 'Film Censorship in Great Britain', *Screen*, vol. 11, no. 3, Summer 1970, pp. 19–30.

Varma, D. P., *The Gothic Flame*, London, Arthur Barker, 1957.

Vas, Robert, 'Arrival and Departure', *Sight and Sound*, Spring 1963, pp. 56–9.

Voight, Michael, 'Pictures of Innocence: Sir Carol Reed', *Focus on Film*, no. 17, Spring 1974, pp. 17–38.

Walker, Alexander, *Stanley Kubrick Directs*, London, Abacus, 1973.

—— *Peter Sellers*, London, Weidenfeld & Nicolson, 1981.

—— *Hollywood, England*, London, Harrap, 1986.

Wardle, Irving, *The Theatres of George Devine*, London, Jonathan Cape, 1978.

Watson, John, 'The Changing Economics of the Cinema', *Three Bank Review*, no. 102, June 1974, pp. 35–53.

Weeks, Jeffrey, *Sex, Politics and Society*, London, Longman, 1989.

Welsh, James Michael, *Peter Watkins: A Guide to References and Resources*, London/Boston, George Prior/G. K. Hall, 1986.

Whannel, Paddy, 'Receiving the Message', *Definition*, no. 3, Spring 1961, pp. 13–15.

Wheen, Francis, *The Sixties*, London, Century, 1982.

White, Barbara, 'Lassally on British Cinematography', *Journal of the University Film Association* (USA), vol. 26, no. 4, 1974, pp. 61–2, 79–80.

Willemen, Paul and Will, David (eds.), *Roger Corman – the Millennic Vision*, Edinburgh Film Festival in association with *Cinema* Magazine, 1970.

Williams, Raymond, *Culture and Society 1780–1950*, Harmondsworth, Penguin, 1963.

—— 'A Lecture on Realism', *Screen*, vol. 18, no. 1, Spring 1977, pp. 61–74.

Willis, Ted, *Woman in a Dressing Gown and Other Television Plays*, London, Barrie & Rockliff, 1959.

—— 'Society and the Writer', *Films and Filming*, September 1957, pp. 15, 34.

Wilmut, Roger, *Tony Hancock, 'Artiste'*, London, Bibliophile Books, 1986.

Wilson, Elizabeth, *Women and the Welfare State*, London, Tavistock, 1977.

—— *Only Halfway to Paradise*, London, Tavistock, 1980.

Wimhurst, Jolyon, 'Movies at a Halt', *Statist*, 30 December 1963, pp. 863–4.

Wistrich, Enid, *'I Don't Mind the Sex It's the Violence': Film Censorship Explored*, London, Marion Boyars, 1978.

Wood, Linda (ed.), *British Film Industry*, London, BFI Library Services, 1980.

Wood, Robin, *Personal Views*, London, Gordon Frazer, 1976.

—— 'New Criticism?' *Definition*, no. 3, Spring 1961, pp. 9–11.

—— 'Michael Reeves: In Memoriam', *Movie*, no. 17, Winter 1969–70, pp. 2–6.

Wood, Robin and Lippe, Richard (eds.), *American Nightmare*, Toronto, Festival of Festivals, 1979.

Woods, Frederick, 'Take *That* You Swine', *Films and Filming*, August 1959, p. 6.

Wright Wexman, Virginia, *Roman Polanski*, Boston, Twayne, 1985.

Wright Wexman, Virginia and Bisplinghoff, Gretchen, *Roman Polanski: A Guide to References and Resources*, London/Boston, George Prior/G. K. Hall, 1979.

Wyndham, Francis, *David Bailey's Box of Pin Ups*, London, Weidenfeld & Nicolson, 1965.

—— 'Stream of Self Consciousness', *Encounter*, October 1965, pp. 38–40.

York, Peter, *Style Wars*, London, Sidgwick & Jackson, 1980.

Young, Colin, 'Tony Richardson: An Interview in Los Angeles', *Film Quarterly*, vol. 13, no. 4, Summer 1960, pp. 10–15.

INDEX

335

341

342

343

346

Robinson, Bernard, 162, 164, 165, 175, 184, 199
Robinson, David, 2, 158, 247, 258
Robinson, Edward G., 93, 94
Rob Roy, 113, 257
Rock Around the Clock, 133
Rockets Galore, 238
Roeg, Nicolas, 34, 64, 72, 122, 159, 187, 213, 230, 234, 264, 265
Rogers, Paul, 54, 216, 226
Rogers, Peter, 250, 251
Rohmer, Eric, 61
Rollins, Sonny, 143
Roman Spring of Mrs Stone, The, 36, 263
Romeo and Juliet, 262
Romulus, 15, 80, 81, 108, 117, 257, 263, 269
Room at the Top, 2, 11–15, 31–2, 33, 35, 52, 54, 63, 80, 112, 120, 122, 149, 257
Rosemary's Baby, 196
Rosenberg, Max J., 189
Ross, Herbert, 267
Rossington, Norman, 239, 250
Rossiter, Leonard, 26, 231
Rotha, Paul, 58
Rothwell, Norman, 85
Rothwell, Talbot, 251
Rough and the Smooth, The, 36, 89, 90, 202
Running Jumping and Standing Still Film, The, 113–14
Running Man, The, 26, 91
Run Wild, Run Free, 269
Rushton, William, 122
Russell, Ken, 72, 223, 241, 242–3, 259–60, 261, 271, 272, 278
Russell, Rosalind, 73
Rutherford, Margaret, 257, 265
Ryan's Daughter, 6, 91
Rydell, Mark, 261

Saad, Margit, 205
Sabotage, 141
Sailor from Gibraltar, The, 6, 72, 258
Salinger, J. D., 20
Saltzman, Harry, 16, 112–13, 218–19, 258, 259–60, 262
Sammy Going South, 47, 92–3, 94
Sanders, George, 228
Sands of the Desert, 250
Sands of the Kalahari, 262
Sangster, Jimmy, 162, 165–6, 168, 170, 176, 187, 195, 199, 204
Sapphire, 38–40, 48, 50, 51–2, 79, 209, 210
Sarafian, Richard, 269
Sarne, Mike, 43, 152–4, 268
Sasdy, Peter, 176, 190
Satanic Rites of Dracula, The, 176
Satan's Skin, 193
Saturday Night and Sunday Morning, 18–21, 25, 28, 32, 35, 63, 73

Saturday Night Out, 78
Saunders, Charles, 211
Saville, Philip, 90
Saville, Victor, 12, 38, 120
Scales of Justice series, 109, 214, 215
Scarlet Blade, The, 173, 183, 191
Scars of Dracula, The, 176, 179
Schaffner, Frank, 263
Schell, Maximilian, 226
Schlesinger, John, 7, 25–6, 63, 71, 72, 109, 111, 122, 124–5, 126, 159, 224, 263, 277, 278
Schneider, Romy, 231
School for Scoundrels, 238–9
Scofield, Paul, 112
Scotland Yard series, 109, 201, 213–14
Scott, Janette, 122–3
Scott, Peter Graham, 183, 250
Scott, Ridley, 182
Screen (journal), 65
Screen Education (journal), 62
Sea Gull, The, 265
Sea of Sand, 36
Seance on a Wet Afternoon, 46, 72, 75, 76
Sears, Heather, 166
Sebastian, 4, 90, 98, 140, 232, 262
Secombe, Harry, 244
Secret Ceremony, 72, 88, 91, 160, 270–1, 273, 277
Secrets of a Windmill Girl, 6
Segal, George, 228
Sekely, Steve, 180
Self and Others (book), 74
Sellers, Peter, 7, 44, 99, 113, 207, 208, 230, 240, 241, 244–6, 247, 252
Sequence (journal), 10, 59
Serious Charge, 40–1, 117, 134
Serjeant Musgrave's Dance (TV), 90
Servant, The, 66, 71, 88–90, 199, 203
Sesselman, Sabina, 213
Seven Days to Noon, 43, 218
Seven Keys, 212
Seventh Veil, The, 59
Severed Head, A, 254
Sewell, Vernon, 196, 212
Sex and Marriage in England Today (book), 142
Sex, Class and Realism (book), 1, 2, 8–9, 29
Shadow of the Cat, The, 173
Shaffer, Anthony, 194
Shakedown, The, 209
Shake Hands With the Devil, 258
Shakespeare Wallah, 72
Shalako, 265
Shapiro, Helen, 114
Share Out, The, 214
Sharp, Don, 168, 169, 171, 183, 197, 212
She, 183
Shelley, Barbara, 8, 170, 171, 184, 213
Shelley, Mary, 162

351

352

353